# Introductory Programming with Object-Oriented C++:
## An IS Perspective

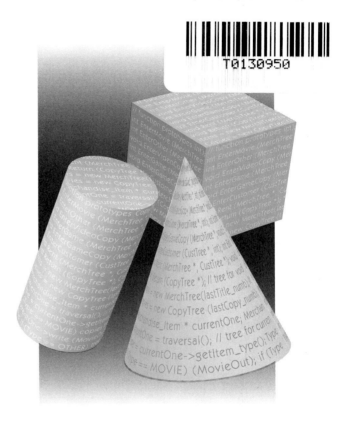

# Jan L. Harrington

Marist College, Department of Computer Science
and Information Systems

## John Wiley & Sons, Inc.

New York  Chichester  Brisbane  Toronto  Singapore  Weinheim

| Acquisitions Editor | Beth Lang Golub |
| Assistant Marketing Manager | Leslie Hines |
| Senior Production Manager | Linda Muriello |
| Production Editor | Melanie Henick |
| | |
| Manufacturing Director | Susan Stetzer |
| Manufacturing Manager | Dorothy Sinclair |

This book was set in Adobe Garamond by Black Gryphon Ltd. and printed and bound by Donnelley/Crawfordsville. The cover was printed by Lehigh Press.

Library of Congress Cataloging in Publication Data

Harrington, Jan L.
    Introductory programming with object-oriented C++ : an IS perspective/ by
Jan L. Harrington
                    p.        cm.
    Includes bibliographical references.
        ISBN 0-471-16371-6      (paper : alk. paper)
        1. Object-oriented programming (Computer science) 2. C++ (Computer
    program language) I. Title.
QA76.64.H377      1997
005.13'3 - - DC20                              96-30953
                                               CIP

Printed in the United States of America

10 9 8 7 6 5 4 3 2

# To the Instructor

If you're holding this book in your hand, then you've probably committed yourself to teaching object-oriented C++ to students without any previous programming background. Most of us who teach introductory object-oriented programming using C++ recognize that this is a difficult thing to do. Why? Because so many of the things that have made C++ the most widely used language for application software development have also made it a very treacherous environment for novice programmers. However, there are some compelling reasons to choose C++ as a first programming language for IS and IT majors:

- Your students' first programming experiences are with the object-oriented paradigm. This means they won't suffer from the difficulties that plague many experienced programmers who try to make the shift from traditional structured programming to object-oriented programming.
- Your students will develop good high-level programming habits as they learn to view the programming world and organize their program with objects.
- The object-oriented concepts learned in a C++ programming class translate easily into object-oriented analysis and design and database management. Students who have taken object-oriented programming therefore are better prepared for upper-level IS and IT courses.
- Students learn a language that is actually used in the real world, a language that not only will provide them with knowledge of programming, but that can also translate into a real job. Although this may not have been a major consideration in your choice of C++ as a teaching language, it figures high in the minds of many students.

This book has been written to capitalize on the benefits of learning object-oriented C++ as a first language, while at the same time providing a safety net that keeps students from making some of the more typical mistakes to which novice programmers are prone. It is designed to provide IS and IT students with marketable skills but also to teach them concepts on which they can build:

- This book is written specifically for students studying information systems or information technology, not for computer science students. If you are teaching in an IS, IT, CIS, or MIS program, then you will find this book better focused on the specific needs of your students than a book designed for computer science students.

- This book uses examples that are meaningful to students whose careers will be in a business environment. Instead of computing the areas of graphic shapes or the velocity of an accelerating object, students will see examples such as computing interest on loans and analyzing the data from a marketing survey. (The book also contains some "fun" program examples, just to keep things from getting too heavy.)

- This book places programming within the context of the organization. It begins by presenting the systems development life cycle, and then shows students where the software development cycle fits within it.

- This book begins with the object-oriented paradigm. Instead of teaching structured programming first, and then expecting students to fit traditional program structures into an object-oriented framework, this book takes a top-down approach by looking at high-level object organization first. Traditional program structures therefore are simply the means by which object behaviors are implemented.

Your students will find this book easy to read. It's written in an informal, conversational style rather than the formal language found in many computer science textbooks.

## Coverage and Organization

One of the biggest issues in creating an introductory programming text is exactly how much of the language to cover. C++ is a very rich language; however, experience in teaching the course for which this book is designed indicates that there simply isn't enough time in a single semester to present every feature of the language. Rather than overwhelm students with more material than they can possibly absorb in one semester, this book covers the fundamentals of the language as it gives students a firm grounding in the object-oriented paradigm.

The book begins in Chapter 1 by introducing students to the organizational process within which software development takes place.

In Chapter 2, students get their first look at how programs are developed and the software used to write and debug them. At this point, you will need to acquaint students with the specific software development environment you expect them to use. The code in this book has been written using only ANSI functions that are available with any ANSI-compliant development software. It has been tested with Turbo C++ for Windows, Visual C++ for Windows, and Metrowerks CodeWarrior C++ for Macintosh. However, because it is ANSI-standard C++, it should run with minimal modifications (for example, changes in header file names) in just about any ANSI-compatible C++ environment.

Chapter 3 presents an overview of the binary number system and its relationship to computer programming. This material will be used throughout the book, but is presented early on to give students some foundation concepts about main memory addresses and how numbers and characters are stored.

Chapter 4 presents the fundamental concepts of the object-oriented paradigm. In Chapter 5, students are introduced to the overall structure of an object-oriented C++ program. In chapter 6, students are introduced to simple variable types; Chapters 7 and 8 introduce declaring and writing simple member functions.

Many instructors have indicated that they would like I/O operations taught early in the course, rather than waiting until the end as in many texts. Chapter 9 therefore presents interactive stream I/O. Chapter 10 extends the concepts of I/O as streams of data by discussing file I/O. These chapters also represent a student's first exposure to using ANSI C++ class libraries.

The procedural portion of C++ is covered in Chapters 11, 12, and 13, where students are introduced to C++ arithmetic operators, to selection, and to iteration.

Chapter 14 focuses on arrays, looking at one- and two-dimensional arrays of numbers. In Chapter 15, students are introduced to arrays of objects, along with the concept of a data structure. This is their first exposure to a container class (the array manager) and the way in which an object-oriented program handles multiple objects created from the same class.

Because so much business programming involves text processing, Chapter 16 covers string manipulation and string functions, and reinforces array concepts by dealing with arrays of strings.

Chapter 17 introduces pointers. Although students will be familiar with the idea of a pointer as a main memory address from their work with arrays and strings, this chapter discusses the wider use of pointers throughout a C++ program. In particular, it covers pointer arithmetic, the this pointer, pass by reference, and binary files.

Chapter 18 completes the coverage of basic object-oriented concepts by discussing inheritance and polymorphism. It also reinforces the use of pointers by emphasizing the use of base class pointers.

The remaining chapters of the book contain more advanced material that you may wish to cover if you have time. Chapter 19, for example, covers linked lists to demonstrate an abstract data type and to reinforce the way in which object-oriented programs handle data structures. A linked list was chosen for this chapter because it is easy for IS and IT students to see how linked lists are useful.

Chapter 20 covers overloading. Function overloading is introduced throughout the earlier chapters of the book and reviewed at the start of this chapter, but operator overloading—one of the more difficult aspects of C++ for novices to understand—has been isolated in this chapter so that it can be omitted if you so choose.

Chapter 21 looks at templates. To help make the templates meaningful, the template examples are based on the sample linked list used in Chapter 19. Students can then see how templates make it easy to reuse classes that were originally very specific.

The final chapter presents a long, summary program: a datebook. This program is designed to show students how everything they have learned throughout the book can come together into a meaningful, useful program. The program uses arrays of pointers to objects, linked lists, and operator overloading, along with everything else taught in the book.

## Acknowledgments

It takes a lot of people to put a book together, and I'd like to take this opportunity to thank them:

- Beth Golub, the editor at Wiley who is a joy to work with.
- Melanie Henick, production editor at Wiley who made the production of this book a breeze.
- Betty Pessagno, copy editor, who has a better eye for oddities in text than most of us!
- The reviewers:
    - John W. Durham, Fort Hays State University
    - Jeff Guan, University of Louisville
    - Michael Milligan, Front Range Community College
    - David G. Zolzer, Our Lady of the Lake University

JLH

# Contents

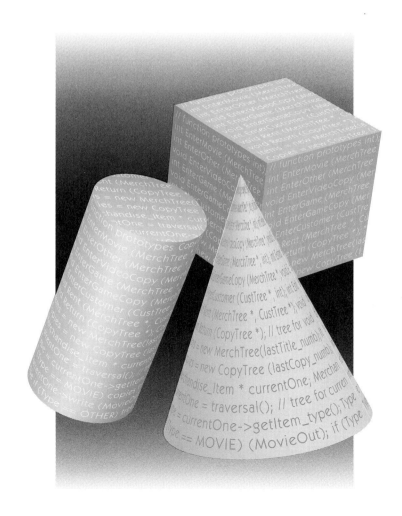

## To the Instructor

## Contents

## Chapter 10: File I/O

## Chapter 11: Doing Arithmetic

## Chapter 12: Making Decisions

# Chapter 15: Arrays of Objects

# Chapter 16: Strings

## Chapter 17: Pointers

## Chapter 18: Inheritance

# Software Development: The Organizational Process

## OBJECTIVES

In this chapter you will learn:

- The process traditionally used to design and implement information systems in an organization.
- Where application development fits into the overall process.

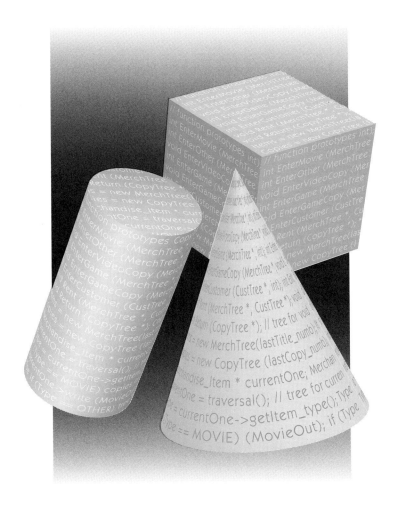

As excited as you must be to dive right into programming, it pays to step back for a moment and look at the organizational process that surrounds software development in a business environment. Experience has taught us that software development requires careful planning to ensure that the programs that are written meet the needs of the organization.

Software development is generally a team activity in which many people collaborate to produce a single, working information system. However, it's not enough just to produce programs that work: If the programs don't do what the users need them to do, the programmers might as well not bother to write the programs in the first place.

A software development team therefore pays special attention to the needs of the users and follows a set of procedures—the *software development life cycle*—that has been shown to provide a solid framework for the development process. This chapter therefore introduces you to the software development life cycle and the behaviors that a development team follows to prepare a good program.

## The Software Development Life Cycle

If you have taken a systems analysis and design course, then you are probably familiar with the *system development life cycle*, the process commonly used to design and implement information systems. Although there are many ways to represent its steps, the systems development life cycle generally includes the following phases:

- Analyzing a business environment to determine user and organizational needs.
- Developing alternative solutions to meet those needs.
- Evaluating and choosing an alternative.
- Designing a system to meet the specifications of the chosen alternative.
- Developing the system (implementation).
- Putting the system in everyday use.

The software development life cycle is a subset of the system development life cycle, focusing on the creation of software. It fits inside the system design and implementation phases of the system development life cycle and includes the following activities:

- Determining user needs. For programs that are part of a systems development project, this activity has already been performed during the analysis phase of the system development life cycle. However, if the program is being added to a system already in use, the programming team will need to determine exactly what the users need the program to do before proceeding any further.
- Designing the program. This takes place during the detailed system design phase of the system development life cycle.
- Writing the program. This takes place during the implementation phase of the system development life cycle.
- Testing the program. This also takes place during the implementation phase of the system development life cycle.

## Determining User Needs

When a program is part of a major system development project, basic user needs are determined during the needs assessment phase of the systems development life cycle. However, once the developers have released a system for everyday use ("put into production use"), it is not unusual for users to realize that they need programs to perform added functions. In that case, an information systems manager may assign the development of a specific program to a programmer (or team of programmers), who is then responsible for the entire software development process.

How do you find out what a user wants a program to do? The most obvious answer is to ask the user. However, that's not as easy as it sounds. Users often have trouble expressing what they need. To make matters worse, what you hear the user saying may not be what the user thinks he or she said. (Remember the "telephone game"?) There are, however, some things you can do to increase the effectiveness of the communication between you and someone for whom you will be writing a program:

- Ask the user to show you, on paper, the output that he or she would like to have. For many people, *showing* what they want is easier than telling you about it.
- Ask the user to demonstrate how he or she intends to use the program. This is another technique that can help people who have trouble verbalizing their needs.

- Repeat back to the user what you thought the user said. Let the user indicate whether what you heard is what he or she meant. This gives you a chance to clear up any misunderstandings in communication.
- After the interview with the user is over, write down what you think the user is asking the program to do. Let the user review the document. This is a further check that you have understood what the user wants (not necessarily what the user said).

A small word of caution is in order at this point. Even if you understand exactly what a user wants, you may not always be able to meet those needs. Some programs are simply infeasible. In other words, it may be that the effort to write and perfect the program will take more organizational resources than the benefits of the program warrant. It may also be that running the program will tie up computing resources disproportionately to the benefit of the output provided by the program.

In most cases, if a programmer or programming team leader (in the case of a team effort) believes a programming assignment to be infeasible, he or she brings those concerns to the attention of the person who originally assigned the program development task. The manager can then reevaluate the user's request for the program and decide whether to go ahead with the project.

## Designing the Program

Program design is performed either by the single programmer assigned to write a program or by members of a programming team. In the case of a team project, the entire team often works together to create a high-level design that defines the major functions the program should perform. Portions of the design are then assigned to individual programmers who flesh out the details.

The process is known as *top-down design* because the overall structure of the program is designed first and the details are filled in later. The major alternative is *bottom-up design*, in which the functional components the program will use are identified first and then assembled into a complete program. The type of programming you will be learning through this book—object-oriented programming—is most effective using a top-down design. Therefore, this is the program design methodology we will be emphasizing.

## Writing the Program

Writing the program is the process of taking the program design and turning it into a program that the user can run. You will be spending most of this semester, using this text, to learn to do just that. However, writing a program often requires more than simply writing the program.

Business software is most often modified by programmers who didn't write the program originally. This means that the programmer doing the modifications must spend time figuring out how the program works before any modifications can be made. If a program is poorly structured or poorly documented, then understanding the program as it currently exists can take longer than rewriting the program from scratch would take.

To make programs easier to modify, many IS departments have developed programming standards. Typical standards include naming conventions, documentation standards, and physical program layout.

### Naming Conventions

Naming conventions govern the naming of elements within a program. By naming items consistently throughout all programs, programmers know what to expect when they are reading a program they didn't write. Although an organization can impose on its programmers any naming conventions it wants, there are some conventions that are used by most programmers who work with the same programming tools. You will discover such conventions throughout this book.

### Documentation Standards

The most common type of documentation that is built into a program is a *comment statement*, a line of explanation that is added to a program when it is being written. A comment statement usually contains information that explains something about how a program works. Although the comment doesn't become part of the version of the program that the user runs, it remains part of the original program so that someone working to modify the program can read it.

Without question it takes time and effort to insert comment statements into a program. Many programmers would prefer not to use them at all. However, well-commented programs can save an organization a great deal of time and money when they make it easier for someone who didn't write a program to understand the program well enough to modify it quickly.

## Physical Layout

As you will see throughout this book, the way in which you physically lay out the parts of a program can seriously affect the program's readability. Programs whose layouts adhere to organizational standards will be easier to understand and therefore easier to modify.

## Software Testing

Software testing is the process through which software developers ensure that a program is as error free as possible. When creating a software testing schedule, programmers must decide who will do the testing and exactly what will be tested. Because software that hasn't been thoroughly tested is a common cause of inaccurate data, it is vitally important that software testing plans be comprehensive.

**Note**
A glitch in a program that prevents a program from operating properly is known as a *bug*. The term supposedly comes from an incident involving one of the world's first computers. A technician discovered that the problem he and his colleagues were having with a program was caused by a moth that had flown in among the computer's vacuum tubes. The moth, which was killed by the heat generated by the vacuum tubes, was retrieved by the technician, who pressed it into the system log with the entry: "Bug found. Problem solved."

## Who Should Test Software

When a programmer writes a program, he or she runs the program to find out if it is working properly. A programmer usually catches many of a program's bugs during this self-testing process. However, should the programmer be the only person to test the software? Who should make the determination that the program is ready to be turned over to the users? As surprising as it may seem, the answer is "not the programmer."

**Note**
A program that runs doesn't necessarily "work." It is possible for a program to run and still contain many problems. To be considered a working program, a program must meet the specifications set down in its design, must run without crashing, and must produce accurate results.

Most programmers unconsciously tend to run their programs in such a way that, once the major bugs have been eliminated, the program works. Programmers know the program intimately and understand how it should be used. Unfortunately, users can't read the programmers' minds and often do things with a program that a programmer didn't anticipate. It is therefore essential that software be tested by people who didn't write it. In particular, users should be involved in the testing process.

Commercial software developers send copies of software that is under development to external users for testing. This "beta test" phase lets people who use the program in their daily activities test it in a realistic manner, using real data in a real business setting. Programs written for in-house use should also be tested by users.

**Note**

There are a number of stories floating around the computer industry about user misunderstandings of software. One of the oldest stories concerns a user calling a technical support line. The user says to the technical support specialist: "It says on the screen to press any key to continue. Where's the 'any' key?" This is exactly the type of software problem that user testing is designed to catch.

## What Should Be Tested and the Testing Plan

How a program is tested is just as important as who does the testing. To be effective, testing should be based on a testing plan that answers the questions

- What should be tested?
- What data should be used?
- How should testing be organized?

The detail with which the testing plan is specified often varies with who is doing the testing. Usually, testing done by programmers is clearly laid out. In some organizations, programmers use a checklist of features that are to be tested along with specifications of the test data they are to use. In particular, programmers want to test extreme values (very high and very low values) and situations where the program either has very little data or is using large amounts of data. They also want to see what happens when someone enters unacceptable values or when something goes wrong with a data file.

When a program is sent to users for testing, instructions are considerably more vague. The intent of outside testing is to let someone who doesn't know the internals of the program use the program naturally. This is often the best way to identify features that don't work as a user expects, that a user finds hard to understand, or that simply don't work at all. Whenever a user finds a problem, he or she fills out a form explaining the problem, which is then transmitted to the programmers for action.

**Note**   You can put a professional programmer's testing methods to work on your own programs. When you test programs written for this class, be sure to test extreme values; test for bad input data and for the failure of file operations. If your instructor allows it, you may also want to let someone else run your program to see if any errors arise that you hadn't anticipated.

## Deciding When the Program Is Ready

One of the toughest decisions in any software development project is deciding when the program is ready to be released to users for everyday use. Typically, this occurs when programmers have fixed most or all of the problems identified during the testing phase. In most cases, errors are documented and checked off as they are fixed. When only a few minor errors remain, a programming team leader or software development manager makes the decision as to whether the program can be released with those errors. The manager weighs the benefits of getting the program to the users quickly against the cost of releasing software containing known bugs.

## Summary

This chapter has looked at the software development life cycle, a sequence of steps that help lead to a successful software development project. Software development is one portion of the system development life cycle, which can be described as consisting of the following steps:

- Analyzing a business environment to determine user and organizational needs.
- Developing alternative solutions to meet those needs.
- Evaluating and choosing an alternative.

- Designing a system to meet the specifications of the chosen alternative.
- Developing the system (implementation).
- Putting the system in everyday use.

The software development life cycle, which occurs during the third and fourth steps of the system development life cycle, breaks the process into four activities:

- Determine user needs.
- Design the program.
- Write the program.
- Test the program.

## Exercises

1. Assume that you have been given an assignment to write a term paper. Write down the steps in the process that you use to do your research, organize the material you find, and write the paper. How closely does your process match the system development life cycle? How might you modify the process so that it more closely matches the system development life cycle? What do you gain, or lose, by making such changes?

2. Assume that one of your relatives has asked you to help choose a new home computer. Using the system development life cycle, describe the process you would use to help your relative make the best purchase for his or her needs.

3. Many things can go wrong in a software development project. For each event in the following list, explain the impact it could have on the successful implementation of the new software. Suggest a way to prevent each event from becoming a major problem.

   - The lead programmer quits in the middle of developing the software.
   - Three users ask for additional programs to be written.
   - A department manager changes the design of a computer screen layout.

- Programmers become very upset when their manager tells them that users will be testing their programs before the system is put into everyday use.
- Programmers don't want to take the time to make computer screens look exactly like the screens that are described in the project's requirements document.

4. Assume that you have been asked to gather the user requirements for a program that manages a checking account. Interview a friend or classmate to find out what he or she would like such a program to do. Then, write down what you thought you heard the interviewee say. Show your writeup to the interviewee and ask him or her if you represented the content of the interview correctly. If your writeup contains some misunderstandings, why do you think they occurred? If your writeup was right on target, what do you think you did that made it possible for you to capture the user's needs correctly?

# 2  Software Development: The Programming Process

## OBJECTIVES

In this chapter you will learn:

- What a computer program really is.
- The components that form the source of a running program.
- The way in which a program's components are processed to create a working program.

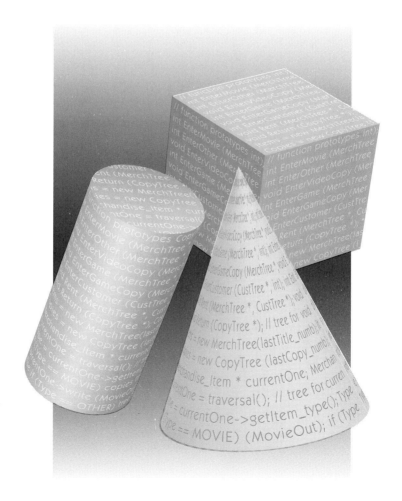

From a user's point of view, a program is something that performs one or more specific tasks. A programmer, however, sees a program in a very different way. In this chapter you will read about what lies underneath the program functionality seen by the user and how a program is processed so that it reaches the form that a person can use.

## Programs, Programming, and Programming Languages

By itself, a computer is merely a dumb box. Unless you tell it specifically what to do, it will just sit on a table or a lap and do absolutely nothing. That's where programs come in: A *program* is a specific, detailed set of directions to a computer. *Programming* is the task of designing, writing, and debugging a program.

**Note**
You will often see or hear the phrase "software program" used in the popular media. That term is rather silly because both words mean the same thing. In other words, "software" refers to a computer program and "program" refers to a computer program. Correct usage is one term or the other, but not both.

There are two general types of software. *Application software* includes programs that do useful work for the user, such as word processors and accounting programs. *Systems software* includes programs that manage the computer's operations. Operating systems, for example, are systems software.

Although people certainly have various opinions about the phases of the programming process, most programmers would agree that the toughest part of a programming project is designing the program. The design of a program includes not only what the user sees (the *user interface*), but also the step-by-step manner in which the program will handle everything that happens while it is running. This is known as the *logic* of the program. Object-oriented programming, about which you will be learning in this book, is, in part, a way of organizing program logic.

**Note**
Programmers often use the word *algorithm* to describe a portion of the logic of a program. An algorithm is a method used for solving a specific problem or arriving at a specific type of output. For example, the formula for finding the area of a circle is an algorithm.

Writing a program involves expressing the program's logical steps in a programming language. Like a spoken language, a programming language has a syntax that you must learn. Fortunately, learning the syntax of a programming language is considerably easier than learning a spoken foreign language.

## Programming Languages

A computer understands only one language—*machine language*—that is made up of a set of codes expressed as patterns of 0s and 1s. Each action that a computer knows how to perform (an *instruction*) has its own unique code. The collection of instructions that a computer understands is known as its *instruction set*.

Machine language is a computer's native language: It can understand and execute instructions in machine language without any translation. In fact, a program must be in machine language before a program can run it. However, t working directly with machine language has two drawbacks.

First, machine language differs between types of CPUs. For example, the machine language used by the Intel Pentium Pro is very different from the machine language used by the Motorola PowerPC. This is why an executable program for Pentium Pro machine can't run on a PowerPC computer and vice versa. If you wanted to produce software for both platforms, you would need to write two completely separate machine language programs.

**Note**

To be completely accurate, it is possible to run software produced for Intel CPUs on a PowerPC CPU, providing you have software that translates the Intel machine language into PowerPC machine language. This process is known as *emulation* because the software running on one CPU is "emulating" the instruction set of another CPU. The translation happens one line at a time, while the Intel program is running. The emulator intercepts each Intel instruction, figures out what it is telling the computer to do, and then executes the corresponding PowerPC instruction to produce the same effect that the program would produce if it were running on an Intel CPU.

Second, it's very difficult for humans to write programs using a relatively meaningless set of codes made up of only 0s and 1s. The programming languages we use are therefore somewhat removed from machine language.

## Assembly Language

One step up from machine language is *assembly language*, in which each instruction code is replaced by a group of letters that are suggestive of the instruction's function (*mnemonic codes*). For example, a mnemonic code to add two numbers might be ADD.

The advantage to assembly language is that a programmer can work directly with a computer's instruction set without needing to worry about the numeric instruction codes. A programmer can therefore write a program that makes the best possible use of the CPU. A well-written assembly language program runs very fast.

Like machine language, however, an assembly language is specific to a single type of CPU. If you want to create a multi-platform program, you will need to write separate programs. To do that, you will need to learn a new language each time you begin to write programs for a different CPU.

**Note**

CPUs come in "families." For example, the Intel 80386, 80486, Pentium, and Pentium Pro are all part of a single family. This means that for the most part they have the same instruction set. However, the more recent, and typically more powerful, CPUs in a family have additional instructions that their older cousins don't have. Software that takes advantage of instructions not present in older CPUs in the same family won't run on the older hardware. Therefore, to write software that is compatible with an entire family of CPUs, a programmer must avoid using instructions that aren't available in the older CPUs.

Because assembly language programs are so closely tied to a CPU's instruction set, assembly language programming can be difficult to learn. Writing a program in assembly language also requires in-depth knowledge of the internal structure of a CPU. In addition, although assembly language mnemonics are suggestive of the instruction they represent, the logic of an assembly language program can be hard to follow.

## High-Level Languages

Although there was a time when assembly language was the first type of programming learned by a student studying computing, today there is an alternative that can make a programmer's life easier: *high-level languages*, which provide an English-like syntax. This approach has two important advantages. First, the programs are easier to understand (and usually easier to write) than assembly language programs. Second, the same program can be transported from one CPU to another. Although a programmer may need to make some changes, especially in the user interface, much of a program can be reused.

On the other hand, a high-level program is significantly divorced from machine language. An assembly language programmer can use the computer's instruction set directly and write a program that works very efficiently. A high-level language programmer doesn't have that close an interaction with the computer hardware and may not be able to write a program that executes as quickly or uses main memory as efficiently as an assembly language program.

In general, most application programs today are written in high-level languages. Small portions of application programs that need to run in a limited amount of memory or that must run very quickly may be written in assembly language.

**Note**

Until the past few years, system software tended to be written in assembly language. However, there has been a shift to writing large portions of operating systems in languages such as C or C++, with only the core of the operating system written in assembly language. The UNIX operating system, for example, is written primarily in C, with only a few thousand lines of assembly language. This is one reason why it has been so easy to move UNIX to multiple platforms.

Many high-level languages are available. One of the easiest to learn is BASIC, which is often used as an introductory language in high schools; Pascal (named after the mathematician Blaise Pascal) is another popular teaching language.

A large proportion of existing business software has been written in COBOL. However, some of today's business software development and much of today's commercial software development use C++, the language you will be learning in this book. As you will learn in Chapter 3, using C++ (or any other object-oriented language) provides some significant advantages for application development.

**Note**

The C language, which predates C++, shares a great deal of syntax with C++, but they are two distinct languages.

## Programming Languages Versus the User Interface

Many of today's operating systems, such as Windows 95 and the Macintosh Operating System, have graphic user interfaces (GUIs). The user interacts with the computer using a pointing device (for example, a mouse, trackball, or graphics tablet). Information is presented visually through a combination of windows, menus, and buttons.

To provide support for a graphic user interface, an operating system comes with a "toolbox" of prewritten programs that a programmer can use. For example, most toolboxes contain programs that draw windows on the screen, redraw windows as they are moved or resized, and detect user actions within a window. However, because a graphic user interface is specific to a given operating system, the way in which a programmer uses the toolbox programs differs from one computing platform to another. In addition, programming a graphic user interface requires an in-depth knowledge of either assembly language or a high-level language.

It is therefore beyond the scope of this book to teach you to create a graphic user interface. As an alternative, we will be working with a text-based, line-oriented interface. Your output to the screen will therefore consist of characters that can be typed at the keyboard; output will appear one character at a time. Input will either be typed at the keyboard or read in from a data file.

If you use a graphic user interface for your daily computing, then a text-based interface may seem rather primitive. However, text-based input and output (I/O) will relieve you from having to deal with the complexities of toolbox programming while you are learning the basics.

The type of I/O we will be using is part of every C++ implementation that adheres to standards set by the American National Standards Institute (ANSI). Throughout this book you will find references to the ANSI standard, especially when we encounter portions of that standard that are relatively new. Some current program development software uses the new portions of the standard; some have adhered to the older version. This means that in a very few instances, how you write C++ will vary depending on the specific development software you are using.

## Program Translation

As you read earlier, a program must be in machine language before a computer can run it. Therefore if a program is written in assembly language or in a high-level language, it must be translated into machine language by another program (a language translator, which is a type of system software) before it can be executed.

Assembly language programs are translated to machine language with *assemblers*. Because each statement in an assembly language program corresponds to one machine language instruction, the translation will be as efficient as the original program.

High-level languages can be translated to machine language by *interpreters* or *compilers*. An interpreter performs the translation line by line while a program is running. This means that if a statement in a program is executed many times, it will be translated to machine language many times, once for each time the program executes that statement. The result is relatively slow execution. In addition, the interpreted program can't be run unless the interpreter is present on the computer. This complicates the process of distributing the program to multiple computers.

A compiler, however, translates a program to machine language all at once, before someone attempts to run the program. Compiled programs run faster than interpreted programs, although they are generally not as efficient as well-written assembly language programs. A compiled program can execute without the presence of the compiler.

The advantage to an interpreter is that you can make changes to a program quickly, one line at a time, without needing to retranslate the entire program. If you change only one line in a compiled program, you will need to recompile more than just that one line. (Exactly how much needs to be recompiled depends on how the program has been structured.) Nonetheless, because interpreted programs run so slowly and won't run without the presence of the interpreter, interpreters are generally used only with teaching languages such as BASIC. Most other high-level languages are compiled.

## The Program Creation Process

The process of creating a program that can be run on a computer involves a bit more than just translating the program to machine language. In this section we will look at the entire sequence of events (summarized in Figure 2.1) that must occur before a program is ready to execute.

Figure 2.1   The program creation process

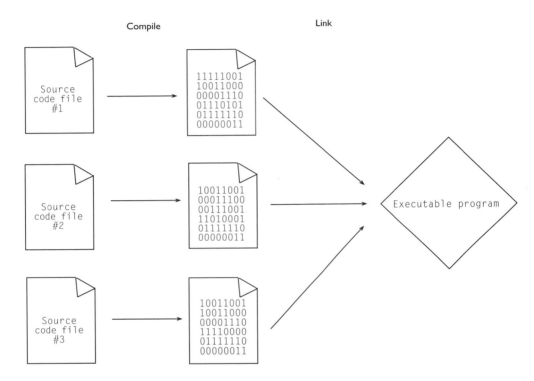

The starting point of a program is *source code*. Source code is contained in a text file that contains programming language statements; most programs are made up of several source code files. You can use any text editor to create program source code. However, most program development software includes a text editor with features that make entering a program easier. Such features include "syntax coloring," where parts of the program are displayed in color to make them easier to identify, and automatic indentation to relieve you from repeatedly pressing the Tab key.

**Warning** Be very careful about using a word processor to enter program source code. Word processors place formatting codes in their documents. Although you typically can't see the codes, they are present and will prevent a program from compiling because they represent something a compiler doesn't understand. Most word processors will save documents as "text only." A text-only word processor document will work for source code, but since program development software typically has its own editor, there is rarely any need to resort to a word processor.

Once you have entered and saved your source code, you can compile it. The result of compilation is *object code*, the machine language translation of the program you entered. However, object code doesn't represent an executable program because it typically is missing some important parts.

Even the simplest of high-level language programs doesn't include its own source code for I/O. Instead, it uses I/O code that has been provided as a part of the program development software. Code of this type, which typically has already been translated into object code, is stored in one or more *libraries*. Libraries not only support I/O, but often provide text handling capabilities, mathematical operations, graphics capabilities, and support for the user interface. Most programs that you write will make at least some use of the contents of program libraries.

In addition to using library code, keep in mind that most C++ programs are made up of more than one source code file. Since each file is compiled separately, there must be some way to put the object code together into a single program. For your program to run, the object code of all your sources files must be combined with the object code of any library program that you've used. This process is known as *linking*. The result of linking is a single executable file (a file with a .EXE extension on a DOS/Windows computer or a file with a hand-in-a-diamond icon on a Macintosh) that can be run from the operating system without the presence of the program development software.

Linking by hand can be a tedious and difficult process. However, most of today's program development software will take care of the linking for you through their *project* capabilities. A project lets you specify all of the source code files whose object code should be linked together for the final program. Depending on the software, you may also need to specify the libraries that contain code used by your source code.

Once you have created a project, you can simply tell the program development software to "run" your program. It will then compile all source code files that have been modified since the last time the program was run. Assuming that the compilation is successful, it will link the program and execute it.

The process needed to prepare a program for execution can therefore be summarized as follows:

- Enter and save source code files.
- Place the names of the source code files in a project.
- If necessary, add program libraries to the project.
- Tell the project to compile, link, and execute the program.

If the compiler detects errors in the source code, it will not attempt to link and run the project. If the linker detects errors, the program will not run.

Unfortunately, there is no simple way to tell you how to create a project because the process varies so much from one development environment to another. For example, if you are using Microsoft's Visual C++ (Figure 2.2), a project only needs to contain the names of the source files. The software identifies the libraries needed by itself. (Borland's Turbo C++ is the same as Visual C++.) However, if you are working with Metrowerks CodeWarrior (Figure 2.3), then your project needs to include both the names of the source code files and the libraries. This means that you will need to get specific directions from your instructor about the process of creating source files, adding them to a project, and running that project.

## Debuggers

A *debugger* is a program designed to help you find logic errors in a program (the hardest kind of errors to find and fix). Like projects, debuggers are specific to the program development environment in which they are found. However, you can expect any debugger to

- Allow you to execute your program, one source code line at a time.
- Let you set breakpoints. A *breakpoint* is a line of code at which execution will stop. Once you tell the debugger to "go," it will execute until the first breakpoint or until the program reaches a natural end.
- Let you "watch" the contents of main memory storage locations as your program executes.

Figure 2.2    A Microsoft Visual C++ project

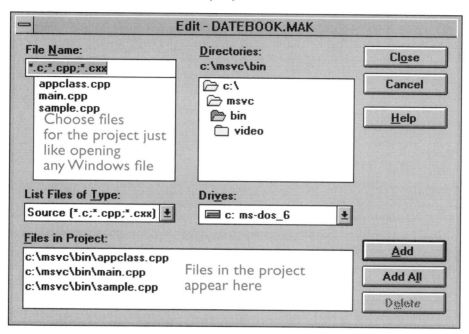

Figure 2.3    A Metrowerks CodeWarrior project

Because a debugger gives you complete control over program execution, you can set breakpoints at places where you know problems occur. Then, you can run the program to a breakpoint. Once you are at a problem location, you execute one line of source code at a time and look at how executing each line changes the data you have stored in main memory or affects what is displayed on the screen. When you find something that isn't as you expect it to be, you will have discovered the source of a problem with your program.

Learning to use a debugger can be a bit daunting at first, but in the long run it will be one of the most useful programming tools you have. You should therefore make the effort to learn to use the debugger that comes with your program development software as soon as possible.

## Summary

A computer program is a sequence of instruction for a computer. The computer only understands instructions in machine language, where each instruction the computer understands is represented by a binary code. To make it easier to write programs, assembly language provides a mnemonic for each instruction. Assembly language, which is translated to machine language with an assembler, is nonetheless difficult to program because it requires an in-depth knowledge of both the instruction set and configuration of a specific CPU.

High-level languages use an English-like syntax for writing program. This allows a programmer to work without knowing the CPU's configuration or instruction set. A high-level language program is translated to machine language with an interpreter (translation while the program is running) or a compiler (translation before the program is run). Most of today's languages are compiled.

To create a working program, the machine language (object code) produced when the text version of a program (source code) is translated, all object code modules must be linked together. Programs often use code modules supplied with the program development software, especially to support I/O, text handling, graphics, and the user interface. This code is usually supplied as object code and collected in libraries. The libraries must therefore be linked with a programmer's object code to create a working program.

## Exercises

1.  You have been given a robot that understands English commands. However, this robot has absolutely no intelligence of its own. It has been left sitting in a chair, turned off and doing nothing. It is your job as the robot's programmer to come up with a sequence of instructions that will get the robot to stand up, walk across the room, turn around, return to its chair, and sit down again. Keep in mind that the robot will do exactly what you tell it to do and nothing more. Write your instructions and then test them on a willing friend. As you test your instructions, formulate answers to the following questions:

    a.  How specific do your instructions need to be?
    b.  What is the effect of testing your instructions on a thinking human being rather than a machine?
    c.  What does this suggest to you about the nature of a computer program?

2.  As you have read in this chapter, the details of creating a project vary from one C++ development environment to another. To help you become comfortable with your development software, in this exercise you will enter, compile, and run a short C++ program.

    a.  Use your development environment's editor to enter the code in Listing 2.1 exactly as it appears. C++ is case sensitive—it knows the difference between upper and lowercase letters—so be sure to match the capitalization exactly. Save your code in a file named *hello.h*.
    b.  Type the code in Listing 2.2 *exactly* as it appears. Save it in a file named *hello.cpp*.
    c.  Type the code in Listing 2.3 exactly as it appears. Save it in a file named *helloapp.cpp*.
    d.  Type the code in Listing 2.4 exactly as it appears. Save it in a file named *main.cpp*.
    e.  Create a new project. Add *hello.cpp*, *helloapp.cpp*, and *main.cpp* to the project. (Do *not* add *hello.h*.)

## Listing 2.1   Hello.h

```
class Hello
{
    private:
        char Prompt1[10], Prompt2[30];
        char Name[25];
    public:
        Hello ();
        void getName ();
        void showMessage ();
};

class HelloApp
{
    public:
        HelloApp ();
        void Run ();
};
```

## Listing 2.2   Hello.cpp

```
#include "Hello.h"
#include <string.h>
#include <iostream.h>

Hello::Hello()
{
    strcpy (Prompt1, "Hello, ");
    strcpy (Prompt2, "Welcome to the world of C++.");
    strcpy (Name,"");
}

void Hello::getName ()
{
    cout << "\nPlease enter your first name: ";
    cin.getline (Name,25);
}

void Hello::showMessage ()
{
    cout << endl;
    cout << Prompt1 << Name << '.' << endl;
    cout << Prompt2 << endl;
}
```

## Listing 2.3   HelloApp.cpp

```
#include "Hello.h"

HelloApp::HelloApp ()
{
    // nothing happens here
}

void HelloApp::Run ()
{
    Hello theGreeting;
    theGreeting.getName();
    theGreeting.showMessage ();
}
```

## Listing 2.4   Main.cpp

```
#include "Hello.h"

void main ()
{
    HelloApp theApp;
    theApp.Run ();
}
```

f.  Run your project. In most cases, "running" a project will compile, link, and execute in a single step. When running properly, the program should ask you for your first name and then echo it back to you, producing a screen display like that in Figure 2.4.

## Figure 2.4   Output of the Hello program

```
Please enter your first name: John

Hello, John.
Welcome to the world of C++.
```

g.  If you encounter errors, at this point they will likely be typographical errors. Therefore, check your typing carefully. Correct your errors and run the program again. Keep trying until it executes successfully.

3. Investigate the debugger that is part of your program development software. The easiest way to do this would be to run the debugger using the program you created for Exercise 2 and explore the various menu options. Answer the following questions:

   a. How do you enter the debugger? (In other words, how do you run it?)
   b. How do you run the program from within the debugger? (*Hint*: Look for a "go" command.)
   c. How does running under the debugger affect a program's user interface?
   d. How do you set a breakpoint? How do you clear a breakpoint?
   e. How do you execute a program one line at a time?
   f. What is the difference between "stepping over" and "stepping in"?
   g. How do you look at main memory? Do you need to explicitly set a "watch," or does the debugger automatically show you all the data you have stored in main memory?

# 3

# The Role of Binary

## OBJECTIVES

In this chapter you will read about:

- How values are represented in the binary number system.
- The relationship between binary numbers and a computer's main memory.
- How binary numbers influence the way numeric values are stored in a computer.
- How characters are stored in a computer.
- How hexadecimal is used as a shorthand for binary.

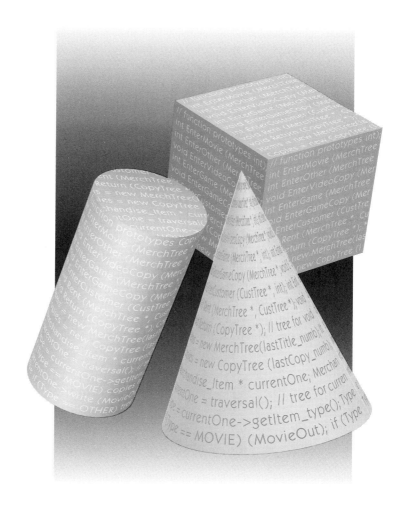

Earlier in this book, you read that a machine language instruction is represented by a code of 0s and 1s. Because the digits in this code have only two possible values, this is a *binary* code. It is a perfect way to represent information in a computer because a computer is made up of electrical circuits, each of which can carry a high voltage or a low voltage. The low voltage represents a 0, the high voltage a 1.

In this chapter we will explore the underlying concepts behind the binary number system and look at how various types of data are represented in a computer using binary.

## The Binary Number System

Besides meaning anything that has two values, the term *binary* also refers to the base 2 number system. In base 2, there are only two digits: 0 and 1. Each single digit in a number is called a *bit* (a contraction of "binary digit"). Computers use base 2 for numbers, character codes, and to organize memory, as well as for instruction codes. It is therefore important for you to have some understanding of how the binary number system works.

Number systems, including the base 10 number system we use every day, are place value systems. This means that each digit in a number represents the value of the place in which the digit resides multiplied by the digit. To make this concept a bit clearer, take a look at Figure 3.1. Each digit in this number is multiplied by a power of 10. We therefore say that 10 is the *base* of this number system.

Notice that the powers are numbered from right to left, beginning with 0. Any number raised to the 0 power is 1. Therefore, the rightmost place represents $1 \times$ the digit occupying the $10^0$ place (in this example, 8). Any number raised to the 1 power is the number itself. The second place from the right therefore represents $10 \times$ the number occupying the $10^1$ place. Since $10^2$ is 100, the value in the third place from the right is $100 \times$ the digit. You can continue to evaluate the remaining place values in the same way.

This concept—multiplying a digit by its place value—can be extended to number systems with bases other than 10. As you have read, the binary number system, which uses a base of 2, is particularly important for computing.

Figure 3.1 Base 10 as a place value system

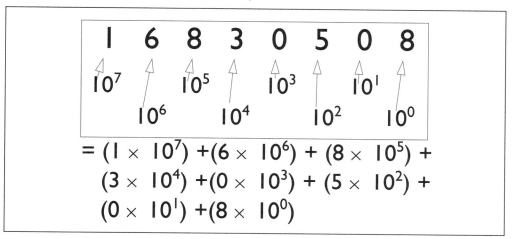

$$= (1 \times 10^7) + (6 \times 10^6) + (8 \times 10^5) +$$
$$(3 \times 10^4) + (0 \times 10^3) + (5 \times 10^2) +$$
$$(0 \times 10^1) + (8 \times 10^0)$$

The places in a base 2 (binary) number represents powers of 2. As an example, consider the number in Figure 3.2. Notice that the place values are numbered just as they are in a base 10 number; the difference is that the base is 2 rather than 10.

The base 2 number in Figure 3.2 is written $10110011_2$. The subscripted 2 at the right of the number indicates the base. To read the number, you say each of the digits: "one zero one one zero zero one one." Saying "ten million one hundred eleven thousand eleven" is incorrect because it doesn't accurately represent the value of the number.

To convert a binary number to base 10, add together the values of all the places in the binary number that contain a 1. (As you can see from Figure 3.2, places with 0s don't participate in the value of the number.) The trick, of course, is to know the base 10 equivalents of powers of 2. To help you get started, Table 3.1 contains some of the more commonly used powers. Why the higher powers are important will become clear shortly.

Counting in base 2 is similar to counting in base 10. The major difference is that instead of moving one place to the left and carrying when the value in a place exceeds 9, you move one place to the left and carry when the value in a place exceeds 1. To see how this works, look carefully at Table 3.2.

Figure 3.2   Base 2 as a place value system

$$1\ 0\ 1\ 1\ 0\ 0\ 1\ 1$$

$$2^7\ \ 2^6\ \ 2^5\ \ 2^4\ \ 2^3\ \ 2^2\ \ 2^1\ \ 2^0$$

$$= (1 \times 2^7) + (0 \times 2^6) + (1 \times 2^5) + (1 \times 2^4) +$$
$$(0 \times 2^3) + (0 \times 2^2) + (1 \times 2^1) + (1 \times 2^0)$$
$$= (1 \times 128) + (0 \times 64) + (1 \times 32) + (1 \times 16) +$$
$$(0 \times 8) + (0 \times 4) + (1 \times 2) + (1 \times 1)$$
$$= 179$$

Table 3.1   Some powers of 2

| Power | Base 10 | Power | Base 10 |
|-------|---------|-------|---------|
| $2^0$ | 1 | $2^{15}$ | 32768 |
| $2^1$ | 2 | $2^{16}$ | 65536 |
| $2^2$ | 4 | $2^{20}$ | 1048576 |
| $2^3$ | 8 | $2^{30}$ | 1073741824 |
| $2^4$ | 16 | $2^{31}$ | 2147483648 |
| $2^5$ | 32 | $2^{32}$ | 4294967296 |
| $2^6$ | 64 | | |
| $2^7$ | 128 | | |
| $2^8$ | 256 | | |
| $2^9$ | 512 | | |
| $2^{10}$ | 1024 | | |

Table 3.2 Counting in base 2

| Base 2 | Base 10 | Base 2 | Base 10 | Base 2 | Base 10 |
|--------|---------|--------|---------|--------|---------|
| 1 | 1 | 1011 | 11 | 10101 | 21 |
| 10 | 2 | 1100 | 12 | 10110 | 22 |
| 11 | 3 | 1101 | 13 | 10111 | 23 |
| 100 | 4 | 1110 | 14 | 11000 | 24 |
| 101 | 5 | 1111 | 15 | 11001 | 25 |
| 110 | 6 | 10000 | 16 | 11010 | 26 |
| 111 | 7 | 10001 | 17 | 11011 | 27 |
| 1000 | 8 | 10010 | 18 | 11100 | 28 |
| 1001 | 9 | 10011 | 19 | 11101 | 29 |
| 1010 | 10 | 10100 | 20 | 11110 | 30 |

## Organizing Memory

A computer's main memory is made up of a large collection of circuits, each of which holds a voltage that represents one bit. A program needs to be able to access specific bits in memory so that it can read instructions, read data, or write data. We must therefore have some way of organizing all the bits in main memory so that a program can easily specify which bit—or group of bits—it wants to access.

Computers group bits together to make then easier to access. The most basic grouping is a *byte* (8 bits), which, for example, can hold one character or an integer in the range -128 to +127. Each byte in a computer's memory is given a unique number (its *address*) by which the byte can be referenced.

Because today's computers have millions of bytes of main memory and hard disk space, we usually refer to larger groupings of bytes:

- *Kilobyte:* $2^{10}$, or 1024 bytes. (Abbreviation: K or Kb)
- *Megabyte*: $2^{20}$, or 1,048,576 bytes. (Abbreviation: Mb or Meg)
- *Gigabyte*: $2^{30}$, or 1,073,741,824 bytes. (Abbreviation: Gb or Gig)

The main memory in a typical PC is measured in megabytes (usually 8 Mb or more in new computers); hard disk space is measured in hundreds of megabytes or gigabytes.

**Note** Because a kilobyte is very close to 1000 bytes, a megabyte close to 1,000,000 bytes, and a gigabyte close to 1,000,000,000 bytes, we often think of these groupings using the simpler numbers. There's rarely any harm in doing so, but when you do, keep in mind that the real quantities are slightly more.

## Storing Integers

A computer uses binary to store numbers. Numbers come in two general groups: integers (whole numbers without fractional portions) and floating point numbers (numbers that can have decimal fractions, such as $3.567 \times 10^{15}$). The details of number storage formats are beyond the scope of this book. However, it is useful to know something about the range of numbers that an integer can handle so you can avoid some common programming errors.

On most PCs, a standard integer is stored in 16 bits, providing a range of -32,768 to +32767 that allocates half of 65,536 possible numbers to positive and half to negative. (Keep in mind that 0 is a positive number.) Looking back at Table 3.1, you'll see that 65,536 is $2^{16}$. When we consider this fact a bit more closely, there seems to be something wrong with it in relation to the number of values we should actually be able to store.

The maximum number of values (including 0) that you can store in any given number of bits is $2^{n+1}$, where $n$ is the number of bits. A 16-bit integer should therefore theoretically be able to store $2^{17}$ (or 131,072) values. Why are we only getting 65,536 values? Because the leftmost bit is being used to hold the sign of the number. If a 16-bit integer is positive, bit 15 will always be 0; if a 16-bit integer is negative, bit 15 will always be 1. There are therefore only 15 bits available to hold the value of the number, making the total number of values equal to $2^{16}$.

If you attempt to store an integer that is outside the 16-bit range, a C++ program won't tell you that anything wrong has occurred. However, you'll notice that the number you get has the opposite sign and probably a different value from what you intended. The reason the sign changes is that the number overflows into the bit reserved for storing the sign, causing it to change.

**Note** Most C++ compilers also provide a "short" integer. Theoretically, this should be an 8-bit integer that holds numbers in the range -128 to +127. You would use a short integer to avoid wasting space when all you needed was storage for a small quantity. However, many of today's C++ compilers use 16 bits for both short integers and regular integers, so there's usually little benefit to be gained by asking for a short integer. Nonetheless, you should check your compiler's documentation to be sure.

If a 16-bit integer doesn't have enough range, you can use a "long," or 32-bit, integer, which provides a range of -2,147,483,648 to +2,147,483,647. As with a 16-bit integer, the biggest signal that you've attempted to store a value outside the range is a number that has the wrong sign and probably the wrong value.

C++ also provides "unsigned" integers. An unsigned integer stores only positive values. This means, for example, that the full 16 bits of a standard integer can be used to store the value of the number, providing a range of 0 to 65,635. If you can get by without negative numbers, you can therefore double the range of values by requesting an unsigned, rather than a signed, integer.

If your value won't fit even in a long integer, you will need to resort to a floating point number. The range of floating point numbers varies from one computer to another, but, on a PC you can typically expect to be able to handle numbers in the range $\pm 2^{127}$, which is approximately equivalent to $\pm 10^{38}$. Each floating point number can occupy from five to eight bytes (depending on the specific floating point format used by your computer). Because this is considerably more space than an integer, you should use floating point numbers only when you specifically need numbers that have decimal fractions.

## Character Codes

A computer stores characters using a binary code, the most commonly used of which is *ASCII* (pronounced "ass-key"). Standard ASCI is a 7-bit code; extended ASCII uses the full 8 bits in a byte.

The ASCII codes for letters and numbers can be found in Table 3.3. There are several very important things to notice about these codes. First, look at the codes for the digits. If you translate the ASCII code for 0 to decimal, you will get 48; the ASCII code for 1 is $49_{10}$, and so on. This is a far cry from the numeric values 0 and 1. In other words, a computer can store a digit in two ways: (1) as an integer; (2) as a character, using its ASCII code. However, if you try to do arithmetic with the ASCII code, the computer will use a value of 48 rather than 0, producing an inaccurate result. The bottom line is that if you

Table 3.3    Some sample ASCII codes

| Character | Code | Character | Code | Character | Code |
|---|---|---|---|---|---|
| 0 | 00110000 | A | 01000001 | a | 01100001 |
| 1 | 00110001 | B | 01000010 | b | 01100010 |
| 2 | 00110010 | C | 01000011 | c | 01100011 |
| 3 | 00110011 | D | 01000100 | d | 01100100 |
| 4 | 00110100 | E | 01000101 | e | 01100101 |
| 5 | 00110101 | F | 01000110 | f | 01100110 |
| 6 | 00110110 | G | 01000111 | g | 01100111 |
| 7 | 00110111 | H | 01001000 | h | 01101000 |
| 8 | 00111000 | I | 01001001 | i | 01101001 |
| 9 | 00111001 | J | 01001010 | j | 01101010 |
| | | K | 01001011 | k | 01101011 |
| | | L | 01001100 | l | 01101100 |
| | | M | 01001101 | m | 01101101 |
| | | N | 01001110 | n | 01101110 |
| | | O | 01001111 | o | 01101111 |
| | | P | 01010000 | p | 01110000 |
| | | Q | 01010001 | q | 01110001 |
| | | R | 01010010 | r | 01110010 |
| | | S | 01010011 | s | 01110011 |
| | | T | 01010100 | t | 01110100 |
| | | U | 01010101 | u | 01110101 |
| | | V | 01010110 | v | 01110110 |
| | | W | 01010111 | w | 01110111 |
| | | X | 01011000 | x | 01111000 |
| | | Y | 01011001 | y | 01111001 |
| | | Z | 01011110 | z | 01111110 |

need to do arithmetic with digits, you must be sure that they are stored as numbers, not as characters.

Next look carefully at the codes for the letters. Uppercase and lowercase letters are different. When a program compares characters, it will be comparing the numeric values of the ASCII codes. Unless a program takes special action to translate characters to the same case, *a* is not equal to *A*.

A computer knows nothing about alphabetical order. However, we often need to be able to sort strings of characters to produce alphabetical listings. The way in which ASCII codes have been assigned to characters makes this easy: Letters that precede others in alphabetical order have lower codes. For example, the code for *a* is numerically less than the code for *b*. Keep in mind that unless a program takes action to translate characters to the same case, all uppercase letters alphabetically precede all lowercase letters.

## Hexadecimal

Because each place in a binary number only represents a power of 2, binary numbers can become very long very quickly. To make it easier to work with binary, we often translate a binary number into base 16, or *hexadecimal.*

Each place in a hexadecimal number represents a power of 16. As you can see in Table 3.4, it doesn't take many hexadecimal places to generate rather large numbers. In Table 3.4 you will also see the powers of 2 that correspond to powers of 16. Notice that each power of 16 is exactly four powers of 2. This is simply because $2^4$ is 16. We can therefore use hexadecimal as a shorthand for a long binary number. All we have to do is substitute one hexadecimal digit for each group of four binary digits.

Writing a hexadecimal number presents a bit of a problem, however. Since hexadecimal is base 16, each place must be able to store a single digit that represents the quantities 0 through 15. Unfortunately, we only have 10 digits (0 through 9). We get around the problem by using letters: A = 10, B = 11, C = 12, D = 13, E = 14, and F = 15. For example, AF12 is a legal hexadecimal number.

To translate a hexadecimal number to decimal, you use the same process we discussed earlier in this chapter for translating binary to decimal: Multiply each digit by its place value and then add the numbers. As an example, take a look at Figure 3.3.

Table 3.4    Some powers of 16

| Base 16 | Base 2 | Base 10 |
|---------|--------|---------|
| $16^0$ | $2^0$ | 1 |
| $16^1$ | $2^4$ | 16 |
| $16^2$ | $2^8$ | 256 |
| $16^3$ | $2^{12}$ | 4096 |
| $16^4$ | $2^{16}$ | 65536 |
| $16^5$ | $2^{20}$ | 1,048,576 |
| $16^6$ | $2^{24}$ | 16,777,216 |
| $16^7$ | $2^{28}$ | 268,435,456 |
| $16^8$ | $2^{32}$ | 4,294,967,296 |
| $16^9$ | $2^{36}$ | 68,719,476,736 |
| $16^{10}$ | $2^{40}$ | 1,099,511,627,776 |

Converting between binary and hexadecimal is much easier than converting to decimal. To convert a binary number to hexadecimal, all you have to do is group the bits into four, beginning at the right edge of the number. Substitute one hexadecimal digit for each group of four binary digits. As you can see in Figure 3.4, you only need to worry about binary numbers with a maximum of four digits!

To convert from hexadecimal to binary, just substitute the equivalent four binary digits for each hexadecimal digit. In Figure 3.5 you can see that the process is exactly the opposite of converting from binary to hexadecimal.

C++ allows you to include hexadecimal values in a program. However, you need to preface each number with 0x to alert the compiler that what follows is being expressed in hexadecimal. For example, 0x1234 and 0xAB09 are legal C++ hexadecimal values. Without the 0x, the compiler will report an error for values that contain letters as digits and interpret a value without letters as a base 10 number.

Figure 3.3   Translating a hexadecimal number to decimal

$$A \quad F \quad 1 \quad 2$$

$$16^3 \qquad 16^1$$
$$16^2 \qquad 16^0$$

$$= (10 \times 16^3) + (15 \times 16^2) +$$
$$(1 \times 16^1) \quad + \quad (2 \times 16^0)$$

$$= (10 \times 4069) + (15 \times 256) +$$
$$(1 \times 16) + (2 \times 1)$$

$$= 40{,}690 + 3{,}840 + 16 + 2$$
$$= 44{,}548$$

Figure 3.4   Converting binary to hexadecimal

| binary | 1111 | 0000 | 1010 | 1111 |
|---|---|---|---|---|
| hexadecimal | F | 0 | A | F |

Figure 3.5   Converting hexadecimal to binary

| hexadecimal | 2 | C | F | 3 |
|---|---|---|---|---|
| binary | 0010 | 1100 | 1111 | 0011 |

## Summary

A computer uses binary (base 2) to represent virtually everything it uses when running a program. Binary is particularly well suited for this task because it has only two digits that match the two voltages carried by computer circuits.

A CPU's instruction set is represented by binary codes. In addition, numbers and characters are stored in binary. Binary is also used to number the addresses of bytes in main memory.

Because binary numbers become very long very quickly, we often use hexadecimal—base 16—as a shorthand for binary. Each hexadecimal place represents four binary places. To convert between binary and hexadecimal, you simply substitute one hexadecimal digit for each binary digit.

## Exercises

1.  Translate the following binary numbers to decimal:

    a.  100011100
    b.  1000001100111
    c.  1111000011110
    d.  0111001100111

2.  Translate the following decimal numbers to binary:

    a.  526
    b.  109
    c.  1512
    d.  8745

3.  Suggest the best type of data storage (for example, integer, unsigned integer, or character) for each of the following values:

    a.  1099
    b.  -5395837
    c.  $6.38 \times 10^{15}$
    d.  c
    e.  A5
    f.  70667
    g.  10678456

4.  Translate the following hexadecimal numbers to decimal:

    a.  B12C
    b.  1234
    c.  A99BE
    d.  FFFF
    e.  FFFFFFFF

5.  Translate the following binary numbers to hexadecimal:

    a.  10000111000111000
    b.  1111110000001110001111
    c.  100000000000000000001
    d.  10101010101000000011110
    e.  101111000111000111110001111

# 4

# Introducing the Object-Oriented Paradigm

## OBJECTIVES

In this chapter you will learn:

- How objects provide a way of looking at the elements of a program's environment.
- About the characteristics of objects.
- About how objects with the same properties are represented as classes.
- How classes work together to structure the logic of a program.

If you look at recent articles in computer journals and magazines, you'll notice an emphasis on something known as *object-oriented programming* (often abbreviated *OOP*). Object-oriented programming is a method for developing and organizing the logic of application programs. Object-oriented concepts have also had an impact on systems analysis and design procedures, operating systems, and database systems. As a whole, object-oriented technology represents a *paradigm* (a theoretical model that can be used as a pattern for some activity).

There are many reasons why application programmers are increasingly choosing to write object-oriented programs. However, you will need to wait until you know something about how the object-oriented paradigm works to understand the advantage to this approach. We will therefore start by looking at an example of the object-oriented approach that has absolutely nothing to do with computers. To make it easier for you to see how object-orientation differs from other ways of solving problems, we'll compare it to a more traditional way of describing and organizing instructions..

Then we'll turn to technology, beginning with a look at how the object-oriented paradigm originated, followed by an introduction to the basic elements of an object-oriented program. Then, as we go, we'll identify those features of object orientation that make it the paradigm of choice for many programmers today.

## Performing a Real-World Task

One of the things we do frequently is prepare a meal. Whether you're cooking a standing rib roast for an elegant dinner or making a peanut butter and jelly sandwich for a quick lunch, there is a general process that you follow.

- First, you must decide what to prepare to eat.
- Next, you must figure out what ingredients the food requires.
- Third, you must look to see if you have the ingredients on hand.
- If you're missing an ingredient, you must either go to the store, or change your mind about what you're going to fix.
- Once all the ingredients are in place, you can follow the recipes and prepare the meal.

The recipes for the items you are preparing can be very simple ("Put peanut butter on one piece of bread; put jelly on a second piece of bread; smash together.") or very complex. Nonetheless, there is a specific set of instructions that you follow whenever you are preparing food in any way.

The preceding bulleted list describes a general process for preparing a meal; it doesn't depend on what specific foods are going to be prepared. However, the ingredients used and the recipe for preparing any given dish are specific to that dish.

Now assume that you have been asked to write instructions for preparing a meal for two people consisting of an egg salad sandwich, carrot sticks, potato chips, and soda. A traditional way to assemble such a set of instructions might appear as in Listing 4.1.

## Listing 4.1    Steps to prepare lunch

```
1. Decide to serve egg salad sandwich, carrot sticks, potato chips, and soda.
2. Put two eggs, mayonnaise, four pieces of bread, lettuce, two carrots, potato
   chips, and two cans of soda on the list of ingredients. Place mixing bowl,
   tablespoon, fork, paring knife, two lunch plates, and two glasses on the
   list of equipment needed.
3. Check the refrigerator for eggs, mayonnaise, lettuce, carrots and soda;
   check the cupboard for bread and potato chips.
4. You have everything except eggs.
5. Do you want to change your mind about the egg salad sandwiches? No. Then go
   to the store and buy eggs. (If yes, go back to Step 1.)
6. Make the egg salad sandwich: Boil two eggs for 15 minutes. Peel the eggs.
   Put the eggs in a bowl and mash them with a fork. Put the mashed eggs in the
   freezer for 15 minutes to cool. Remove from the freezer. Add two tablespoons
   of mayonnaise and mix. Divide the mixture evenly between two pieces of
   bread. Cover with lettuce. Spread mayonnaise on two remaining pieces of
   bread. Place break on top of lettuce. Place each sandwich on a separate
   lunch plate.
7. Prepare carrot sticks: Wash two carrots. Peel the carrots. Cut each carrot
   in half lengthwise; cut each half in half again. Place on a lunch plate next
   to the sandwiches.
8. Prepare potato chips: If necessary, rip open the bag of potato chips. Shake
   approximately one cup of chips onto each lunch plate.
9. Prepare the soda: Place one can of soda and a glass on the table next to each
   lunch plate.
```

As you read through these instructions, you're probably thinking that they seem fairly straightforward: They tell someone what to do in a step-by-step manner. In fact, until the advent of object-oriented programming, the instructions that made up computer programs were organized in a very similar way. This type of program organization is known as *structured programming*.

Listing 4.1 illustrates some of the basic principles of structured programming. First, and most importantly, instructions are executed in order, beginning at the first instruction, until something in the set of instructions indicates that you should do something different.

At several places in the instructions you are asked to make a decision. For example, you need to figure out whether you have the ingredients needed. If you don't, you have to decide whether to go to the store or to change your mind about what you are preparing. In our particular example, we decided to go to the store. However, if you were to change your mind about the dish, you would need to return to Step 1 and start again with a different decision about what to serve. Making decisions between two sets of alternative actions is something that computers also do frequently.

So, what's wrong with this picture? If the instructions and the way they have been prepared seem so straightforward, why would people try to find another way to describe them? To understand the problem, consider what would happen if you *did* decide to make something other than an egg salad sandwich. In other words, at Step 5, you decided to return to Step 1 and make tuna fish sandwiches instead. Notice the problem: the instructions that follow are no longer appropriate for what you're going to make. Instead of eggs, you need tuna fish. Rather than boiling, mashing, and cooling eggs, you need to open the can of tuna and drain the liquid.

The instructions, as written, are specific to one particular menu. If we want a different menu, we need to modify almost all the instructions. We could avoid needing to redo the instructions if we separated the instructions into pieces. One type of "piece" could be a dish that we know how to prepare. The ingredients and the instructions for preparing a given dish belong to the dish. When we want information from the dish, we ask for it. If we rewrite the meal preparation instructions under the assumption that the dishes will give us information when we ask for it, then the instructions might look like Listing 4.2.

Listing 4.2   Steps to prepare lunch when the dishes we prepare can give us information

```
1. Decide which dishes to prepare (Dish1, Dish2, Dish3, Dish4)
2. Ask each dish to list its ingredients.
3. Verify that we have all the ingredients.
4. If an ingredient is missing, either go to the store or go back to Step 1.
5. Ask a dish to tell us how to prepare it. Follow the instructions given to us
   by the dish.
6. If all dishes are prepared, stop. Otherwise, go back to Step 5.
```

There are two major differences between Listing 4.2 and Listing 4.1, aside from Listing 4.2 being much shorter:

- The specific ingredients and recipe needed to prepare any given dish are hidden from the list of instructions. We have to ask the dish to give us information when we need it.
- Because the ingredients and the recipe aren't included in the instructions, a change in the dishes that are being prepared doesn't require a change in the instructions.

The second set of instructions that we have been studying exhibits many of the characteristics of object orientation. In this particular example, there are actually five objects: the four dishes being prepared and the set of instructions itself. The dishes we prepare are typical objects: they have data that describe them (the ingredients and amounts of those ingredients needed) and they have things that they know how to do ((1) tell us the ingredients and (2) tell us how to prepare the dish). They hide the details of how they do their work from the object that is manipulating them (the set of instructions).

The beauty of working with the dishes as objects is that the set of instructions that uses the objects can be written generically. We can switch objects at any time (for example, swap egg salad with tuna fish) without making any other changes. Our set of instructions doesn't need to include the details about preparing a given dish; all it needs to do is ask the dish for the ingredients and recipe when appropriate.

Object-oriented programming takes much the same approach, hiding the details of objects from objects of other types. When an object needs information from another object or needs another object to perform a task, it sends a message to the object requesting whatever it needs. As a result, object-oriented programs can be written more generically than structured programs. Usually, making changes to the programs is then easier than changing structured programs.

Objects that have the same data that describe them and know how to do the same things in the same way are said to belong to the same *class*. For example, the egg salad sandwich, the tuna fish sandwich, carrot sticks, potato chips, and soda objects all belong to one class, which we might name *LunchFood*.

If we want to add a new dish to our collection of things that we can have for lunch, we use *LunchFood* as a pattern for creating the new dish. The class definition tells us what data any object of the class will have (the ingredients and the amounts of those ingredients) and what objects of the class know how to do (tell us about the ingredients and tell us the recipe). A class therefore functions as a template for creating objects.

Classes are independent of where they are used. For example, we are currently using objects created from the *LunchFood* class in a set of instructions that tells us how to prepare lunch. However, we could also use objects created from the *LunchFood* class in a set of instructions that tell us how to prepare a printed cookbook. Because class is independent of the instructions that are using it, the class can be reused in many programs. The ability to reuse classes is another major benefit of object orientation.

Now that you have a general understanding of why many people believe the object-oriented approach is better than a sequential approach, let's take a more formal look at how objects are used in computer programs.

## A Bit of History

The object-oriented paradigm was developed in 1969 by Dr. Kristin Nygaard, a Norwegian who was trying to write a computer program that described the movement of ships through a fjord. He found that the combination of tides, the movements of the ships, and the shape of the coastline were difficult to deal with using existing programming methods. Instead, he looked at the items in the environment he was trying to model—ships, tides, and the fjord's coastline—and the actions each item was likely to take. Then he was able to handle the relationships between them.

The object-oriented technology we use today has evolved from Dr. Nygaard's original work on ships and fjords. The paradigm retains the concept of combining the description of the items in a data processing environment with the actions performed by those items.

## Objects

At the heart of the object-oriented paradigm is the *object*, an entity in the data processing environment that has data that describe it and actions that it can perform. An object can be something that has a physical existence, such as a boat, product, or computer (or a lunch dish that we know how to prepare!). It can also be an event (for example, the sale of a product, a professional conference, or a business tip), a place, a part of a program's user interface (for example, a menu or a window), or even the program itself (an *application object*).

Any given object-oriented program can handle many objects. For example, a program that handles the inventory for a retail store uses one object for each product carried by the store. The program manipulates the same data for each object, including the product number, product description, retail price, number of items in stock, and the reorder point.

Each object also knows how to perform actions with its own data. The product object in the inventory program, for example, knows how to create itself and set initial values for all its data, how to modify its data, and how to evaluate whether enough items are in stock to satisfy a purchase request. The important thing to recognize is that an object consists of *both* the data that describe it and the actions it can perform.

An object in a computer program isn't something you can touch. When a program is running, most objects exist in main memory. Objects are created by a program for use while the program is executing. Unless a program explicitly saves an object's data to a disk, the object is lost when the program ends.

An object performs one of its actions when it receives a *message* instructing it to do so. A message includes an identifier for which action the object is to perform, along with the data the object needs to do its work. Messages therefore constitute an object's window to the outside world.

## Classes

The template from which objects of the same type are created is known as a *class*. A class contains specifications for the data that describe an object along with descriptions of the actions an object knows how to perform. These actions are known as *services*, *methods*, or *member functions*. The term *member function* is most commonly used with C++ because a *function* is a self-contained block of C++ source code.

**Note**

One of the greatest ironies of object-oriented programming is that member functions must be written using an older programming paradigm known as *structured programming*, the paradigm to which object-oriented program is a major alternative. This means that although you will be using object-oriented programming to create the high-level program organization of your programs, you will also need to learn structured programming to provide the details of the actions your objects will perform.

A class also includes all the data needed to describe objects created from the class. These are known as *attributes* or *variables*. The term *attribute* is used in object-oriented analysis and object-oriented databases; the term *variable* is used in object-oriented programs.

## Identifying Classes

It seems relatively straightforward to state definitions that define classes, objects, member functions, and variables. However, the task of identifying the classes that make up a program can be challenging. It means looking at the environment that a program is to serve and being able to view it in terms of objects and object relationships.

The design of an object-oriented program takes place during the design phase of the software development cycle. Designing an object-oriented program means using the needs of the users and knowledge of the environment the program will serve to create a structure for the program.

Unfortunately, there aren't any simple rules for determining what the classes should be for any given program: identifying classes can be as much of an art as a science. The process is somewhat imprecise because there is often more than one way to design an object-oriented program. Choosing between alternative designs involves weighing the advantages and disadvantages of each; it's not unusual for there to be no clear-cut best design. To make the process a bit easier, let's start by looking at an example. At the end of the chapter, we'll generalize some guidelines you can use when you approach your own programs.

## The Office Supply Inventory

Hard times have hit the major international management consulting firm of Rye Associates Inc. Top management has ordered financial cutbacks in every aspect of the organization, including the purchasing of office supplies. Instead of simply ordering whatever anyone needs, office managers have been instructed to keep detailed records of office supply levels. In other words, corporate management wants to know the state of the current office supply inventory at any given time. It also wants office managers to reorder only when levels drop below a predetermined reorder point.

Although the demand to keep track of office supplies is a major burden for many office managers, the head of Information Systems has come up with a relatively simple solution. She asks one of the C++ programmers to create a program that will track current inventory levels of office supplies. At the end of each month, one of the department secretaries will take a physical inventory of all the office supplies. (The monthly physical inventory is a lot simpler than trying to capture data every time someone takes something out of the supply cabinet.) These data will be entered into the program, which will then print out a summary of the inventory. By comparing summaries from many months, the IS manager can get a good picture of how supplies are being used.

The program will also generate a monthly order list. All supplies for which the current stock level has dropped below the reorder point will be placed on that list, which can then be sent directly to Purchasing.

In this case, the needs of the user (the IS manager) have been well specified. The first task facing the C++ programmer therefore is deciding what classes to use in the program. The office supply inventory program actually deals with only one thing: the office supplies that make up the inventory. However, just what is the class?

The class is a type of office supply, in this particular situation called Inventory Item. From that class the program will create one object for each type of supply used by the IS department, such as floppy disks, black fine-line pens, or Post-It notes. The class might be diagrammed as in Figure 4.1. Each item is described by an item number, a text description of the item, the number on hand as of the most recent physical inventory, and the reorder point.

Figure 4.1  The Inventory Item class and the data that describe it

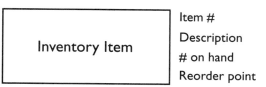

One of the most common mistakes made by people who are just starting to work with object-oriented concepts is to look at the entire inventory, rather than the inventory item, as the class. Keep in mind, however, that a class is a template from which you stamp out objects. Each object represents one real-world occurrence, or *instance*, of the class. If the inventory were the class, then each object would represent a separate inventory (the contents of a separate supply cabinet, if you will). This is clearly not what the C++ programmer is trying to represent. In this example, the inventory is actually the collection of all the objects created from the Inventory Item class.

**Note**

Because an object represents an instance of a class, the verb *instantiate* is often used to refer to the process of creating an object from a class.

The C++ programmer must also define the actions that the Inventory Item class will perform. Given the requirements defined by the IS manager, the programmer comes up with the following list:

- Create a new inventory item.
- Modify the data describing an inventory item.
- Delete an item from the inventory.
- Check to see if the item needs to be reordered.
- Return information about the item's current stock level.
- Return information about the item's description.

This list illustrates one very important characteristic of member functions. Each member function acts on only one object at a time. Therefore, there is no member function to print a report of items that need to be reordered. Instead, there is a function that checks a single object to see if it needs to be reordered.

To prepare the report of items that need to be reordered, the program needs another class that can manipulate the many objects that have been created from the Inventory Item class. In a simple object-oriented program, this class will be the application class.

For this particular example, one object will be created from the application class, which will create objects from the Inventory Item class and organize them in some way. If we were to diagram the object used by the supply inventory program, we might draw something like Figure 4.2. The application object can be thought of as the manager of or container for the Inventory Item objects.

Figure 4.2    The objects used by the inventory supply program

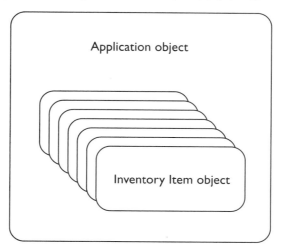

**Note**

There are many ways to organize multiple objects created from the same class. You will learn about two of those methods—arrays and linked lists—in this book.

Then, it will access the Inventory Item objects one at a time to determine which items need to be ordered, and will add only those that do need to be reordered to the report.

The last two member functions in the Inventory Item class send data from an object back to whatever is manipulating the object. In this particular object, the application object uses these functions to create the monthly inventory summary report. They are necessary because an object's data are hidden from any function using the object (*information hiding*). The inventory program's application object, however, needs the item description and stock level for the monthly inventory summary report

## Inheritance

Classes are often related in a hierarchy that moves from general to specific. For example, assume that you are writing a program that computes an amortization table for three types of loans (fixed-payment, variable-payment, and mortgage).

All of the types of loans share some attributes (principal and interest rate). However, in addition to the common attributes, each type of loan has some attributes that are specific to it:

- Fixed-payment: payment amount
- Variable-payment: payment percent, minimum payment, and minimum interest
- Mortgage: number of payment periods, number of payment periods per year, and payment amount

One way to structure the loan program is to create three separate classes, each of which duplicates the principal and interest rate attributes. However, the objects can be related in a hierarchy that captures the idea that there is a generic class—a loan—from which other specialized classes branch. This type of relationship, which goes from a general class to specialized classes, is known as *inheritance*. For our particular example, it might be diagrammed as in Figure 4.3. The Loan class is known as a *base* class; the other three classes are *derived* classes.

Figure 4.3   Classes in the loan program

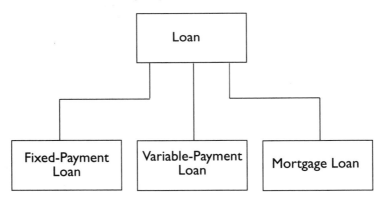

When the classes are declared in a program, the Loan class will include the principal and interest rate attributes. The derived classes include only their class-specific attributes. They "inherit" the common attributes from Loan.

Using inheritance has two major advantages:

- It avoids duplicating attributes in related classes.
- It imposes organization on the classes in a program, making the structure of a program easier to understand and maintain.

**Note**  Member functions can also be inherited, but the situation is a bit more involved than with data.

It isn't always easy to determine when inheritance is appropriate for a program. To explore the situation a bit further, we'll look at two examples.

## The Office Supply Company

One of the companies from which Rye Associates purchases office supplies is Country-Wide Supplies. Country-Wide uses an object-oriented C++ program to keep track of the supplies in its catalog. The program manages information about all available merchandise items, including their price, shipping weight, and other descriptive characteristics.

As you might expect, the underlying class in Country-Wide's program is the office supply item. The entire program could therefore be based on a single class like that in Figure 4.4. The problem with this design, however, is that the descriptive characteristics that are stored about the items vary, depending on the general type of the item; not every type of product has values for every data item. For example, paper products are described by their size and color, whereas writing products are described by type of tip, size of tip, and color.

Figure 4.4    A class to handle an office supply company's merchandise

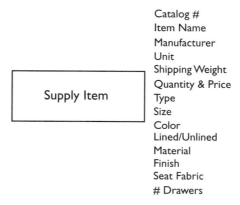

Your first thought may be that Country-Wide can simply leave data items that don't apply to any given type of merchandise without values. Although such a solution will certainly work, it isn't very efficient in terms of storage space. Whenever an object is created, space is allocated in main memory for the entire object. That means that even if no values are assigned to some data items, those data items still consume storage. The unnecessary storage may also consume extra disk space when the object is transferred to external storage.

The fact that there are many variations on one type of object suggests that Country-Wide is dealing with some generic properties of an item (the price and shipping weight, for example) along with other properties that apply to more specific types of items. Such a situation can be handled through inheritance.

A portion of a possible class hierarchy for Country-Wide appears in Figure 4.5. (Because an office supply company typically handles so many types of products, showing the entire class hierarchy in one drawing isn't particularly practical!) Notice that the hierarchy begins with the base class—Supply Item—and is then made more specific with derived classes. For this example, there are three derived classes on the second level of the hierarchy—Writing Instrument (pens and pencils), Paper Product, and Furniture. The Furniture class has two derived classes—Chair and Desk.

Only the four classes with black circles in their boxes in Figure 4.5 (Writing Instrument, Paper Product, Chair, and Desk) are actually used to create objects. When an object is created, it receives its own data along with the data of its base class. For example, a Writing Instrument object inherits all the data that are defined as part of the Supply Item class.

The Furniture class also inherits the data defined as part of the Supply Item class. The Desk class therefore inherits not only the data defined as part of the Furniture class, but also the data that the Furniture class inherited from the Supply Item class.

The major advantage to using the design in Figure 4.5 is that no storage space is wasted when objects are created: Every data item is used for every object. However, in this particular example, using the class hierarchy instead of a single class can make the objects harder to use. For example, if the program using this class hierarchy needs to display or print every product carried by Country-Wide, then the program must use separate code for each class; the output will be inaccurate if the programmer happens to forget about a class. If the coding is based on a single class, the programmer only has to write code that processes one class and runs no risk of missing any objects.

Figure 4.5    A portion of the class hierarchy for an office supply company

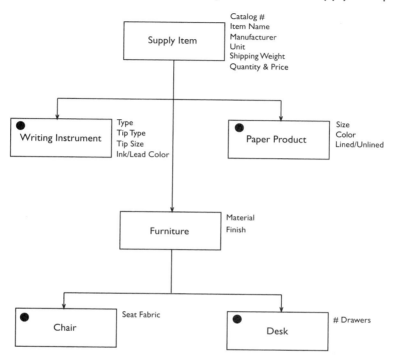

Which design is better, one class or a class hierarchy? The answer is "It depends." The best design depends in large measure on how the class or classes will be used. If the program is intended for telephone salespeople who answer questions about specific products or types of products, then the class hierarchy is probably the best choice. It is the most efficient in terms of storage, allowing more objects to reside in main memory, speeding up the program. However, if the program is designed for more general use, including a need to provide a listing of every product, then the single-class design is probably best. Although it may waste a bit of storage and its performance may suffer when objects must be loaded from disk during execution, it simplifies access to the merchandise as a whole.

## The Corner Pharmacy

The Corner Pharmacy is a full-service drug store owned and operated by George and Gladys Bellows. It has been in the Bellows family for three generations and currently isn't part of any national chain. In addition to containing a pharmacy, the store sells cosmetics, personal care items, and other merchandise typically found in a drug store. Both Mr. and Mrs. Bellows are registered pharmacists; the store employs two other pharmacists as well as a 10-person sales staff.

The Bellows are concerned that their business may be suffering because they aren't managing their prescriptions on a computer like the drug stores that belong to national chains. Among other things, the national chains advertise that they can check for drug interactions. The Bellows are therefore going to have someone write a program that will handle prescriptions.

**Note**

The Bellows looked at existing pharmacy management software packages, but discovered that those packages were designed for much larger stores and provided functions the Bellows didn't need. The cost of custom programming that would exactly match the Bellows's specifications was less than the purchase of a ready-made package with capabilities that would never be used.

As you know, the first step in the process is to analyze the needs of the users of the program. The Bellows sat down with the programmer and identified three major things about which they needed to store data: customers, drugs, and prescriptions. They stated that it is vital that data about drug interactions be part of the program. The Bellows also emphasized that there is a slight difference in the handling of prescriptions for controlled and noncontrolled substances.

After listening carefully to the Bellows's description of the data the program needs to store and what the program needs to do, the programmer produced the classes shown in Figure 4.6. There are three stand-alone classes (Customer, Drug, and Prescription). The Prescription class also has two derived classes, one for a controlled substance and the other for a noncontrolled substance.

Figure 4.6 Classes to manage a pharmacy's prescriptions

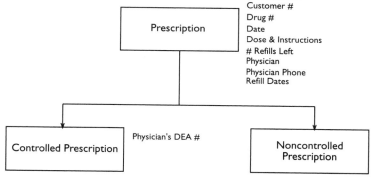

There is certainly a relationship between the three stand-alone classes. Each prescription is for one customer and one drug. Why, then, isn't Prescription a derived class of Customer and Drug? If the classes were designed in that way, the class hierarchy would look like Figure 4.7. (Deriving a class from more than one base class is known as *multiple inheritance*.)

This design may initially seem very intuitive, especially if you've taken a data management course and are familiar with the design of relational databases. However, keep in mind that with inheritance, the derived class inherits all the data items of the base class. In other words, every time a Prescription object was created, it would include *all* the customer data as well as *all* the drug data. Inheritance isn't a logical relationship between classes; it's a migration of class data and functions down a hierarchy.

There is one primary reason why, in this particular example, inheritance isn't appropriate. Consider first how these classes might be used. An object is created from each Customer class for every person for whom a prescription is

Figure 4.7   Attempting to use inheritance in the prescription class hierarchy

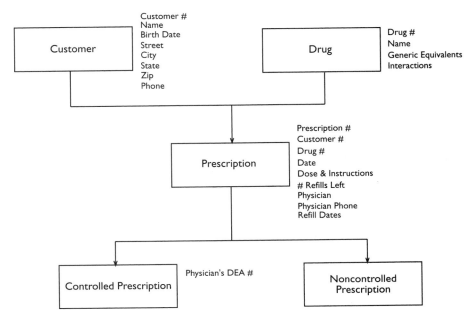

filled; an object is created from the Drug class for every drug carried by the pharmacy. (Note that drugs include nonprescription substances because over-the-counter medications can interact with prescription drugs.)

When a prescription is filled for the first time, an object is created from the Prescription class. Although the Prescription object inherits all the data from the Customer and Drug classes, it's unlikely that customer data (other than the Customer #) and drug data (other than the Drug #) would be repeated. Repeating the data introduces a lot of unnecessary duplication into the program. The duplicated data don't take up any extra room—the space for the inherited data items is allocated regardless of whether values are entered—but this type of duplication introduces a major risk of inaccurate data. How can you guarantee that each time a customer's name and address are entered they are entered in exactly the same way, every time? How can you guarantee that the generic equivalents of a drug and the drugs with which a drug interacts are entered in exactly the same way, every time? In addition, will a pharmacist want to take the time to reenter all the drug information each time he or she fills a new prescription?

Given that the bulk of the data from the base classes aren't going to be repeated in the derived class, inheritance isn't appropriate in this case. Instead, the Customer, Drug, Controlled Prescription, and Noncontrolled Prescription classes will be managed as stand-alone classes. The application program that manipulates objects created from these classes will use the Customer # and Drug # to search Customer and Drug objects to locate objects related to any given prescription.

## Classes and the User Interface

As you know, classes aren't restricted to entities that store data. They are also used to represent items in a program's user interface. As an example, consider the four types of windows in Figure 4.8. Although all are rectangular and approximately the same size, they have different characteristics. The document window at the top left of Figure 4.8 has scroll bars, a title bar, a close box, a size box, and a zoom box. The shadowed window to its right and the alert window below have none of those characteristics but instead have distinctive borders. The round-cornered window at the lower right has a title bar and close box, but no scroll bars, grow box, or zoom box; its title bar is also rather different from the title bar of the document window.

Because these windows are variations of a generic rectangular window, they lend themselves to a class hierarchy like that shown in Figure 4.9. The base class, Window, includes a unique ID number for a window along with the coordinates of the window's position on the screen. These coordinates also represent the window's size.

There is one derived class for each type of window in Figure 4.8. The Document class includes data that describe all the possible types of elements that a programmer might choose to include in a window; the same is true for the Round-cornered class. However, the Shadow and Alert classes don't have any data other than what they inherit from the base class.

Why, then, are the Shadow and Alert classes necessary? The answer lies in the member functions. In particular, each class has a member function that draws the window on the screen. The way in which that function acts varies among the four types of windows because each type of window looks different. Even though the Alert and Round-cornered classes don't add any data to that of the base class, the way in which they respond to a "draw yourself" message is different.

Figure 4.8    Sample window types

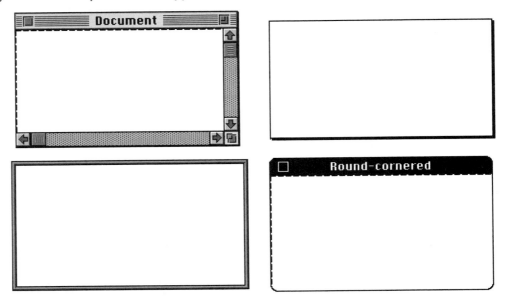

Figure 4.9    A window class hierarchy

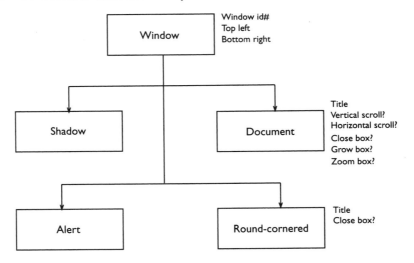

## Some Guidelines for Defining Classes

Based on your reading of the preceding examples, several general principles should have emerged for defining classes, class hierarchies, and member functions. When defining classes, you should pay attention to the following guidelines:

- Choose classes to represent the most specific entities in the data processing environment. When representing an inventory of items, for example, choose classes for the items in the inventory, rather than the inventory itself.
- Consider inheritance when you have similar types of items that share some data, but have data specific to a given item type. Create a base class that contains the common data and use derived classes to represent the item-specific data.
- Consider inheritance when you have similar types of items that react differently to the same message.
- After identifying classes that will store program data, consider classes that will be used to manage the user interface.
- Create one class that will represent the application itself. As you have read, you will create only one object from this class.

When deciding what member functions to define for a class, consider the following:

- Each class needs at least one function that is run when the object is created (a *constructor*). You may also want to include a function that will be run when the object is destroyed (a *destructor*). Constructors and destructors are discussed in more depth beginning in Chapter 8.
- A member function acts on just one specific object rather than on all objects of the same class. Therefore, a member function must represent an action appropriate for a single object. If all objects of the same class need to be processed, then it is the responsibility of a class specifically designed to handle multiple objects of another type to do so.
- Because the data that describe an object are hidden from the program manipulating the object, classes often need member functions that return data values to whatever is manipulating the object.

- In addition to functions that return data values, classes also need functions to change the values in their attributes.

## Summary

The object-oriented paradigm is a way of organizing the high-level logic of a program. It has the following major characteristics:

- Entities in the programming environment—data, the user interface, and the program itself—are represented as objects.
- Objects have data that describe them (variables) and things they know how to do (member functions).
- The general pattern from which an object is created is known as a class.
- A class's variables are usually private (hidden from functions outside the class).
- The way in which functions are called is public. The details of how functions operate are private (known as information hiding or encapsulation).
- General classes (base classes) share their variables and member functions with more specific classes created from them (derived classes); this is known as inheritance.
- Objects communicate by sending messages to one another. A message indicates the object that is to receive the message, the member function that is to be executed, and the data that are to be used as input to the member function.

## Exercises

Draw a diagram like those used in this chapter to describe the classes you would create for the programs described in the following. On a separate page, list the member functions you would need for each class.

1.  A program that would manage a student's calendar, including class schedule, reading assignments, assignments to hand in, and exam schedules. The program should also track school holidays.

2.  A program that keeps track of grades a student receives during the semester, identified by course, type of graded item, and the weight of that item in the overall course grade.

3.  A program that helps someone building a house pick the options for that house, including siding material and color, inside wall covering and color/pattern, and floor coverings for each room.

4.  A program that manages a video store, including the movies in inventory, the people who rent them (the customers), and the actual rentals of those items.

5.  A program that a salesperson could use to manage his or her contacts with customers, including when each contact was made, the substance of the contact, and how the contact should be followed up.

6.  A program that a student could use to manage a bibliography for a term paper, including sources of research material, quotations taken from the research, and data to be used in writing the paper.

7.  A program to manage a Human Resources department (formerly called "Personnel"), including employees, their job history with the company, and their dependents.

8.  A program that a hobby shop could use to control its inventory. The program should track items in inventory along with the sales of those items. (*Hint:* Don't forget about the people making purchases.)

9.  A program to manage the service department of an automobile dealership. The program should handle cars and their owners, service appointments, and work done during those appointments.

10. A program to handle accounts payable (money a company owes). The program should track the vendors to whom money is owed, the statements that are received from those vendors, and payments made. When developing your classes, consider the effect of writing checks on a company's bank account.

# 5

# Anatomy of a C++ Program

## OBJECTIVES

In this chapter you will read about:

- The elements that are found in almost every object-oriented C++ program.
- The basic structure of C++ functions.
- The basic structure of C++ class declarations and how they are prepared for use in a program.

For one of the exercises at the end of Chapter 2, you entered and ran a complete object-oriented program, without being able to identify the parts of the program or how those parts fit together. In this chapter we'll take care of that problem: You will be introduced to the elements that you will find in almost every object-oriented C++ program. This will give you a framework for the more in-depth discussions of variables and member functions that you will encounter in Chapters 6 and 7.

As an example of a simple (and silly) short program that contains all the basic elements needed for a complete object-oriented C++ program, we'll be looking at an age analysis program that asks you for your age and the ages of your parents when you were born. It then figures out how old you were (or will be) when your parents are twice your age. The dialog the program conducts with the user can be found in Figure 5.1.

Figure 5.1  Playing with ages

```
What is your current age? 26
How old was your mother when you were born? 23
How old was your father when you were born? 29

Your mother was twice your age when you were 23 years old.
Your father will be twice your age when you are 29 years old.
```

A C++ program is a collection of *functions*. As you have read, a function is a self-contained block of executable program code. A function can belong to a class (a member function) or it can be stand-alone (not part of a class). Although you can use C++ to write a program without ever using a class or a member function, such a program isn't object-oriented. In fact, an object-oriented C++ program has only one function that isn't a member function: the main function.

**Note**   Some programming languages—for example, SmallTalk and Java—force you to write object-oriented programs. Many people therefore consider them to be "pure" object-oriented languages. However, because C++ lets a programmer write programs that aren't object-oriented, it is up to the programmer to ensure that a program adheres to object-oriented principles.

## The main Function

As you have just read, an object-oriented C++ program has only one function that isn't part of a class. It is always named `main`. (This is the only place where C++ stifles your creativity in terms of naming things.) `main` is the first function executed by the computer. It is required because the compiler must have some way to know where a program begins.

As you will see throughout this book, in an object-oriented program the `main` function is extremely short: The `main` function used in this book contains only two executable statements. Its whole purpose is to create an application object and to send a message to the application object to run the program. Because it jump-starts program execution, the `main` function is sometimes called the program's *driver*.

You can find the `main` function used by the age analysis program in Listing 5.1. It has a very specific structrure:

```
return_data_type main ()
{
    body of function
}
```

In this notation, anything that appears in italics needs to be replaced with a value that you choose. Everything that appears in regular type is used just as it appears. We will use this notation throughout this book to present C++ syntax patterns.

### Listing 5.1    A sample main function (stored in *main.cpp*)

```
#include "appclass.h"

void main ()
{
    AppClass theApp;
    theApp.Run();
}
```

The first element of the `main` function is a "return data type." To understand what this means, you need to know two things:

- A function can send one value from inside the function to the outside world. This is known as *returning* a value. The value itself is called the *return value*. Where does the value go? In the case of a main function, it goes back to the computer's operating system. Theoretically, an operating system can make use of a main function's return value to determine whether the program ended correctly. However, many of today's program's don't bother to send a value back to the operating system.

**Note**

You will learn a great deal more about return values throughout this book. Only the main function sends a value back to the operating system. Member functions return values to other functions.

- The function's declaration must indicate the type of data (for example, integer or floating point value) that the function will be running. If there is no return value, you use the word void as a placeholder. By default, a main function returns an integer, but today we often simply use void to indicate no return value.

**Note**

Many early C++ compilers would let you get away without indicating a return data type for the main function. If you left it out, the compiler simply assumed you wanted an integer. However, most of today's compilers will flag a missing return data type as an error.

The braces ({ and })that you see surrounding the body of the main function are used throughout C++ programs for grouping. In this case, they let the compiler know where the function begins and ends. Anything within the braces belongs to main and therefore constitutes the *body of the function.*

The first line in the body of the function creates an object (theApp) from a class named AppClass. The second line executes, or *calls*, the object's Run function. All of the program's work is then handled by Run. You will learn more about the syntax used in this function in Chapter 8.

Because a main function is *executable code*—program code that the computer can run—we store the source file in a text file with a *.cp* or *.cpp* extension. Most compilers require an extension of *.cp* or *.cpp* for executable source code files. The portion of the file name preceding the extension is up to you. However, most of the time you should try to use something that is suggestive of the contents of the file. In this example, the main function is stored in *main.cpp.*

## Class Declarations

The age manipulation program uses two classes: an application class to represent the program itself and a class to represent the ages that relate to one person. Before a program can create objects from any class, the class must be *declared*. Declaring a class means that you must give the class a name, name the elements that will store its data, and describe the functions that will perform actions with objects.

Declarations aren't executable program code. Instead, the computer uses them to figure out how to allocate storage for values used by the program and to recognize functions that the program will use. Typically, we place class declarations in different files from executable code, using one file for each class. Known as *header files*, they are stored with a file name extension of *.h*.

Because the age manipulation program uses two classes, it has two header files: *appclass.h* (Listing 5.2) and *age.h* (Listing 5.3). If you look closely at the contents of these two files, you'll notice that they have some syntax in common. In particular, you can see that each class declaration begins with the keyword `class`, followed by the name of the class. The body of the class is surrounded by braces, just like the `main` function we just discussed. However, unlike the `main` function, the class declarations end with a semicolon.

Listing 5.2   The declaration of the application class (stored in *appclass.h*)

```
class AppClass
{
    public:
        AppClass();
        void Run();
};
```

Listing 5.3   The declaration of the age class (stored in *age.h*)

```
class age
{
    private:
        int childAge, motherAge, fatherAge;
    public:
        age();
        void init (int, int, int);
        int getChild();
        int getMother();
        int getFather();
};
```

A class declaration has the folowing general syntax:

```
class class_name
{
    private | protected | public:
        definitions of private elements (usually stored data)

    private | public:
        definitions of public elements (usually functions)
};
```

This syntax is an extension of the general syntax you saw when we looked at the syntax for the `main` function. As before, any part of the syntax that appears in regular type (for example, `class`) represents a part of the syntax that you should use exactly as it appears. Any part that appears in italics (for example, `class_name`) is a description of something that you must add, something that is determined by exactly what you are doing. In the example above, you must choose and enter a class name.

When you see items separated by a vertical bar (|), that means you must choose one option from among those listed. For example, in the class declaration syntax, you must choose one of `private`, `protected`, or `public`. Because these appear in regular type, it means you choose one and use it exactly as it appears. Since we will be discussing the meaning of these words more extensively in Chapter 7, it will suffice for now to say that they determine the access that program elements outside the class have to parts of the class. For example, if access to the data stored by a program to describe an object should be restricted to the object itself, then the data are private. Public elements of a class are accessible to all parts of the program. Most member functions, for example, are public.

As mentioned earlier, class declaration begins with the keyword `class`, followed by the name of the class. Class names can include letters, numbers, and underscores and must not be the same as any C++ keyword. In almost every case, we try to give classes names that are suggestive of what they represent. The body of the class definition is surrounded by braces (`{` and `}`) and ends with a semicolon.

As another example, consider the class declaration in Figure 5.2. This class is named `Product`. It contains private data (data whose contents are accessible only to member functions) for a product number, product name, product description, product price, and the product on hand. The member functions are all public, meaning that they can be called by any other function, even those outside the class. The functions initialize an object's data, format a display of all data about a product, send the product price back to a calling function, and update the number of items on hand.

Figure 5.2   A sample class declaration

```
class Product  ←──────── class name
{
    private:  ←──── Access for Data storage      Data storage
        int prod_numb;                           declarations
        char prod_name[26]; prod_desc[81];
        float prod_price, numb_on_hand;
    public:  ←────────── Access for functions
        Product(int, char[], char[], float, float);
        void viewProduct();
        float getPrice();
        void updateOnHand (int);  ←──── Function declarations
};
```

## Class Implementations

The source code for the implementation of a class's member functions is executable code. It is therefore stored in text files with *.cp* or *.cpp* extensions. Typically, we place the implementation of each class in a separate file. This means that the age manipulation program requires two more files, one for the application class (Listing 5.4) and one for the age class (Listing 5.5).

Each function implementation has the same general structure. Notice that a function begins with a header line that contains, among other things, the name of the function, and that its body is surrounded by a pair of braces. We will look at the structure of functions in depth in Chapter 7.

## Obtaining Classes

Where do classes come from? In the examples you have seen to this point, the classes have been written by the programmer who was responsible for creating the program. However, as you read in Chapter 2, we often also use classes that are written by someone else. Classes that provide I/O support, for example, are written by others and supplied to us as part of a program library that accompanies a C++ software development package.

**Listing 5.4    The implementation of the age manipulation program's application class (stored in *appclass.cpp*)**

```cpp
#include "appclass.h"
#include "age.h"
#include <iostream.h>

AppClass::AppClass()
{
    // This is a comment line that the compiler ignores
}

void AppClass::Run()
{
    age thePerson; // create one object from the age class
    int ichild, imother, ifather;

    // collect data from the user
    cout << "What is your current age? ";
    cin >> ichild;
    cout << "How old was your mother when you were born? ";
    cin >> imother;
    cout << "How old was your father when you were born? ";
    cin >> ifather;

    // initialize the object
    thePerson.init (ichild, imother, ifather);

    // analyze the ages and display the correct sentence
    if (thePerson.getMother() < thePerson.getChild())
        cout << "\nYour mother was twice your age when you were ";
    else
        cout << "\nYour mother will be twice your age when you are ";
    cout << thePerson.getMother() << " years old.";

    if (thePerson.getFather() < thePerson.getChild())
        cout << "\nYour father was twice your age when you were ";
    else
        cout << "\nYour father will be twice your age when you are ";
    cout << thePerson.getFather() << " years old.";
}
```

In general, there are three sources for classes:

- You can declare and implement your own classes. These will always be available to you as source code.
- You can use classes that someone else has written and given or sold to you. Whether you have source code for such classes, or are lim-

Listing 5.5    The implementation of the age manipulation program's age class
(stored in *age.cpp*)

```cpp
#include "age.h"

// This function initializes all the data storage to 0 when an object is created from the class
age::age()
{
    childAge = 0;
    motherAge = 0;
    fatherAge = 0;
}

// This function places data into an object
void age::init (int child, int mother, int father)
{
    childAge = child;
    motherAge = mother;
    fatherAge = father;
}

// "Get" functions send private values to another function
int age::getChild()
    { return childAge; }

int age::getMother()
    { return motherAge; }

int age::getFather()
    { return fatherAge; }
```

ited to using object code for the implementation of the classes, will
vary from one set of classes to another.
- You can use classes from the program libraries that accompany your
C++ development software. The implementations of these classes
are typically supplied as object code.

Regardless of where you obtain the classes you use in a program, keep in
mind that you must have access to the declarations of the classes. Even if the
implementations have been compiled and supplied to you as object code, you
must have the text version of the class declarations for your compiler to use.

## Classes and Header Files

As you have seen, class declarations—those of classes you write yourself and those of classes that are part of the libraries supplied with your program development software—are typically stored in their own source code files, separate from the implementations of their member functions. These are the header files that were mentioned earlier in this chapter.

There is a major benefit to using header files: You can make the same class declaration available to many programs without duplicating the declaration. This type of software reuse is not limited to object-oriented programming, but as you will discover as you become more familiar with C++, an object-oriented program makes software reuse much easier.

To gain access to the contents of a header file, a file that contains the implementation of functions of the class declared in the header file or a file that creates objects from the class declared in the header file *includes*, or merges, the header file using a *compiler directive*. A compiler directive is an instruction to the compiler that is processed during compilation. Compiler directives begin with a pound sign (#).

The directive to merge the contents of a header file into a file containing function source code is

```
#include file_name
```

Most compilers support two slightly different versions of this directive. The first instructs the compiler to look for the header file in a disk directory that has been designated as the repository for header files. For example, if you want to use the class library that supports the I/O you will learn about in Chapter 9, the command is written

```
#include <iostream.h>
```

Notice that the name of the header file is surrounded by the less than and greater than symbols. However, if the header file is in a different directory, you surround its path name with double quotes, as in

```
#include "/my.headers/custom.h"
```

**Note**

Although the C++ discussed in this book adheres to the ANSI standard, C++ compilers do differ. In particular, the names given to the header files that support the libraries shipped with the compiler may not be the same. The header file names used in this book are those typically used with the MS-DOS and Macintosh operating systems. Therefore, if you are working on a different platform, check your compiler's documentation to verify header file names.

If you look back at Listing 5.1, you will notice that the age analysis program's *main.cpp* file includes the header file *appclass.h*. This makes the declaration of the application class in Listing 5.2 available to the main function. By the same token, the implementation of the age class in *age.cpp* (Listing 5.5) includes the declaration of the class being implemented. The implementation of the application class in Listing 5.4 includes both header files (*appclass.h* and *age.h*) because the implementation of the application class requires an object from the age class.

Because header files are included in source code files, they aren't added to project files. In fact, if you attempt to compile a file that contains nothing but declarations, the compiler will report a number of errors. You should therefore only place files containing executable code (files with *cp* or *.cpp* extensions) in projects.

## Summary

A C++ program is a collection of functions. In an object-oriented C++ program, only the main function isn't a member function (part of a class). Program execution begins with the main function.

Object-oriented C++ programs use at least one class: an application class from which an object is created to represent the program itself. In most cases, a program uses at least one other class to hold data being manipulated.

Classes must be declared before objects can be created from them. Class declarations are placed in header files, which are then included, or merged, into executable source code files.

## Exercises

The first two exercises below will give you a chance to debug (find the errors in) some simple C++ programs. The errors that are in these programs are typical errors that people make when learning to program in C++ and involve the structural elements of a C++ program that were presented in this chapter. You can enter the programs yourself or obtain the source code files from your instructor. In either case, however, you will need to create a project file for each program.

The remaining exercises provide extra practice with some of the important concepts that you've learned.

1.  Shipping companies often ask you to compute the total dimensions of a package by adding the package's width, length, and height. In Figure 5.3 you can see the output of a program that performs the computation for you. When you have the program running correctly, it should conduct a dialog with you just as you see in the illustration.

**Figure 5.3    Output of the package size computation program**

```
Enter the width of the package: 10
Enter the length of the package: 15
Enter the height of the package: 20

The size of the package is 45 inches.
```

a.  Enter the header files in Listing 5.6 and Listing 5.7.

**Listing 5.6    The declaration of the pkgSize class (save as *size.h*)**

```cpp
class pkgSize
{
    private:
        int length, width, height;
    public:
        pkgSize();
        void init (int, int, int);
        int totalSize ();
}
```

**Listing 5.7    The declaration of the application class (save as *appclass.h*)**

```cpp
class AppClass
{
    public:
        AppClass();
        void Run();
};
```

b.  Enter the source code in Listing 5.8, Listing 5.9, and Listing 5.10.

## Listing 5.8    The main function for the package size program (save as *main.cpp*)

```
#include "appclass.h"

main()
{
    AppClass theApp;
    theApp.Run();
```

## Listing 5.9  The implementation of the application class (save as *appclass.cpp*)

```
#include "appclass.h"
#include "size.h"
#include <iostream.h>

AppClass::AppClass()
{
    // nothing happens here
}

void AppClass::Run()
{
    int iwidth, ilength, iheight;
    pkgSize thePackage; // create an object

    cout << "Enter the width of the package: ";
    cin >> iwidth;
    cout << "Enter the length of the package: ";
    cin >> ilength;
    cout << "Enter the height of the package: ";
    cin >> iheight;

    thePackage.init (iwidth, ilength, iheight);

    cout << "\nThe size of the package is " << thePackage.totalSize() << "
    inches.";
}
```

c.  Create a project for the program and add the *.cpp* files to the project.
d.  Run the program to see what errors the compiler detects. There are three errors in it that you must correct before it will compile and execute. (*Hint:* One error is in *pkgSize.h*, and the other two are in *main.cpp*.)

## Listing 5.10    The implementation of the pkgSize class (save as *size.cpp*)

```
#include "size.h"

pkgSize::pkgSize()
{
    length = 0;
    width = 0;
    height = 0;
}

void pkgSize::init (int ilength, int iwidth, int iheight)
{
    length = ilength;
    width = iwidth;
    height = iheight;
}

int pkgSize::totalSize()
    { return length + width + height; }
```

2.  One of the facts of life in business today is the need to add sales tax to retail sales in most states. In Figure 5.4 on page 78 you can find sample output from a program that computes the tax due on a purchase. The program uses two classes: an application class and a class that describes a purchase by its prices and tax rate. When you have your version of the program running properly, the program should conduct a dialog with you similar to that in the illustration.

## Figure 5.4  Output of the tax computation program

```
Enter the purchase price of the item: 25.95
Enter the tax rate as a fractional percentage (0.XX): 0.0725

The tax is $1.88.
```

a.  Enter the header files in Listing 5.11 and Listing 5.12.
b.  Enter the source code files in Listing 5.13, Listing 5.14, and Listing 5.15.
c.  Create a project for the program and add the *.cpp* files to the project.
d.  Run the program to see what errors the program detects. There are two errors that you must find and correct before the program will run correctly. (*Hint:* One error is in *main.cpp*; the other is in *tax.cpp*.)

**Listing 5.11    Application class header file for the tax computation program (save as *appclass.h*)**

```
class AppClass
{
    public:
        AppClass();
        void Run ();
};
```

**Listing 5.12    Tax class header file for the tax computation program (save as *tax.h*)**

```
class tax
{
    private:
        double taxRate, price;
    public:
        tax ();
        void init (double, double);
        double compute ();
};
```

**Listing 5.13    The main function for the tax computation program (save as *main.cpp*)**

```
#include "appclass.h"

void main ()

    AppClass theApp;
    theApp.Run();
}
```

3.  A student adds the following files to a project:

    - *main.cpp*
    - *appclass.h*
    - *appclass.cpp*
    - *dataclass.h*
    - *dataclass.cpp*

    When the student tries to run the program, the compiler reports many errors. What is wrong with the files that have been included in the project? How would you fix the problem?

## Listing 5.14 The implementation of the application class for the tax computation program (save as *appclass.cpp*)

```cpp
#include "tax.h"
#include "appclass.h"
#include <iostream.h>
#include <iomanip.h>

AppClass::AppClass()
{
    //
}

void AppClass::Run ()
{
    double iRate, iPrice;

    tax thePurchase; // create an object

    cout << "Enter the purchase price of the item: ";
    cin >> iPrice;
    cout << "Enter the tax rate as a fractional percentage (0.XX): ";
    cin >> iRate;
    thePurchase.init (iRate, iPrice);

    cout << setiosflags (ios::fixed) << setprecision (2);
    cout << "\nThe tax is $" << thePurchase.compute() << ".";
}
```

## Listing 5.15 The implementation of the tax class (save as *tax.cpp*)

```cpp
tax::tax()
{
    taxRate = 0.0;
    price = 0.0;
}

void tax::init (double iRate, double iPrice)
{
    taxRate = iRate;
    price = iPrice;
}

double tax::compute ()
    { return (taxRate * price); }
```

4.  One of the program libraries that you will use frequently provides functions for handling strings of characters. The declarations for the string functions are found in the file named *string.h*. Assume that you place the following line in a source code file:

    ```
    #include "string.h"
    ```

    Will this syntax cause a problem? If so, why? How would you fix the problem?

5.  Why must every C++ program have a `main` function? How is the `main` function different from other functions in an object-oriented C++ program?

6.  What purpose do braces ({ and }) serve in a C++ program?

# 6

# Variables

## OBJECTIVES

In this chapter you will read about:
- How variables provide access to data stored in main memory.
- The way in which types of data affect how much storage is allocated for pieces of data.

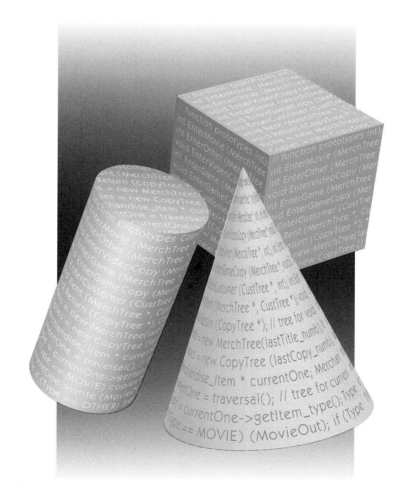

When a programmer writes a description of a class, he or she must specify exactly what data describe each object that will be created from the class. The class declaration must include a name by which each piece of data can be referenced; it must also indicate the type of data that will be stored. The compiler can then set aside storage in main memory for data whenever an object is created from the class.

What can a program do with the data stored in main memory? A program might, for example, perform arithmetic computations with the values. It can make comparisons between values to determine which is greater. It can also display the values on the screen, write them to a data file, or send them to a printer.

In this chapter, you will learn about declaring main memory storage for data. The data may describe objects, or the data may be used temporarily while the program is manipulating objects. You will read about how storage is allocated, how it is accessed, and how you can place values in that storage.

## Variables as Main Memory Storage

Assume, for example, that you are declaring a class that describes pet foods in a pet store's inventory. The class is called Food. Each of the objects created from the class is described by the following pieces of data:

- Manufacturer
- Product name
- Species (e.g., dog, cat, bird, fish)
- Size (e.g., 5 lbs., 10lbs.)
- Type (e.g., dry, semi-moist, canned)
- Price

Regardless of the number of different types of pet foods carried by the store, each can be completely described by its own individual object, each with its own values for the class's descriptive data. In addition, as a program manipulating the objects runs, the values for any given object's data can change. Because the data we store about objects can change during the program run, the storage locations for those data are known as *variables*. Conceptually, it may also help to think of a variable as a container for data. You can put something into a variable; you can take something out of a variable.

When objects from the Food class are created by a computer program, the program must maintain those data in main memory and provide a way for a program to access those data when needed. A program therefore declares names (*variable names*) to represent each storage location the program will use. Variable names act as labels assigned to storage locations in main memory. Whenever the program needs to reference a value, it asks for the contents of a specific variable of a specific object.

The idea that a variable is a label for a main memory storage location isn't new with object-oriented programming. It is the traditional way in which high-level language programs have referenced program data. The major benefit of having variables is that programmers don't have to deal directly with main memory addresses.

Because variables represent storage locations in main memory, they share some characteristics with main memory that, as you will see throughout this book, affect how we use them:

- A variable can hold only one value at a time. This is because each circuit that makes up the memory allocated to a variable can have either a low voltage or a high voltage, but not both. (You can think of a variable as a very shallow container.)
- When you assign a new value to a variable, the new value replaces the old value. Again, this is because changing the value in a main memory location means physically changing the electrical properties of the memory. The old value is lost when new voltages are applied to memory. (If we are looking at a variable as a container, then visualize each new value that's placed into the container as having a small explosive charge that vaporizes the old value when the new value is inserted, as in Figure 6.1.)

## Data Types

When you declare a variable, you are asking a high-level language compiler to set aside main memory storage for that variable. As you will remember from Chapter 2, the amount of storage you need for a value depends on what type of data you are storing: A character, for example, takes up only one byte, while an integer might take up two or four bytes. A variable therefore has a *data type*, which specifies what kind of data it will store, and tells the computer exactly how much space to allocate for it.

Figure 6.1   Variables as containers for one value at a time

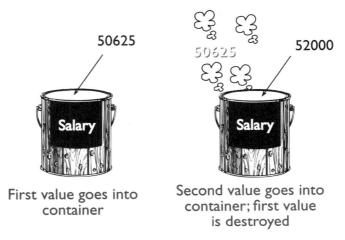

First value goes into container

Second value goes into container; first value is destroyed

The data types that are available to a programmer depend on the language with which he or she is working. In C++, you can choose from a number of simple data types, including the following:

- int: A 16-bit integer (two bytes of storage)
- long: A 32-bit integer (four bytes of storage)
- float: A floating point number (five to eight bytes of storage)
- double: A floating point number with more range and precision than float (five to eight bytes of storage). The precise range and precision vary from one computer to another.
- char: A character (one byte of storage)

As you will see later in this chapter, there are at least two ways to extend the available data types. However, for the moment, we will work with just the preceding five.

Programs used in business make extensive use of text data. Multiple characters assembled into words and sentences are known as *strings*. C++ doesn't have a simple data type that can store a string. Programmers must therefore use more complex variable structures to manage text data. You will learn about strings in Chapter 16.

## Variable Names

Each variable must have a name that identifies it. To avoid confusion with other elements of the C++ language, variable names must adhere to the following rules:

- Variable names can contain letters, numbers, or underscores (_).
- Variable names must start with a letter or an underscore.
- Variable names cannot contain spaces.
- Variable names, like the rest of C++, are case sensitive. In other words, `theVariable` is distinct from `TheVariable`, which is also distinct from `tHEvARIABLE`.

Ordinarily, you want to give variables names that are suggestive of the purpose of the data stored in the variable ("meaningful" variable names) to make the program easier to understand. For example, the number of inventory items in stock in a store might be stored in a main memory location labeled `numb_on_hand` or `NumbOnHand`. Notice that we use either underscores or embedded uppercase letters to indicate breaks between words because variable names can't contain spaces.

If the emphasis on meaningful variables names seems somewhat trivial, take a look at the two class declarations in Listing 6.1. The first class (named A) uses meaningless variable names. It's impossible to tell what the variables will be storing. Even if you understand what the variables mean when you write the program, a few days later, you will probably forget. (You may not believe this now, but when you start writing your own programs, you'll see how quickly you forget why you wrote a program in a particular way.)

On the other hand, it is very clear what the second class will represent. Its name is Employee, so we know that each object created from the class will represent one person who works for a particular company. In addition, each of the variables has an English name that is indicative of what it will store. For example, `monthlyTarget` will hold the employee's monthly sales goal; the `currentSales` variable will hold the amount of sales to date for the current month. Even months later, the class declaration will tell you, or anyone who happens to be using the class, exactly what each variable is intended to represent.

## Listing 6.1   Meaningful versus meaningless variable names

```
// Meaningless variable names
class A
{
    private:
        int a, b, c;
        float x1, x2, x3;
    public:
        A();
        void B (int, int, int, float, float, float);
        float C ();
};

// Meaningful variable names
class Employee
{
    private:
        int employeeNumb, roomNumber, phoneExtension;
        float salary, monthlyTarget, currentSales;
    public:
        Employee ();
        void init (int, int, int, float, float, float);
        float computeSalesDifferential ();
};
```

**Note**  Programs that contain information that describe themselves are known as *self-documenting*. Because it is so easy to forget why a program was written in a particular way and because a program may be modified by someone who didn't write the program originally, it is important that source code contain as much information as possible describing how the program works. This can significantly cut down on the amount of time needed to maintain the program; programmers won't need to spend as long figuring out the logic of the program.

## Declaring Variables

When you declare a class for use in a program, you include declarations of all the class's variables. To declare a variable, you use the data type followed by the name of the variable. For example, you could set aside storage for one integer with the following:

```
int anInteger;
```

The declaration is terminated by a semicolon (;), the character that terminates all C++ declarations and statements. (Remember from Chapter 5 that class declarations end with semicolons, but functions do not.)

**Note**  Although it might seem a bit of a bother to be required to put a semicolon at the end of every declaration and statement in a program, the semicolon is actually quite useful. A C++ compiler doesn't assume that a declaration or statement ends until it encounters a semicolon. Therefore, you can break declarations and statements into multiple lines in your source code file to make the source code easier to read, without worrying about the compiler becoming confused. Using multiple lines for source code and indentation to show program structure is another way of making your code self-documenting. Don't be upset if your instructor insists that you use indentation in your source code in a particular way; this isn't an attempt to make you a conformist. It's a way of helping you to be able to read and understand what your programs do, especially as your programs become longer.

If you have more than one variable of the same data type, you can include it in the same declaration, as long as you separate the variable names with commas. For example, if you need to declare three integers:

```
int Integer1, Integer2, Integer3;
```

Most C++ compilers ignore spaces and carriage returns in a source code file. Therefore, the following declarations are equivalent:

```
int firstNumb, secondNumb, thirdNumb;

int firstNumb,secondNumb,thirdNumb;

int     firstNumb,
        secondNumb,
        thirdNumb;
```

When an object is created, space is allocated in main memory for all the object's variables. The storage locations are placed one next to another. As an example, assume that a class contains the following variable declarations:

```
int EmployeeNumb;
int OfficeNumb;
float Salary;
```

```
long territorySize;
```

The way in which storage is allocated for these variables can be found in Figure 6.2. In this illustration, each small rectangle represents one byte of storage. The darker rectangles surrounding the bytes indicate how the bytes are allocated to data types that require more than one byte of storage. In particular, each integer is given two bytes, the floating point variable five bytes, and the long integer four bytes. As mentioned earlier, the storage locations are contiguous (right next to one another). Space is allocated in this way so that there is no wasted space. The order of the variables in memory is determined simply by the order of the variable declarations in the class.

**Figure 6.2**   Variable storage in main memory

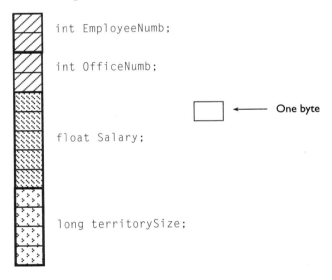

When a program creates an object, it sets aside space for all of the object's variables. Although contiguous allocation means that there is theoretically no wasted space, a program is not required to place a value in an allocated storage location. Even if a program doesn't use a variable, the space is still allocated.

Do variable storage locations have something in them when storage is first allocated? Maybe. Unless it is changed explicitly by a program, a main memory circuit retains its current value. Allocating storage doesn't change main memory values. This means that you can never be certain what value a newly allocated variable will have. Your programs must therefore explicitly give each variable a value before you attempt to use the value. This is known as *initialization*.

There are two ways to initialize a variable: assignment, which is discussed in the next section of this chapter, and acceptance of data from an external source, usually either the keyboard or a data file. You will read about external input in Chapters 9 and 10.

## Giving Variables Values: Assignment

*Assignment* occurs when a program inserts a value directly into a variable. The computer places that value into main memory at the location allocated to the variable. Because a storage location can hold only one value at a time, the effect of assignment is to replace any existing value with the value being assigned.

In C++, the *assignment operator* is an equals sign. To write an assignment statement, you place the variable on the left of the equals sign and the value being assigned on the right:

```
int oneValue, twoValue;
oneValue = 16;
twoValue = oneValue;
```

The value on the right of an assignment operator comes in one of three forms. First, it can be a *literal value*. Literals are values such as 1, 196, *c*, or *This is a test* that appear directly in your source code. When you place literals in your source code, such values aren't stored in main memory like values placed in variables, but instead are translated into the source code when the program is compiled.

The second source of a value for assignment is another variable. When you use a variable on the right of an assignment operator, the computer takes the contents of that variable and *copies* it to the destination location, indicated by the variable on the left of the assignment operator. The content of the source variable on the right of the assignment operator is modified.

Finally, you can place some sort of expression on the right of the assignment operator. An *expression* is a combination of operations that are performed on data. Typical expressions perform arithmetic, manipulate strings, or evaluate whether a condition is true or false. We will begin talking about a wide variety of expressions beginning in Chapter 11.

## The Importance of Initialization

As you read earlier, you can never be sure what value will be in a variable's storage location when space for the variable is first allocated. It is therefore important that you initialize every variable before you use it. Why this is so important may not be immediately obvious, so let's take a look at an example.

Assume that you are performing some addition in a program:

```
sum = sum + firstValue;
sum = sum + secondValue;
sum = sum + thirdValue;
```

Because the assignment operation is a *replacement* operation, these arithmetic statements make sense to a computer. They say "perform the addition on the right side of the assignment operator and store the result in the storage location indicated by the variable on the left side of the assignment operator." To perform the first addition, the computer does the following:

1. Looks up the value in sum.
2. Looks up the value in firstValue.
3. Adds the two values.
4. Stores the result in the location labeled by sum. The original value in sum, which was used in the computation, is erased. The value in firstValue remains the same.

Now, let's give the variables some values:

```
sum contains 0
firstValue contains 10
secondValue contains 20
thirdValue contains 30
```

Given these values, the final value in sum is 60. However, what if sum doesn't start out with 0? What if, for example, the location assigned to sum has 212 in it, a value left over from a program that was previously occupying the same place in main memory? In that case, the final value in sum would be 272, a value that is clearly incorrect in terms of what our program is trying to achieve.

The solution to the problem is to initialize sum before beginning the arithmetic:

```
sum = 0;
```

In this way, we can be certain that we start accumulating from 0, rather than from some unknown value. If you remember to initialize all variables before attempting to use them on the right side of an assignment operator, you will go a long way toward avoiding the production of incorrect results from your programs.

## Variables That Don't Change: Constants

As contradictory as it might seem, C++ programs use a special type of variable whose value can't be changed. Known as a *constant*, this type of variable can make it easier to keep track of literal values. Remember that literal values are values that are a part of your source code, such as 1, 0, 2.45, *c* and *This is a string*.

Good C++ programming attempts to avoid using any meaningful literal values in the body of a program. For example, the current hourly pay rate for all clerical employees could be placed in a program as a literal:

```
float grossPay;
grossPay = hoursWorked * 12.45;
```

The second statement takes the contents of a variable named hoursWorked and multiplies it by the literal pay rate ($12.45 an hour). This literal is meaningful in the context of the program; it represents important information that a program would use when computing an employee's gross pay. The program will certainly work when written in this way, but placing the meaningful literal in the program causes two problems.

First, the literal makes the program difficult to read and understand. When you or someone else looks at the program at a later date, it is likely that you will have forgotten what the literal means.

Second, the literal makes the program difficult to modify. When the hourly pay rate changes, you will have to search through all the source in the program, looking for every place where the literal has been used.

The solution is to use a constant, a word that represents the literal. For example, if you see the word PAY_RATE, you know exactly what it means. Using constants therefore helps make your program more self-documenting.

In addition, assigning words to literals makes the program easier to modify. Constant declarations are usually placed in the same file as the declaration of the class whose member functions will be using the constants. This means that if you need to change a literal, you don't need to search through all your source code to find every place where you've used the literal. You change the declaration of the constant and change it just once.

C++ provides two ways of giving literals names, one inherited from C and the other unique to C++. There is at least one advantage to using the C++ version, which is discussed shortly.

## The #define Directive

The #define directive, which C++ inherited from C, creates a *macro* whose contents are inserted into the code when the program is compiled, just as if you had typed the literal directly into program statements. For example, we could define the constant for the hourly pay rate as follows:

```
#define float PAY_RATE 12.45
```

The directive is followed by the data type of the literal, the name of the macro, and then by the macro's definition. (If the literal is an integer, you can leave off the data type.) Because #define is a compiler directive and not a C++ statement, it doesn't end with a semicolon.

**Note**

By convention, the names of constants are all uppercase letters.

**Note**

Throughout this book you'll find many more programming styles to which C++ programs adhere "by convention." No one enforces these styles, but because they are so widely used they make reading and understanding programs much easier. You will therefore be a better C++ programmer if you adhere to common programming style practices.

Once you have declared the macro, you can use it in the program:

```
grossPay = hoursWorked * PAY_RATE;
```

When the program is compiled, the compiler substitutes the value 12.45 for PAY_RATE. A constant declared with #define therefore isn't like a variable. Instead, it is simply a placeholder for the literal. The object code generated from the source code contains the actual value of the literal represented by the macro.

Because the value of the macro generated by the #define directive is inserted directly into the code when a program is compiled, the #define directive can be responsible for unnecessary repeated code. However, when #define is used to put a name on a literal, the values are short. This is therefore a minor drawback.

## The const Statement

The C++ const statement defines a *constant*—a variable whose contents can't be changed. (Yes, the idea of a "constant variable" is an oxymoron. Nonetheless, this is the terminology that's used.) This means that when the program is compiled, space is set aside for the constant, just as space is set aside to hold the value of a variable. When the program uses the constant, it looks in the main memory storage location where the value of the constant is stored.

The const statement looks much like an assignment statement. To declare a constant, you must give the constant a data type and name, and indicate the value the constant is to contain:

```
const float PAY_RATE = 12.45;
```

Notice that the keyword const is followed by the data tyhpe of the constant, the name of the constant, the assignment operator, and the value of the constant. Because const is a C++ statement, it is terminated by a semicolon.

A constant defined with the const statement behaves much like a variable. In particular, you can examine its value with a debugger, which can make finding problems in a program somewhat easier. However, a compiler won't allow you to assign a value to a constant once the constant has been defined. In other words, a constant is a read-only variable.

Although it is generally better to use const with a C++ program, many of the function libraries you will be using (for example, the string processing libraries) come from C; you will therefore also see some use of #define.

## Creating Your Own Variable Types

One of the things that makes C++ a very flexible language is the ability to create your own variable types. As you will see in Chapter 16, this can greatly simplify working with complex data types such as strings. It can also help make a program easier to understand. (Yes, we're back to that self-documentation business again ...)

At this point, you will be introduced to two mechanisms for defining custom data types: the typedef and enum statements. You will see many uses for them (especially typedef) throughout this book.

## Using typedef

The typedef statement assigns a new variable type name to any existing C++ data type. For example, the statement

```
typedef int BOOLEAN;
```

creates a new variable type named BOOLEAN that holds an integer value. (A "Boolean" is a value that is either true or false.) The new variable type can then be used to define variables for use in a class declaration or member function. You would probably, for example, use the BOOLEAN variable type for variables that indicated whether some condition in the program was true:

```
BOOLEAN More, Finished, Done;
```

It might not be immediately clear why defining the BOOLEAN variable type is any better than simply declaring the three variables as int. However, declaring them as BOOLEAN makes the way in which the variables will be used very clear; the program will therefore be easier to understand.

## Enumerated Variables

An *enumerated variable* is a special integer variable type that can also help make a program easier to understand. When you declare an enumerated variable type, you provide a list of the permissible values for variables of that type. The list typically contains words that represent the values. For example, you might set up an enumerated variable type to hold sizes of the merchandise you sell:

```
enum Sizes {SMALL, MEDIUM, LARGE, X_LARGE};
```

The C++ compiler numbers the values surrounded by braces, beginning with zero. In this particular example, SMALL is 0, MEDIUM is 1, and so on.

Once the variable type has been defined, you can use it to declare variables:

```
enum Sizes T_ShirtSizes;
enum Sizes DressSizes;
```

## Summary

A variable is a label placed on a storage location in main memory so that a program can have access to data stored in that location. A variable can hold only one value at a time; when a program places a new value in a variable, the old value is destroyed.

A variable has a data type that indicates the type of data that will be stored. The data type determines how much storage is allocated. Typically, integers receive two bytes, long integers four bytes, characters one byte, and so on. A compiler allocates variable storage contiguously, with no unused space between variables.

Variables must be declared before they can be used. They should also be initialized because the declaration process doesn't erase any previous value the main memory storage location may have had.

A C++ program often uses constants to represent meaningful literals within a program. Constants let you use words instead of literals, making programs easier to understand and modify.

A C++ program can create its own data types with the typedef statement, providing a custom name for an existing data type. The enum statement also sets up a custom data type in which the compiler assigns integer values to all permissible values for the variable.

## Exercises

In this set of exercises, you will first work with some variable and constant declarations with pen and paper. Then you'll get a chance to declare variables and constants in a sample program, as well as to debug some errors involving constant and variable declarations. You may either type in the source code for the programs or obtain the text files from your instructor. In either case, you will need to create your own project.

1.  Write the following variable declarations:

    a.  A character variable that will hold a letter that represents the size of a piece of clothing.

    b.  An integer variable that will count the number of people who visit a web site.

    c.  A character variable that will hold a single-letter response to a question asked by the computer.

    d.  Two integer variables, one for a student's test score at the beginning of a one-week training course and the other for the same student's test score at the end of the training course.

    e.  A floating point variable that will hold the price of a gallon of home heating oil.

    f.  Three floating point variables that will hold the winning times of the first three heats of a foot race.

2.  Write the following constant declarations, using both the `#define` and `const` syntaxes:

    a.  An integer constant for the number of people who responded to a survey.

    b.  Two integer constants, one for the number of salespeople employed by a company and another for the number of consultants employeed by the same company.

    c.  Three character constants to represent the three sizes that are available for a line of sweatshirts (medium, large, and extra large).

    d.  A floating point constant for the commission rate that salespeople receive on their sales.

    e.  Two floating point constants, one for the regular hourly pay rate and the second for the overtime pay rate.

3.  Identify the problems with the following declarations:

```
a. float Sales, float Commission;
b. float Sales, int Commission;
c. float Sales, Commission
```

```
d. char yes_no; maybe;
e. define NUMB_PEOPLE 18
f. #define CONTACTS = 12;
g. const NUMB_PEOPLE 18;
h. #const NUMB_PEOPLE = 18;
i.  const NUMB_PEOPLE = 25
```

4. For this exercise, you will work with a slightly modified version of the tax computation program that you first saw at the end of Chapter 5. This version conducts a very simple dialog with the user:

```
Enter the amount of the purchase: 85.99
The tax on $85.99 is $6.23
```

Rather than asking the user for the tax rate, the tax rate is a constant.

a. Enter the header file for the purchase class that you see in Listing 6.2. Replace the first blue line in the file with a declaration for a constant named TAX_RATE. Set the tax rate equal to the sales tax rate in your state; if your state has no sales tax, use 0.05. Replace the second blue line in the file with a declaration for a variable named price. You must use these exact names, including matching the case of the letters, because they are used elsewhere in the program.

**Listing 6.2 Header file for the purchase class (save as *purchase.h*)**

```
// replace this line with a constant named TAX_RATE

class purchase
{
    private:
// replace this line with a floating point variable named price
    public:
        purchase ();
        void init (float);
        float computeTax ();
};
```

b. Enter the header file for the application class (Listing 6.3).
c. Enter main function (Listing 6.4).

**Listing 6.3    Header file for the application class (save as *appclass.h*)**

```
class AppClass
{
    public:
        AppClass();
        void Run ();
};
```

**Listing 6.4    Main function (save as *main.cpp*)**

```
#include "appclass.h"

void main ()
{
    AppClass theApp;
    theApp.Run();
}
```

      d.  Enter the implementation of the purchase class that you see in Listing 6.5. You will need to write two assignment statements to complete this implementation. Replace the first blue line with an assignment statement that assigns 0.0 to the variable `price`. Replace the second blue line with an assignment statement that assigns the value in the variable `iprice` to the variable `price`. (*Hint:* Don't forget that the destination of an assignment goes on the left of the assignment operator and that the source goes on the right.)

**Listing 6.5 Implementation of the purchase class (save as *purchase.cpp*)**

```
#include "purchase.h"

purchase::purchase()
{
    // replace this line with an assignment statement that initializes the "price" variable with 0.0
}

void purchase::init (float iprice)
{
// replace this line with an assignment statement that assigns the value in the "iprice" variable to the "price" variable
}

float purchase::computeTax ()
    { return price * TAX_RATE; }
```

e. Enter the implementation of the application class that you see in Listing 6.6. Replace the blue line with the declaration of a floating point variable named iprice.

Listing 6.6    Implementation of the application class (save as *appclass.cpp*)

```
#include "purchase.h"
#include "appclass.h"
#include <iostream.h>
#include <iomanip.h>

AppClass::AppClass()
{
    //
}

void AppClass::Run()
{
    // replace this line with the declaration of a floating point variable named "iprice"

    purchase thePurchase; // create an object

    cout << "Enter the amount of the purchase: ";
    cin >> iprice;

    thePurchase.init (iprice);

    cout << setprecision (2) << setiosflags (ios::fixed);
    cout << "The tax on $" << iprice << " is $" << thePurchase.computeTax();
}
```

f. Create a project for the program. Add the *.cpp* files to the project.

g. Run the program. Find and correct your errors.

h. Which version of this program do you like better? The version from Chapter 5 where the program asked the user to enter the tax rate every time the program was run or this version where the tax rate is built in as a constant? Why? Would your answer change if you knew the tax rate would be changing in the next month? Why?

5. When a doctor asks a patient to monitor his or her own blood pressure, the doctor often suggests that the patient takes three readings, each about ten minutes apart, and then compute the average of the readings. For this exercises, you will be finding the errors in a program that asks the user for the

three readings and then produces the average. It finishes by telling the user whether his or her blood pressure is high. A sample dialog that the program conducts with the user can be found in Figure 6.3.

**Figure 6.3    Sample output of the blood pressure program**

```
Enter the first readings (systolic first, then diastolic): 180 110
Enter the second readings: 210 100
Enter the third readings: 140 100

Your average blood pressure is 166/113
Your blood pressure is high.
```

   a.   Enter the header files in Listing 6.7 and Listing 6.8.

**Listing 6.7    Header file for the pressure class (save as *pressure.h*)**

```
const SYSTOLIC   140
const DIASTOLIC   90

class pressure
{
    private:
        int systolic1; systolic2, systolic3;
        diastolic1, diastolic2, diastolic3;
    public:
        pressure();
        void init (int, int, int, int, int, int);
        int systolicAvg ();
        int diastolicAvg ();
};
```

**Listing 6.8    Header file for the application class (save as *appclass.h*)**

```
class AppClass
{
    public:
        AppClass();
        void Run();
};
```

   b.   Enter the `main` function in Listing 6.9 and the class implementations in Listing 6.10 and Listing 6.11.

**Listing 6.9    Main function for the blood pressure program (save as *main.cpp*)**

```
#include "appclass.h"

void main ()
{
    AppClass theApp;
    theApp.Run();
}
```

**Listing 6.10    Implementation of the pressure class (save as *pressure.cpp*)**

```
#include "pressure.h"

pressure::pressure()
{
    // initializations missing here
}

void pressure::init (int iSys1, int iSys2, int iSys3, int iDias1, int iDias2,
    int iDias3)
{
    systolic1 = iSys1;
    systolic2 = iSys2;
    systolic3 = iSys3;
    diastolic1 = iDias1;
    diastolic2 = iDias2;
    diastolic3 = iDias3;
}

int pressure::systolicAvg ()
    { return ((systolic1 + systolic2 + systolic3)/3); }

int pressure::diastolicAvg()
    { return ((diastolic1 + diastolic2 + diastolic3)/3); }
```

    c.  The implementation of the Pressure class in *pressure.cpp* is missing variable initializations. Replace the blue line in Listing 6.10 with assignment statements that initialize each variable in the Pressure class to 0.

    d.  Create a project for the program and add the *.cpp* files to the project.

    e.  Run the project. The compiler will catch some errors that you must find and correct before the program will execute properly. (*Hint:* The errors are all in *pressure.h*.)

## Listing 6.11    Implementation of the application class (save as *appclass.cpp*)

```cpp
#include "appclass.h"
#include "pressure.h"
#include <iostream.h>

AppClass::AppClass ()
{
    //
}

void AppClass::Run()
{
    int iSys1, iSys2, iSys3, iDias1, iDias2, iDias3;

    pressure Readings; // create an object to hold the readings

    cout << "Enter the first readings (systolic first, then diastolic): ";
    cin >> iSys1 >> iDias1;
    cout << "Enter the second readings: ";
    cin >> iSys2 >> iDias2;
    cout << "Enter the third readings: ";
    cin >> iSys3 >> iDias3;

    Readings.init (iSys1, iDias1, iSys2, iDias2, iSys3, iDias3);

    int sysAvg, diasAvg;

    sysAvg = Readings.systolicAvg();
    diasAvg = Readings.diastolicAvg();

    cout << "\nYour average blood pressure is " << sysAvg << "/" << diasAvg;
    if (sysAvg > SYSTOLIC || diasAvg > DIASTOLIC)
        cout << "\nYour blood pressure is high.";
    else
        cout << "\nYour blood pressure is OK.";
}
```

# 7

# Declaring Member Functions

## OBJECTIVES

In this chapter you will read about:

- Declaring member functions that describe what an object knows how to do.
- Writing complete declarations for classes.

In Chapter 5 you were introduced to the overall structure for declaring a class. In Chapter 6 you studied variables, a part of classes, in great depth. In this chapter we'll finish our discussion of class declarations by looking at declarations for member functions. By the end of the chapter, you will be able to write your own classes from scratch.

## Member Functions

The actions that an object knows how to perform are specified in its class's member functions. The body of a member function therefore contains executable C++ statements. Typically, however, executable statements aren't part of a class declaration. The declaration contains only *prototypes* for member functions.

A *function prototype* is a declaration of the function's name, the data the function needs from the outside world to perform its work, and the type of data that the function will send back to the outside world when it has finished its task. The data that the function receives from the outside world are known as *parameters*, and together with the function's name, make up the function's *signature*.

A function prototype has the following general syntax:

```
return_data_type FunctionName (parameterDataType1, ...);
```

For example, assume that a class needs a function to compute the sum of two integers. The function should do its arithmetic and then send the sum back to the outside world. The function prototype could be written:

```
int Sum (int, int);
```

The first `int` is the data type of the value the function will be sending back. The `int`s inside parentheses represent two values that will be received by the function from the outside world. Notice that the input parameters haven't been given names; at this point, they exist only as data types. However, it is legal to name input parameters in a function declaration:

```
int Sum (int Value1, int Value2);
```

Should you choose to name input parameters, the parameter declarations look just like variable declarations. This is because the input parameters become variables that the member function can use when doing its work.

A member function doesn't need to have input parameters. However, you must include the parentheses that would surround parameters in the prototype. For example, if the Sum function had no parameters, its prototype would be written:

```
int Sum ();
```

By the same token, a member function doesn't need to return a value to the outside world. If a function has no return value, you replace the return value data type with void. For example, if the Sum function were to store its result in an object rather than return the value, the prototype could be written:

```
void Sum (int, int);
```

The only function in a C++ program that doesn't need a prototype is the main function.

**Note**

## Special Function Types

Most classes have two special types of member functions: constructors and destructors. A *constructor* is a member function that is executed automatically by a program whenever an object is created from a class. A *destructor* is executed automatically whenever an object is destroyed (removed from main memory).

The prototypes of constructors and destructors are somewhat different from those of other member functions. A constructor has no return value data type, and its name is always the name of the class. It can have input parameters but isn't required to do so. For example, if you are declaring a class named Calculator, the declaration will contain a constructor with the following prototype:

```
Calculator ();
```

A declaration of this type—a constructor with no input parameters—is often called a *default constructor* because if it isn't included in a class declaration, most compilers will provide it.

The name of a destructor is a tilde (~) followed by the name of the class. Like a constructor, a destructor has no return data type; it also has no input parameters. For example, the Calculator class would have a destructor with the following prototype:

```
~Calculator ();
```

## Function Overloading

A class may contain many constructors. For example, one constructor might expect all of its input to come from its parameters; another might expect its input to come from a data file; and yet another might take its data from another object of the same class. All of these constructors will have the same name (the name of the class) but will have different parameters. (Remember that a C++ compiler looks at both a function's name and its parameters to identify the function.) Including more than one function with the same name but different parameters in a class is known as *function overloading*, a technique that can be used with all types of member functions. (You will see examples of it throughout this book.)

Function overloading provides one of the advantages of object-oriented programming: a consistent interface to the programmer. To help you understand what this means, let's look at an example. Assume that you have a class that describes the employees of your business. Some employees are paid monthly; others are paid hourly, with overtime if they work more than 40 hours per week. You would like to include a member function named computePay. However, the way in which the pay is computed is different for the two types of employees. You need two member functions, one for each type of employee:

```
float computePay ();
float computePay (float, float);
```

The first function—the one without any input parameters—uses the monthly salary stored within the class. The second function uses an hourly pay rate stored within the class in combination with the number of straight-time hours worked (the first parameter) and the number of overtime hours worked (the second parameter). The programmer needs to remember only one function name; only the parameters depend on the type of employee. The function over-loading therefore makes it easier for the programmer to know which member function to use in a given circumstance.

**Note**

Because a destructor has no input parameters, it cannot be overloaded. A class therefore has at most one destructor.

## Variable and Member Function Accessibility

The variables and functions that are part of a class are accessible to other parts of the class, but they aren't necessarily accessible to functions that belong to other classes or to the main function. Variables are typically *private*, which means that functions that belong to the class can use them, but other functions cannot.

In contrast, most member functions are *public*, which means that they can be called by functions outside the class. A function's prototype provides the function's interface to other functions that wish to call it. To call a function, another function identifies the object whose function is to be executed, and provides the name of the function and values for the function's parameters.

The body of a public function—the executable statements that perform the function's actions—is still hidden from other functions (even other functions that belong to the same class). This characteristic is a major feature of the object-oriented paradigm, known as either *encapsulation* or *information hiding*. Although other functions can call a member function using its signature, the details of how the function performs its work are encapsulated within the function implementation, hidden from the outside world. The major benefit that this feature provides is that a programmer can change the body of a member function—the specific way in which a function performs its work—without having to change any code that calls the function.

There is a third type of access—*protected*—that is used in conjunction with inheritance. If a variable or member function is protected, it is accessible to any classes derived from the class in which the variable or member function is declared. However, the variable or member function is still hidden from classes outside the inheritance hierarchy.

## Sample Class Declarations

You have now seen all the elements of a class definition that are typically stored in a header file. To tie it all together, let's look at some class definitions that include member function prototypes.

As you look at these classes, remember that each has a constructor, a member function that has the same name as the class. A constructor, which is run automatically whenever an object is created from a class, has no return data type. Constructors, however, can have input parameters. Whether you use them depends on the way in which a program creates and references objects.

## The Application Class

As you have been reading, the foundation class for an object-oriented program is its application class. In its simplest form, an application class doesn't need any variables. It requires only two member functions, a constructor and a second function that is typically called `Run`. For the initial programs that you write for your C++ course (and all the sample programs you have seen so far), the declaration of the application class will look like Listing 7.1.

### Listing 7.1    An application class

```
class AppClass
{
    public:
        AppClass (); // The constructor, which has no return data type
        void Run ();
};
```

## Currency Conversion

Because today's business world has such an international focus, many companies need a way to to make a quick conversion between local currency and the currency of a country with which they are doing business. The basis for a C++ program that performs such conversions is a class called `Converter` (Listing 7.2).

The `ConversionFactor` variable holds the value by which local currency is multiplied or divided to do the conversion. The `Method` variable determines whether the operation performed is multiplication or division.

### Listing 7.2 The Converter class

```
class Converter
{
    private:
        float ConversionFactor;
        char Method;

    public:
        Converter (void); // Constructor
        void ModConversion (float, char);
        float DoConversion (float);
        float GetFactor (void);
        char GetMethod (void);
};
```

This class needs five member functions. The first (Converter) is the constructor. The second, the ModConversion function, takes data from the program using an object of this class and puts those values into an object. It can be used to initialize an object or modify an object. A currency conversion is performed by the DoConversion function. Finally, the GetFactor and GetMethod functions are used to send the contents of the private variables to a program using the class. As you will see in Chapter 10, these last two functions are used when writing the contents of objects to a data file.

## Marketing Survey Analysis

The Andrews Shoe Company has conducted a large marketing survey to track the types of shoes people own and how many pairs they purchase each year. The survey is anonymous, identifying respondents only by a number. The survey also records a respondent's age and gender, along with shoe ownership and purchasing habits for four types of footwear.

The program that analyzes the survey data uses a class name OneSurvey to represent a single survey completed by one person. The declaration can be found in Listing 7.3.

The OneSurvey class that forms the basis of the shoe company's marketing research efforts is used in a different way than the Converter class. The Converter class acts on its data to perform a mathematical operation. However, the OneSurvey class is primarily a storage device for the results of a survey. The actual data analysis is performed on groups of data, working with many objects created from the OneSurvey class.

## Listing 7.3   The OneSurvey class

```
const SWAP_MADE = 1;
const NO_SWAP = 0;

class OneSurvey
{
    private:
        int Survey_numb;
        char Gender;
        int Age, AthleticOwned, AthleticBought, DressOwned, DressBought,
            BootsOwned,BootsBought, SandalsOwned, SandalsBought;

    public:
        OneSurvey(); // constructor
        void InitSurvey (int, char, int, int, int, int,
            int, int, int, int, int);
        char GetGender (void);
        int GetAge (void);
        int GetAthleticOwned (void);
        int GetAthleticBought (void);
        int GetDressOwned (void);
        int GetDressBought (void);
        int GetBootsOwned (void);
        int GetBootsBought (void);
        int GetSandalsOwned (void);
        int GetSandalsBought (void);
// The copy function copies one object into another. It is used when sorting an array
// of survey objects. You will see how it is used in Chapter 15.
        void copy (OneSurvey);
```

The OneSurvey class makes individual values available to the object that uses objects created from OneSurvey. Therefore, the member functions consist primarily of functions that return individual values to the calling program. The copy function is used to copy data from one object to another. It is used when sorting groups of OneSurvey objects.

The two constants at the beginning of the class's header file are used when sorting objects of the OneSurvey class. Because the constants are declared outside the class, they are *global* and therefore accessible to any function of any class in the survey analysis program.

## Comments

This class also contains *comments*, lines of text added to source code to provide documentation. A compiler ignores comments. You can—and should—add them frequently to help you remember what portions of your source code do.

C++ supports two types of constants, one shared with C and another unique to C++. In Listing 7.3, you will find the C++ comment syntax: a line or portion of a line beginning with two slashes (//). The compiler ignores everything from the // to the end of the line.

The C comment syntax brackets the comment with /* and */, as in:

```
/* This is a C style comment */
```

The comment can be placed on a line by itself or at the end of another line, or it can span several lines.

Which style should you use? It really doesn't matter. However, as you can see in the following example, it's often easier to use the C syntax for long comments:

```
// When you use C++ comments for multi-line comments
// you must precede each line with the double slashes.
// This can be a bit of a bother for a long comment.

/* With the C syntax, you can run a comment onto
multiple lines without needing special characters to
indicate that a line belongs to a comment. However,
you must be very careful to close the comment. If you
don't, the rest of your source code will be considered
to be part of the comment! */
```

## The Hi/Lo Game

One of the first games written for personal computers was a "hi/lo" guessing game. The computer generates a random number between 0 and 100. The user then has seven tries to guess the number. Each time the user guesses, the computer lets the user know whether the guess was above or below the correct answer.

The object-oriented version of the hi/lo game uses one class to represent a game. It needs only two variables: the correct answer and the current guess made by the user (Listing 7.4).

## Listing 7.4   The Game class

```
class Game
{
    private:
        int answer, guess;

    public:
        Game (void);
        int evaluateGuess (int);
        int GetAnswer (void);
};
```

The class has three member functions: a constructor, a function to deter-mine whether a guess is above or below the correct answer (`evaluateGuess`), and a function to send the correct answer back to the application object run-ning the game (`GetAnswer`).

## Summary

In this chapter you learned to add function prototypes to class declarations, which, along with variables, constitute complete class declarations.

Each variable and member function is assigned an access mode. Private access, generally used for variables, means that only functions that are members of the class can access those variables. When inheritance is involved, variables are often Protected, providing access to member functions of the class and any derived classes. Public access, used primarily for functions, lets any function call the function; a public variable can be accessed by any function. Private member functions are accessible only to other member functions in the class. Protected access doesn't apply to member functions.

Member functions are most often declared by including just their proto-types. A function prototype includes the function's return value type, the func-tion's name, and its parameter list.

A prototype's parameter list includes the data types of the values that will be passed into the function. Variable names aren't required for simple data types, but may be required for some complex data types, such as two-dimen-sional arrays.

Each class has at least one special member function called a constructor. A constructor, which has the same name as the class, is run automatically whenever an object is created from the class. A class may also have a destructor, a member function that is run automatically when an object created from the class is destroyed. The name of a destructor is a tilde (~) followed by the name of the class.

# Exercises

For the first six exercises below, you will write complete class declarations on paper. Be sure to use meaningful variable names and to add comments where necessary. (You'll be writing code to manipulate these many classes throughout this book. Some classes will also be modified to add text data once you have learned to manipulate strings. You should therefore document your classes so that you can remember the meaning of each variable, even if you haven't worked with the class for some time.)

Following the pen-and-paper exercises, you will find a program for which you will complete the class declaration and then run the program. The last exercise lets you do some debugging.

1.  A picture frame: Write a class declaration for an order for the custom framing of a picture. Include the following variables:

    *   Job ticket number (a unique number assigned to each order)
    *   The width of the frame in inches
    *   The length of the frame in inches
    *   The price of the frame per running inch
    *   The price of mounting the picture
    *   The price of glass
    *   The price of labor

    The member functions for this class should include

    *   A constructor
    *   A function to place data into an object
    *   A function to compute the cost of framing (including the frame, glass, mounting, and labor)
    *   Functions to return each variable in the class

2. An oil storage tank: Write a declaration for a class that describes a tank in an oil tank farm. Include the following variables:

   - Tank #
   - Capacity in gallons
   - Current number of gallons of oil in the tank

   The member functions for this class should include

   - A constructor
   - A function to place data into an object
   - A function to compute how full the tank is expressed as a percentage of the capacity
   - A function to compute the available space in the tank expressed as a percentage of the capacity
   - Functions to return each variable in the class

3. A paycheck: Write a class declaration for a paycheck. Include the following variables:

   - Check #
   - ID# of employee receiving the check
   - Date of check (stored as six digits: MMDDYY)
   - Net pay (amount of pay before deductions)
   - Federal tax amount
   - State tax amount
   - Social Security tax amount
   - Gross pay (amount of pay after deductions)

   The member functions for this class should include

   - A constructor
   - A function to place all data except the gross pay into an object
   - A function to compute the gross pay
   - Functions to return each variable in the class

4.  Service performed on an automobile: Write a class declaration for one type of service (for example, a tune-up) performed on a car. This class could become part of a program that manages the service department of an automobile dealership. Include the following variables:

    - The car's vehicle ID # (VIN)
    - The date the service was performed (stored as six digits: MMDDYY)
    - The service code (a three-digit code that identifies the type of service)
    - The number of hours of labor used to perform the service
    - The cost of parts and other supplies used to perform the service
    - The total cost of the service

    The member functions for this class should include

    - A constructor
    - A function to place all data except the total cost into an object
    - A function to compute the total cost of the service
    - Functions to return each variable in the class

5.  A check generated by an accounts payable system: Write a class for a check used to pay a bill owed by a company. This class could become part of an accounts payable program. Include the following variables:

    - Check #
    - Bank account # from which the check is drawn
    - ID# of the payee
    - Date of check (stored as six digits: MMDDYY)
    - Amount of the check

    The member functions for this class should include

    - A constructor
    - A function to place all data into an object
    - A function to deduct the amount of the check from the correct bank account
    - A function to deduct the amount of the check from the balance due to the payee
    - Functions to return each variable in the class

6.  A statement or payable invoice received from an organization or person to which a company owes money: Write a class for a statement or invoice. This class could become part of an accounts payable program. Include the following variables:

    - ID# of the organization or person from which the statement or invoice was received
    - Invoice or statement #
    - Date statement or invoice was received (stored as six digits: MMDDYY)
    - Amount of the statement or invoice
    - Account code to which the amount of the invoice should be posted

    The member functions for this class should include

    - A constructor
    - A function to place all data into an object
    - A function to post the amount of the statement or invoice to the correct account
    - A function to add the amount of the statement or invoice to the balance due the organization or person from which the invoice or statement was received
    - Functions to return each variable in the class

7.  The XYZ company wants a report that displays some statistics about its web site. As you can see in Figure 7.1, the program asks the user for the number of hits taken by the web site, the number of e-mail messages left, and the number of files downloaded. The program then displays a nicely formatted report with the values the user entered. Your job in this exercise is to write the declaration for the webStats class on which the program is based.

    a.  The declaration of the webStats class must follow the specifications below. (If you don't adhere to function and variable names, the program won't run.)

        - Include three integer variables named `hits`, `messages`, and `downloads`. All three variables are private.
        - Include a constructor that has no parameters.

Figure 7.1    Output of the web statistics program

```
Enter the number of hits: 1509
Enter the number of messages left: 350
Enter the number of files downloaded: 2560


Here are your web site statistics
=================================
Hits   Messages  Downloads
----   --------  ---------
1509   350       2560
```

- Include a function named init that has three integers as input parameters. The function doesn't return a value.
- Include a function named getHits that has no input parameters and returns an integer.
- Include a function named getMessages that has no input parameters and returns an integer.
- Include a function named getDownloads that has no input parameters and returns an integer.
- Make all functions public.
- Save the class declaration in *webstats.h*.

b.  Enter the application class declaration in Listing 7.5.

Listing 7.5    Application class declaration (save in *appclass.h*)

```
class AppClass
{
    public:
        AppClass();
        void Run ();
};
```

c.  Enter the main function in Listing 7.6 and the class implemetations in Listing 7.7 and Listing 7.8.
d.  Create a project for the program and add the *.cpp* files to the project.
e.  Run the program. Find and fix any errors you have made.

## Listing 7.6    The main function (save as *main.cpp*)

```
#include "appclass.h"

void main ()
{
    AppClass theApp;
    theApp.Run();
}
```

## Listing 7.7    Implementation of the webStats class (save as *webstats.cpp*)

```
#include "webStats.h"

webStats::webStats ()
{
    // Assignment statements to initialize class variables
    hits = 0;
    messages = 0;
    downloads = 0;
}


void webStats::init (int iHits, int iMessages, int iDownloads)
{
    // Assignment statements to place values into an object's variables
    hits = iHits;
    messages = iMessages;
    downloads = iDownloads;
}


int webStats::getHits()
    // Send back the number of hits to a calling function
    { return hits; }


int webStats::getMessages()
    // Send back the number of messages to a calling function
    { return messages; }


int webStats::getDownloads ()
    // Send back the number of downloads to a calling function
    { return downloads; }
```

**Listing 7.8    Implemention of the application class (save as *appclass.cpp*)**

```
#include "appclass.h"
#include "webStats.h"
#include <iostream.h>
#include <iomanip.h>


AppClass::AppClass()
{
    // default constructor does nothing
}


void AppClass::Run()
{
    int iHits, iMessages, iDownloads;

    webStats theStats;

    cout << "Enter the number of hits: ";
    cin >> iHits;
    cout << "Enter the number of messages left: ";
    cin >> iMessages;
    cout << "Enter the number of files downloaded: ";
    cin >> iDownloads;

    theStats.init (iHits, iMessages, iDownloads);

    cout << endl << endl;
    cout << "Here are your web site statistics" << endl;
    cout << "=================================" << endl;
    cout << "Hits    Messages    Downloads" << endl;
    cout << "----    --------    ---------" << endl;
    cout << setw (7) << setiosflags (ios::left) << theStats.getHits();
    cout << setw (11) << theStats.getMessages() << theStats.getDownloads();
}
```

8. In Figure 7.2 you can see the output of a simple program that computes the total cost of an oil change for a passenger car. The cost includes the base price of the service, the charge for the number of pints of oil used (in whole pints), and the cost of the oil filter (if any). Your job in this exercise is to find the errors in the program so that you can get it up and running.

   a. Enter the main function in Listing 7.9
   b. Enter the header files for the application and oilChange classes (Listing 7.10 and Listing 7.11, respectively.)
   c. Enter the implementation of the application class in Listing 7.12.

## Figure 7.2   Output of the oil change program

```
Enter the number of pints of oil used: 6
Enter the price of the oil filter (0 if no filter used): 6.95

The total cost of the oil change is $30.24
```

## Listing 7.9   Main function for the oil change program (save as *main.cpp*)

```cpp
#include "appclass.h"

void main ()
{
    AppClass theApp;
    theApp.Run ();
}
```

## Listing 7.10   Header file for the application class (save as *appclass.h*)

```cpp
class AppClass
{
    public:
        AppClass();
        void Run();
};
```

## Listing 7.11   Header file for the oilChange class (save as *oil.h*)

```cpp
const float BASE_CHARGE = 17.95;
const float OIL_PRICE = 0.89

class oilChange
{
    private:
        oil_used;
        float filter_price;
    public:
        oilChange();
        init (int, float);
        float totalCost ()
};
```

    d.   Enter the implementation of the oilChange class in Listing 7.13.

    e.   Create a project for the program and add the *.cpp* files to the project.

    f.   Run the program. Correct the errors in *oil.h* reported by the compiler.

## Listing 7.12    Implementation of the application class (save as *appclass.cpp*)

```cpp
#include "oil.h"
#include "appclass.h"
#include <iostream.h>
#include <iomanip.h>

AppClass::AppClass()
{
    // default constructor does nothing
}

void AppClass::Run()
{
    int iUsed;
    float iPrice;

    cout << "Enter the number of pints of oil used: ";
    cin >> iUsed;
    cout << "Enter the price of the oil filter (0 if no filter used): ";
    cin >> iPrice;

    oilChange theChange; // declare an object
    theChange.init (iUsed, iPrice);

    cout << setprecision (2) << setiosflags (ios::fixed);
    cout << "\nThe total cost of the oil change is $" << theChange.totalCost();
}
```

## Listing 7.13    Implementation of the oilChange class (save as *oil.cpp*)

```cpp
#include "oil.h"

oilChange::oilChange()
{
    oil_used = 0;
    filter_price = 0.0;
}

void oilChange::init (int iUsed, float iPrice)
{
    oil_used = iUsed;
    filter_price = iPrice;
}

float oilChange::totalCost()
    { return (BASE_CHARGE + (oil_used * OIL_PRICE) + filter_price); }
```

# 8 Writing and Using Member Functions

## OBJECTIVES

In this chapter you will read about:
- How functions can return a value.
- How objects are created from classes.

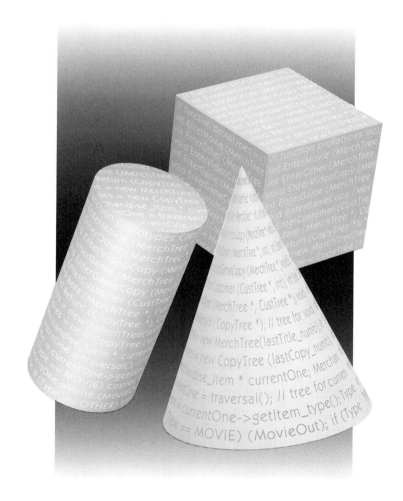

To this point, you have been reading about classes and their functions without considering how objects are created, how functions are called, and how everything fits together to make a program that runs. In this chapter we will therefore extend your knowledge of the basic source code parts that make up an executable C++ program. We will also look at notation for implementing functions and at how some simple member functions are written.

# The Source Code Elements of an Executable C++ Program

As you know, a C++ program is a collection of functions. The compiler looks for a function named `main` and assumes that program execution begins with that function. All C++ programs must therefore include a `main` function that isn't part of any class.

The remaining portions of an object-oriented C++ program are member functions. In this book, we are going to assume that the main function has only two tasks:

- Create an object of an application class
- Call the application object's `Run` function to begin the program's real work

The application class will have at least two member functions: a constructor and `Run`. In its `Run` function, an application object will usually do all of the following:

- Create objects from the classes needed by the program.
- Call member functions to perform input and output (I/O), including handling of the user interface and the capture of user interaction with the computer.
- Call member functions to perform data manipulation.

As an example, consider the shoe purchasing survey analysis program whose data class—OneSurvey—you saw in Chapter 7. To count the number of people who own sandals, the application object's `Run` function must

- Create one object from the `OneSurvey` class for each survey.
- Read data from a data file to place data into the objects' variables.
- Organize the objects so that so they are accessible to the application object.

At this point, the programmer has a choice to make: The Run function can do all the work needed to count owners of sandals, or it can call another function. Because this program will manipulate the survey data in a variety of ways, it makes sense to place each type of analysis in its own function. This will keep the Run function short and easy to read; it will also make the entire program more understandable because each specific task performed by the program is in its own function. In addition, the modularity will make the program easier to modify.

The programmer therefore adds a function to the application class named countSandals. This new function does the following:

- For each object of the OneSurvey class, it calls the object's member function that returns the number of pairs of sandals owned by the survey respondent.
- If the number of pairs of sandals is greater than zero, it adds one to the count of people who own sandals.
- It performs I/O to display the result to the user.

The issue of where I/O is performed is a tricky one. If you are working with a GUI, I/O is typically separate from classes that manipulate data because I/O requires special objects of its own. For example, a dialog box that collects data from the user is represented by an object. The object manipulating the dialog box captures the data entered by the user and then passes it to an object that stores data. If you want to print the data in an object, the program may use a special printout object. By the same token, a window object is usually separate from the object that represents whatever is seen in the object. The advantage to this approach is that you can change the I/O—for example, the layout of a dialog box or printout—without having to change the structure of classes that store and manipulate data.

When we are working with a line-oriented text-based interface as we are in this book, I/O is often part of a data manipulation class. In the example we have been considering, the OneSurvey class probably knows how to read the data for one object from a file. It probably also knows how to display the data for one survey. On the other hand, I/O that relates to summaries of data, such as the count of the number of people who own sandals, is handled by the application object because it relates to all the OneSurvey objects as a whole rather than to a single object. In this book we will generally not be using separate objects for I/O—the exception is menus from which users can choose program actions—but do keep in mind that when you work with a GUI, you will need to separate I/O from classes that store data.

Because an object-oriented C++ function is a collection of member functions, much of what you read about in the rest of this book deals with writing functions. In this section you will be introduced to the structure of functions and look at how some simple functions are written.

By convention, member functions are placed in files with a *.cp* or *.cpp* extension. We typically place all the functions for one class in a single file. It is rare for a file to contain functions for more than one class.

Because the functions that make up a C++ program are typically stored in at least three files (one for the application class's member functions, one for the member functions belonging to a class being manipulated by an application object, and one containing the `main` function) and because C++ programs use functions stored in precompiled libraries, the program must be linked into one run-time module for execution.

As you read in Chapter 2, the way in which you let a compiler know which source files make up one program is typically with a project file. The project file identifies the source code files that make up the program and—depending on the requirements of specific program development software—perhaps the libraries that should be linked with the source code.

You must create a new project for every program you prepare: Each project is specific to one given program. For example, a project file for the survey analysis program might contain

```
survyApp.cpp
survey.cpp
main.cpp
```

The *SrvyApp.cpp* file contains the member functions for the application class; the *survey.cpp* file contains the member functions for the `OneSurvey` class; and the *main.cpp* file contains the `main` function. Notice that no header files are included in the project file. This is because the contents of the necessary header files are "included" in all three of the *.cpp* files when the program is compiled.

## Function Structure

The implementations of all member functions have the same basic structure:

```
return_data_type className::FunctionName (parameterList...)
{
    body of function goes here
}
```

Notice that this structure is similar to that of the declaration of a class. However, there is no semicolon after the closing brace. This is because the declaration of a class represents a request for data storage, just like the declaration of a simple variable. In contrast, the implementation of a function (the *definition* of the function) is executable source code. The braces surrounding the body of the function simply tell the compiler where the function begins and ends.

The class name is followed by two colons, which are known as the *scope resolution operator*. You will see this operator used throughout C++ programs to identify the class to which a member function or variable belongs.

A function's parameter list is slightly different from that used in the function's prototype: variable names *must* be included for each parameter, along with the parameter's data type. This declares the variables that will be passed into the function; the variables don't need to be redeclared within the function. You will then be able to use the parameters in the body of the function to gain access to the values they represent.

The variables in a function's parameter list must match the parameters in the function's prototype. There must be the same number of parameters; they must also have the same data types. For example, the DoConversion function that belongs to the Converter class has the following prototype:

```
float DoConversion (float);
```

and the following associated implementation structure:

```
float Converter::DoConversion (float Dollars)
{
    body of function goes here
}
```

The init function from the OneSurvey class has the prototype

```
void InitSurvey (int, char, int, int, int, int,
    int, int, int, int, int);
```

and an implementation structure of

```
void OneSurvey::InitSurvey (int iSurvey_numb, char iGender, int
    iAge, int iAOwned, int iABought, int iDOwned, int iDBought,
    int iBOwned, int iBBought, int iSOwned, int iSBought)
{
    // body of function goes here
}
```

## Local Variables

To this point, you have been introduced to one type of variable: variables that are part of classes. However, those aren't the only variables that a program uses. Variables are often needed within member functions to hold temporary values that are generated as the function does its work.

Variables declared within a function that are designed for use only within that function are called *local* variables. Space for local variables is allocated when the function that uses those variables is called. By default, local variables are destroyed (their member allocation released) when the function in which they were created finishes execution.

For example, the function that counts the number of pairs of sandals owned by all survey respondents needs a local variable to hold the count while the function is accessing all of the OneSurvey objects. The function might therefore have the following general structure:

```
int surveyApp::countSandals()
{
    int count;

    // rest of body of function goes here
}
```

Notice that the local variable is declared inside the braces that enclose the body of the function. The declaration looks just like the declaration of variables that are part of a class.

To be completely accurate, by default a local variable is destroyed when the set of braces in which it is declared are closed. As you will see beginning in Chapter 11, braces perform a variety of grouping functions in a C++ function, and many sets of braces can appear within a single function.

If you don't want a local variable destroyed when the braces in which it was declared are closed, you can change the variable's *storage class*. The default—auto—says to destroy the variables. However, if you precede the variable declaration with the keyword `static`, the variable will be left in memory until the program ends. To make the count of the number of survey respondents who own sandals a static variable, a program would include:

```
static int count;
```

## Simple Constructors and Initializing Variables

As you know, a constructor is a special member function that a program calls automatically whenever an object is created from a class. The purpose of a simple constructor is to *initialize* the variables in an object.

Initializing a variable means that you give the variable a starting (or initial) value. Usually, we set numeric variables to zero and character variables to *null* (a special value that means no character is present).

As you will remember, we initialize variables because although creating an object allocates space in main memory for all the object's variables, it doesn't clear out the previous contents of the memory. Space has been allocated, but the contents of the space hasn't been altered from the space's previous use. This means that unless a program explicitly assigns a value to a memory location, the memory location may contain a value that is unrelated to the current program and may therefore cause inaccurate results if used unaltered.

To initialize a variable declared from one of the simple data types to which you have been introduced, you assign it a value using the assignment operator, just as you learned in Chapter 6. Each variable in the class must be handled separately. As an example, take a look at the default constructor for the `OneSurvey` class in Listing 8.1.

## Listing 8.1    The constructor for the OneSurvey class

```
OneSurvey::OneSurvey ()
{
    Survey_numb = 0;
    Gender = '';
    Age = 0;
    AthleticOwned = 0;
    AthleticBought = 0;
    DressOwned = 0;
    DressBought = 0;
    BootsOwned = 0;
    BootsBought = 0;
    SandalsOwned = 0;
    SandalsBought = 0;
}
```

Notice that initializing the integer variables requires simply a zero on the right side of the assignment operator. However, something different happens with the character variable `Gender`: A null is indicated by typing two single quotes next to each other. As you can see, a null is therefore quite different from a blank, which is a character like any other.

**Note**

A null is also often represented as '\0'. Although there are two characters within the single quotes, a compiler recognizes that the \0 mean a null and substitutes the ASCII code for null.

**Warning**

C++ interprets single and double quotes differently. Use single quotes to surround one character at a time for use with the `char` data type. Double quotes are reserved for strings, which require a different type of data storage and very special handling. We will look at string variables beginning in Chapter 16.

You should initialize local variables as well as variables that belong to classes. One of the easiest ways to do so is to include the initialization in the variable declaration:

```
int count = 0;
```

Alternatively, you can perform the initialization separately from the declaration:

```
int count;
count = 0;
```

**Note**

You can't initialize variables that are part of a class in the class declaration. You must therefore perform the initialization in the constructor, using assignment statements that are separate from the variable declarations.

## Functions That Return Private Data

The simplest member functions are those that send the value of a private variable back to the program calling the function (*get* functions). In most cases, you will write one get function for each class variable whose value is likely to be output by a program manipulating objects created from the class.

Such functions often have names that begin with Get, like those that are part of the OneSurvey class. Each get function has only one statement in its body: return. The return statement sends one value back to the program that called the function and terminates execution of the function. For example, the GetAge function is written:

```
int OneSurvey::GetAge ()
{
    return Age;
}
```

The value that the function returns must be of the same data type as the declared return data type. For example, if a class contains a floating point variable named price, the following function will be detected as an error:

```
int Shopping::getPrice ()
    { return price; }
```

**Note**

Remember that C++ compilers don't pay any attention to the spacing of your source code. In the two examples you have just seen, the body of the first was spread over three lines; the entire body of the second was on one line. It makes absolutely no difference to the compiler how the functions are physically laid out. We typically use physical code layouts that make the structure of the code easier to read. If a function has only one statement, it's all right to put the entire function body on one line. However, if a function has more than one statement, it is clearer to use multiple lines that are indented from the surrounding braces.

## Creating Objects

Two methods can be used to create objects from classes. One lets you handle objects much like variables; the other requires you to use the starting addresss of the main memory storage allocated to the object (a *pointer*). Although we'll defer a discussion of pointers (main memory addresses) until Chapter 17, it's important that you understand the difference between the two methods of creating objects and the criteria for deciding when to use each method.

## Static Versus Dynamic Binding

When an object is created, space is set aside to hold the object's data, and the member functions of the class from which the class was created are linked to the object. In other words, the object doesn't receive its own complete copy of its class's member functions; the object is only connected to the functions.

This object to function linking is known as *binding*. The difference between the two methods for creating objects has to do with when binding actually occurs. Binding can be performed when a program is compiled (*static binding*). The space set aside for the objects remains allocated, and the binding remains intact while the program is running. Static binding is therefore most appropriate for objects that are needed throughout the entire run of the program. To get static binding, you define objects as if they were variables.

Alternatively, you can allocate space for objects and bind objects to member functions while the program is running (*dynamic binding*). The benefit of dynamic binding is that you can create and destroy objects as needed, providing more efficient use of memory. It is therefore appropriate for objects that are used temporarily or for large programs that must continually free memory to continue operation. To get dynamic binding, you obtain the address of the object's place in memory with the new operator.

**Note** As you have been reading, the main memory address of the starting location of an object's or a variable's data storage is called a *pointer*. It is very difficult to write more than simple programs in C++ without using pointers in some way. You will therefore begin to learn about using pointers in Chapter 17.

## Defining Objects Using Static Binding

To allocate space for an object as you would a variable, resulting in static binding, you define a variable whose data type is the class from which you want to create an object. For example, we might want to use three objects in the currency converter program, one each for the conversion rates of Germany, Great Britain, and France. The object declarations would therefore bet written

```
Converter Germany, Great_Britain, France;
```

Space is allocated for three objects—one to convert German currency, one to convert the currency of Great Britain, and one to convert French currency.

We can use this same syntax to create an application object in a `main` function. If we assume that the application class is named `AppClass`, then the application object is created using

```
AppClass theApp;
```

## Calling Functions Using Static Binding

To tell an object to execute one of its member functions, you send a message to the object. More commonly, we say that a program *calls* a function. The syntax for a function call depends on whether you are using static or dynamic binding.

To call a function that returns no data (in other words, has a return data type of `void`) using static binding, you use the name of the object, followed by a period, the name of the function, and the function's input parameters. If the function has no input parameters, you must include the parentheses that would otherwise surround the parameter list.

This notation—known as *dot notation*—can be used to call an application object's `Run` function:

```
theApp.Run();
```

At this point, you know everything you need to write and understand a complete `main` function:

```
#include "appclass.h"

void main ()
{
    AppClass theApp; // create the object
    theApp.Run(); // call the Run function
}
```

The body of the function contains only two lines of executable code. The first creates an application object. The second calls the application object's `Run` function. Notice that the function must include the header file that declares the application class so that `main` will have access to the class's public members. We will use a similar `main` function for every program in this book.

If a member function returns a value, you can choose whether to capture that value in a variable. Assume, for example, you have a function with the following prototype that is a member function of a class named `Compute`:

```
float exponentiate (float, float);
```

This function takes the value in the first parameter and raises it to the power contained in the second parameter. The function then returns the result as a floating point value.

The function's implementation begins with the following header:

```
float Compute::exponentiate (float value1, float value2);
```

Keep in mind that the parameter list in the function implementation declares the variables for use inside the function.

To call the function and capture the result, you must declare a variable for the result and then assign the function's result to that variable using the assignment operator:

```
float result; // a variable to hold the result
float first = 1.2, second = 5.0; // some data to use
Compute theObject; // create the object
//
// other code goes here
//
result = theObject.exponentiate (first, second);
```

Notice that the parameter list in the member function call contains just the names of the variables holding the values that are to be sent to the member function; data types aren't used. The parameters are mapped to the member function's parameter list in order. In this particular example, the contents of the first variable are sent to the value1 variable; the contents of the second variable are sent to the value2 variable. Parameters in the function call must match the data types of the parameters in the first line of the function. However, parameters in the call don't need to have the same variable names as parameters in the function.

When you pass parameters in this way, the computer sends a *copy* of the parameter to the function being called. The original values—in our example, stored in first and second—are left untouched. This means that value1 and value2 are completely distinct storage locations. Changing the contents of value1 and value2 in the exponentiate function has absolutely no effect on the contents of first and second. This type of parameter passing is therefore known as *pass by value*, because a copy of the parameter's value is actually transferred to the function.

**Note**

Because you can initialize local variables when they are declared, you can place a function call in an initialization. The first time a variable is used in a function, you can declare and initialize it with the result of a function in the same statement:

```
float result = theObject.exponetitate (first, second);
```

If you do this, keep in mind that the declaration (represented by the variable's data type) must occur only once in the function. The next time the function uses the variable, the data type should not be used.

## Summary

The execution of an object-oriented C++ program begins with a function named main, which is the only function that is not part of a class. The purpose of a main function is to create an application object and to call the application object's Run function, which triggers the remainder of the program's actions.

Member function implementations begin with the function's return data type, followed by the name of the class to which the function belongs, the scope resolution operator, the function name, and the function's parameter list. The parameters are declared (given data types and names) in the list.

Functions send a single value back to the calling function with the return statement.

Functions can use variables that are part of their class and variables that are declared as input parameters. Functions can also declare local variables for use just within the function.

Because variables that belong to classes cannot be initialized in the class declaration, constructors—functions executed automatically when an object is created—are used to initialize variables that belong to a class.

Objects can be created from a class in two ways. To use static binding, objects are declared just like variables; instead of the data type, the declaration uses the class name. Space in memory for the object is allocated when the program is compiled. The alternative—dynamic binding—allocates space for an object when the program is running. Dynamic binding provides a pointer to the location of an object in memory. The major advantage of dynamic binding is that it allows dynamic memory management; unneeded objects can be removed from memory, freeing up space under low-memory conditions.

To call a function using static binding, you use the name of the object, followed by a period (the dot operator), the name of the member function, and any input parameters needed by the function. This is known as dot notation.

# Exercises

1.  To begin your programming experience, you will write a `main` function to drive a C++ program.

    a.  In Listing 8.2 you will find a class declaration for an application class. Enter this class into a file named *AppClass.h*.

## Listing 8.2    AppClass.h

```
class AppClass
{
    public:
        AppClass();
        void Run();
};
```

    b.  The implementation for this class can be found in Listing 8.3. Enter the member functions into a file named *AppClass.cpp*.
    c.  Write a `main` function to drive this program. Store it in a file named *main.cpp*.
    d.  Create a project for the program.
    e.  Run the program. When working properly, it will ask you for your age, how many brothers you have, and how many sisters you have. Press Return after each entry. After you have entered the three values, the program should display them back to you.
    f.  What local variables does this program use? What happens to them when the `Run` function finishes executing?

2.  In this exercise you will write a constructor and some get functions for a class. The program performs the same input and output as Exercise 1, but rather than simply echoing your input back to you immediately, it stores the data in an object.

    a.  Enter the class declaration in Listing 8.4 into a file named *student.h*.

## Listing 8.3    AppClass.cpp

```
#include <iostream.h>

AppClass::AppClass()
{
    // In this simple program, the constructor doesn't do anything
}

void AppClass::Run()
{
    int age, brothers, sisters;

    cout << "\nHow old are you?";
    cin >> age;
    cout << "\nHow many brothers do you have?";
    cin >> brothers;
    cout << "\nHow many sisters do you have?";
    cin >> sisters;
    cout << "\n\nYou are " << age << " years old." << endl;
    cout << "You have " << brothers << " brothers and ";
    cout << sisters << " sisters.";
}
```

## Listing 8.4    Student.h

```
class Student
{
    private:
        int age, brothers, sisters;
    public:
        Student();
        void Init (int, int, int);
        int getAge();
        int getBrothers();
        int getSisters();
};
```

    b.  Complete the implementation of the class's member functions using the function stubs in Listing 8.5. You should finish the constructor by assigning a zero to each of the class's variables. For each of the get functions, return the required variable. Store the implementation in *student.cpp*.

    c.  If you completed Exercise 1, use the *appclass.h* file from that exercise. Otherwise, enter the application class declaration in Listing 8.2 and save it as *appclass.h*.

## Listing 8.5    Student.cpp

```
Student::Student()
{
    // put your initializations here
}

void Student::Init (int iAge, iBrothers, iSisters)
{
    age = iAge;
    brothers = iBrothers;
    sisters = iSisters;
}

int Student::getAge ()
{
    // put your return statement here
}

int Student::getBrothers ()
{
    // put your return statement here
}

int Student::getSisters ()
{
    // put your return statement here
}
```

d. Enter the code in Listing 8.6 as the implementation of the application class for this program. Save it as *appclass.cpp*.

e. Write a `main` function for this program and save it as *main.cpp*.

f. Create a project for this program.

g. Run the program. When working properly, it should conduct the same dialog as the program from Exercise 1.

h. Look carefully at the `Run` function. Identify the following:

- Local variables
- The statement where an object of class `Student` is created
- All calls to member functions of class `Student`

## Listing 8.6   AppClass.cpp

```
#include <iostream.h>

AppClass::AppClass()
{
    // default constructor does nothing
}

void AppClass::Run()
{
    int iAge, iBrothers, iSisters;
    Student theStudent;

    cout << "\nHow old are you?";
    cin >> iAge;
    cout << "\nHow many brothers do you have?";
    cin >> iBrothers;
    cout << "\nHow many sisters do you have?";
    cin >> iSisters;
    theStudent.Init (iAge, iBrothers, iSisters);
    cout << "\n\nYou are " << theStudent.getAge() << " years old." << endl;
    cout << "You have " << theStudent.getBrothers() << " brothers and ";
    cout << theStudent.getSisters() << " sisters.";
```

**Warning**

We often use the same file names in different programs, especially where application classes and `main` functions are concerned. You can avoid running into the problem of accidentally overwriting a file by creating a separate file directory for each program you write. Put all of the source code files and the project file in that special directory. Not only will this help you avoid destroying a file you want to keep, but it will also help you organize your disk.

# 9

# Stream I/O

## OBJECTIVES

In this chapter you will read about:
- Viewing I/O as a stream of characters.
- Working with the default I/O streams.
- Using the I/O stream classes.
- Initializing objects with keyboard input.

One of the most basic things a computer program must do is move data from the outside world into the computer and from the computer back to the outside world. Input and output (I/O) using C++ can be performed in several ways. However, the easiest to use and most universal is *stream I/O*, so named because input and output are viewed as a stream of characters moving from a source to a destination. Sources of stream I/O typically include the keyboard and data files. Typical stream I/O destinations include the screen, a data file, or a printer.

In this chapter you will learn to use stream I/O to create text-based screen displays and to accept keyboard input. You will also learn how to use C++'s assignment operator to take the data a program receives from an I/O stream and initialize variables and objects. As you do this, you will learn how to write more member functions.

## Stream I/O Classes and Objects

An ANSI-compliant C++ development environment includes classes that support stream I/O as part of its C++ libraries (the libraries that you link with your object code when preparing a program). Typically, the class declarations for screen and keyboard I/O are found in a header file named *iostream.h*. To gain access to the stream I/O classes, you must include the necessary header file in any source code file that uses those classes.

An I/O stream is an object. It has member functions that you can call. In addition, it has operators that put data into the stream and take data from the stream. To use an I/O stream, you first create an object from the stream class.

When you run a C++ program, however, three I/O stream objects are created automatically for you: cin (for keyboard input), cout (for screen output), and cerr (for error output, usually directed to the screen). To use them, you only need to be sure to include *iostream.h* in a source code file that is using the objects.

## Introducing cin and cout

In Listing 9.1 you will find a very simple program that uses the cin and cout stream objects. The program isn't object-oriented; all the code is contained in a main function. Although this is something you would never do in practice, it will serve as a short introductory example.

Listing 9.1    Age.cpp: An extremely simple program to capture someone's age and display it on the screen

```
#include <iostream.h>

void main()
{

    int Age;
    cout << "What is your age? ";
    cin >> Age;
    cout << "John/Jane, you are " << Age << " years old.";
}
```

The program in Listing 9.1 contains three stream I/O statements. Running the program produces something like the following:

```
What is your age? 19
John/Jane, you are 19 years old.
```

## Using cout

The first executable statement in the Age program uses cout to display the "What is your age?" prompt on the screen. The statement begins with the name of the stream object (cout) followed by <<, the *stream insertion operator*. The stream insertion operator puts a value into a stream so that it can be sent to the stream's destination. In this example, the value being inserted is a literal string, surrounded by double quotes. (Remember that you use single quotes around individual characters but double quotes around strings of characters.)

The third executable statement in Listing 9.1 also uses the cout stream. It inserts three values into the stream, one after the other. The first is a literal string, the second the contents of a variable, and the third another literal string. Each individual value sent to the stream is prefaced by its own stream insertion operator. When you place a variable in a cout stream, cout displays the contents of the variable on the screen.

It may seem a bit odd that the stream insertion operator points into the stream name when the intent of the operator is to perform output. To help you fix in your mind why the operator points *toward* the stream, take a look at Figure 9.1. Values are placed into the stream, to travel toward the output location (in this case, the screen).

Figure 9.1    Inserting values into a stream

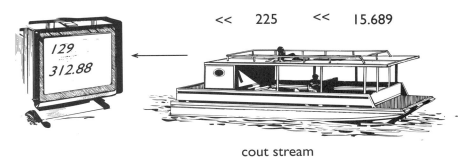

cout stream

(Items flow toward the screen)

The behavior of cout varies slightly from one compiler to another. Some compilers automatically begin a new line of output with each use of cout; others begin output exactly where the previous screen display ended. If your compiler doesn't automatically begin a new line, there are two ways to do so. First, you can insert an endl at the end of an output stream, as in:

```
cout << "This is a test" << endl;
cout << "This one starts on a new line";
```

Alternatively, you can use an *escape character* (a value that sends formatting information to an output device). The new line escape character is \n:

```
cout << "This is a test";
cout << "\nThis one starts on a new line";
```

The backslash (\) alerts the I/O stream that what follows is a formatting code rather than a value to be displayed. In the preceding example, the \n could be placed at the end of the first string or the beginning of the second.

**Note**

If your compiler automatically inserts a new line with each use of cout, using endl or \n will insert an extra line in the output. As you will see, there are many situations in which you will explicitly use endl and/or \n to place blank lines in output for formatting purposes.

## Using cin

The second executable statement in Listing 9.1 uses `cin` to accept a value from the keyboard. The statement begins with the name of the stream (`cin`), followed by >>, the *stream extraction operator*. The stream extraction operator takes a value from a stream and places it into the variable whose name follows the operator. The operator points away from the stream name because we are taking values *out* of the stream (just the opposite of the stream insertion operator).

The `cin` stream can handle more than one input value. For example, if you have one integer variable—`Age`—and one character variable—`Gender`—the following statement will accept both values:

```
cin >> Age >> Gender
```

The values are separated by a space, a tab, or the Enter key. The drawback to this is that you can't use `cin` to enter a string of text because `cin` sees each word as a separate value. As you will see in Chapter 16, string input requires the use of a `cin` member function.

The `cin` stream does virtually no data type checking. It won't warn you, for example, if you enter a floating point value instead of an integer for a person's age. The value will simply be truncated to an integer when it is stored; the decimal fraction portion of the number will be lost. C++ also won't warn you if you enter a character instead of an integer; the character is simply translated to an integer value based on its ASCII code.

The `cin` stream has one little "gotcha" of which you should be aware: it will wait forever for a value. This means that you can't use `cin` if you want the user to be able to press Enter without entering a value to signal the end of input. In Chapter 16, however, you will be introduced to some `cin` member functions you can use when you need to be able to trap for no input.

## A Simple Text Menu Class

You can combine `cin` and `cout` to provide a simple text menu class for controlling a program. Although you will be introduced to a more flexible menu class once you've learned to handle strings, this technique can make your programs easy to use with the knowledge you already have.

The currency converter program, which you will see in its entirety in Chapter 12, provides three options to its users: set a conversion rate, perform a conversion, and exit the program. The display of the menu options and the capture of a user's choice are handled by a menu object.

The declaration of the `menu` class can be found in Listing 9.2. The class's `display` function shows the menu options on the screen; the `choose` function prompts the user to make a choice and returns that choice to the calling function.

**Listing 9.2    menu.h**

```
class menu
{
    private:
        int option;
    public:
        menu();
        void display ();
        int choose ();
};
```

As you can see in Listing 9.3, the implementation of the `menu` class uses `cout` and `cin` to display and capture values. Why keep the `display` and `choose` functions separate? There are two reasons. First, keeping them separate gives the programmer the choice of either displaying the menu options or asking for a menu choice without needing to do both. For example, if the user entered a choice that wasn't valid, you might want to ask for a choice again without displaying the menu. Second, it makes the code clearer, making it easier to understand and to modify (for example, adding or removing items from the menu).

To use this class, the currency converter program's application object's Run function must first declare an object of the `menu` class:

```
menu theMenu;
```

Then, whenever it wants to display the menu, it calls the menu object's `display` function:

```
theMenu.display();
```

## Listing 9.3    menu.cpp

```cpp
#include <iostream.h>
#include "menu.h"

menu::menu()
{
    option = 0;
}

void menu::display()
{
    cout << "\n\nPick a menu option:" << endl;
    cout << "  1. Set conversion rate" << endl;
    cout << "  2. Do a conversion" << endl;
    cout << "  9. Quit" << endl;
}

int menu::choose()
{
    cout << "\nWhich one? ";
    cin >> option;
    return option;
}
```

Finally, to make a menu choice, the Run function must declare a local variable to hold the chosen option and call the choose function.

```cpp
int menuChoice;
//
// some other code goes here
//
menuChoice = theMenu.choose();
```

**Note**

Yes, it takes a bit of extra time and coding to create understandable menus for your programs. However, a program is only as good as its usability. You should therefore always be thinking about the interface your program presents to the user and how you can make the interface as easy to use as possible.

## Grabbing a Single Character

There is one small drawback to the menu class: The user must press Enter after typing menu selection. Since the menu choice is a single number, why not simply have the computer grab whatever the user enters without requiring Enter? You can do this with a cin member function.

The cin stream is an object created from a class named iostream. It therefore can use any of the member functions defined for its class. One of those functions is get(), which returns a single character. The get() function is called like any other member function. For example, the line

```
cin >> option;
```

could be replaced with

```
option = cin.get();
```

In both cases, the character that the user types appears on the screen. The difference between the two is that the first requires a press of the Enter key to transmit the keyboard input to the cin stream; the second takes a single character without waiting for the Enter key.

Because the get() function returns a value just like any other function, the last two executable statements of the choose function in Listing 9.3 (the cin and the return) could actually be replaced by just one statement:

```
return cin.get();
```

Combining the two statements into one avoids using a storage location for the menu choice. It also avoids taking the time to write the result of the get() function to a storage location in main memory and then retrieve that value to return it to the calling function. The program therefore uses just a little bit less memory and runs just a little bit faster.

## Simple cout Formatting

By default, cout displays one value after the other, without any formatting or special spacing. The stream I/O class hierarchy, however, provides some functions that can help format stream output. To gain access to these *manipulators*, include the header file *iomanip.h* in the program that uses them.

The currency converter program uses manipulators to display the result of a currency conversion. Because the results are currency, the floating point values should be displayed with two digits to the right of the decimal point. This is known as setting the *precision* of the number. You do so by calling the setprecision member function:

```
cout << setprecision(2);
```

The setprecision function takes one input parameter: the number of digits that should appear to the right of the decimal point. It stays in effect until cout encounters another call to the function.

Two other manipulators similar to setprecision that you might find useful are setw and setfill. The setw function sets the width of the field in which a value is displayed. It takes one parameter—the width of the field, which is often entered as a constant. If the value contains fewer characters than the field, it is right justified in the field. If the value is larger than the field, it is truncated. Unlike other manipulators, the width setting returns to the default after each stream insertion. In other words, if you use

```
cout << setw(10) << Number1 << Number2;
```

only Number1 will appear in a field 10 characters wide; Number2 takes up just enough space to display its value. If you want both values in 10-character-wide fields, you must use

```
cout << setw(10) << Number1 << setw(10) << Number2;
```

The setfill function determines what character will appear in the empty space surrounding a value that doesn't fill the entire width of its field. The default fill character is a space. However, you can set it to any character. For example, you might want to use asterisks as leading characters for currency values. Assuming that you have the value 156.895 stored in a floating point variable, you will find that the statement

```
cout << setprecision(2) << setw(10) << setfill('*')
    << Float_Number;
```

produces the output value ****156.89.

## Putting Data into Objects

When you use static binding to create objects, you typically don't have data for the objects at the time memory is allocated for the objects. Thus, all a constructor can do is initialize the objects; you need member functions to place data into objects' variables. In this section you will see how to write member functions that put data into objects. You will also see how to call those member functions from a function that is manipulating the objects and how member function calls relate to stream I/O.

The sample program for this section is a "bucket management" program. It keeps track of our buckets, storing data about their capacity and how many holes they have. The class declaration—stored in *bucket.h*—appears in Listing 9.4. The program has a main function (Listing 9.5) and an application class with a Run function (Listing 9.6), just as you have seen earlier.

---

**Note**

Because the main function and application class declaration are the same for most programs in this book, we won't repeat them from here on. However, if an application class contains functions other than a constructor and Run, you will see the class declaration.

---

Listing 9.4    bucket.h: Header file for the bucket management program

```
class Bucket
{
    private:
        int numbHoles;
        float capacity;

    public:
        Bucket(void);
        void InitBucket (int, float);
        int GetnumbHoles (void);
        float Getcapacity (void);
};
```

Listing 9.5    main.cpp: main function for the bucket management program

```
#include "appclass.h"

void main ()
{
    AppClass theApp;
    theApp.Run();
}
```

Listing 9.6    appclass.h: Header file for the bucket management program's
               application class

```
class AppClass
{
    public:
        AppClass();
        void Run();
};
```

## Member Functions That Put Data into Objects

The Bucket program uses static binding to create objects. Because data aren't available when the objects are created at the start of program execution, the class must contain a member function that puts data into the object. This function (InitBucket in Listing 9.7) receives data through its parameter list. It then assigns the values in the input variables to the object's variables.

Listing 9.7    InitBucket: A function to place data into a Bucket object

```
void Bucket::InitBucket (int Holes, float Gallons)
{
    numbHoles = Holes;
    capacity = Gallons;
}
```

Classes include "init" functions whenever objects will receive data after the objects are created. This type of function can also be called to modify the data in an object at any time.

An alternative to an "init" function is a group of "set" functions, each of which places a value in one of a class's variables. If we were to structure the Bucket class in that way, we would need two "set" functions:

```
        void setHoles (int);
        void setCapacity (float);
```

Their implementations can be found in Listing 9.8. Although writing a group of "set" functions is more tedious than creating a single "init" function, the "set" functions are more flexible. They give a programmer the choice of changing the contents of only those variables that need to be changed, without requiring the programmer to specify an input value for every variable in the class.

### Listing 9.8   "Set" functions for the Bucket class

```
void Bucket::setHoles (int Holes)
    { numbHoles = Holes; }

void Bucket::setCapacity (float Gallons)
    { capacity = Gallons; }
```

The application class Run function that manipulates Bucket objects can be found in Listing 9.9; running the program produces output such as that in Figure 9.2. The Run function defines three Bucket objects (Bucket1, Bucket2, Bucket3). It then asks the user to enter the number of holes and the capacity of each bucket. When it has the data for one bucket, it calls the InitBucket member function to place the data it has collected from the user into a Bucket object.

## Member Functions and cout

If you look carefully at the last three statements in Listing 9.9, you'll notice that the cout statements contain calls to member functions of Bucket objects. These member functions, which appear in Listing 9.10, return the values stored in a Bucket object's private variables.

The way in which these functions are embedded in the cout seems to be in direct contrast to the way in which member functions that return values are called: There's no variable to hold the return value, and there's no assignment operator. Actually, the return value does come back to the calling function. Rather than being assigned to a variable, the return value is inserted into the cout stream. In general, cout can evaluate executable C++ statements that generate a value and display the result produced by executing the statement.

You could certainly assign values to variables and use those variables in the cout, as in Listing 9.11. However, if you're not going to use the values other than for output, there's no reason to ask the computer to store the values

**Listing 9.9    The Run function that manipulates Bucket objects**

```
void AppClass::Run()
{
    Bucket Bucket1, Bucket2, Bucket3;

    int iHoles;
    float iGallons;

    cout << "How many holes in bucket #1? ";
    cin >> iHoles;
    cout << "How many gallons does bucket #1 hold? ";
    cin >> iGallons;
    Bucket1.InitBucket (iHoles, iGallons);

    cout << "How many holes in bucket #2? ";
    cin >> iHoles;
    cout << "How many gallons does bucket #2 hold? ";
    cin >> iGallons;
    Bucket2.InitBucket (iHoles, iGallons);

    cout << "How many holes in bucket #3? ";
    cin >> iHoles;
    cout << "How many gallons does bucket #3 hold? ";
    cin >> iGallons;
    Bucket3.InitBucket (iHoles, iGallons);

    cout << setprecision(2) << setiosflags (ios::fixed | ios::showpoint) <<
    endl << endl;
    cout << "Bucket #1 holds " << Bucket1.Getcapacity() << " gallons and has "
        << Bucket1.GetnumbHoles() << " holes." << endl;
    cout << "Bucket #2 holds " << Bucket2.Getcapacity() << " gallons and has "
        << Bucket2.GetnumbHoles() << " holes." << endl;
    cout << "Bucket #3 holds " << Bucket3.Getcapacity() << " gallons and has "
        << Bucket3.GetnumbHoles() << " holes." << endl;
}
```

in main memory and then retrieve them for display. Your code will be shorter and the program will execute faster if you simply place the function calls in the cout, without first storing the values in memory.

## I/O and Class Structure

In the program you have just seen, the I/O is managed by the application class. Alternatively it could have been handled by the Bucket class. This is a choice that you will face with every object-oriented program you write: Should I/O be part of an object that stores data or should it be handled by another class?

Figure 9.2    Output of the Bucket program

```
How many holes in bucket #1? 5
How many gallons does bucket #1 hold? 4.5
How many holes in bucket #2? 10
How many gallons does bucket #2 hold? 12
How many holes in bucket #3? 99
How many gallons does bucket #3 hold? 2.5


Bucket #1 holds 4.50 gallons and has 5 holes.
Bucket #2 holds 12.00 gallons and has 10 holes.
Bucket #3 holds 2.50 gallons and has 99 holes.
```

Listing 9.10  GetnumHoles and Getcapacity: Functions to return private data
                from a Bucket object

```
int Bucket::GetnumbHoles ()
{
    return numbHoles;
}


float Bucket::Getcapacity ()
{
    return capacity;
}
```

Listing 9.11   Using variables rather than function calls in cout

```
iHoles = Bucket1.GetnumbHoles();
iGallons = Bucket1.Getcapacity();
cout << "Bucket #1 hold " << iGallons << " gallons and has "
        << iHoles << " holes." << endl;
```

Before we examine the issues surrounding the choice, let's look at a revised version of the bucket management program that includes I/O as part of the Bucket class.

The Bucket class has been modified so that its class declaration appears like Listing 9.12. Notice that the "init" and "get" functions are gone. They are no longer necessary because there will be no need to move data from other functions into a Bucket object or from a Bucket object back to another function. Keep in mind, however, that this is a very small class with very limited capabilities; it is not typical of most of the classes you will encounter. Even if you do I/O as part of a class, you may often also need to include "set" and "get" functions.

Listing 9.12    The Bucket class with I/O functions as part of the class

```
class Bucket
{
    private:
        int numbHoles;
        float capacity;

    public:
        Bucket(void);
        void input ();
        void display ();
};
```

The new functions added to the Bucket class can be found in Listing 9.13. The cout and cin statements look very much like they did when they were part of the application class's Run function in Listing 9.9. However, the text of the prompts that are displayed to the user are more generic, without reference to a specific object name (e.g., Bucket #1 or Bucket #2) because there is no way to know how objects will be named.

Listing 9.13 Input and Display functions for the Bucket class

```
void Bucket::input ()
{
    cout << "How many holes are in this bucket? ";
    cin >> numbHoles;
    cout << "How many gallons does this bucket hold? ";
    cin >> capacity;
}

void Bucket::display ()
{
    cout << "This bucket holds " << capacity << " gallons and has "
        << numbHoles << " holes." << endl;
}
```

As a result, the Run function (Listing 9.14) takes care of displaying information that identifies the specific objects it uses. Program execution therefore looks a bit different from the original (see Figure 9.3), although the end result is exactly the same.

## Listing 9.14   The Run function modified to handle I/O as part of the Bucket class

```
void AppClass::Run()
{
    Bucket Bucket1, Bucket2, Bucket3;

    cout << "\nBucket #1: " << endl;
    Bucket1.input();

    cout << "\nBucket #2: " << endl;
    Bucket2.input();

    cout << "\nBucket #3: " << endl;
    Bucket3.input();

    cout << setprecision(2) << endl << endl;
    cout << "\nBucket #1: " << endl;
    Bucket1.display();

    cout << "\nBucket #2: " << endl;
    Bucket2.display();

    cout << "\nBucket #3: " << endl;
    Bucket3.display();
}
```

## Figure 9.3   Output of the modified Bucket program

```
Bucket #1:
How many holes are in this bucket? 5
How many gallons does this bucket hold? 4.5

Bucket #2:
How many holes are in this bucket? 12
How many gallons does this bucket hold? 99

Bucket #3:
How many holes are in this bucket? 99
How many gallons does this bucket hold? 2.5




Bucket #1:
This bucket holds 4.50 gallons and has 5 holes.

Bucket #2:
This bucket holds 99.00 gallons and has 12 holes.

Bucket #3:
This bucket holds 2.50 gallons and has 99 holes.
```

Now let's compare the two versions of the bucket management program. When I/O is handled by the application object, we gain the following:

- The class that handles data (`Bucket`) is separate from I/O. This means that we can change the I/O code—perhaps even moving to a GUI—without modifying the class that manipulates data.
- The I/O (in particular, the prompts that the user sees) can be tailored to the way in which the objects are being used in a program.

On the other hand, if we make the I/O part of the class that handles data, we also gain something:

- The application class becomes completely separate from the class that handles data. We can change the I/O without having to modify the application class.
- The application class's `Run` function is much shorter and clearer.
- The data handling class is complete; it includes all the code necessary for any program to use objects from the class. It therefore is easier to reuse the class in many programs.

Which of these two overall program structures should you use? Should you make I/O part of classes that handle data or should I/O be part of the class that manipulates data handling classes? As you can see from the preceding discussion, there is no straightforward answer. Your choice depends on what you are trying to achieve with a given class. You will therefore see both structures in use throughout this book. It will be up to you and your instructor to decide which structure makes the most sense for any given program.

## Summary

C++ views input and output as a stream of characters. Streams can accept input from a file or from the keyboard; streams can send output to a computer screen, to a file, or directly to a printer. Stream I/O is performed in the same manner, regardless of the source or destination of the data being transferred.

C++ supports two default I/O streams: `cin` for keyboard input and `cout` for screen output. Keyboard input is extracted from the `cin` stream with the stream extraction operator (>>) and stored in program variables. Output is inserted into the cout stream with the stream insertion operator (<<) and displayed on the screen. Data for the cout stream may be stored in program variables or can be inserted as constants.

The cout stream can be formatted using manipulators. Manipulators set characteristics such as the width of the field in which data appear, the base in which numbers are displayed, whether a decimal point appears, and the character that fills empty space left in a print field.

Stream output is often used to accept data that are then passed to a member function that assigns values to an object. This technique is particularly useful for objects created using static binding because data are usually not available when the objects are created.

## Exercises

1. Write and test a program that lets a person pick six numbers for playing a biweekly state lottery. Accept the six numbers from the keyboard. (*Hint*: The single class for this program is the lottery ticket. You will need to create just one object from the class.) Print the lottery ticket to the screen and printer. The lottery ticket might look something like Figure 9.4.

Figure 9.4    A sample lottery ticket

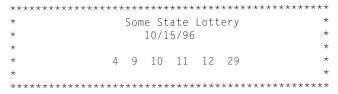

2. Write and test a program that prints sales flyers for a grocery store. Create a class for a grocery store product, including the regular price and the sale price of the object. Create objects for ground beef, milk, yogurt, and lettuce. Ask the user to enter the regular and sale prices for each item, storing the data in the appropriate objects. Then, use the objects to print the sales flyer. It might look something like Figure 9.5.

Figure 9.5    A sample grocery store sales flyer

```
                    Jones' Corner Grocery

                        SALE PRICES
                Week of 10/10/96 - 10/16/96


                   REGULAR PRICE    SALE PRICE
Ground Beef          $1.79/lb        $1.09/lb
2% Milk               1.75/gal        .99/gal
Plain Yogurt           .79 each       .49 each
Lettuce                .99/head       .49/head
```

3.  Write and test a program that stores emergency phone numbers. In this case, the class is a phone number. Its single variable is a phone number, stored as an integer. Create objects for police, fire, and ambulance. Include the following capabilities in your program:

    *   Accept data for each object from the user.
    *   Store the data in a file each time the program ends.
    *   Read stored data from the file each time the program begins. Display the data for the user immediately after reading it.

4.  In many medical practices, the diagnoses that are determined for a patient are coded using numeric codes. Write and test a program that handles data about a diagnosis made for a patient. The program should handle a patient number, a diagnosis code, and a date (stored as a six-digit integer). Each run of the program corresponds to the diagnoses for one patient (up to five per patient). Allow the user to enter the patient number and date only once. Then collect the five diagnosis codes. After you've initialized objects, display a report that summarizes what the user has entered. Make your own choices about the structure of the class and its member functions.

# 10

# File I/O

## OBJECTIVES

In this chapter you will read about:
- Using stream I/O with files.
- Initializing objects with file input.
- Using stream I/O for simple printing.

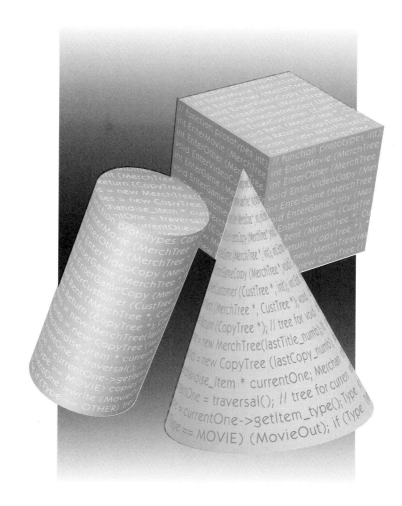

One of the problems with the way in which we have been using objects is that when a program run ends, the data stored in objects are lost. However, many business applications rely on saving data in some permanent way. For example, if a program performs accounting functions for a business, then there must be a way to store data about income and expenditures between program runs.

In traditional data processing, data were stored in special files called *data files*. Today, most file processing systems and their data files have been replaced with *database management systems*. A database management system (DBMS)—among other things—takes care of the details of file input and output, relieving an application programmer from having to write file I/O.  However, despite the fact that most of your real-world C++ programming experience will probably involve interaction with a DBMS rather than directly with data files, you need to know how to perform some simple file I/O so that you can save data while you are learning C++ techniques.

In this chapter you will learn to create and use stream objects that send data to and from files, and how to use file input to initialize objects. You will also learn to extend the stream I/O concept to include simple output to a printer.

## C++ Files

As far as C++ is concerned a file can be a source of data, just like a keyboard. By the same token, a file can be a destination to which data are sent, just as the keyboard. To write data to or read data from a file, you create a stream object that acts as a pathway between the computer and the file, just as cout acts as a pathway between the computer and the screen and cin acts as a pathway between the keyboard and the computer.

C++ supports two types of files: text and binary. *Text files* store data as ASCII codes. Single values, such as numbers and single characters, are separated by spaces. Assume, for example, that you want to store the data from the bucket management program  from Chapter 9 in a data file. Each time the program begins its run, it reads the data from the data file, displays it to the user, and then gives the user the chance to change the data. Just before it ends, the program writes its data back to the data file. The revised program is based on the first version of the bucket managment program, where all I/O takes place in the Run function. All changes have therefore been made just to Run; all the rest of the code is the same. The program now produces a dialog with the user as in Figure 10.1.

Figure 10.1   Output of the revised bucket management program

```
The current bucket data are:


Bucket #1 holds 12.00 gallons and has 5 holes.
Bucket #2 holds 3.00 gallons and has 15 holes.
Bucket #3 holds 5.00 gallons and has 88 holes.


Now you can change the data:

How many holes in bucket #1? 10
How many gallons does bucket #1 hold? 12
How many holes in bucket #2? 5
How many gallons does bucket #2 hold? 8
How many holes in bucket #3? 0
How many gallons does bucket #3 hold? 20


Bucket #1 holds 12.00 gallons and has 10 holes.
Bucket #2 holds 8.00 gallons and has 5 holes.
Bucket #3 holds 20.00 gallons and has 0 holes.
```

Since the program manipulates three objects, the data file will contain three sets of data. In Listing 10.1, you can see the contents of a text file that is manipulated by a revised version of the bucket management program. The first value in each pair is the size of the bucket; the second value is the number of holes. Notice that there is a space after each number. (Although you can't see it, there is a space after the last number.)

Listing 10.1   The data file that stores bucket data

```
12 5 3 15 5 88
```

Text files can be used for data storage or to create images of printed output that can be sent to a printer later. However, because by default values are separated by spaces, reading text files that contain string data can become a bit complicated. This section therefore looks at handling files of simple variable types; we'll revisit text files in Chapter 16 once you've learned to handle strings.

*Binary files* store streams of bits, without any attention to ASCII codes or separating spaces. They are convenient for storing objects. However, using binary files requires using the address of a storage location. We will therefore defer a discussion of them until Chapter 17.

## Opening Files

Before a program can read to or write from a file, it must *open* the file. The process of opening a file identifies the file's location to the program. To open a C++ text file for reading, you create an object (a stream) of the `ifstream` class; to open a file for writing, you create an object of the `ofstream` class. You can then use the names of the streams you created with the stream insertion and extraction operators.

Like the default `cin` and `cout` streams, ANSI file I/O streams can transfer data in only one direction. This means that you must open and manipulate separate streams for reading from and writing to text files.

**Note**

Can you have more than one stream associated with a single file at a time? In particular, can you have read and write streams open to the same file? Although some operating systems support multiple streams on the same file at the same, as you will see shortly it usually isn't wise to try to read from and write to the same file at the same time. However, if necessary, a program can manage more than one input stream for the same file at the same time without a problem.

## Opening a File for Reading

The revised bucket management program uses a file named *Buckets* to store the data from its objects. To open the file for reading at the start of every program run, the program includes the statement

```
ifstream fin ("Buckets");
```

Notice that this looks very similar to other statements you have seen that create objects for static binding. The `ifstream` object is named `fin`. It is associated with a file whose path name is inside the parameter list. This parameter is passed to the class's constructor, which uses it to locate and open the file.

**Note**

Many programmers use `fin`, short for "file input,"as the name for a file input stream.

If the file name is entered as a constant, as it is in the preceding example, it must be surrounded by double quotes to make it a string. You may, however, wish to ask a user to enter a file name. In that case, the file name would be stored in a variable that contains a string. You will learn how to do this when we study string I/O in Chapter 16.

## Opening a File for Writing

The revised bucket management program rewrites the *Buckets* file each time the program ends. It therefore opens the file for writing with the statement

```
ofstream fout ("Buckets");
```

By default, if a program attempts to open a file for writing and the file doesn't already exist, the program will create the file.

**Note**

Many programmers use `fout`, short for "file output," as the name for a file input stream.

When an existing file is opened in this way, it is truncated to length zero. This means that opening the file destroys all its previous contents; you must rewrite the entire file to preserve its contents.

The alternative to truncating an existing file on opening is to open the file for appending. In that case, anything you write to the file is added on the end. To open in append mode, you add a second parameter to the parameter list. The parameter is a variable that is part of the `ios` class, the base class from which all stream I/O classes are derived. As you can see below, in this case the variable is called `app`:

```
ofstream fout ("Buckets", ios::app);
```

You indicate that it comes from `ios` by preceding the name of the variable by the name of the class and the scope resolution operator.

## Controlling File Replacement

If you want to open a file only when a file doesn't exist, you can use the `ios` variable `noreplace` to prevent opening an existing file. In that case, the statement to open the file is written:

```
ofstream fout ("Buckets", ios::noreplace);
```

## Controlling File Creation

In some cases, you may want to open a file for writing only if a file already exists; if a file doesn't exist, you *don't* want to create a new one. To prevent a new file from being created, place the `nocreate` flag into the file object's parameter list, as in

```
ofstream fout ("Buckets", ios::nocreate);
```

**Note**

After trying to opening a file, you need to check to see if the file has been opened. You will find out how to do so in Chapter 12.

## Writing to a Text File

Writing the contents of simple variables to a text file is just like writing them to the screen using the `cout` stream. As you can see in Listing 10.2—the revised version of the bucket management program's `Run` function—the stream insertion operator is used to send the values returned by "get" functions to the `fout` stream. For example, the program writes the contents of the `Bucket1` object with

```
fout << Bucket1.Getcapacity() << ' '
     << Bucket1.GetnumbHoles() << ' ';
```

Some C++ implementations automatically place a blank after each numeric or character value written to a text file; others do not. It is therefore good practice to explicitly insert a blank after each value, as was done in the preceding example and Listing 10.2. This will ensure that one blank appears between the values. Even if your compiler would automatically insert a blank, you will still end up with just one blank.

## Listing 10.2    Updated application class Run function for the bucket management program

```
void AppClass::Run()
{
    Bucket Bucket1, Bucket2, Bucket3;

    int iHoles;
    float iGallons;

    // Open a file for reading by creating a file input stream object
    ifstream fin ("Buckets");

    // Extract values from the file input stream
    fin >> iGallons >> iHoles;
    Bucket1.InitBucket (iHoles, iGallons);
    fin >> iGallons >> iHoles;
    Bucket2.InitBucket (iHoles, iGallons);
    fin >> iGallons >> iHoles;
    Bucket3.InitBucket (iHoles, iGallons);
    // close the file
    fin.close();

    cout << "The current bucket data are: " << endl;

    cout << setprecision(2) << setiosflags (ios::fixed | ios::showpoint)
        << endl << endl;
    cout << "Bucket #1 holds " << Bucket1.Getcapacity()
        << " gallons and has " << Bucket1.GetnumbHoles() << " holes." << endl;
    cout << "Bucket #2 holds " << Bucket2.Getcapacity()
        << " gallons and has " << Bucket2.GetnumbHoles() << " holes." << endl;
    cout << "Bucket #3 holds " << Bucket3.Getcapacity()
        << " gallons and has " << Bucket3.GetnumbHoles() << " holes." << endl;


    cout << "\n\nNow you can change the data: " << endl << endl;

    cout << "How many holes in bucket #1? ";
    cin >> iHoles;
    cout << "How many gallons does bucket #1 hold? ";
    cin >> iGallons;
    Bucket1.InitBucket (iHoles, iGallons);

    cout << "How many holes in bucket #2? ";
    cin >> iHoles;
    cout << "How many gallons does bucket #2 hold? ";
    cin >> iGallons;
    Bucket2.InitBucket (iHoles, iGallons);
```

Continued next page

**Listing 10.2 (Continued)    Updated application class Run function for the
bucket management program**

```
cout << "How many holes in bucket #3? ";
cin >> iHoles;
cout << "How many gallons does bucket #3 hold? ";
cin >> iGallons;
Bucket3.InitBucket (iHoles, iGallons);

cout << setprecision(2) << setiosflags (ios::fixed | ios::showpoint)
    << endl << endl;
cout << "Bucket #1 holds " << Bucket1.Getcapacity()
    << " gallons and has " << Bucket1.GetnumbHoles() << " holes." << endl;
cout << "Bucket #2 holds " << Bucket2.Getcapacity()
    << " gallons and has " << Bucket2.GetnumbHoles() << " holes." << endl;
cout << "Bucket #3 holds " << Bucket3.Getcapacity()
    << " gallons and has " << Bucket3.GetnumbHoles() << " holes." << endl;

// Open a file for writing by creating a file output stream object
ofstream fout ("Buckets");

// These lines write data to the text file. Notice the space that follows each value.
fout << Bucket1.Getcapacity() << ' ' << Bucket1.GetnumbHoles() << ' ';
fout << Bucket2.Getcapacity() << ' ' << Bucket2.GetnumbHoles() << ' ';
fout << Bucket3.Getcapacity() << ' ' << Bucket3.GetnumbHoles() << ' ';
}
```

## Reading from a Text File

Reading numeric and character data from a text file is just like reading values
from the keyboard using the `cin` stream. In Listing 10.2 the stream extraction
operator is used to take two values from the `fin` stream and store them in local
variables. The values in these variables are then used as parameters in a call to a
function that initializes an object. For example, the following code reads one
value into `iGallons` and a second value into `iHoles`, and then sends those
data to the `Bucket1` object:

```
fin >> iGallons >> iHoles;
Bucket1.InitBucket (iHoles, iGallons);
```

To read a value from a file, a program reads characters until it encounters
a blank. Anything between two blanks is considered a single value. As long as
there are no strings in the file, the program will skip over the blanks to reach
the next value.

If you compare the file output and input statements for the bucket management program, you'll notice that the statements are very careful to read the data in the same order in which they were written. In this case, since the size of the bucket was written first, followed by the number of holes, the file input statement reads the size followed by the number of holes.

There is nothing automatic about this ordering. It is up to the programmer to ensure that a program reads data from a file in exactly the same order in which it was written. When the data are written to the file, they lose all their meaning; they become nothing but a series of characters. The data can be used effectively only if the program that reads them knows how the data were written and can read them in that way.

**Note**

This close relationship between a data file and the programs that use the data is characteristic of file processing systems. It means that if you change the layout of the file, you have to change the programs that use the file. Because database management systems isolate programs from file storage details, they generally mean that you can change file storage without needing to change application programs. This is one of the reasons why DBMSs have to a large extent replaced file processing in business.

## Closing Files

The revised bucket management program reads from and writes to the same file. However, many operating systems won't let you have the same file open for reading and writing at the same time. (If this seems a bit odd, consider what would happen if you opened a file for reading and then immediately opened it for writing in truncate mode.) The *Buckets* file must therefore be closed after it is read, before it is opened for writing.

Files are closed automatically when the function in which the file's object was created ends. That means that you don't have to worry about closing files at the end of a program. However, as in the case mentioned in the previous paragraph, there are times when you need to close a file explicitly. To do so, you use the `ifstream` or `ofstream` member function `close()`, calling it just as you would any other member function. For example, the stream `fin` is closed with the statement

```
fin.close();
```

## Performing File I/O from Within a Member Function

You may be wondering at this point why you haven't seen a second version of the bucket management program that works with files, a version analogous to the second version of the program you saw in Chapter 9, where the I/O is performed by a member function. Given the amount of C++ that you know right now, it can't be done, and it is important that you understand why so that you can avoid some making time-consuming errors in your own programs. To make this clear, let's look at two possible ways to handle the problem: opening the file in the member function and opening the file in the application object's Run function.

If a program opens a file in a member function, the file's contents are truncated (for all intents and purposes, erased) when the file is opened. The member function then writes its data to the file. When the member function ends, the file is closed. This will therefore work just fine for the first object. But what happens when the member function is called for the second object? The member function opens the file and truncates its contents, erasing the data that were written for the first object. No matter how many objects you attempt to write to the file, the file will never contain more than the data for the last object.

Alternatively, you could open the file in the member function and tell the program to append data to the file rather than allowing the default truncation. This works fine for the second object and beyond—assuming that the first object opened the file and erased the previous contents before writing.

Now you can see the problem: Before writing the first object, you need to open the file and erase; when writing all other objects, you need to open the file and append. There is no way to write a single member function to do this, because the member function won't know when it's writing the first object to the file.

The other major strategy is to open the file output stream in the application object's Run function. However, in that case the member function doing the writing has no information about the stream. (The cin, cout, and cerr streams are automatically made available to the entire program; all other streams are known only to the function in which they are created.) To send a stream to a member function, so that the member function can use the stream, you must pass the stream as a parameter to the function. This is actually how the problem is solved. However, streams are passed as references to main memory addresses, and we will therefore defer a discussion of stream passing until Chapter 17.

## Printing to PC Printers

The way in which you create printed output from a program varies a great deal depending on the type of computer and its operating system. Macintosh printing, for example, requires calls to routines in the ToolBox and is therefore outside standard functions of the C++ language. On the other hand, most MS-DOS/Windows C++ compilers support predefined "file names" for printers connected directly to a single computer: PRN, LTP1, and LPT2. These streams actually represent ports on a PC. They are associated with specific physical ports in the system's CONFIG.SYS file. You might, for example, map PRN to a parallel port and LPT1 and LPT2 to serial ports.

**Note**

Although some PC compilers provide extensions to the C++ language to support sophisticated printing, the printing described in this section is limited to the characters in the MS-DOS character set. It is suited for printers that print one character at a time (for example, dot-matrix printers).

To print directly to a PC printer, you open an output stream to the port to which the printer is connected. For example, assuming that PRN is the parallel port, you can open a stream to a dot-matrix printer with

```
ofstream printer ("PRN");
```

This statement creates a stream named printer that can then be used just like any other I/O stream.

To write to the printer, you insert data into the printer I/O stream. For example, the short but nonobject-oriented program in Listing 10.3 asks the user for the number of buckets purchased along with the total cost of the buckets. The prompts for input appear on the computer's screen. However, the output is sent to a printer rather than back to the monitor.

## Listing 10.3    Printing to a PC printer

```
#include <streamio.h>

void main (void)
{
    int numbBuckets;
    float price;

    ofstream printer ("PRN"); // Opens a stream to the printer

    cout << "How many buckets did you buy?";
    cin >> numbBuckets;
    cout << "How much did they cost?";
    cin >> price;

// You can use manipulators to format printed output just as you can file output or
// output to the screen
    printer << setprecision(2);
    printer << "You spent " << price << " on ";
    printer << setprecision(0);
    printer << numbBuckets << ". How could you?";
}
```

## Printing Alternatives

If your compiler doesn't support PRN, LPT1, LPT2, there is still an easy way to create text-only printed output. The process involves using a text file as a substitute for the printer. Once the text file exists, you can print it. To use a text file as a substitute for a printer:

1. Open a text file as an output stream.
2. Write output to the file as if you were writing to the printer.
3. Exit the program that created the file.
4. If you are working in an MS-DOS environment, use the PRINT command to print the text file. From Windows, open the file with the Write application and print the file. In a UNIX environment, use the lp command or your system's equivalent. On a Macintosh, open the file with a text editor or word processor and set the font to Monaco or Courier (or any other monospaced font). Then print the file.

## Summary

There are two types of C++ files. Text files store data as streams of individual ASCII codes, separating values with spaces. Binary files store streams of bits, without regard to ASCII codes and without spaces separating values.

To read from or write to a text file, a C++ program opens an I/O stream to the file. Data are then written to an output file's stream using the stream insertion operator; data can be read from an input file's stream using the stream extraction operator. Text file I/O streams can also be formatted using manipulators.

MS-DOS C++ compilers typically support default file names for direct output to printers. However, these are suitable only for one-character-at-a-time output. More sophisticated printing on most platforms is supported by extensions that aren't a part of the standard C++ language.

## Exercises

1. Write and test a program for a college admissions office. The class on which this program is based is an academic year. Include the following variables, all of which are integers:

   - Academic year
   - Number of people who asked for information about admission to the college
   - Number of people who applied for admission
   - Number of people who were accepted
   - Number of those accepted who actually attended

   Create the following member functions:

   - A constructor
   - An initialization function that accepts data from the calling functions and places them in an object
   - Functions that return each class variable to a calling function

   The program should create four objects, one for each of the past four years, and do the following:

   - Read current data values from a file when the program begins.
   - Write data values to a file when the program ends.

- Give the user the opportunity to change the data in all objects (excluding the year, of course).
- Prepare a nicely formatted report showing all the data.

2.  Write and test a program that a teacher might use to store student grades. The class for this program is a student. It has the following variables:

- Student number (integer)
- Percentage grade on midterm exam (floating point)
- Percentage grade on final exam (floating point)
- Percentage grade for class participation (floating point)
- Percentage grade for assignment 1 (floating point)
- Percentage grade for assignment 2 (floating point)
- Percentage grade for assignment 3 (floating point)
- Percentage grade for assignment 4 (floating point)

For this exercise, it will be up to you to decide what member functions you need. The program should do the following:

- Create and manipulate five objects (it's a very small class).
- Store data in a data file.
- Read data into main memory so that it can be manipulated while the program is running.
- Give the user the opportunity to change data in each object. (*Hint*: Present the current data values with cout; then let the user input a value.)
- Present a nicely formatted report that shows the current grades for each student.

3.  Write and test a program that manages data about the distance driven by cars in a corporation's fleet. For each car, the program should store its vehicle identification number (VIN) and the number of miles driven each day in a seven-day period. The data should be stored in a text file. Write the program to handle five cars. Allow the user to enter data for each day and then display the data in a nicely formatted report. It is up to you to decide how the class for this program should appear. You should also determine the member functions that are required.

# Doing Arithmetic

## OBJECTIVES

In this chapter you will read about:

- The types of arithmetic operations supported by C++ operators.
- Arithmetic operations that must be performed using library functions.
- The syntax for constructing arithmetic statements.

The first commercial computers were designed to perform repeated numeric calculations. Although today's computers handle text and graphics as easily as they handle numbers, the driving force behind the development of computers was the automation of arithmetic.

Computers are still rather good at arithmetic. In fact, one of the things computers do very well is to perform repeated calculations on a lot of numbers very quickly. In this chapter you will therefore learn about how you can request a computer to perform arithmetic by coding arithmetic expressions.

An *expression* is any part of a C++ statement that can be evaluated to produce a single value. Expressions can be used in several ways, including assigning their values to variables using the assignment operator and displaying their values by inserting them into a cout stream. You will learn other uses for expressions throughout this book.

Expressions fall into two general categories: arithmetic and logical. *Arithmetic expressions* perform some calculation that produces a numeric value; *logical expressions* evaluate values and return either "true" (some value other than 0, but usually 1) or "false" (0). Logical expressions are used in statements that allow a program to make choices; you will learn how to construct them and how they are used in Chapters 12 and 13.

## Arithmetic Operators and Arithmetic Expressions

An arithmetic expression is created by combining one or two numeric values with a single *arithmetic operator*, which specifies what action the computer should take with the numeric value or values. Those operators that work with a single value are called *unary operators*; those that work with two values are called *binary operators*. In this section you will read about both types of C++ operators and learn what they do to numbers.

## The Unary Plus and Minus Operators

The unary plus and minus operators act on the sign of a number. Placing the unary plus operator (+) in front of a number preserves the sign of the number. For example, executing the following statements places a 6 in the result1 variable and -6 in the result2 variable:

```
int firstNumb = 6, secondNumb = -6;
int result1, result2;
result1 = +firstNumb;
result2 = +secondNumb;
```

The unary minus operator changes the sign of a number. It makes a negative number positive and a positive number negative. For example, assume that the variable `firstNumb` holds 6 and `secondNumb` holds -6. After executing the code below, the `cout` statements displays -6 and 6:

```
result1 = -firstNumb;
result2 = -secondNumb;
cout << firstNumb << ' ' << secondNumb;
```

## The Computational Operators

C++ provides five basic computational operators, all of which are binary operators:

- + Addition
- - Subtraction
- * Multiplication
- / Division
- % Modulus

The first four perform arithmetic operations with which you are familiar; you may not have run into the modulus operator before.

### Addition and Subtraction

You create an addition or subtraction expression by placing a numeric value on either side of the operator. The value can be specified as a literal, a constant, or a variable name. The following expressions are therefore all legal:

```
int sum, difference, first = 6, second = 10;
sum = first + second;
difference = first - second;
sum = first + 10;

const INCREASE = 10;
sum = second + INCREASE;
```

The result of each of the preceding arithmetic expressions has been assigned to a variable. Keep in mind that when you perform assignment, you replace the existing value in the variable. As you saw earlier in this book, this means that the following statement is legal in a computer program, although it might not make sense in algebra:

```
sum = sum + INCREASE;
```

This statement is telling the computer to retrieve the value stored at the location labeled sum, to add the value to the value of the constant INCREASE, and then to store the result back in the location labeled sum. The original value of sum is replaced by the new value. This type of statement appears frequently in computer programs.

There is no limit to the number of arithmetic expressions you can place in a single C++ statement. For example, a compiler will accept both of the following:

```
sum = 10 + first - second + INCREASE;
cout << first - second + 200 - INCREASE;
```

In the second example, the arithmetic expression has been placed in a cout statement. The computer calculates the value of the expression and inserts it into the cout stream, causing the value to be displayed on the computer screen. The value isn't stored anywhere.

As a first program that performs some simple arithmetic, let's look at a program that conducts a simple survey to find out how casual someone likes to dress. The survey's dialog with the user can be found in Figure 11.1.

Figure 11.1    Output of the clothing survey program

```
Please answer questions with 1 for 'yes' and 0 for 'no'

Do you own more than four pairs of jeans? 1
Do you own more than four pairs of sneakers? 0
Do you own a jean jacket? 1
Do you own more than 10 T-shirts? 1
Do you purposely wear clothes with holes in them? 0


You answered 'yes' to 3 questions.
```

Underlying the program is a class named Survey, declared in Listing 11.1. The class stores a user's response to a question about his or her clothing in the answer variable. Each of the member functions asks the user one question and sends the response (1 for *yes* and 0 for *no*) back to a calling function. As you can see in Listing 11.2, the I/O for the questions is part of the member functions.

Listing 11.1    survey.h: Header file for the clothing survey class

```
class survey
{
    public:
        int answer;
    public:
        survey();
        int Quest1 ();
        int Quest2 ();
        int Quest3 ();
        int Quest4 ();
        int Quest5 ();
};
```

To figure a user's score on the survey, the application object's Run function (Listing 11.3) creates a local variable named `total`. It then adds the value returned by a call to one of a Survey object's member functions to the total. After all the member functions have been called—and all responses added—the Run function displays the final result.

In Listing 11.3, each function call has been placed in a separate addition statement. However, this isn't the shortest or most efficient way to write this sequence of operations. One alternative is to put all the additions in one statement:

```
total = theSurvey.Quest1() + theSurvey.Quest2() +
    theSurvey.Quest3() + theSurvey.Quest4() +
    theSurvey.Quest5();
```

The preceding single statement will execute more quickly than the separate additions because a value is only stored in main memory once. However, we could get away with storing any value at all by placing the addition in the `cout`. In that case, the entire Run function looks like Listing 11.4. Although the function in Listing 11.4 is shorter and will run faster than Listing 11.3, it is not as easy to understand. If you choose to write compact code like Listing 11.4, be sure to use lots of comment statements so that you will remember what you did.

## Listing 11.2    survey.cpp: Implementation of the clothing survey class

```cpp
#include "survey.h"
#include <iostream.h>

survey::survey()
{
    answer = 0;
    // Constructor displays instructions so they will only appear once
    cout << "\nPlease answer questions with 1 for 'yes' and 0 for 'no'" << endl
        << endl;
}


// Each member function displays one question and collects its answer. The answer must be captured in a
// local variable because there is no way to combine a cin and a return statement.
int survey::Quest1 ()
{
    cout << "Do you own more than four pairs of jeans? ";
    cin >> answer;
    return answer;
}

int survey::Quest2 ()
{
    cout << "Do you own more than four pairs of sneakers? ";
    cin >> answer;
    return answer;
}

int survey::Quest3 ()
{
    cout << "Do you own a jean jacket? ";
    cin >> answer;
    return answer;
}

int survey::Quest4 ()
{
    cout << "Do you own more than 10 T-shirts? ";
    cin >> answer;
    return answer;
}

int survey::Quest5 ()
{
    cout << "Do you purposely wear clothes with holes in them? ";
    cin >> answer;
    return answer;
}
```

Listing 11.3   appclass.cpp: Implementation of the application class for the clothing survey program

```cpp
#include "survey.h"
#include "appclass.h"
#include <iostream.h>

AppClass::AppClass()
    {   }  // constructor does nothing

void AppClass::Run ()
{
    survey theSurvey;  // create an object

    int total = 0;  // variable to hold total "yes" responses

// Call each member function in turn, adding the result to the total
    total = total + theSurvey.Quest1 ();
    total = total + theSurvey.Quest2 ();
    total = total + theSurvey.Quest3 ();
    total = total + theSurvey.Quest4 ();
    total = total + theSurvey.Quest5 ();

    cout << "\n\nYou answered 'yes' to " << total << " questions.";
};
```

Listing 11.4   The revised Run function

```cpp
void AppClass::Run ()
{
    survey theSurvey;  // We still need an object

    // Now, all we need is one cout statement
    cout << << "\n\nYou answered 'yes' to " << theSurvey.Quest1() +
        theSurvey.Quest2() + theSurvey.Quest3() + theSurvey.Quest4() +
        theSurvey.Quest5() << " questions.";
}
```

## The Issue of Data Type

In the examples you have just seen, all of the values in the expressions have been integers. But what happens if the values aren't all of the same data type? For example, what will be stored in sum if you execute the following?

```cpp
int sum, value1 = 10;
float value2 = 20.5;
sum = value1 + value2;
```

In this case, the answer will be 30. Here's what happens:

- The computer promotes the data type of `value1` to a floating point number. Whenever you have different data types in an expression, the computer upgrades all values so that they are the same data type as the type with the greatest range and precision.
- The computer adds the two floating point values, generating a result of 30.5.
- The computer assigns the result to the integer variable `sum`, truncating the floating point value to an integer. This means that the digits to the right of the decimal point are dropped; the number is not rounded.

The changing of the data types is known as *typecasting*. In this example, the typecast is implicit, performed automatically by the computer without a request from the programmer.

C++ will always attempt to evaluate expressions you give it, typecasting when necessary to ensure that it is working with the same type of data throughout an expression. This can be good because it frees you from worrying about the consistency of data types in expressions. However, if you are not aware that the typecasting is going on, you may accidentally end up with inaccurate results. For example, consider the following:

```
float value1 = 0.5;
int result, value2 = 1;
result = value2 = value1;
```

The result of evaluating the expression on the right of the assignment operator is 0.5. However, the .5 is truncated when the result is assigned to the `result` variable, which will then contain 0.

C++ converts character data as well as numeric data. When `char` data are used in an expression with integers, C++ converts the characters to integer, handling the ASCII codes as if they were numeric values. As you will see in Chapter 12, this comes in handy when you want a program to choose actions based on the value in a `char` variable.

Although C++ tries automatically to convert data types wherever possible, under some circumstances conversion isn't possible. In particular, variables that hold pointers (main memory addresses) can't be converted to an arithmetic data type. When a C++ compiler encounters a conversion it cannot make, it generates a compiler error. This is often a hint that you are using a variable in a way that you didn't intend. For example, you might be telling C++ to use a main memory address instead of the value that is stored at that address.

**Note**

Because C++ is so forgiving of multiple data types in the same expression, we say that the language is *weakly typed*.

## Multiplication

When doing arithmetic by hand, we use × to represent the multiplication operator. However, in computer languages, that operator is replaced with an asterisk (*). Arithmetic expressions involving multiplication are therefore written like the following:

```
int product, source1 = 15, source2 = 3;
product = source1 * source2;
source1 = source1 * product;
product = source1 * 10 * source2;
```

As discussed in the previous section, C++ will perform implicit typecasting when performing multiplication. For example, after executing the following statements, `result1` contains 5.25, but `result2` contains 5.

```
float result1, value1 = 0.5;
int result2, value2 = 10.5;
result1 = value1 * value2;
result2 = value1 * value2;
```

Because one of the values in the multiplication expression is a floating point number, the computer performs a floating point multiplication and produces a floating point result. When the result is assigned to a floating point variable, the digits to the right of the decimal point are retained; the data type of the result isn't changed. However, when the result is assigned to an integer variable, the fractional portion of the value is truncated, typecasting the value into an integer.

To see multiplication at work, let's look at a very simple object-oriented program that performs a useful peice of business multiplication. It computes the amount of money that an employee should submit for car expenses, based on the number of miles driven and a current rate of 29¢ per mile. The program conducts a very simple dialog with the user:

```
How many miles did you drive? 658.9
You can put $190.82 on your expense report.
```

The underlying class is car, which is declared in Listing 11.5. It has only one variable: the number of miles driven. The member functions include a constructor, an init function to place data into the object, and a function named reimbursement to calculate how much the user should put on his or her expense report. Notice also that the amount paid per mile is included in the header file as a constant. This makes the value easy to change whenever the mileage rate changes.

### Listing 11.5    car.h: Header file for the mileage program

```
const float MILEAGE_RATE = 0.29;

class car
{
    private:
        float miles_driven;
    public:
        car();
        void init (float);
        float reimbursement ();
};
```

The implementation of the car class can be found in Listing 11.6. As you can see, a multiplication expression appears in the reimbursement function. The single line in the body of the function tells the computer to perform the multiplication and then send the value back to the calling function.

### Listing 11.6    car.cpp: Implementation of the car class

```
#include "car.h"

car::car()
    { miles_driven = 0.0; }

void car::init (float imiles)
    { miles_driven = imiles; }

float car::reimbursement ()
    { return miles_driven * MILEAGE_RATE; }
```

Alternatively, the `reimbursement` function could have been written as follows:

```
float car::reimbursement ()
{
    float result;
    result = miles_driven * MILEAGE_RATE;
    return result;
}
```

In this case, the function first declares a local floating point variable. (Remember that a local variable is a variable that is declared within a function body for use only within that function.) The function then performs the multiplication and stores the value in the local variable. Finally, the function looks up the value in the local variable and returns that value to the calling function.

This second version of the function produces exactly the same result as the first. However, it takes up more memory because it requires space for the local variable. It also takes longer to run because it must allocate space for the local variable, store a value in that variable, and then look up the value to return it. Unless you are planning to use a value more than once, there is no need to store it in a variable. Your program will use less space, and it will run faster without the unneeded storage.

The application class's `Run` function employs a similar technique (Listing 11.7). Notice that the call to the `reimbursement` function for the object named `theCar` has been placed in the `cout` stream. This instructs the computer to call the function and insert the function's return value into the stream, causing the result to appear on the computer's screen. Since the function's return value isn't going to be used again, there is no reason to store it in a local variable.

## Division

You can indicate division in a hand-worked problem in several ways, including

```
value1 ÷ value2

value1
value2
```

Listing 11.7    appclass.cpp: Implementation of the application class for the
                mileage program

```cpp
#include "car.h"
#include "appclass.h"
#include <iostream.h>

AppClass::AppClass ()
    {  }   // default constructor does nothing

void AppClass::Run ()
{
    int imiles;

    car theCar; // create an object

    cout << "How many miles did you drive? ";
    cin >> imiles;
    theCar.init (imiles); // send value to the object

// The call to the reimbursement function is placed in the cout stream. The computer calls the function
// and then inserts its return value into the stream, causing the result to appear on the screen
    cout << "You can put $" << theCar.reimbursement()
        << " on your expense report.";
}
```

Unfortunately, the ÷ operator isn't a part of the standard ASCII character set (although it is available in some extended ASCII character sets). By the same token, it isn't possible to use the "one value on top of another" notation within a computer program. Programming languages, including C++, therefore use a slash (/) as the division operator.

The following statements perform legal division operations:

```cpp
float result1, value1 = 10.0, value2 = 20.0;
int result2, value3 = 6;
result1 = value1 / value2;
result2 = value3 / 3;
```

After the preceding statements have been executed, result1 contains 0.5 and result2 contains 2.

As with other arithmetic operations, implicit typecasting can have an impact on division. Assume that a program contains the statements below:

```cpp
float result1, value1 = 10.0, value2 = 20.0;
int result2, value3 = 6;
result2 = value1 / value2;
result1 = value3 / 3;
```

After execution, `result2` contains 0 and `result1` contains 2.0. Why does `result2` contain 0? Although the computer performs a floating point division and generates 0.5 as a result, the value is truncated to 0 when it is assigned to an integer storage location.

## Modulo Division

Modulo division, the operation performed by the modulus operator (%), is the only C++ operator that is restricted to integers. It divides two integers and returns the *remainder* of the division; the quotient is discarded. For example, the following statements place 5 in `result`:

```
int result, value1 = 12, value2 = 7;
result = value1 % value2;
```

# The Increment and Decrement Operators

C++ has two additional arithmetic operators: increment (++) and decrement (--). The increment operator increases a value by 1; the decrement operator decreases the value by 1. When the increment or decrement occurs depends on whether the operator precedes or follows the variable value that is being modified.

When an increment or decrement operator precedes a variable, the value in the variable is modified *before* the result of the expression is evaluated. As an example, consider the following:

```
int result = 100, counter = 10;
result = ++counter + result;
result = --counter + result;
```

To execute the expression containing the preincrement operator, a computer adds 1 to `counter`, producing 11, and then adds that to `result`, generating a final result of 111. To execute the expression containing the preincrement operator, a computer subtracts 1 from `counter`, producing 9, and then adds that to result, generating a final result of 109.

When an increment or decrement operator follows a variable, the value in the variable is modified *after* the result of the expression is evaluated. Consider what happens when a computer executes the following:

```
int result = 100, counter = 10;
result = result + counter++;
result = result + counter--;
```

Evaluating the expression containing the postincrement operator first adds result and counter, giving the expression a final result of 110. The computer then increments counter, changing its value to 11. Similarly, to evaluate the expression containing the postdecrement operator, the computer performs the addition, generating the same final of result of 110. It then subtracts 1 from counter, changing its value to 9.

The increment and decrement operators really aren't necessary parts of C++. They are shorthand for assignment statements such as

```
int index;
index = index + 1;
index = index -1;
```

Can you get by without using increment and decrement operators? Absolutely. However, as you will see throughout the rest of this book, they can simplify and shorten your source code. They are also used widely by C++ programmers and their use is considered good programming style.

## Assignment Shorthand

The increment and decrement operators aren't the only shorthand operators available with C++. As you have seen, assignment statements often store their results in one of the storage locations used in the expression on the right side of the assignment operator. For example, a program might accumulate a total with

```
sum = sum + newNumb;
```

C++ provides a shorthand for this type of assignment. The preceding statement can be written

```
sum += newNumb;
```

In this notation, notice that the arithmetic operator precedes the assignment operator. There are assignment shorthand operators for each of C++'s arithmetic operators, which are summarized in Table 11.1.

Table 11.1   Assignment statement shorthand

| Shorthand | Equivalence |
|---|---|
| `sum += newNumb;` | `sum = sum + newNumb;` |
| `sum -= newNumb;` | `sum = sum - newNumb;` |
| `sum *= newNumb;` | `sum = sum * newNumb;` |
| `sum /= newNumb;` | `sum = sum / newNumb;` |
| `sum %= newNumb;` | `sum = sum % newNumb;` |

## Precedence and Parentheses

When different arithmetic operators appear in the same expression, a computer must make a choice about which operator to evaluate first. To see why this is important, consider the following:

```
int result, one = 1, ten = 10, twenty = 20;
result = one + ten * twenty;
```

If the expression is evaluated from left to right, the addition is performed first, followed by the multiplication. The result is 220. However, if the multiplication is performed first, the result is 201.

C++ has a set of rules that govern the order of evaluation of operators, known as *precedence*. As you can see in Table 11.2, the unary positive and negative operators have the highest precedence, following the preincrement and predecrement operators, multiplication and division, modulo, addition and subtraction, and finally postincrement and postdecrement. If an expression contains more than one operator with the same precedence, they are evaluated from left to right.

Table 11.2   The C++ Arithmetic Operators, listed in order of
precedence

| Operator | Function |
|:---:|:---|
| + | Positive |
| - | Negative |
| ++i | Preincrement i |
| --i | Predecrement i[a] |
| * | Multiplication |
| / | Division[b] |
| % | Modulo |
| + | Addition |
| - | Subtraction |
| i++ | Postincrement i |
| i-- | Postdecrement i[c] |

a.   Preincrement and predecrement have the same precedence.
b.   Multiplication and division have the same precedence.
c.   Postincrement and postdecrement have the same precedence.

What can you do if you don't want the computer to use its default precedence rules? You can change the order or evaluation by using parentheses to group parts of an expression. For example, if you want to force the computer to perform an addition before a multiplication, you would use

```
result = (one + ten) * twenty;
```

The computer will evaluate the expression within parentheses first. In essence, parentheses have higher precedence than any operator.

Parentheses are also used to clarify C++ expressions. For example, what should a compiler do with the expression below?

```
sum + + + idx
```

Is this a postincrement followed by an addition, an addition followed by a preincrement, or a postincrement followed by a unary positive (an error)? To make the sense of the expression clear, we group operators with the values they affect inside parentheses. Either of the following is valid:

```
(sum++) + idx
sum + (++idx)
```

Sets of parentheses can be nested, one within the other. In that case, a computer evaluates the expression in the innermost set of parentheses first. In the expression

```
result = ((one + ten) * twenty) + one;
```

the computer adds one and ten, producing 11. It then multiplies the 11 by twenty, producing 220. Finally, it adds one to the 220, generating the final result of 221.

When you nest parentheses, you must be very careful that the parentheses are "balanced." In other words, you must have a closing parenthesis for each opening parenthesis. For example, the following expressions are *not* legal:

```
((number + 10) + sales
cost - ((cost * discount_percent) )) * sales_tax_rate
```

The first expression has two opening parentheses but only one closing parenthesis. The second expression has two opening parentheses and three closing parentheses.

Depending on the context in which unbalanced parentheses occur, a compiler may or may not be able to determine that a syntax problem is caused by unbalanced parentheses. Nonetheless, unbalanced parentheses will always cause a compiler to report an error of some type.

## Explicit Typecasting

Just as you can alter default precedence with the use of parentheses, you can also control typecasting by explicitly telling C++ how you want data types to be converted. To perform explicit typecasting, you precede a variable with the data type you want the variable to take. The typecasted data type is surrounded by parentheses.

You can, for example, use typecasting to force C++ to perform integer division, even if one of the values in the expression is stored in a floating point variable:

```
float value1 = 20.16;
int value2 = 5, result;
result = (int) value1 / value2;
```

To evaluate the assignment statement, C++ first converts `value1` to an integer, truncating any digits to the right of the decimal point. It then performs an integer division.

## Using Math Library Functions

There are some commonly performed arithmetic operations for which C++ doesn't have operators, including exponentiation (raising a number to a power) and taking a square root. These operations are available, however, by using functions stored in a library.

Two sets of libraries are supplied with most C++ compilers: the C++ libraries (e.g., the library in which `cout` is found) and the C libraries. The C libraries contain nonobject-oriented utility functions, of which you will most often use math and string functions.

Depending on your compiler, the prototypes for math functions will be found in either *math.h* or *fp.h*. You must include the appropriate header in your source code to have access to any of the library's functions.

Assuming that you have identified and included the correct header file, a program can then perform exponentiation using the `pow` function, which computes $x^y$:

```
double pow (double x, double y)
```

This function takes two parameters, both double-precision floating point numbers. It returns a double-precision floating point value. If you give the function integer or single-precision floating point values, C++ will typecast them to double-precision floating point.

The `pow` function is very flexible. It can accept fractional and negative powers as well as positive, integer powers. For example, you might use it to compute $109.15^{-0.55}$:

```
double result, base = 109.15, power = -0.55;
result = pow (base, power);
```

You compute the square root of a number with the `sqrt` function:

```
double sqrt (double x)
```

For example, you could display the square root of 12.5 with

```
cout << sqrt (12.5);
```

## An Arithmetic Program

To help you see how all these arithmetic expressions can fit into a program, let's look at a slightly longer program that performs a variety of operations on two numbers (see Figure 11.2). The program uses the same `main` function and application class that you have already seen.

### Figure 11.2   Output of the simple arithmetic program

```
Enter the first number: 12.5
Enter the second number: 6

The sum of these numbers is 18.5
The difference between these numbers is 6.5
The product is 75
The floating point quotient is 2.08333
The integer quotient is 2
The remainder of an integer division is 0
The first number raised to the power of the second number is 3.8147e+06
The square root of the first number is 3.53553
The square root of the second number is 2.44949
```

The arithmetic is handled by the `Numbers` class (Listing 11.8). As you can see in Listing 11.9, each member function takes one or two of the values stored in the class and performs some arithmetic manipulation. You should notice two important things as you study these functions:

- The result of an arithmetic expression isn't stored in a variable. Instead, the expression is placed in a `return` statement. The computer evaluates the expression and then returns the result of the expression directly to the calling function.
- The two functions that perform integer arithmetic (`intDivide` and `modulo`) use explicit typecasting to convert the floating point values stored in the class into integers.

## Listing 11.8    Numbers.h

```
class Numbers
{
    private:
        float value1, value2;
    public:
        Numbers();
        void init (float, float);
        float addition ();
        float subtraction ();
        float multiplication ();
        float floatDivide ();
        int intDivide ();
        int modulo ();
        float power ();
        float root1 ();
        float root2 ();
};
```

The application class `Run` function that produces the output in Figure 11.2 can be found in Listing 11.10. It begins by creating an object from the `Numbers` class. It then asks the user for two values, which it sends to the `Numbers` object by calling the `init` function.

The remainder of the `Run` function is a series of `cout` statements in which calls to `Number` class member functions have been embedded. Because the function results are for display only, there is no reason to store them in variables.

## Summary

C++ supports the typical set of arithmetic operators found in a high-level programming language. However, there is no exponentiation operator; exponentiation is typically performed by using a library function. C++ also provides special operators for quickly incrementing and decrementing a value by one. C++ supports the typical logical operators of AND, OR, and NOT, along with bit-wise logical operators that perform logical operations on the individual bits in two storage locations.

During arithmetic operations, C++ automatically converts data types so that all values in the expression are the same data type. By default, conversion is to the data type with the greatest range and precision. A programmer can over-

## Listing 11.9  Numbers.cpp

```cpp
#include <math.h>
#include "numbers.h"

Numbers::Numbers()
{
    value1 = 0;
    value2 = 0;
}

void Numbers::init (float ivalue1, float ivalue2)
{
    value1 = ivalue1;
    value2 = ivalue2;
}

float Numbers::addition()
    { return value1 + value2; }

float Numbers::subtraction()
    { return value1 - value2; }

float Numbers::multiplication()
    { return value1 * value2; }

float Numbers::floatDivide()
    { return value1 / value2; }

int Numbers::intDivide()
    { return (int) value1 / (int) value2; }

int Numbers::modulo()
    { return (int) value1 % (int) value2; }

float Numbers::power ()
    { return pow (value1, value2); }

float Numbers::root1()
    { return sqrt (value1); }

float Numbers::root2()
    { return sqrt (value2); }
```

ride automatic data conversion with typecasting, which forces a conversion to a specific type of data. Typecasting is the only way to force C++ to perform a floating point division with two integers.

### Listing 11.10 The application class's Run function

```
void AppClass::Run()
{
    Numbers theNumbers;  // create a Numbers object
    float ivalue1, ivalue2;

    cout << "Enter the first number: ";
    cin >> ivalue1;
    cout << "Enter the second number: ";
    cin >> ivalue2;
    theNumbers.init (ivalue1, ivalue2);

    cout << "\nThe sum of these numbers is " << theNumbers.addition() << endl;
    cout << "The difference between these numbers is "
        << theNumbers.subtraction() << endl;
    cout << "The product is " << theNumbers.multiplication() << endl;
    cout << "The floating point quotient is " << theNumbers.floatDivide()
        << endl;
    cout << "The integer quotient is " << theNumbers.intDivide() << endl;
    cout << "The remainder of an integer division is " << theNumbers.modulo()
        << endl;
    cout << "The first number raised to the power of the second number is "
        << theNumbers.power() << endl;
    cout << "The square root of the first number is " << theNumbers.root1()
        << endl;
    cout << "The square root of the second number is " << theNumbers.root2()
        << endl;
}
```

## Exercises

1. Write and test a program that uses the class for a picture frame that you wrote for Exercise 1 at the end of Chapter 6. Create one object from the class. (The program handles one order for framing at a time.) The program should do the following:

   - Enter data to describe a picture framing order.
   - Compute and display the cost of the framing order. (*Hint:* Keep in mind that the total inches of framing used in the frame is twice the width plus twice the length.)
   - Display all the data for the picture framing order.

2. Write and test a program that uses the class for an oil storage tank that you wrote for Exercise 2 at the end of Chapter 6. Create one object from the class. (The program handles one oil storage tank at a time.) The program should do the following:

   • Enter data to describe an oil tank.
   • Display the amount of oil in the tank expressed as a percentage of the tank's capacity.
   • Display the amount of available space in the tank expressed as a percentage of the tank's capacity.
   • Display all data for the storage tank.

3. Write and test a program that uses the class for a paycheck that you wrote for Exercise 3 at the end of Chapter 6. Create one object from the class. (The program should process one paycheck at a time.) The program should do the following:

   • Enter employee data, including ID#, gross pay, and amount of deductions.
   • Compute the employee's net pay.
   • Display a nicely formatted paycheck and pay stub, showing all deductions.

4. Write and test a program that uses the class for service performed on an automobile that you wrote for Exercise 4 at the end of Chapter 6. Create one object from the class. (The program should process one service order at a time.) The program should do the following:

   • Enter the automobile and service data, including the service code, amount of labor, and cost of supplies.
   • Compute the total amount of the service.
   • Display a nicely formatted receipt for the customer, showing how much time was spent performing the work, the cost of supplies used, and the total cost of the service.

5. Create a class that stores information about costs to produce a product, including the number of units produced in the past month, the direct materials cost per unit, the direct labor cost per unit, and the overhead per

unit. Include a member function that computes the total cost for all units produced in the past month. Write a program that lets the user enter data for a product and then displays the total cost for that product.

6. Add a member function to the program you write for Exercise 5 at the end of Chapter 7. This function should compute the following:

- The percentage of people who inquired about information that actually applied to the college.
- The percentage of people who inquired that were accepted.
- The percentage of people who were accepted that actually attended the college. (Colleges call this the "conversion" rate.)

Prepare a nicely formatted report that displays these values for each of the four objects handled by the program.

# 12 Making Decisions

## OBJECTIVES

In this chapter you will learn about:
- Logical expressions.
- The way in which computers can choose between alternative sets of actions.
- C++ syntax for writing logical expressions and the statements in which they can be embedded.

In addition to arithmetic operations, another of the things that a computer does commonly is to make a choice between alternative groups of actions, a process known as *selection*. In this chapter you will learn about how a program instructs a computer to make a choice, including how to construct the logical expressions that a computer evaluates when deciding which alternative to take. You also will be introduced to the two C++ statements that are used to contain logical expressions and group the statements that are to be executed depending on the value of those logical expressions.

A logical expression is an expression that can be evaluated as either true or false. In many ways, a logical expression is like a question that can be answered as either yes or no. For example, we could write a logical expression that asked whether an employee's salary was greater than $50,000 or whether the number of purchase orders a program is counting is less than or equal to the total number of purchase orders.

Another term for an expression that produces a result of only true or false is a *Boolean expression*, named after George Boole (1815–64), an English mathematician and logician who developed the operations that can be performed with true and false values. All of the manipulations of true and false that you read about in this chapter come from what is known as *Boolean algebra*, which underlies the design of circuits in a computer. If you take a course in Discrete Math, you will learn a great deal more about Boolean algebra.

## Basic Relationship Operators

A programmer can use six relationship operators to create expressions that can be evalutated as either true or false:

- ==                    equal to
- !=                    not equal to
- \>                     greater than
- \>=                    greater than or equal to
- <                     less than
- <=                    less than or equal to

All of these are binary operators. This means that legal expressions have a value on either side of the operator.

Assume, for example, that we want a program to decide whether an employee's salary is greater than $50,000. The logical expression would be written

```
salary > 50000
```

Notice that when we use the literal value on the right of the operator, we omit any formatting, such as a dollar sign and comma.

When the computer encounters an expression like the preceding example, it evaluates the expression to decide whether it is true or false. If an expression is false, the computer gives the expression a value of 0. If it is true, the expression is given a value that isn't zero. Although most C++ programs assign a value of 1 to a true expression, there is a slight chance that you may encounter a compiler that uses some other nonzero value.

When you are first learning to use the relationship operators, it can be difficult to keep the greater than and less than operators straight. It helps if you remember that the closed end of the operator points to the smaller value and that the open end of the operator points to the larger value when reading the expression from left to right. For example, this expression is true:

```
2 > 1
```

The expression is read "two greater than one." We know that the operator is greater than because when we read the expression from left to right we encounter the open end of the operator first. In contrast, this expression is false:

```
2 < 1
```

You read the expression "two less than one." As you can see, we come across the closed end of the operator first, when reading from left to right. This lets us know that the operator is indeed less than.

**Warning**

The == operator (two equal signs next to each other) tests for the equality of two numbers or characters. Be very careful not to confuse it with the assignment operator (=). For example, this statement checks to see if a variable that is counting the number of values processed is the same as the total number of values:

```
count == NUMB_VALUES
```

However, the following is also a legal expression (an assignment statement):

```
count = NUMB_VALUES
```

If you use the assignment statement in a situation where you actually intended to place a logical expression, a C++ compiler will accept the assignment statement. (Some C++ compilers will warn you of a "possible unintended assignment," but don't count on it.) The program will perform the assignment and then evaluate the contents of the count variable. If count contains something other than zero, the expression will evaluate to true.

The less than or equal to and greater than or equal to operators are a shorthand for the combination of two expressions. For example, the expression

```
count >= NUMB_VALUES
```

tests to determine whether the value in the count variable is the same or greater than the constant NUMB_VALUES. This is the same as evaluating the following two expressions separately:

```
count == NUMB_VALUES
count > NUMB_VALUES
```

## Binary Logical Operators

When you want to combine more than one arithmetic operation into a single expression, you simply add the needed operators and values to the expression; the operators themselves act as connectors for the parts of the expression. The situation with logical expressions is a bit more involved. The simple logical expressions that you create with the relationship operators are combined into complex logical expressions with two binary logical operators: && (AND) and || (OR).

AND and OR take the results of the logical expressions on either side of them and determine whether the entire expression is true or false. The decision is made based on the logical truth table for each operator.

## AND

An expression including AND is true only if both expressions on either side of the operator are true. We can summarize this by looking at its truth table in Table 12.1.

Table 12.1   AND truth table

| AND | true | false |
|---|---|---|
| true | true | false |
| false | false | false |

As examples, consider the following logical expression:

```
2 > 1 && 3 > 4
```

The expression is read "two greater than one and three greater than four." The first half of the expression is true. However, the second half is false. The entire expression is therefore false.

## OR

An expression including OR is true if either expression surrounding the OR is true. This rule is summarized in the truth table in Table 12.2.

Table 12.2   OR truth table

| OR | true | false |
|---|---|---|
| true | true | true |
| false | true | false |

If we rewrite the preceding example using OR, the expression appears as

```
2 > 1 || 3 > 4
```

and is read "two greater than one or three greater than four." In this case, the entire expression evaluates as true. Although the simple expression on the right side of the OR is false, the expression on the left side is true. With OR, only one of the expressions needs to be true for the entire expression to be true.

## The Unary NOT Operator

C++ provides only one unary logical operator: the NOT operator (!), which inverts the value of a logical expression. If an expression is true, placing ! in front of it changes the value to false; if an expression is false, placing ! in front of it changes the value to true. For example, the following expressions are false:

```
!(2 > 1)

int count = 1;
!(count)
```

In both examples, a computer first evaluates the logical expression inside the parentheses. The first inner expression evaluates to true because two is greater than one; the second is true because the value in count is nonzero. In fact, the second inner expression is a shorthand for count == 1. The NOT operator changes the value of both true inner expressions to false.

By the same token, the following expressions are true:

```
!(1 > 2)

int count = 0;
!(count)
```

The expression inside the parentheses of the second expression is a shorthand for count == 0, and is false because the value in count is zero. In both examples, the NOT operator inverts the false inner values to true.

## Bit-wise AND and OR

**Warning**

C++ provides two additional binary logical operators: bit-wise AND (&) and bit-wise OR (|). In most of your programming you won't need to use them, and their presence in the language can be the source of error if you accidentally use one of them when you intend to use the && or || operator.

The bit-wise operators perform logical operations on the individual bits in two values, interpreting 1 as true and 0 as false. The truth tables are the same as those for the && and || operators, but instead of working on the values as a whole, the bit-wise operators work on one pair of bits at a time. As an example, assume that you are performing a bit-wise OR between the two values below:

```
1000 0001
0111 0001 |
```

The result will be 1111 0001. Where did this come from? Look at the two binary numbers, reading *down* each pair. When both numbers are 0, place a 0 in the result; when either number is 1, place a 1 in the result. If you look at this carefully, you'll notice that the following is true:

```
a | 1 = 1
a | 0 = a
```

In other words, if you OR a bit with 0, you preserve the value of the bit. If you OR a bit with 1, you set the bit to 1, regardless of the bit's original value. This means that if you want to set one bit in a storage location to 1, you OR the current contents of the location with a value that contains a 1 in the position of the bit you want to set and 0s in all other positions.

This ability to set individual bits underlies one circumstance in which the bit-wise OR operator can be of use: it can help provide additional formatting for numbers in cout displays. The function that provides this formatting is called setiosflags. The "flags" in the function name are individual bits in an input parameter. Each bit represents a different type of formatting. When a bit is set, it tells the cout stream to apply that formatting.

The setiosflags function takes one input parameter: a 32-bit integer in which specific bits have been set to indicate the formatting that should be used. The function call is placed in the cout stream, just like other formatting functions such as setprecision.

The ios flags are defined as enumerated variables of the ios class. Those that you are likely to use can be found in Table 12.3. Each value has a 1 in the bit assigned to that particular flag; the rest of the bits in the value are 0.

To format currency values, we often use the showpoint and fixed flags along with setprecision(2). This ensures that a decimal point appears, followed by two digits to the right of the decimal point, even if either of those digits is 0. The parameter sent to the setiosflags function must therefore have two bits set (one for each flag); the rest of its bits must be zero.

Table 12.3   Flags for the setiosflags function

| Flag | Function |
|------|----------|
| `left` | Left justify output in its field. |
| `right` | Right justify output in its field. |
| `showpoint` | Display a decimal point for a floating point number. |
| `showpos` | Display a plus sign (+) in front of positive numbers. |
| `scientific` | Display floating point numbers in scientific format. |
| `fixed` | Display floating point numbers in fixed point notation. |

To create the input parameter, we perform a bit-wise OR on the two flags. The call therefore looks like

```
cout << setiosflags (ios::showpoint | ios::fixed);
```

Notice that each flag name is preceded by the scope resolution operator to indicate the class from which it comes. The bit-wise OR is placed in the parameter list. The computer will perform the bit-wise OR before sending the parameter to the function. If you want more formatting flags, just add the names of the flags to the parameter list with additional bit-wise OR operators.

Keep in mind that this formatting only affects how the number appears. It won't, for example, place a dollar sign in front of a currency value. It we want a value to appear in the format $XXX.XX, then we have to do something like the following:

```
float theCurrency = 5689.1;
cout << setprecision(2)
     << setiosflags (ios::fixed | ios::showpoint);
cout << "The value is $" << theCurrency;
```

Running this code produces:

```
The value is $5689.10
```

Notice that the dollar sign was displayed by making it the last character in the literal string that was sent to the `cout` stream just prior to the value in the `theCurrency` variable.

The `ios` flags stay in effect for a given stream until the stream object is destroyed (usually when you exit the function) or until the flags are explicitly reset with `resetiosflags`. For example, to turn off the `showpoint` and `fixed` formats, you would use:

```
cout << resetiosflags (ios::showpoint | ios::fixed);
```

## Precedence, Parentheses, and Logical Expressions

There is theoretically no limit to the number of simple logical expressions you can string together into a complex logical expression using AND and OR. For example, the following expression is valid:

```
count < MAX && sales > 100000 || contacts > LIMIT
```

Faced with such an expression, which part of it should the computer evaluate first? As with arithmetic operators, there is a precedence associated with logical operators: AND takes precedence over OR, which takes precedence over NOT and the relationship operators.

In the preceding example, the AND will be evaluated first. However, what the programmer really intends is the following:

```
count < MAX && (sales > 100000 || contacts > LIMIT)
```

The OR should be evaluated first. The programmer therefore places the two simple logical expressions joined by OR within parentheses to indicate that the computer should evaluate the contents of the parentheses first.

Just as you saw with arithmetic expressions, you use parentheses to group portions of a logical epression. Whatever is inside parentheses is evaluated first. Whenever parentheses are nested, the contents of the innermost set has precedence. For example, in this statement

```
count < MAX && (sales > 100000 && (district == 6 || district == 2))
```

the computer evaluates the OR inside the innermost parentheses first, checking the district in which a salesperson works. Then the computer performs the AND with the sales amount. Finally, the computer performs the AND involving the count of the number of salespeople that have been processed.

When you use nested parentheses, don't forget that the parentheses must be balanced: There must be one opening parenthesis for every closing parenthesis.

## The if Statement

The logical expressions about which you have been reading are placed inside C++ statements that group alternative sets of actions that are to be taken depending on whether a logical expression evaluates to true or false. The most widely used of these statements is if.

## Simple if Statements

A simple if statement has the following general syntax:

```
if (logical expression)
    statement to execute if true;
else
    statement to execute if false;
```

The following rules apply to constructing if statements:

- The else portion of the statement is optional.
- The logical expression following if must be placed in parentheses.
- If the statement following if or else is a single executable statement, then it can follow without any braces or grouping. However, if there are multiple executable statements following if or else, then each set of statements must be grouped within braces.

As a first example, here is an if statement that the concurrency conversion program uses to determine which of two arithmetic operators to use to perform a conversion:

```
if (Method == 'm' || Method == 'M')
    return ConversionFactor * Dollars;
else
    return Dollars / ConversionFactor;
```

Notice the semicolon after the statement following if, as well as one after the statement following else. However, there are no semicolons directly after if or else.

How does a computer execute such a statement? To help you visualize what is occurring, we'll be using a technique known as a *flowchart*. Through the early 1980s, flowcharts were considered to be the best way to depict the logic of a computer program, and programmers were encouraged to draw flowcharts before starting to write code. Although flowcharts have largely fallen into disuse, their symbols can make it easier to understand small bits of program logic.

Let's first consider an if statement that has no else. The programmer's intention is to execute the statements following if when the logical expression following if is true. If the expression is false, then the program should continue without taking any special action. This is diagrammed in Figure 12.1. The logical expression is represented by the diagram (often called a "decision box"). If the question in the decision box can be answered "yes" (or true), program execution follows the right-hand path out of the decision box. The program executes the statements following if and then continues execution with whatever follows the if. However, if the question in the decision box can be answered "no" (or false), the program skips the statements following if entirely and continues with the statement directly following the if.

Figure 12.1    Executing an if

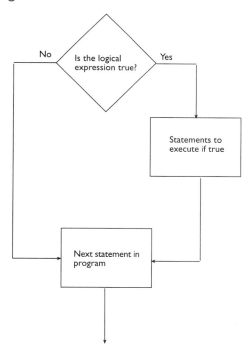

Consider the following code:

```
overtime = hours = 40;
pay = 0;
if (overtime > 0)
    pay = rate * 1.5 * overtime;
pay = pay + (hours - overtime) * rate);
```

A program using this code first computes the number of hours of overtime an employee has worked. It then uses an if to determine whether there is actually any overtime. If the employee has worked more than 40 hours, then the overtime variable will contain a value greater than 0, and the computer will compute overtime pay at time-and-a-half. Execution continues with the statement below the if, which completes the pay computation. However, if the employee has not worked any overtime, then the program skips the overtime pay computation completely and goes directly to the statement that computes pay at the regular rate (the statement below the if).

When an if statement includes an else, the computer has two possible paths to take—one if the logical expression is true and the other if it is false. As you can see in Figure 12.2, a program chooses between the two sets of actions. If the logical expression is true, the program executes the statements following if. If the logical expression is false, the program executes the statements following else. In both cases, execution continues with the next statement below the else.

Looking back at the if/else example you saw earlier, notice that if the conversion method is either m or M, the computer performs a multiplication. Otherwise, it performs a division. The important thing to realize is that when an else is part of an if, the computer performs one set of actions, but not both.

Because we can use braces to group executable statements, it is easy to instruct a computer to perform multiple actions following either if or else. The following if statement is therefore legal:

```
if (hours > 40)
{
    cout << "\nThere has been an error." << endl;
    cout << "No one should be working overtime."
}
else
    pay = rate * hours;
```

Figure 12.2   Executing an if/else

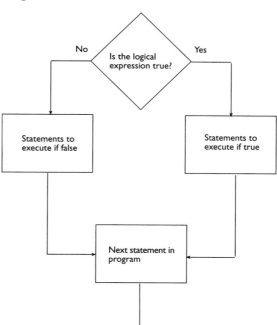

Because two `cout` statements follow `if`, they must be grouped within braces. However, only one statement follows `else`. It therefore doesn't need braces, although a compiler won't consider it an error if you do use them.

We can use the `if` statement to prepare a more user-friendly version of the clothing survey program you first saw in Chapter 11. The original version of the program worked only because we forced the user to enter a 1 for *yes* and a 0 for *no*. A better interface would let the user type a *y* or *n*. The program would then need to evaluate the character the user entered and decide whether to add 1 to the total.

Making these modifications first requires changing the class declaration so that the question member functions (`Quest1`, `Quest2`, and so on) return a character and that the `answer` variable will hold a character, as in Listing 12.1. Then, the only modification required in implementation of the member functions is a change in the return data types (see Listing 12.2).

Listing 12.1    Revised survey.h file for the clothing survey program

```
class survey
{
    public:
        char answer;
    public:
        survey();
        char Quest1 ();
        char Quest2 ();
        char Quest3 ();
        char Quest4 ();
        char Quest5 ();
};
```

On the other hand, the application class's Run function in Listing 12.3 looks significantly different. The function now does the following:

- Creates a Survey object.
- Declares a local variable to hold the number of *y* responses.
- Declares a character variable to hold the user's response.
- Calls the member function that asks question 1, capturing the response in a local variable.
- Uses an if statement to determine whether the user entered a *y* or a *Y*. If the logical expression evaluates as TRUE, then the function increments the contents of the total variable using the postincrement operator.
- Repeats the preceding two steps for the remaining four questions.
- Displays the contents of the total variable.

When we were using integers to capture a user's responses to the survey, we could make the Run function very short by embedding the function calls and addition in an output statement. However, when we are working with characters, there isn't any way to shorten the function because we must explicitly evaluate the response to each question. You will find that this happens frequently: Making a program easier for the user often requires a lot more work for the programmer.

## Listing 12.2   Revised survey.cpp file for the clothing survey function

```cpp
#include "survey.h"
#include <iostream.h>

survey::survey()
{
    answer = 0;
    cout << "\nPlease answer questions with 1 for 'yes' and 0 for 'no'" << endl
    << endl;
}

// Notice that the only difference between these functions and those you saw in Chapter 11 is the return
// data type of each function, which has been changed from int to char
char survey::Quest1 ()
{
    cout << "Do you own more than four pairs of jeans? ";
    cin >> answer;
    return answer;
}

char survey::Quest2 ()
{
    cout << "Do you own more than four pairs of sneakers? ";
    cin >> answer;
    return answer;
}

char survey::Quest3 ()
{
    cout << "Do you own a jean jacket? ";
    cin >> answer;
    return answer;
}

char survey::Quest4 ()
{
    cout << "Do you own more than 10 T-shirts? ";
    cin >> answer;
    return answer;
}

char survey::Quest5 ()
{
    cout << "Do you purposely wear clothes with holes in them? ";
    cin >> answer;
    return answer;
}
```

Listing 12.3   Revised application class Run function for the clothing survey
program

```
void AppClass::Run ()
{
    survey theSurvey; // create an object

    int total = 0; // variable to hold total "yes" responses
    char answer;

    answer = theSurvey.Quest1 ();
    if (answer == 'y' || answer == 'Y')
        total++;
    answer = theSurvey.Quest2 ();
    if (answer == 'y' || answer == 'Y')
        total++;
    answer = theSurvey.Quest3 ();
    if (answer == 'y' || answer == 'Y')
        total++;
    answer = theSurvey.Quest4 ();
    if (answer == 'y' || answer == 'Y')
        total++;
    answer = theSurvey.Quest5 ();
    if (answer == 'y' || answer == 'Y')
        total++;

    cout << "\n\nYou answered 'yes' to " << total << " questions.";
}
```

## Nesting if Statements

Any executable statement can follow if or else, including another if statement. Placing one if inside another is known as *nesting*.

For example, the hi/lo guessing game program that you will see in its
entirety in Chapter 13 uses the following nested if construct to evaluate a
guess:

```
if (guess == answer)
    return EQ;
else
    if (guess < answer)
        return LO;
    else
        return HI;
```

The structure of this statement is diagrammed in Figure 12.3. If the logical expression in the first if is true, the program returns the value of the constant EQ, taking the rightmost path in Figure 12.3. However, if the logical expression is false, the program immediately encounters the second if, which is the single statement following else. The computer therefore evaluates the second expression, and, if that second expression is true, it takes the right branch from the second decision box in the diagram, returning LO to calling function. If the second expression is false, the program takes the leftmost branch and returns Hi.

Figure 12.3  Executing a nested if/else statement

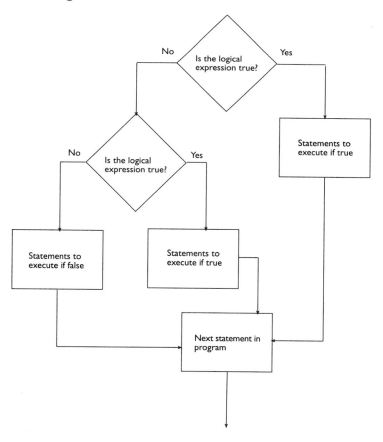

There is no limit to how deep you can nest `if` statements. However, when they are nested more than two or three levels deep, they can become difficult to understand. Later in this chapter you will therefore read about the `switch` statement, which in some cases can greatly simplify a situation where nested `if`s would be cumbersome.

**Warning**

When you nest `if` statements that are followed by groups of statements surrounded by braces, you must be careful to completely nest one set of braces within another. To make this a bit clearer, take a look at Figure 12.4. We commonly use indentation in our source code to make it easy to see how braces group sets of nested statements. However, a compiler ignores spacing in a source code file.

**Figure 12.4    Incorrect and correct nesting of if statements**

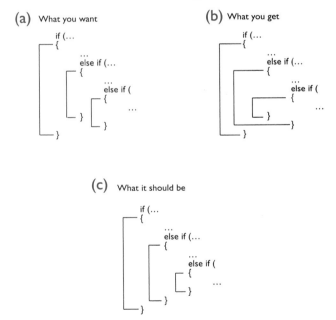

In Figure 12.4(a), a program has used indentation in an attempt to indicate the pairing of braces. Notice that the programmer's intention is to close the middle set of braces before closing the innermost set. Regardless of how the braces have been placed in the source code file, the compiler interprets the grouping as in Figure 12.4(b). This occurs because *a compiler always*

*associates a closing brace with the most recently encountered opening brace*. Therefore, unless sets of braces are completely nested within one another—as they are in Figure 12.4(c)—a program will not behave as you expected.

## Checking the Result of File Operations

One of the characteristics of a well-written computer program is *error trapping*. This is program code that looks for things that might go wrong and when they do, either recovers gracefully without the user ever knowing that a problem has occurred or, if recovery is either not possible or desirable, lets the user know what has happened. Error trapping insulates the user from his or her mistakes and in many cases can prevent a program from crashing.

In particular, a good program checks the result of file I/O operations. If a program doesn't catch a problem with opening a file, for example, any attempt to read from or write to the file will usually cause the program to crash.

Depending on your compiler, you will use one of two ways to check if a file has been opened successfully. The older method is to use the unary NOT operator to determine whether the file stream object is valid:

```
ifstream myFile ("File_name");
if (!myFile)
{
    cout << "\nCouldn't open input file.";
    return;
}
else
{
    // code to read file goes here
}
```

Notice that if the value of the file stream object is zero (in other words, the file stream object isn't valid), the program displays an error message for the user. This structure therefore prevents the program from attempting to read from a nonexistent file.

The newer version of the ANSI standard includes a function that checks whether files are open:

```
ifstream myFile ("File_name");
if (!myFile.is_open())
{
    cout << "\nCouldn't open input file.";
    return;
}
else
{
    // code to read file goes here
}
```

The function is_open can be used by both ofstream and ifstream objects. However, the only way to determine whether you should use is_open or the earlier method for checking file streams is to consult your compiler's documentation.

One program that we have seen already that desperately needs to check whether a file is open is the bucket management program that you saw in Chapter 10. The revised application class Run function can be found in Listing 12.4.

The checks for proper file opening appear in two places, at the beginning when the program attempts to open an input file for reading and at the end when the program attempts to open an output file for writing. In both cases, the if statement that contains the call to the is_open function appears immediately after the statement that creates the file stream object.

What a program does when a file hasn't been opened properly is up to the programmer. A user-friendly interface lets the user know what has happened and, if appropriate, lets the user choose whether to continue running the program. If you look at Listing 12.4, you'll see that this is exactly what happens if an input file can't be opened. The function asks the user if he or she wants to continue running the program. If the user responds with n or N, the function issues a return, which causes the function to stop execution. Because the call to this Run function is the last statement in the main function, the program stops.

However, if the user wants to continue running the program, the function must make sure that it doesn't attempt to read from a nonexisting file. (Otherwise, the program might crash.) The function therefore places all the file input statements inside an else, which is skipped if the file wasn't opened

Listing 12.4    The bucket management program's application class Run
                function modified to include verifying the opening of files

```
void AppClass::Run()
{
    Bucket Bucket1, Bucket2, Bucket3;

    int iHoles;
    float iGallons;
    char yes_no; // This will hold the user's response to a yes/no question

    ifstream fin ("Buckets");
    // Here's where the first file checking goes
    if (!fin.is_open()) // This will be true if the file wasn't opened properly
    {
        cout << "No input file found. Continue? ") // Message to user
        cin >> yes_no;
        if (yes_no == 'n' || yes_no == 'N')
            return; // User wants to quit, so exit the function
    }
    else // This else makes sure that you don't attempt to read from a non-existing file
    {
        fin >> iGallons >> iHoles;
        Bucket1.InitBucket (iHoles, iGallons);
        fin >> iGallons >> iHoles;
        Bucket2.InitBucket (iHoles, iGallons);
        fin >> iGallons >> iHoles;
        Bucket3.InitBucket (iHoles, iGallons);
    }

    fin.close();

    cout << "The current bucket data are: " << endl;

    cout << setprecision(2) << setiosflags (ios::fixed | ios::showpoint)
        << endl << endl;
    cout << "Bucket #1 holds " << Bucket1.Getcapacity() << " gallons and has "
        << Bucket1.GetnumbHoles() << " holes." << endl;
    cout << "Bucket #2 holds " << Bucket2.Getcapacity() << " gallons and has "
        << Bucket2.GetnumbHoles() << " holes." << endl;
    cout << "Bucket #3 holds " << Bucket3.Getcapacity() << " gallons and has "
        << Bucket3.GetnumbHoles() << " holes." << endl;

    cout << "\n\nNow you can change the data: "  << endl << endl;
```

Continued next page

**Listing 12.4**(Continued)    The bucket management program's application class
Run function modified to include verifying the opening of files

```
cout << "How many holes in bucket #1? ";
cin >> iHoles;
cout << "How many gallons does bucket #1 hold? ";
cin >> iGallons;
Bucket1.InitBucket (iHoles, iGallons);

cout << "How many holes in bucket #2? ";
cin >> iHoles;
cout << "How many gallons does bucket #2 hold? ";
cin >> iGallons;
Bucket2.InitBucket (iHoles, iGallons);

cout << "How many holes in bucket #3? ";
cin >> iHoles;
cout << "How many gallons does bucket #3 hold? ";
cin >> iGallons;
Bucket3.InitBucket (iHoles, iGallons);

cout << setprecision(2) << setiosflags (ios::fixed | ios::showpoint)
    << endl << endl;

cout << "Bucket #1 holds " << Bucket1.Getcapacity() << " gallons and has "
    << Bucket1.GetnumbHoles() << " holes." << endl;

cout << "Bucket #2 holds " << Bucket2.Getcapacity() << " gallons and has "
    << Bucket2.GetnumbHoles() << " holes." << endl;

cout << "Bucket #3 holds " << Bucket3.Getcapacity() << " gallons and has "
    << Bucket3.GetnumbHoles() << " holes." << endl;

ofstream fout ("Buckets");

// Second file checking goes here
if (!fout.is_open)
{
    cout << "Couldn't open output file."; // Message to user
    return; // Get out of the function without attempting to write to a file
}
// No else is required here because the preceding return got the user out of the function
fout << Bucket1.Getcapacity() << ' ' << Bucket1.GetnumbHoles() << ' ';
fout << Bucket2.Getcapacity() << ' ' << Bucket2.GetnumbHoles() << ' ';
fout << Bucket3.Getcapacity() << ' ' << Bucket3.GetnumbHoles() << ' ';
}
```

properly. On the other hand, if the file was opened properly, the logical expression following if is false. The function drops immediately to the statements following else and reads the data from the file.

The Run function also checks to make sure that an output file was opened properly. If the file couldn't be opened (for example, because the disk was full), the function lets the user know what happened. At this point, the function simply ends; there really are no options for the user. If the file was opened properly, the logical expression following if will be false and the function drops to the line below the if, where writing to the file begins.

Why aren't the file output statements placed in an else like the file input statements? Because if the file hasn't been opened properly, the function executes the return statement and never even has a chance to execute the file input statements.

## The switch Statement

As mentioned earlier, athough if statements can be nested without limit, deeply nested ifs are difficult to debug and modify. When a program needs to evaluate many possible values for a single variable (for example, deciding what to do based on an option in a menu), it is cleaner to use a statement called switch. In fact, if you need to take actions based on more than two values of the same variable, you should use a switch rather than an if.

A switch statement provides the equivalent of several logical expressions, all involving an integer variable and the equal to operator. Assume, for example, that you are working with the menu class for the currency converter program to which you were introduced in Chapter 9. The menu has three options: set the conversion rate, do a conversion, and quit the program.

The code to determine which option the user picked could be written with nested ifs, as in Listing 12.5. However, if the actions the program takes for each menu option are at all complex, the program's structure will become very difficult to understand.

Alternatively, we could use a switch (Listing 12.6). The switch evaluates the value in the choice variable. It begins checking all the values following case, looking for a match. As soon as it finds a match, it executes all the statements below.

Unlike if/else, switch doesn't automatically skip the remainder of the construct once it finds code to execute. If you want to exit the switch without executing any additional code, you must place a break statement at

## Listing 12.5   Using nested ifs to process menu choices

```
int choice;
choice = theMenu.choose();
if (choice == 1)
{
    // do option one things here
}
else
    if (choice == 2)
    {
        // do option two things here
    }
    else
    {
        // handle program exit choice here
    }
```

## Listing 12.6   Using a switch to process menu choices

```
int choice;
choice = theMenu.choose();
switch (choice)
{
    case 1:
        // do option one things here
        break;
    case 2:
        // do option two things here
        break;
    case 9:
        // handle program exit choice here
        break;
    default:
        cout << "\nYou've entered an invalid menu option."
}
```

the place where you want the program to leave the switch. If the user chooses 1 in the example we are considering, the program stops when it encounters case 1 and executes whatever statements follow case until it reaches the break, at which point the program jumps to whatever statement follows the closing brace of the switch. If, however, the user entered a value that wasn't accounted for by a case, the computer ends up at default. Use this option to group actions that execute when no case is matched. In this particular case, the program prints an error message to the user.

The switch statement has the following general syntax:

```
switch (integer_variable)
{
    case integer_value1:
        statements to execute
        break;
    case integer_value2:
    case integer_value3:
        statements to execute
        break;
    :
    :
    default:
        statements to execute if no case is matched
}
```

There are several syntactical details to which you should pay attention when writing a switch structure:

- The entire body of the switch is surrounded by a single set of braces.
- Each case is associated with one integer value. However, multiple case statements can be associated with the same set of actions, as occurs with integer_value2 and integer_value3 in the preceding general syntax.
- The integer value can be an integer variable, an integer constant, a literal integer, a character variable, a character constant, or a literal character. When the value is a character, C++ automatically type-casts it into an integer, using its ASCII code.
- Each case is followed by the statements that are to be executed when the value in the switch variables matches the value following case.
- The break statement at the end of a group of executable statements causes the switch to branch to the statement below the closing brace. Although not required as far as a compiler's syntax checking is concerned, a break prevents the computer from evaluating any other case statements within the switch.

**Note**

The `break` statement causes a program to immediately jump out of the innermost set of braces in which it is contained. As you will see in Chapter 13, `break` has uses in addition to its function in the `switch` statement.

- The statements following `default` are executed if the value in the `switch` variable matches none of the preceding `case` values. A `default` statement is optional. If no `default` is present and the value in the `switch` variable doesn't match any `case` values, the `switch` statement simply does nothing.

## The Currency Converter Program

To see how a programmer uses choices to organize a program, let's take a look at the entire currency converter program. This program uses the same `main` function and application class as the other programs you have seen, so we won't duplicate their listings here. It also uses the `menu` class you saw in Chapter 9.

As written, the program converts between U.S. dollars and British pounds, French francs, and Japanese yen (see Figure 12.5). The first menu choice lets the user enter a conversion rate and method. If one unit of the target currency is equal to many dollars, then the method requires division; if one unit of the target currency is a portion of a dollar, then the method requires multiplication. The second menu choice actually performs a conversion.

The application object manipulates three objects of the class `Converter` (Listing 12.7). Each object contains data about the conversion factor and the method that should be used to perform a conversion (multiplication or division).

The class declaration also contains five member functions, all of which use techniques to which you have been introduced in Chapters 9 and 10. The code for these functions is stored in a file named *converter.cpp* (Listing 12.8):

- `Converter` (the constructor): Uses assignment to initialize an object's variables.
- `ModConversion`: Uses assignment to place variables into an object's variables. This function can be used to set values for a new object or to modify existing values.

Figure 12.5   Sample output of the currency converter program

```
Pick a menu option:
   1. Set conversion rate
   2. Do a conversion
   9. Quit

Which one? 1
Country ( E)ngland, F)rance, or J)apan ): e
Conversion factor: 2.45
Method ( M)ultiply or D)ivide): d


Pick a menu option:
   1. Set conversion rate
   2. Do a conversion
   9. Quit

Which one? 2
Country: ( E)ngland, F)rance, or J)apan )e

Dollar amount to be converted? 10

10.00 Dollars = 4.08 Pounds.
```

Listing 12.7   Converter.h

```cpp
class Converter
{
    private:
        float ConversionFactor;
        char Method;

    public:
        Converter (void);
        void ModConversion (float, char);
        float DoConversion (float);
        float GetFactor (void);
        char GetMethod (void);
};
```

- DoConversion: Based on the value in the Method variable, converts U.S. dollars into a foreign currency. This function contains an if statement to choose the correct conversion process and arithmetic operations to perform the conversion.
- GetFactor: Returns the value in the conversion factor variable.
- GetMethod: Returns the value in the conversion method variable.

## Listing 12.8    Converter.cpp

```
#include "converter.h"

Converter::Converter()
{
    ConversionFactor = 0.0;
    Method = '\0';
}


void Converter::ModConversion (float iFactor, char How)
{
    ConversionFactor = iFactor;
    Method = How;
}


float Converter::DoConversion (float Dollars)
{
    if (Method == 'm' || Method == 'M')
        return ConversionFactor * Dollars;
    else
        return Dollars / ConversionFactor;
}


float Converter::GetFactor ()
{
    return ConversionFactor;
}


char Converter::GetMethod ()
{
    return Method;
}
```

The application class Run function that manipulates Converter objects can be found in Listing 12.9. The function makes extensive use of switch constructs to organize the actions to be taken for each menu option. There are two major advantages to using the switch rather than nested if statements. First, the code is easier to understand. Second, it is easier to modify. Adding a new menu option requires simply adding another case to the switch, along with statements that are to be executed when the new option is chosen.

## Listing 12.9    Application class Run function for the currency converter program

```
void AppClass::Run()
{
    Converter England, France, Japan; // create three converter objects
    menu theMenu; // create a menu object

    ifstream Read_File ("Data");

    int option = 0;
    char country, How;
    float Factor, Dollars, Amount;

    if (Read_File.is_open())
    {
        Read_File >> Factor >> How;
        England.ModConversion (Factor, How);
        Read_File >> Factor >> How;
        France.ModConversion (Factor, How);
        Read_File >> Factor >> How;
        Japan.ModConversion (Factor, How);
        Read_File.close();
    }
    while (option != 9)
    {
        theMenu.display(); // show the menu
        option = theMenu.choose();
        switch (option)
        {
            case 1:
                cout << "Country ( E)ngland, F)rance, or J)apan ): ";
                cin >> country;
                cout << "Conversion factor: ";
                cin >> Factor;
                cout << "Method ( M)ultiply or D)ivide): ";
                cin >> How;
                switch (country)
                {
                    case 'e':
                    case 'E':
                        England.ModConversion (Factor, How);
                        break;
```

Continued next page

**Listing 12.9**(Continued)    Application class Run function for the currency
                    converter program

```
                case 'f':
                case 'F':
                    France.ModConversion (Factor, How);
                    break;
                case 'j':
                case 'J':
                    Japan.ModConversion (Factor, How);
                    break;
                default:
                    cout << "You've entered a country I can't handle.";
            }
        break;
    case 2:
        cout << "Country: ( E)ngland, F)rance, or J)apan )";
        cin >> country;
        cout << "\nDollar amount to be converted? ";
        cin >> Dollars;
        cout  << setprecision(2) << setiosflags
            (ios::fixed | ios::showpoint);
        switch (country)
        {
            case 'e':
            case 'E':
                Amount = England.DoConversion (Dollars);
                cout << "\n" << Dollars << " Dollars = " << Amount
                    << " Pounds." << endl;
                break;
            case 'f':
            case 'F':
                Amount = France.DoConversion (Dollars);
                cout << "\n" << Dollars << " Dollars = " << Amount
                    << " Francs." << endl;
                break;
            case 'j':
            case 'J':
                Amount = Japan.DoConversion (Dollars);
                cout << "\n" << Dollars << " Dollars = " << Amount
                    << " Yen." << endl;
                break;
```

Continued next page

Listing 12.9(Continued)    Application class Run function for the currency
                converter program

```
        default:
            cout << "\nYou've entered a country I can't handle.";
        }
        break;
    case 9:
        ofstream Write_File ("Data");
        if (Write_File.is_open())
        {
            Write_File << England.GetFactor() << England.GetMethod();
            Write_File << France.GetFactor() << France.GetMethod();
            Write_File << Japan.GetFactor() << Japan.GetMethod();
        }
        break;
    default:
        cout << "You've entered an unavailable option.";
    }
  }
}
```

**Note**

This Run function contains some code that we haven't discussed yet (the statement that begins with `while`). The purpose of this statement is to instruct the program to repeat actions. You will learn how to use it in Chapter 10.

As you study this program, notice that the `default` option in the `switch` provides an error message for the user, indicating that he or she has picked a value not in the menu.

Notice also that the code following the first two `case` statements (menu options 1 and 2) includes an embedded `switch`, the purpose of which is to determine the country (and thus the object to be used) for conversion. This is perfectly legal: A `case` can be followed by any executable statement. The inner `switch` structures look for literal characters rather than literal integers. As mentionned earlier, C++ automatically typecasts a character to an integer, making its evaluation based on the charater's ASCII code.

## Summary

C++ supports two structures that enable a program to make choices between alternative sets of actions: `if` and `switch`.

The `if` structure tests a logical expression. The logical expression is made up of relationship operators (==, <, >, <=, >=, !=), values, and the logical operators (!, &&, and ||). The expression is surrounded by parentheses.

If an `if` statement's logical expression is true, then the statement following `if` is executed. If the expression is false, the statement is skipped and program execution continues with the statement following the entire `if` structure.

If an `if` statement is followed by an `else`, the program will execute the statement following `else` when the logical expression following `if` is false. The "statement" after `if` or `else` may be a single line of executable code or a compound statement grouped by braces.

When many values of a single integer variable need to be evaluated, a `switch` structure can make program logic clearer. (A `switch` can also be used with a character variable because the computer can use the numeric value of the character's ASCII code.) The `switch` includes a number of `case` statements, each of which traps one value of the structure's control variable. A `case` statement is followed by the statements that are to be executed when the value in the control variable matches the value of the `case`. Each group of statements ends with a `break`, which branches out of the `switch` structure.

## Exercises

1. Write and test a program that computes the cost of janitorial services performed for a business. The cost of cleaning an office depends on the size of the office:

   - If the office is less than 2000 sq. ft, then the cost is $0.20 per sq. ft. per month.
   - If the office is greater than 2000 sq. ft. but less than 10,000 sq. ft., the cost is $0.15 per sq. ft. per month.
   - For offices equal to or greater than 10,000 sq. ft, the cost is $0.10 per sq. ft. per month.

   Create a class to represent the cleaning of one office. Let the user enter the square footage. Then compute and display the monthly cleaning cost.

2.  Write and test a program that a semiconductor manufacturer can use to compute the cost of an order for computer chips. The pricing of the chips is as follows:

    - < 1000: $3.95 each
    - 1000 – 4999: $3.50 each
    - 5000–9999: $3.00 each
    - 10,000–14,999: $2.50 each
    - > 15,000: $2.00 each

    In addition, if a customer pays on delivery (C.O.D.) rather than within 30 days, the customer receives a 10 percent discount.

    Create a class that represents an order, including the number of chips ordered and whether the order will be shipped C.O.D. Let the user enter data for the order. Then prepare a nicely formatted display of the total cost of the order. If the customer should receive the C.O.D. discount, be sure to show the total before the discount and the total after the discount.

3.  Write and test a program that uses a decision tree to identify a living creature that the user describes to the program. The way in which the program should make its decisions is diagrammed in Figure 12.6. The program collects information by asking the user questions such as "How many legs does the creature have?" and "Does the creature live in water?" Design your own class for this program. Define one object from that class. (The program should handle one creature at a time.)

4.  Create a class to handle the conversion between 12-hour and 24-hour time. The class should include variables for the time (a four-digit integer) and whether it represents 12- or 24-hour time. Include a member function that performs the conversion based on the value in the "12 or 24" variable. Then display the result in an appropriate format. For example, 12-hour time should be displayed as HH:MM PM or HH:MM AM, where HH is the hour and MM is the minutes; 24-hour time should be displayed simply as HH:MM.

Figure 12.6   A decision tree for identifying a living creature

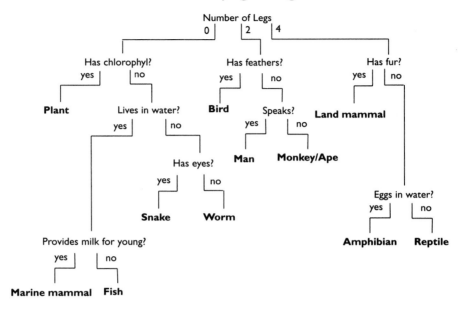

# 13 Repeating Actions

## OBJECTIVES

In this chapter you will read about:
- The logic behind instructing a computer program to repeat a set of actions.
- The C++ syntax used to repeat sets of actions.
- Making choices between the alternative ways to repeat actions.
- Generalized procedures for calling various types of functions.

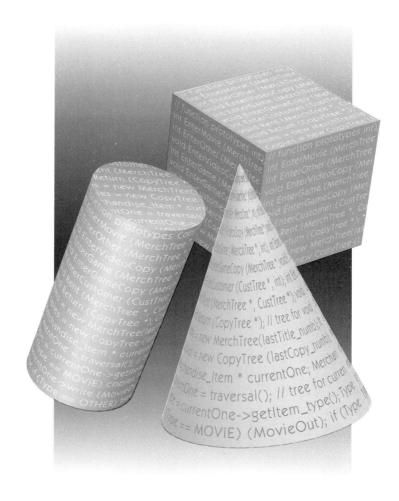

A computer program needs to be able to repeat actions, as well as to be able to make choices between alternative sets of actions. For example, if a program has to compute a sum, it needs a way to repeatedly add values to accumulate the total.

Repeating actions within a computer program is known as *iteration* or, more casually, *looping*. A set of actions that are repeated are known as a *loop*. C++ provides three looping statements: while, do while, and for. In this chapter you will learn how these statements work and the circumstances under which each one makes most sense.

## Basic Loop Operation

A program loop is a set of executable statements (grouped by braces if there is more than one statement) that is executed repeatedly as long as a logical expression (the *control condition*) evaluates to true. Assume, for example, that you want to total the amount of sales made by each of your salespeople this month. The logic of the loop might be described as follows:

1. Initialize a counter variable and a sum variable to 0.
2. Add the monthly sales made by a salesperson to the sum.
3. Increment the counter variable by 1.
4. Check to see if the value in the counter variable is equal to the total number of salespeople. If equal, stop looping. Otherwise, return to Step 2.

We can also diagram this loop using the flowchart symbols you first saw in Chapter 12 (see Figure 13.1). As you can see in the illustration, a decision is made at the bottom of the loop. This particular type of loop can be programmed with the C++ do while statement. If you look closely at the loop, you will see that the body of the loop (Steps 2 and 3 in the series of steps above) will always be performed at least once. The computer goes through the body of the loop before it encounters the test condition.

More commonly, however, you will use loops where the test of the control condition is at the beginning of the loop, before the computer encounters the body of the loop. As you can see in Figure 13.2, this type of loop has its decision box at the very beginning of the loop. If the control condition is false the first time the program encounters the loop, the body of the loop will never be executed. You will use the while and for statements to create loops of this type.

Figure 13.1   A loop in which the test occurs at the bottom

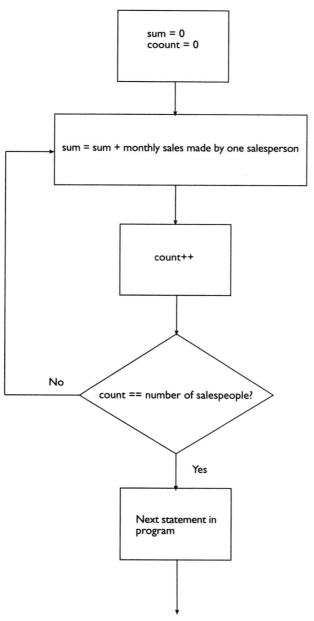

Figure 13.2   A loop in which the test occurs at the top

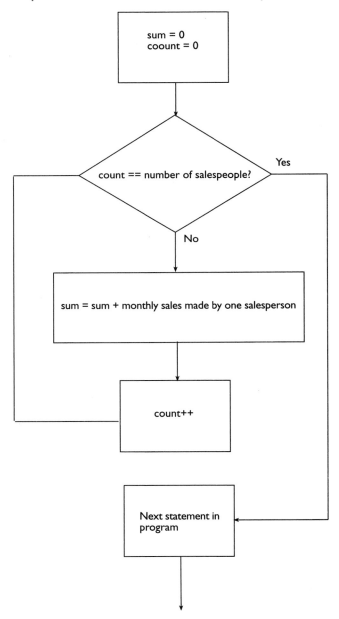

## Using the while Statement

The while is the most common C++ looping structure. It has the following general syntax:

```
while (logical_expression)
{
    body of loop
}
```

If the body of the loop is only one statement, the surrounding braces aren't needed.

A common use of a while is to keep a program going until the user chooses a Quit option from a menu. If the Quit option is 9, then the loop could be written:

```
int Option = 0;

while (Option !=9)
{
    choose a menu option
    process the menu option in some way
}
```

If you look back at Listing 12.9 on page 229, the application class Run function for the currency converter program, you'll see that this is exactly what allows that program to continue to present the user with the menu and take actions based on menu choices until the user selects the Quit option.

The important thing to remember about a while is that the logical expression in parentheses is evaluated at the top of the loop. This means that a loop might never be executed. As an example, let's modify the code you just saw slightly:

```
int Option = 0;

Option = 9;
while (Option !=9)
{
    choose a menu option
    process the menu option in some way
}
```

Because the logical expression is false the first time the program encounters the while, control passes to the statement below the body of the loop, without ever executing the statements in the loop.

This is not necessarily a bad thing. Consider, for example, the code in Listing 13.1. The purpose of the code is to move the decimal point in a positive floating point number so that the number is in the format .XXXX. It also needs to keep track of how many times the decimal point is moved. If the original number is greater than or equal to 1, it should be multiplied by 0.1; if the number is less than 0.1, it should be multiplied by 10. Listing 13.1 contains two while loops, one for each condition. Rather than using an if to decide which loop to execute, the code takes advantage of the fact that the original value in Number will pass the test of no more than one while, ensuring that only the correct transformation is performed. (If the number is already in the correct format, neither loop will execute.)

**Listing 13.1    Loops that intentionally may never be executed**

```
float Number;
int timesMoved = 0;
:
:
while (Number >= 1)
{
    Numb *= 0.1;
    timesMoved++;
}
while (Number < .1)
{
    Number *= 10;
    timesMoved++;
}
```

## Coding a while Statement

One limitation of the programs that we have used as examples so far is that because you hadn't been introduced to loops, the programs could only perform an action once. (If you needed to do something more than once, you had to include duplicated code.) At this point, however, we can begin to modify those programs so that they give the user the choice of performing actions many times.

As a first example, let's look at a modified version of the mileage computation program that was introduced in Chapter 11. When a while loop is placed in the application class's Run function, the user can do repeated computations without leaving the program, as in Figure 13.3. The program stops when the user enters a 0 for the number of miles driven.

Figure 13.3   Running the mileage computation program after a loop has been added

```
How many miles did you drive? 95
You can put $27.55 on your expense report.

How many miles did you drive? 268
You can put $77.72 on your expense report.

How many miles did you drive? 0
```

The modified Run function can be found in Listing 13.2. The way in which the while has been used in this function is typical of while statements. Notice first that the control variable is imiles, the local variable that holds the user's input. The user knows that entering a 0 will stop the program. The control condition is therefore:

```
imiles != 0
```

The loop will continue as long as the value in imiles is not equal to 0.

**Note**

There's no magic to use of the value of 0 as the stop value: The programmer chose 0 and then told the users that they should enter a 0 when finished. The stop value could just as easily have been 9999 or 1111, or any arbitrary number that wasn't a likely legitimate value for the number of miles driven.

The Run function must initialize the control variable to ensure that there is a meaningful value in imiles when the function encounters the while statement for the first time. In our particular example, this initialization takes the form of a cin statement that accepts the first value of miles driven. It appears just before the while.

Listing 13.2    Modified application class Run function for the mileage
                computation program using a while loop

```cpp
void AppClass::Run ()
{
    int imiles;

    car theCar; // create an object

    // Initializes the control variable; makes sure user can get out without ever executing the loop
    cout << "How many miles did you drive? ";
    cin >> imiles;

    while (imiles != 0)
    {
        // Object initialization and output to the user are performed inside the loop so that they aren't
        // accidentally executed if the user enters 0 miles immediately after the program begins
        theCar.init (imiles); // send value to the object
        cout << "You can put $" << theCar.reimbursement()
            << " on your expense report.";
        // Must repeat statements that affect the control variable to make sure that this loop will stop
        cout << "\n\nHow many miles did you drive? ";
        cin >> imiles;
    }
}
```

The nice thing about this particular placement of the initialization is that if the user decides that he or she doesn't want to continue working with the program, he or she can enter 0 and exit immediately. The 0 ensures that the while loop never executes. However, if the user enters a value other than 0, the function executes the body of the loop.

Inside the loop, the mileage is sent to the object named theCar. Then, the function displays the output, including the result of the call to the reimbursement function.

The function ends with a repeat of the statement that places a value in imiles. This statement makes sure that the value in imiles changes each time through the loop. It is essential if a function is going to avoid an infinite loop.

## Avoiding Infinite Loops

An *infinite loop* is a loop that never stops repeating. It is a major reason why programs "hang," or seem to freeze. Although there occasionally are reasons to write an infinite loop, in most cases you want to make sure that your program doesn't accidentally get stuck in a loop.

To see how an infinite loop could occur, let's look at a loop that computes total monthly sales:

```
int count = 0;
float sum = 0, sales = 0;
const NUMB_SALESPEOPLE = 20;
    :
    :
while (count < NUMB_SALESPEOPLE)
{
    cout << "\nSales amount: ";
    cin >> sales;
    sum = sum + sales;
}
```

There is a major problem with this loop: The value of the *control variable* (count) never changes; its value will never be equal to NUMB_SALESPEOPLE, the condition that would stop the loop. This loop is therefore an infinite loop. To correct the problem, the programmer must insert the statement

```
count++;
```

before the closing brace below the body of the loop.

*To avoid an infinite loop, you must be certain that you modify some aspect of the control condition within the body of the loop.* This usually means incrementing a counter or switching the state of a Boolean value.

## Using the do while Statement

The do while is a variation of the while in which the test of the control condition occurs at the bottom of the loop:

```
do
{
    body of loop
}
while (logical_expression);
```

Notice that the logical expression that contains the control condition appears at the bottom of the loop. A do while will therefore always execute at least once, until it reaches the while at the bottom where the control condition is actually evaluated. Also notice that the logical condition after while is followed by a semicolon; this is not the case with the while statement.

Given that the body of a do while is executed at least once, you might be tempted to use it frequently. You might, for example, want to use it to control a loop that terminates when the user chooses a Quit option from a menu. The loop would then have the structure:

```
const QUIT = 9;
int Option;

do
{
    display mennu
    Option = call appropriate menu object function;
    take action based on value of Option
}
while (Option != QUIT);
```

The advantage of this structure is that you don't have to give Option a value before the loop begins. If you use a while, the code must be written:

```
const QUIT = 9;
int Option = 0;

while (Option != QUIT)
{
    display menu
    Option = call appropriate menu object function;
    take action based on value of Option
}
```

In this example, Option must be initialized to something other than the value of QUIT so that the loop will execute the first time.

Nonetheless, using do while can make a program harder to understand and debug because the while (logical_expression); at the end of the loop looks an awful lot like a while without a body. Many programmers therefore prefer to avoid using do while as much as possible, even if it means remembering to initialize while control values.

## Using the for Statement

The for statement is useful when you need a loop that increments a numeric control variable and stops when that variable reaches some predetermined value. For example, it could be used in place of a while in the loop you saw earlier that computes total sales.

The for structure has the following general syntax:

```
for (initialization; terminating_condition; control_update)
{
    body of loop
}
```

The sales totaling loop could therefore be written:

```
for (count = 0; count < NUMB_SALESPEOPLE; count++)
{
    cout << "\nSales amount: ";
    cin >> sales;
    sum = sum + sales;
}
```

The parentheses following for actually contains three separate C++ statements. (Remember that the semicolon marks the end of a statement.) The first statement initializes the loop. Typically, this takes the form of initializing a control variable. In this case, it is count, a variable that has been declared earlier in the program. The second statement within the parentheses is a logical expression. The loop continues as long as the condition is true.

The final statement is an arithmetic expression that changes the control condition in some way, usually incrementing a control variable. In this particular example, the loop continues as long as the control variable is less than the total number of salespeople (stored in the constant NUMB_SALESPEOPLE). Each time the loop repeats, the control variable is incremented by 1.

As a simple example of a for loop, let's rewrite the application class's Run function from the mileage program once more. The dialog with the user changes slightly, as you can see in Figure 13.4. In particular, the user must specify the number of cars at the beginning of the program. (We'll talk more about this aspect of the interface in a bit.)

The application class Run function that produced the output in Figure 13.4 can be found in Listing 13.3. There are some major differences between this function and the one in Listing 13.2 that uses a while:

- The for loop needs to know how many times it will repeat before the loop begins. This means that the function must ask the user for that information.
- All of the code relating to the mileage computation is within the loop, including the cin statement that asks for the number of miles

Figure 13.4    Output of the mileage program written with a for loop

```
For how many cars do you want to compute the mileage? 3

Car #:1 How many miles did you drive? 66
You can put $19.14 on your expense report.

Car #:2 How many miles did you drive? 2509
You can put $727.61 on your expense report.

Car #:3 How many miles did you drive? 475
You can put $137.75 on your expense report.
```

Listing 13.3    Modified application class Run function for the mileage
computation program using a for loop

```cpp
void AppClass::Run ()
{
    int imiles, numb_cars;

    car theCar; // create an object

    // We need to know exactly how many cars to process before the for loop begins
    cout << "For how many cars do you want to compute the mileage? ";
    cin >> numb_cars;

    // If the user enters 0, the for loop will never execute
    // Therefore, we can put the input of imiles inside the loop
    for (int i = 1;i <= numb_cars; i++) // Variable i exists only for the duration of the loop
    {
        cout << "\nCar #:" << i << " How many miles did you drive? ";
        cin >> imiles;
        theCar.init (imiles); // send value to the object
        cout << "You can put $" << theCar.reimbursement()
            << " on your expense report." << endl;
    }
}
```

driven. This is possible because if the user enters 0 for the number of cars, the for loop will never execute, meaning that none of the statements in the body of the loop will be executed.

Which is the better way to write this function? With the while or the for? Both versions of the function do what we need them to do, but which is easier for the user? The version with the while. In most cases, it is unreasonable to ask a user how many times he or she wants to do something. It is much easier for a user to remember a single stop value, such as the 0 used with the while version of this function. If you find that you need to ask the user to input a value for the number of times a loop should repeat, then you should jolt yourself awake and replace the for with a while!

## The break and continue Statements

As you saw in Chapter 12, the break statement is used within a switch to branch out of the switch after the program has matched a case value and executed the associated statements. The break statement, however, can be used in other ways, including branching out of a loop at any time. In particular, break can be very useful when there are many conditions that can terminate a loop, too many to put into a single logical expression.

The continue statement causes a loop to iterate (repeat) immediately, without executing any of the following statements in the body of the loop. Its use can speed up program execution by preventing a program from evaluating if statements whose logical expression can't be true because a preceding if's logical expression is true.

As an example of both break and continue, consider the code in Listing 13.4. Notice that the logical expression for this while generates an infinite loop. This was done on purpose: A loop of this type relies on if statements that contain breaks to terminate the loop.

The first if in the body of the loop traps values greater than 100. In this case, the loop should iterate after performing the multiplication. Although it wouldn't hurt to leave out the continue—the value won't meet any of the following if's logical expressions—the program will execute faster if the computer doesn't have to evaluate the remaining ifs.

The remaining three if structures in the loop contain logical expressions that terminate the loop. Although the logical expressions in the ifs could have been combined into a single while logical expression, doing so would have created a complicated logical expression that would be hard to understand. The structure in the example is easier to understand.

There is one drawback to placing logical expressions that terminate a loop inside the body of the loop (rather than in the while): The program can be harder to debug and modify because it isn't immediately obvious which conditions in the body actually stop the loop. Most programmers therefore try to limit the use of break in a while to situations where a while's logical expression would be impractically complicated.

Listing 13.4    A while statement that uses break and continue statements

```
while (1 < 2)
{
    cin >> SomeValue;
    if (SomeValue > 100)
    {
        NewValue += SomeValue * 2;
        cout << SomeValue;
        continue;
    }
    if (SomeValue >= 50 && SomeValue <= 100)
    {
        NewValue += SomeValue / 2;
        cout << NewValue;
        break;
    }
    if (SomeValue > 25 && SomeValue <= 50)
    {
        NewValue += SomeValue = 2;
        cout << NewValue;
        break;
    }
    if (NewValue < 1)
    {
        cout << SomeValue;
        break;
    }
}
```

## The Hi/Low Game

As a more extensive example of how loops are used in a program, let's look at the very simple number guessing game two which you were first introduced in Chapter 7. The computer picks a random number between 1 and 100, and the user has seven guesses to figure out the answer. The implementation of the game that appears here also keeps statistics on how well the player is doing. As you can see in Figure 13.5, the program counts the number of games played, how many have been won, and at the end of play, reports the winning percentage.

## The Classes

The Hi/Lo game program uses two classes: the Game class, which handles the play of one game, and an application class. Let's first look at the Game class. As you can see in Listing 13.5, the game has two variables: the correct answer,

Figure 13.5   Sample output from the Hi/Lo Game program

```
--- Welcome to the Hi/Lo Guessing Game ---

Enter your guess: 50
Your guess was too high.
Enter your guess: 25
Your guess was too high.
Enter your guess: 15
Your guess was too low.
Enter your guess: 20
Your guess was too low.
Enter your guess: 21
Your guess was too low.
Enter your guess: 22
You win!
Another game? (y or n): n

You played 1 and won 1
for a winning percentage of 100%.
```

which the player is trying to guess, and the current guess made by the player. There are also prototypes for four functions: a constructor (Game), a function to initialize a new game by generating a new answer (InitGame), a function to determine whether a guess is above, below, or equal to the answer (evaluateGuess), and a function to return the correct answer for display by the application object (getAnswer).

## Listing 13.5   Game.h

```cpp
// class for hi/lo game
// game.h

const HI = 1;
const LO = -1;
const EQ = 0;
const MAX_GUESSES = 7;
const RAND_FACTOR = 325;

class Game
{
    private:
        int answer, guess;
    public:
        Game();    // constructor
        void InitGame();
        int evaluateGuess (int);
        int getAnswer ();
};
```

The declaration for the application class can be found in Listing 13.6. Unlike the application classes we have used to this point, this particular class has variables and functions other than Run. The two variables hold the number of games played during a single program run (games_played) and the number of games won during a single program run (games_won). The three private member functions will be called by the Run function to increment the number of games played, increment the number of games won, and display the final result.

**Listing 13.6   AppClass.h**

```
class AppClass
{
    private:
        int games_played, games_won;
        void incrementPlayed ();
        void incrementWon();
        void displayFinal();
    public:
        AppClass();
        void Run ();
};
```

Why do we have these three private functions? Couldn't their actions be handled just as easily by the Run function? Yes, the actions taken in those functions could be placed in the Run function. However, the private functions perform distinct actions on the application class's variables. Therefore, the class will be easier to modify if actions on those variables are separated into their own functions. For example, you might want to change the layout of the final display. A programmer won't need to search through the Run function looking for where the class's variables are used; changes can be made directly to the private functions, without having to modify the Run function at all.

## Game Class Member Functions

The source code for the Game class member functions is stored in the file *game.cpp* (Listing 13.7). As you would expect, the constructor simply initializes the class variables. The InitGame function uses the rand function from the standard C libraries to generate a random number and then scales that number so that it is in the range 0 to 100.

## Listing 13.7    Game.cpp

```cpp
#include <stdlib.h>
#include "game.h"

Game::Game()
{
    answer = 0;
    guess = 0;
}

void Game::InitGame()
{
    // generates the answer as random # between 0 and 100
    answer = rand() / RAND_FACTOR;
}

int Game::evaluateGuess (int guess)
{
    if (guess == answer)
        return EQ;
    else
        if (guess < answer)
            return LO;
        else
            return HI;
}

int Game::getAnswer()
{
    return answer;
}
```

The rand function, whose prototype appears in *stdlib.h*, generates a number in the range 0 to $2^{15}$. Because this program requires a number between 0 and 100, the random number is divided by the constant RAND_FACTOR (defined as 325 in *game.h*).

Each successive call to rand produces a different number, based on a starting number supplied at the beginning of the program run. To avoid getting the same sequence of random numbers each time you run the program, you need to initialize the random number generator when the program run begins. Do this with a call to srand, another function from the C libraries whose prototype appears in *stdlib.h*. Call srand only once:

```cpp
srand (time(NULL) % 37);
```

The srand function requires a seed value as a parameter. Although there is no way to generate a truly random seed value, you can approximate it by grabbing the current time from the system clock and then performing a modulo division to scale it back to an integer. To read the current time, use the time function. (Its prototype appears in *time.h*.) The function's single parameter is a pointer to a variable that will hold the time. However, in this case the time isn't stored anywhere, but instead is divided by 37. The remainder of the division is then used directly by the srand function. There is no need to keep the time; a NULL can therefore be used instead of a pointer to a variable.

The evaulateGuess member function contains the nested if structure you saw in Chapter 12 to examine one guess made by the user. The constants HI, LO, and EQ that the function returns are defined in the header file. The remaining member function—getAnswer—simply returns the correct answer to the main program for display.

**Note**

There is no secret to figuring out the scale factor for a random number. You just need to do a bit of algebra to find it:

$$scale\_factor = 2^{15} / maximum\_number\_wanted$$

## Application Class Member Functions

The member functions for the Hi/Lo game's application class can be found in Listing 13.8. The constructor initializes both of the class's variables. Those two variables are incremented by the incrementPlayed and incrementWon functions.

The display of the results of all the play that appears at the end of a program run is generated in the displayFinal function. Notice that the computation for the percentage of games won has been placed within a cout statement; the result of the computation is for display only and therefore doesn't need to be captured in a variable. Notice also that the computation typecasts the games_won variable to a floating point value so that the computer will perform a floating pointer, rather than integer, division. This is essential because the result of the division before it is multiplied by 100 will be a fraction and would be truncated to 0 by an integer operation.

## Listing 13.8   AppClass.cpp

```cpp
#include "appclass.h"
#include "game.h"
#include <iostream.h>
#include <stdlib.h>
#include <time.h>
#include <ctype.h>

AppClass::AppClass ()
{
    games_played = 0;
    games_won = 0;
}

void AppClass::incrementPlayed()
    { games_played++; }

void AppClass::incrementWon()
    { games_won++; }

void AppClass::displayFinal()
{
    cout << "You played " << games_played << " and won " << games_won << endl;
    cout << "for a winning percentage of " <<
        (float) games_won/games_played * 100 << "%.";
}

void AppClass::Run()
{
    int choice, count, result, guesses_made;
    char keep_going = 'Y';
    Game gamePlayed;
    srand (time(NULL) % 37); // initialize random number generator
    cout << "--- Welcome to the Hi/Lo Guessing Game ---" << endl << endl;

    while (toupper(keep_going) == 'Y')
    {
        count = 0;
        guesses_made = 0;
        result = LO;
        gamePlayed.InitGame();
        incrementPlayed();
```

Continued next page

**Listing 13.8**(Continued)    AppClass.cpp

```cpp
        while (guesses_made++ < MAX_GUESSES && result != EQ)
        {
            cout << "Enter your guess: ";
            cin >> choice;
            result = gamePlayed.evaluateGuess (choice);
            switch (result)
            {
                case EQ:
                    cout << "You win!" << endl;
                    break;
                case LO:
                    cout << "Your guess was too low." << endl;
                    break;
                case HI:
                    cout << "Your guess was too high." << endl;
                    break;
            }
        }
        if (guesses_made > MAX_GUESSES && result != EQ)
        {
            cout << "You've exceeded your allotted " << MAX_GUESSES
                << " guesses." << endl;
            cout << "The correct answer was " << gamePlayed.getAnswer()
                << "." << endl;
        }
        else
            if (result == EQ)
                incrementWon();
        cout << "Another game? (y or n): ";
        cin >> keep_going;
        cout << endl;
    }
    displayFinal();
}
```

Game play is controlled by the application class's Run function. The function's basic structure is two `while` loops, one nested within the other. The outer loop iterates once for each game played. The inner loop handles the play of one game. It iterates until the user either makes the maximum number of guesses or guesses the correct answer.

**Warning**    When you nest `while`, `for`, and `do` loops, you must make sure that each loop is completely contained within another, just as you had to make sure that nested `if` statements were completely nested one within the other. To help you avoid the problem, use the same indentation for the opening and closing brace of each nested loop. Then make sure that no loops cross each other, as they do at the top of Figure 13.6. Also remember that the compiler associates a closing brace with the most recently encountered opening brace, regardless of how the braces are indented in the source code!

Figure 13.6    Nesting loops

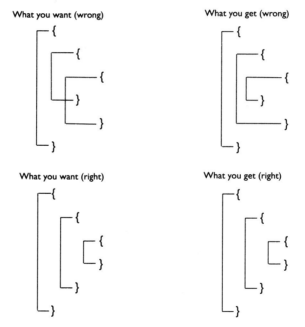

As you study the `Run` function, notice that there is no way to determine exactly which of the two conditions causes the inner loop to stop. The program must therefore use an `if` structure to explicitly test the two conditions and take action based on whichever it finds.

At the end of a game, the user is given the option of continuing to play another game or ending the program. The outer loop uses the value in the keep_going variable to decide whether to begin another game. Because a user might enter either an upper- or lowercase letter, the while in the outer loop uses the toupper function to convert the contents of keep_going to uppercase. (The prototype for this C library function can be found in *ctype.h*.) If keep_going already contains an uppercase character, toupper has no effect.

After the outer loop terminates, the Run function has one more task: It calls its own displayFinal function to show the user the number of games played, the number of games won, and the percentage of games won.

**Note**

The program structures you have studied in the past two chapters are fundamental to *structured programming*. In a structured program, all program logic is made up of three simple structures: sequence (executing one statement after another), selection (making choices), and iteration (looping). It is ironic that although we use the object-oriented paradigm to create the high-level structure of an object-oriented program, we must nonetheless resort to structured programming techniques to implement member functions.

## Summary

C++ supports three iteration structures: while, do while, and for. The while structure places the test for stopping the loop at the top of the loop. It can therefore be used for all loops, even those that should not be executed under certain circumstances. The do while structure places the test for stopping the loop at the bottom of the loop. It is therefore always executed at least once. The for loop is a shorthand version of a while that bases the condition for stopping the loop on some value that it iterated each time the loop is executed.

Functions are called by using the name of the function and its formal parameters. Calls to member functions for objects created with static binding must be preceded by the name of the object on which the function is to operate and a period.

Simple variables used as parameters that are passed through a function's formal parameter list are passed by value. Even if the values are changed inside the function, the changed values aren't returned to the calling program.

# Exercises

1. Write and test a program that computes the pay for three categories of sales associates (junior sales associates, sales associates, and senior sales associates). Create a single class for a sales associate with variables for a sales associate's monthly sales goal, the commission rate paid if the goal is met, the commission rate paid if the goal isn't met, and base salary (may be zero). Create one object for each type of sales associate.

   Store the data for each object in a file. Read the data in at the beginning of each program run; write the data out at the end of each program run.

   Give the user a menu from which he or she can choose the following options:

   - Enter data for each type of sales associate. (This function is used to both initialize and modify the data stored in the objects.)
   - View the current data for each type of sales associate.
   - Compute a sales associate's gross pay, based on monthly sales and the type of sales associate. (The monthly sales and type of associate are entered by the user.) Once the program has decided which commission rate to use, the gross pay is equal to:

   ```
   commission rate * monthly sales + the base pay
   ```

   - Quit the program

2. Create a class that handles the pricing of purchases of athletic uniforms for a uniform supply company. The class should include an ID number for the uniform, a price for the top, a price for the bottom, a price for purchasing the combination of top and bottom, and the percentage discount if 50 or more complete uniforms are purchased. Include a member function that computes the price of an order for uniforms. Write a program that demonstrates that the class and the member function work, where the user enters the prices and the number of uniforms being purchased. Include a menu that lets the user enter data and compute the total of a purchase. The program should also allow the user to compute prices for many purchases without exiting the program.

3.  Create a class for a local water and electric utility that handles a customer's monthly bill. The class should include the customer account number, the gallons of water used, and the number of kilowatt-hours (kwh) of electricity used. Include a member function that computes the amount of the bill based on the following rules:

    *   The first 1500 gallons of water cost $0.011 per gallon.
    *   Each gallon over 1500 costs $0.015 per gallon.
    *   The first 500 kwh of electricity cost $0.044 per kwh.
    *   501 to 1000 kwh of electricity cost $0.065 per kwh.
    *   More than 1000 kwh of electricity cost $0.097 per kwh.

    Write a program that demonstrates that your bill computation function works. The user should enter the gallons of water and the number of kwh of electricity used along with the customer number. The program should print out the customer number and the total bill. Because a utility company handles many customers, the program should allow the user to print the bills for many customers without exiting the program.

4.  Write and test a program that computes the amount of principal in a certificate of deposit, where the interest paid is added to the principal each month. The formula for the principal after interest is paid for a given month is:

    ```
    Principal = Amount of initial deposit *
        (1 + Monthly interest rate)Number of months on deposit
    ```

    Decide what the class should be for this program. Create any necessary object(s).

    Give the user the opportunity to enter the *annual* interest rate. (The program should compute the monthly interest rate.) Also give the user the choice of term for the CD (12, 24, or 26 months). Display the amount of principal on deposit for each month during the term of the CD.

# 14

# Introducing Arrays

## OBJECTIVES

In this chapter you will learn about:

- Variables called arrays that can store more than one value.
- How to declare, initialize, and access data stored in one-dimensional arrays.
- One method for sorting data stored in arrays.
- How to declare, initialize, and access data stored in two-dimensional arrays.

One of the rules under which we have been working to this point is that a variable holds only one value at a time. However, we often need to be able to manipulate many similar, related values, and we could do so most easily if those values were grouped under the same variable name. For example, if you needed to work with the sales figures for a 12-month period, it would be awkward to manipulate 12 individual variables (for example, `sales1`, `sales2`, `sales3`, and so on).

Program structures that organize multiple, related values are known as *data structures*. The simplest data structure is an *array*, a complex variable that can store multiple values of the same data type. The data type can be any of the simple data types with which we have been working to this point, or it can be a class. For example, you can have an array of integers or an array of objects created from the same class.

In this chapter we will look at arrays that are declared as class or local variables to hold integers, floating point values, or characters. In Chapter 15, you will be introduced to handling arrays of objects.

## Understand Array Storage and Access

An array is a convenient way of handling logically related values of the same data type. Assume, for example, that you want to compute the average sales made by a company over a 12-month period. (You will see this program in the next section of this chapter.) You could store the data in 12 individual variables:

```
long Month1, Month2, Month3, Month4, Month5, Month6;
long Month7, Month8, Month9, Month10, Month11, Month12;
```

It would then take 12 lines of code to initialize these variables and 24 lines of code to prompt the user to enter values using the `cout` stream and accept those values using the `cin` stream. Imagine how long and repetitive programming would become if you decided to expand the computations to handle 24 months!

An array can solve this type of problem by letting you store all of the values under a single name. Each value is then accessible by its position within the grouped variable. To see how this works, take a look at Figure 14.1. Conceptually, all the sales values are stored in a list. Each value, known as an *element*, occupies one numbered position in the list (the element's *index*). In C++, array indexes are numbered beginning with 0.

Figure 14.1    One-dimensional array storage

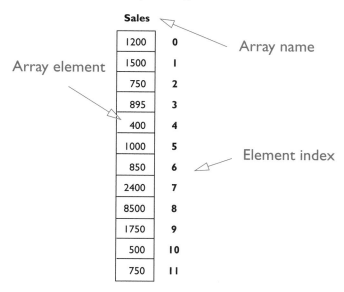

Any element in an array is referenced by the name of the array and the element's index. For example, if the array to hold sales data has been named `Sales`, the first element is:

```
Sales [0]
```

Notice that the array index is surrounded by brackets ([ and ]). You can use an array element referenced in this way just as you would any simple variable, such as `Sales1`.

This type of array is known as *one-dimensional*, because we can visualize its contents as if they were organized into a single column with multiple rows. This single dimension is often thought of as height. However, we also often use arrays with many columns and many rows (dimensions of height and width). You will read about such *two-dimensional arrays* later in this chapter.

**Note**

C++ supports arrays with more than two dimensions. For example, a three-dimensional array might be visualized as a cube (height, width, and depth). However, because arrays with more than two dimensions are conceptually complex, they are rarely used.

## Declaring a One-Dimensional Array

An array must be declared, just like a simple variable. However, when declaring an array, you must also indicate the maximum number of elements the array will contain:

```
const NUMB_SALES = 12;
long Sales [NUMB_SALES];
```

This declaration sets up an array variable named Sales and instructs the computer to allocate 12 storage locations for long integers.

**Note**

It is good programming practice to define constants to use for the total number of elements when declaring arrays. It makes the program easier to read because the name of the constant tells you something about the meaning of the array. It also makes the program easier to modify because you don't have to go hunting through the program to find the array declaration; you only need to change the constant, which is typically located at the beginning of a header file.

## Initializing a One-Dimensional Array

Like simple variables, arrays can be initialized when they are declared. However, the syntax is slightly different and can have an impact on the way storage is allocated for the array in main memory.

Assume, for example, that you want to declare an array to hold integers and you know what those integers are when you declare the array. There are two syntaxes you can use:

```
int array[ ] = {12, 6, 25, 44, 8};
int array[10] = {12, 6, 25, 44, 8};
```

Notice that in both cases, the values that are to be assigned to the array as initial values are surrounded in braces and separated by commas. However, in the first syntax, the array isn't given a size. In that case, the compiler will allocate exactly enough space to hold the initial values. As you can see in Figure 14.2, the result is an array with five elements.

Figure 14.2    Initializing arrays and array storage allocation

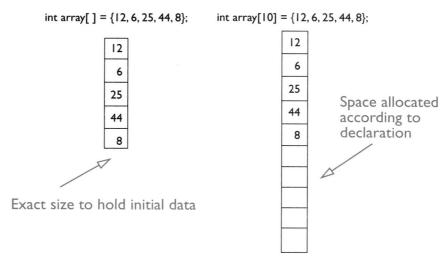

In the second syntax, the array has been given a size. The compiler will therefore allocate space according to the number of elements specified in the declaration and initialize as many elements as there are data. In Figure 14.2, for example, the compiler fills the first five elements in the array and leaves the last five empty.

Use the first syntax, where the compiler allocates exactly the right amount of space to hold initial values, when you are declaring an array that will never need any more elements than those used when the array is declared. However, if the number of elements in the array at any time during a program run will be more than the initial data you have available, then you'll need to use the second syntax.

## Accessing Array Values

To assign a value to an array element, you also use the name of the array and the element's index:

```
Sales [0] = 0;
```

The index can be specified as a literal, as it is in the preceding example, or it can be specified as any expression that generates an integer when it is evaluated, including the name of a variable:

```
int index = 0;
Sales [index] = 0;
Sales [index + 1] = 0;
```

The fact that we can use a variable as an array index means that we can place an array inside a loop, changing the value of the index variable to provide access to successive members of the array. For example, the following code initializes the array that stores 12 monthly sales figures:

```
for (i = 0; i < NUMB_SALES; i++)
    Sales [i] = 0;
```

Assuming that the Sales array was a variable that belonged to an object, we would place the code above in the class's constructor.

By the same token, we can use a loop to display all the values in an array:

```
for (i = 0; i < NUMB_SALES; i++)
    cout << "Month #" << i+1 << ": " << Sales[i];
```

The preceding code fragment produces a display something like the following:

```
Month #1: 12345
Month #2: 396
Month #3: 12
  :
  :
```

There are two important things about this example. First. we are using the for loop's index in the cout statement. Although it is being used as the loop's control varaible, it is a variable like any other whose contents can be retrieved at any time. Second, we want the user to see numbered values that begin with 1; that is the way we normally count things. However, array elements are counted beginning with 0, and the for loop's index varaible therefore gets an initial value of 0. We must therefore add 1 to i before displaying it. Because the result of this addition expression is inserted into the cout stream and not stored anywhere, it does not affect the value in i.

We can also use a loop to add up the values in an array:

```
long sum = 0;
for (i = 0; i < NUMB_SALES; i++)
    sum = sum + Sales[i];
```

Notice that like the preceding examples, we access each element in the array by using the name of the array followed by the array element in brackets.

**Warning**

The name of an array represents the address in main memory where the array begins. This means that you can't initialize an array by assigning a single value to the array name; you must initialize each element, one at a time. In fact, if you try something like:

```
Sales = 0;
```

you will probably cause your computer to crash sometime during the program run. The preceding assignment statement changes the location of the array to main memory address 0, a location that the operating system almost always uses. When the program assigns a value to the relocated array, it will be overwriting something needed by the operating system!

## Array Overflows

When you declare an array, a computer always allocates enough space for the entire array. Each element takes up the amount of space needed for a single value of the array's data type. However, you don't need to use every array element. Unused array elements simply sit around in memory, taking up space. The only harm from this is wasted memory. The situation is far different—and potentially far more destructive—when an array isn't large enough.

C++ doesn't warn you if you attempt to store data in nonexistent array elements. For example, assume that we are working with the same Sales array that stores 12 months worth of sales totals. What do you think would happen if a program included the following statement?

```
Sales [12] = 0;
```

Because array elements are numbered beginning with 0, Sales[12] references a thirteenth element, for which space hasn't been allocated.

Exactly what happens in this case is diagrammed in Figure 14.3. Once a compiler sets aside storage for an array, a computer doesn't keep track of how big the array was declared to be. It only knows where the array's storage begins in main memory (stored in the array name) and the size of each element. In this case, the array has been declared to hold long integers (four bytes each). Therefore, to find the thirteenth element, the array multiplies 12 times four bytes and adds that value to the starting address of the array. Assuming that the variable Total is also a long integer, the Sales[12] will overwrite the entire location assigned to Total, wiping out its value.

Figure 14.3    Array overflow

| | |
|---|---|
| 1200 | **Sales[0]** |
| 1500 | **Sales[1]** |
| 750 | **Sales[2]** |
| 895 | **Sales[3]** |
| 400 | **Sales[4]** |
| 1000 | **Sales[5]** |
| 850 | **Sales[6]** |
| 2400 | **Sales[7]** |
| 8500 | **Sales[8]** |
| 1750 | **Sales[9]** |
| 500 | **Sales[10]** |
| 750 | **Sales[11]** |
| 56679 | **Total** |
| Y | **keep_going** |

Sales[12] references this location

Accessing an element outside the declared size of an array is known as *array overflow*. The strongest indication that this has occurred is values in variables that change without direct program intervention, and the best way to be certain that this is indeed the problem is to use a debugger.

The solution array overflow is *array bounds checking*, code that you add to your program that ensures that the program never attempts to store an element that really isn't part of an array. One way to perform array bounds checking is to use a `for` loop when processing all the elements in the array, as was done earlier in this chapter to initialize the contents of an array.

Another technique is to use a variable to count the number of elements that are stored in an array and to check that value to ensure that it doesn't exceed the number of elements in the array. As an example, consider the code fragment in Listing 14.1. Within the `while`, the code explicitly checks to see whether the variable that contains the last-used array index is less than the total number of elements in the array. If the two are equal, then the array is full. Otherwise, there is still room in the array for more values. Keep in mind that although you declare arrays by indicating the total number of elements in the array (beginning the counting with 1), the actual elements are numbered beginning with 0. Therefore, the index of the last element in the array is always one less than the total number of elements.

## Listing 14.1    Performing array bounds checking

```
const ARRAY_SIZE = 25;
const QUIT = 9;

int lastArrayIndex = 0;
:
:
while (option != QUIT)
{
    if (lastArrayIndex < ARRAY_SIZE)
    {
        lastArrayIndex++;
        // process a new element for the array here
    }
    else
    {
        cout << "The array is full.";
        cout << "Can't add anything else.";
    }
    :
    :
}
```

**Note**

The method of locating array elements described earlier in this section should give you a clue as to why array elements are numbered beginning with 0. Assume, for example, that you want to access the first element in an integer array. The computer multiplies the size of the element (two bytes) by the array index (0) and adds the result (0) to the starting address of the array. The address of the first element is therefore the starting address of the array. Given this method for accessing the elements in an array, you would never be able to access the first element if numbering began with 1.

## Using One-Dimensional Arrays

As a first example of a program that uses an array for data storage, let's look at the implementation of the Sales Average program. In Figure 14.4 you can see that the program does three things: collects input from the user, displays the average of the input values, and displays the contents of the array holding the values.

The array is part of the YearlySales class (Listing 14.2). As you can see, the class has only one variable, the Sales array that holds 12 long integer values. The four member functions include the constructor, a function to place a value into one element in the array (InitSales), a function to compute the average of values stored in the array (AvgSales), and a function to return one value from the array to the application object that is manipulating a YearlySales object (getSales). The member functions can be found in Listing 14.3. The constructor sets each element in the array to zero, using the for loop technique that you saw earlier.

The InitSales member function requires two parameters: the value to be inserted into the Sales array and the index of the element into which the value should be placed. The function uses these parameters to assign the value to the correct element in the array. Values are therefore inserted into the array one at a time.

The AvgSales member function sums the contents of the array and divides by the total number of elements in the array. Notice that to do this, the function must use a for loop to access the array elements individually. Although the values stored in the array are integers, it's unreasonable to assume that the average will also be an integer. The statement that computes the average therefore typecasts the result to a floating point value.

Figure 14.4    Output of the Sales Average program

```
Pick a menu option:
1. Enter sales data
2. Compute average yearly sales
3. See monthly sales
9. Quit

Which one? 1

Enter sales for month # 1:  1200
Enter sales for month # 2:  1500
Enter sales for month # 3:  750
Enter sales for month # 4:  895
Enter sales for month # 5:  400
Enter sales for month # 6:  1000
Enter sales for month # 7:  850
Enter sales for month # 8:  2400
Enter sales for month # 9:  8500
Enter sales for month #10:  1750
Enter sales for month #11:  500
Enter sales for month #12:  750

Pick a menu option:
1. Enter sales data
2. Compute average yearly sales
3. See monthly sales
9. Quit

Which one? 2

Average sales for the year were $1707.92

Pick a menu option:
1. Enter sales data
2. Compute average yearly sales
3. See monthly sales
9. Quit

Which one? 3

The sales for this year are:
   Month # 1:    1200
   Month # 2:    1500
   Month # 3:     750
   Month # 4:     895
   Month # 5:     400
   Month # 6:    1000
   Month # 7:     850
   Month # 8:    2400
   Month # 9:    8500
   Month #10:    1750
   Month #11:     500
   Month #12:     750
```

The final member function, getSales, accepts an index value as its single parameter. Its purpose is to return the contents of one element in the array to the calling program.

## Listing 14.2   Sales.h

```
const NUM_MON=12;

class YearlySales
{
    private:
        long Sales [NUM_MON];
        int whichMonth;

    public:
        YearlySales();
        void InitSales(int, long); // Pass in array index and value
        float AvgSales();
        int getSales(int); // Pass in index value
};
```

## Listing 14.3   Sales.cpp

```
#include "sales.h"

YearlySales::YearlySales()
{
    int i;

    for (i = 0; i < NUM_MON; i++)
        Sales[i] = 0;
    whichMonth = 0;
}

void YearlySales::InitSales (int i, long Amount)
{
    Sales[i] = Amount;
}

float YearlySales::AvgSales()
{
    long sum, i;

    sum = 0;
    for (i = 0; i < NUM_MON; i++)
        sum += Sales[i];
    return (float) sum/NUM_MON;
}

int YearlySales::getSales(int i)
{
    return Sales[i];
}
```

The Run function for the application class that manipulates a YearlySales object can be found in Listing 14.4. This function manipulates two objects: one created from a simple menu class (theMenu) and another created from the YearlySales class (SalesObject).

The structure of the function is based on a while loop that continues to repeat until the user chooses the Quit option from the menu. Within the loop, a switch identifies the chosen menu option and takes action based on that choice.

As you study the Run function, notice that the function can access the Sales array that is part of the YearlySales object one element at a time by passing the index of the desired element to a member function. This is the method used to insert data into the array (the InitSales member function, used to process menu option #1) and to display the contents of the array (the getSales member function, used to process menu option #3).

The Run function can also receive a value from the YearlySales object after the object has processed the entire array. For example, the AvgSales function (used to process menu option #2) returns the average of the contents of the array. In this case, the Run function doesn't interact directly with the array.

## Sorting One-Dimensional Arrays

One of the things that we need to do frequently with data stored in arrays is to place those data in some sort of order, usually numeric, alphabetical, or chronological. There are many ways to sort an array. One of the easiest to understand and program is the *bubble sort*. It is also relatively efficient when the values originally are more in order than out of order (only a few values need to be rearranged) and when the number of values to be sorted are relatively few.

A bubble sort looks at successive pairs of values and swaps their position in the array if they are in the wrong order. For example, if the value in array element 2 is greater than the value in array element 3, the bubble sort swaps the values in those two elements. The sort then proceeds to examine elements 3 and 4, 4 and 5, and so on to the end of the array. Reaching the bottom of the array, the sort returns to the top to begin examining pairs of values again. Once the program makes a scan through the entire array without swapping any values, the array is in the correct low-to-high order.

## Listing 14.4 · The application class Run function for the Sales Average program

```
void AppClass::Run()
{
    int menuChoice = 0, idx;
    long oneMonth;
    YearlySales SalesObject; // create sales object
    mainMenu theMenu; // create menu object

    while (menuChoice != 9)
    {
        theMenu.display();
        menuChoice = theMenu.choose();
        switch (menuChoice)
        {
            case 1:
                for (idx = 0; idx < NUM_MON; idx++)
                {
                    setiosflags (ios::right);
                    cout << "Enter sales for month #" << setw(2) << idx+1
                        << ": ";
                    cin >> oneMonth;
                    SalesObject.InitSales(idx, oneMonth);
                }
                break;
            case 2:
                cout << setiosflags (ios::showpoint | ios::fixed)
                    << setprecision(2);
                cout << "Average sales for the year were $"
                    << SalesObject.AvgSales() << endl;
                break;
            case 3:
                cout << "The sales for this year are: " << endl;
                cout << setiosflags (ios::right);
                for (idx = 0; idx < NUM_MON; idx++)
                    cout << "  Month #" << setw(2) << idx+1 << ": " << setw(6)
                        << SalesObject.getSales(idx) << endl;
                break;
            case 9:
                break;
            default:
                cout << "You've entered an unavailable option." << endl;
        }
    }
}
```

As an example, consider the simple array in Figure 14.5. In the first pass through the array, a sort function makes four swaps (exchanges four pairs of elements). Notice that the effect is to move the largest element into place at the bottom of the array.

Figure 14.5   Performing a bubble sort

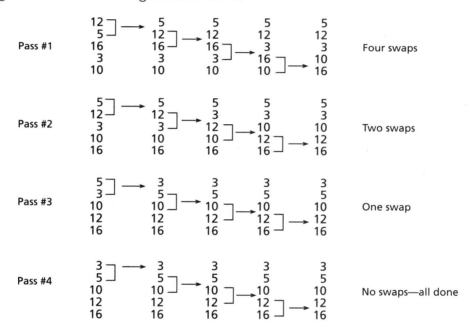

During the second pass, only two pairs of elements are out of order. Again, the effect is to percolate the largest values to the bottom. Pass three makes one swap to place the array in correct order. However, the sort function must make one more pass without swaps to detect that fact.

As an example of sorting an array, we'll add a fourth menu option to the sales average program that sorts the sales and displays them in order. The new code, which can be found in Listing 14.5, has been placed in the switch structure in the application object's Run function.

## Listing 14.5   Coding the bubble sort

```
case 4:
    int result, i;
    long Value, ValueBelow, temp;

    cout << "The sales in ascending order are: " << endl;
    result = SWAP_MADE;
    while (result == SWAP_MADE)
    {
        result = NO_SWAP;
        for (i = 0; i < NUM_MON -1; i++)
            {
            Value = SalesObject.getSales (i);
            ValueBelow = SalesObject.getSales (i+1);
            if (Value > ValueBelow)
            {
                // put current data into temporary variable
                temp = Value;
                // copy data from object below into current object
                SalesObject.InitSales (i, ValueBelow);
                // copy into current from temporary object
                SalesObject.InitSales (i+1, temp);
                result = SWAP_MADE;
            }
        }
    }
    for (i = 0; i < NUM_MON; i++)
        cout << "  Month #" << setw(2) << i+1 << ": " << setw(6) <<
            SalesObject.getSales(i) << endl;
    break;
```

To perform the sort, the function uses two loops. The outer—a `while`—keeps going until the `result` variable indicates that no swaps have been made. (This is where the `SWAP_MADE` and `NO_SWAP` constants come in.) The inner loop—a `for`—makes one pass through the array.

Each time the program begins a pass through the array, it makes the assumption that no swaps have been made (in other words, that the array is in the correct order). It therefore sets the `result` variable to `NO_SWAP` just before entering the `for` loop. The value of this constant is arbitrary. Since it is only being used as a flag, it can have any value, as long as that value is different from the value assigned to the `SWAP_MADE` constant.

Within the `for` loop, the `sort` function uses the `getSales` function to retrieve a value from an array element (`Value`) and the element below (`ValueBelow`). Then, it compares the two elements. If `Value` is greater than `ValueBelow`, the elements are out of order and must be swapped.

Whenever the need for a swap is detected, the bubble sort copies the array element with the lower index into a temporary storage location (in this case, the variable named temp). The program can then copy the value below into the location of the value being held in temporary storage. Finally, the value in temporary storage can be copied into its new location in the array (one array element below where it was originally located). The function finishes the swap process by assigning SWAP_MADE to result, ensuring that at least one more pass will be made through the array.

Notice that if all the values in the array are in order, the expression that compares Value and ValueBelow will never be true. This means that the program won't reach the block of code that performs a swap, and—more importantly—changes the value in result from NO_SWAP to SWAP_MADE. This means that the program will exit the for loop without making any swaps, in which case the while will also stop.

**Note**

There is one drawback to the sorting we have just done: It destroys the original array. In other words, we no longer know which value was entered first, and so on. Therefore, in many cases where you want to preserve the original ordering of your data, you may want to create a second array into which you copy the original values. You can then sort the second array, leaving the original intact.

## Understanding Two-Dimensional Arrays

As mentioned earlier in this chapter, programs often make use of two-dimensional arrays, arrays with multiple rows and columns. A two-dimensional array can be visualized as a table or grid. Each element in the array is referenced by the combination of its row number and column number. For example, assume that you have an array that is three rows down by three columns across, such as the array at the top of Figure 14.6. The top left element has the coordinates 0,0; the bottom right element has the coordinates 2,2. (Don't forget that C++ arrays start element index numbers with 0 rather than 1.)

To declare this array, a C++ program contains a statement with the following general syntax:

```
data_type array_name [# of rows] [# of columns];
```

Assuming that each element in the three row by three column array stores a single character, you can see that the array could be declared as:

```
char grid [3][3];
```

Figure 14.6   Two-dimensional array storage

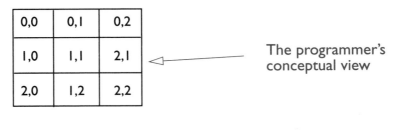

The programmer's
conceptual view

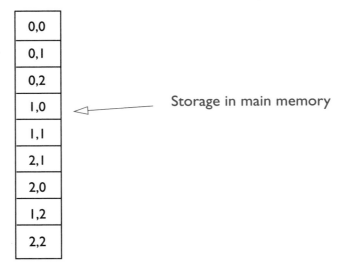

Storage in main memory

Two-dimensional arrays aren't stored in main memory as two-dimensional grids; they're stored linearly, as in the bottom portion of Figure 14.6. In the three by three array, element 0,0 is followed by 0,1; 0,2; 1,0; 1,1; 1,2; 2,0; and so on. Notice that the second index value varies more quickly. This first index changes only after all of the second index values have been used. This means that it makes no difference which index you use for columns and which for rows. You and your program simply have to be consistent in how you access and assign elements to the array. By convention, however, the first index represents rows and the second, columns.

To make a program easier to understand and modify, a programmer wants to avoid using meaningful numeric constants wherever possible. A C++ program is therefore likely to contain the following three statements that define the two-dimensional array:

```
const ROWS = 3;
const COLS = 3;
char grid [ROWS][COLS];
```

## Initializing Two-Dimensional Arrays

Like one-dimensional arrays, two-dimensional arrays can be initialized when they are declared. You can either allocate exactly enough space to hold initial values or have initial values placed in a larger array.

```
int array [][] = {{1, 2, 3, 4},
                  {5, 6, 7, 8},
                  {9, 10, 11, 12}};

int array [5][5] = {{1, 2, 3, 4},
                    {5, 6, 7, 8},
                    {9, 10, 11, 12}};
```

In both syntaxes, each row of data is surrounded by braces. Rows are separated by commas, and the entire set of initial values is surrounded by braces. However, in the first syntax, the compiler allocates an array that has columns and three rows. In the second syntax, the compiler allocates an array with five columns and five rows, but places data only in the first four columns of the first three rows.

## Accessing Two-Dimensional Arrays

As with one-dimensional arrays, you must access the elements in a two-dimensional array individually, using each element's index. However, because the elements in two-dimensional arrays are represented by a column number and a row number, each element requires *two* index values, one for the column and one for the row. To access a single element in a two-dimensional array, you must therefore use two indexes, each surrounded by brackets:

```
grid [1][1] = 'X';
```

The indexes can be integer constants or integer variables. It's up to you as a programmer to keep track of which index represents the row and which represents the column. However, if you stick to the convention of using the left index for rows and the right index for columns, you'll never get them mixed up.

Because there are two indexes, you need to use nested loops to process every element in a two-dimensional array. For example, the following code initializes every element in the grid array to null:

```
int i,
for (i = 0; i < ROWS; i++)
    for (j = 0; j < COLS; j++)
        grid [i][j] = '';
```

When you are simply initializing a two-dimensional array, it makes no difference whether the row index is the inner or outer loop. However, when you want to display the elements in the array, the order in which the elements appear depends on which index varies faster. For example, the following code displays data from each row on a single line:

```
int i, j;
for (i = 0; i < ROW; i++)
{
    cout << '\n'; // new line between rows
    for (j = 0; j < COLS; j++) // one row across
        cout << grid[i][j] << ' ';
}
```

On the other hand, if you want the data from a single column to appear across a line (in effect reversing the dimensions), the code will be written:

```
int i,j;
(for i = 0; i < COLS; i++)
{
    cout << '\n'; // new line between columnar data
    for (j = 0; j < ROWS; j++)
        cout << grid[j][i] << ' ';
}
```

**Note**

Throughout this book we have been using and emphasizing the importance of meaningful variable names. Array indexes, however, are the one situation in which programmers often use single-letter variables names. The letter *i* is used when working with a single array index; a second array index is usually named *j*. Use *k* and *l* for additional indexes.

## Using Two-Dimensional Arrays

The array named `grid` that we have been using as an example of a two-dimensional array can be used as a playing field for a tic-tac-toe game in which a human plays against the computer. Play begins within the user choosing to play X or O and making the first move. (The first move alternates between the player and the computer for each successive game.) The computer then makes its move. After the computer moves, the program displays the game grid (Figure 14.7). Play continues to alternate between the user and the computer until either a winner is detected or the grid is filled, signifying a draw. At that point the user can play again or exit the program (Figure 14.8).

The tic-tac-toe program has two classes: an application class and a class to represent an entire game (`tttGame`). As you can see in the header file (Listing 14.6), the class contains an array for the playing grid along with variables to hold index values, the number of moves made by the player and the computer (used to detect a draw), and the marker (X or O) used by the player and the computer.

## Game Class Member Functions

There are eight member functions in the `tttGame` class. These functions fall into three categories: setting up the game, making moves, and determining the status of the game at the end of a move. As we discuss these functions, notice how they illustrate the way in which a `tttGame` class object and an application object can interact with a two-dimensional array.

Figure 14.7   Opening play for the tic-tac-toe game

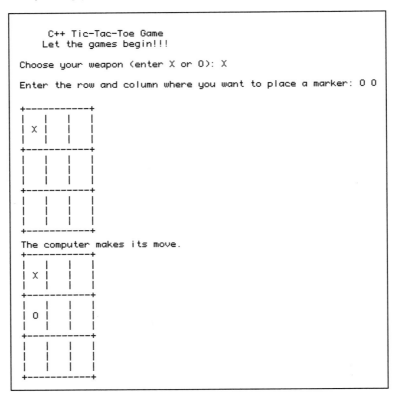

## Setting Up the Game

The first `tttGame` class member function encountered by the application object's `Run` function is the constructor (Listing 14.7). Because the grid and variables such as the number of player and computer moves have to be reinitialized for each new game, there's no point in using the constructor to perform initialization. Instead, it initializes the random number generator.

The `InitGame` function (Listing 14.8) is called every time a new game begins. It assigns a blank to each element in the grid. (A blank is used rather than a null to ensure that the grid displays correctly on the screen even if an array element isn't occupied by an X or O. Keep in mind that a blank is

Figure 14.8   End of game play for the tac-tac-toe program

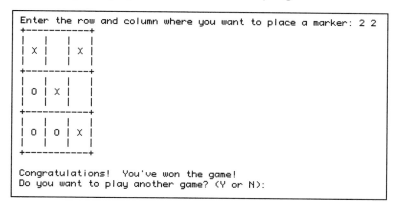

a character, just like X or O.) Notice that just as with one-dimensional arrays, the only way to insert values is to access each element individually. As you saw earlier, the typical way to accomplish this task is to use nested `for` loops.

The third setup function, `chooseMarker` in Listing 14.9, accepts the character chosen by the user as its single input parameter. It then assigns that character to the player and assigns the unused marker to the computer. Like `InitGame`, it is executed once for each new game.

### Displaying the Grid

The function that displays the contents of the two-dimensional array (`displayGrid` in Listing 14.10) intentionally violates the principle that input from the user and output to the user should not be part of a data manipulation class's member functions. In cases where games use a specialized display for portions of game play, it is up to the programmer to decide whether it is more important to hide the details of the display from the application object manipulating the `tttGame` object or to keep the class system-independent by relieving it of any I/O responsibilities. This particular program chooses to hide the details of the display of the grid from the application object. However, if the game were to be ported to several operating systems, a programmer might choose to remove this I/O from the member function.

Another reason for keeping the display code entirely within the class is that it simplifies coding. The grid array is a private variable; an application object using a `tttGame` object can't access the contents of the array directly. If an application object were to perform the display, a member function would

## Listing 14.6 ttt.h

```
// Number of elements in the array
const ROWS = 3;
const COLS = 3;

// Flags to indicate result of making one move
const WIN = 1;
const TIE = 0;
const PLAY_ON = -1;  // neither win nor lose so "play on"

// Flags to indicate whether player or computer goes first
const PLAYER = 1;
const COMPUTER = 0;

const RAND_FACTOR = 10923;  // used to scale random number between 1 and 3

// Flags to indicate whether a player's move attempts to place a marker in an element
// that is already occupied
const GOOD = 1;
const BAD = 0;

class tttGame
{
    private:
        char grid [ROWS][COLS];  // game board
        int row, column;  // array indexes used in member functions
        int player_moves;  // number of moves made by player; used to detect a draw
        int computer_moves;  // number of moves made by computer
        char player, computer;  // X or O

    public:
        tttGame();     // constructor; doesn't need to do anything
        void InitGame();  // initializes a new game
        void chooseMarker(char);  // let player choose X or O
        void displayGrid();   // display the grid
        int playerMove(int, int);  // send in row and column of space
        void computerMove();  // generate a move for the computer;
        int checkGrid();  // check for draw or winner
        int whoWon();  // find out who won
};
```

## Listing 14.7 tttGame class constructor

```
tttGame::tttGame()    // constructor initializes random number generator
{
    srand(time(NULL) % 37);   // initialize random number generator
}
```

## Listing 14.8   tttGame::InitGame function

```
void tttGame::InitGame()
{
    int x,y;

    for (x = 0; x < ROWS; x++)
        for (y = 0; y < COLS; y++)
            grid [x][y] = ' ';
    row = 0;
    column = 0;
    player_moves = 0, computer_moves = 0;
}
```

## Listing 14.9   tttGame::chooseMarker

```
void tttGame::chooseMarker (char marker)
{
    player = marker;
    if (player == 'X')
        computer = '0';
    else
        computer = 'X';
}
```

## Listing 14.10   tttGame::displayGrid

```
void tttGame::displayGrid()
{
    int x, y;

    for (x = 0; x < ROWS; x++)
    {
        cout << "+-----------+" << endl;
        cout << "|   |   |   |" << endl;
        cout << "|";
        for (y = 0; y < COLS; y++)
        {
            cout << " " << grid[x][y] << " |";

        }
        cout << "\n|   |   |   |" << endl;
    }
    cout << "+-----------+" << endl;
}
```

need to be written that returns one element of the grid array. The function would need to have the row and column indexes passed in as parameters. To use such a function, the application object would then use nested for loops to access each element in the array, one at a time. By hiding this logic in a member function, the application object using a tttGame object is simpler.

To display the grid, the displayGrid function uses nested for loops. The outer loop controls displaying one row at a time, including the bar at the top of a row and the blank line below the bar. The inner loop then displays all columns for the row, followed by another blank line. After all three rows have been displayed, the function finishes by displaying the bar at the bottom of the grid. Notice that just like initializing the array, the only way to access the contents of the array is one element at a time, using both a row and column index to identify each element.

### Making Moves

There are two types of moves, one made by the player and the other by the computer. The player move (handled by playerMove in Listing 14.11) function accepts the row and column indexes from the application object. If the array element indicated by the indexes contains a blank, the player's marker is inserted into the element using an assignment statement and the total number of moves made by the player is incremented. Otherwise, the element is occupied, and a flag indicating that the move isn't valid is returned to the calling program.

Listing 14.11    tttGame::playerMove

```
int tttGame::playerMove (int prow, int pcol)
{
    if (grid[prow][pcol] != ' ')
        return BAD;
    grid[prow][pcol] = player;  // insert the player's marker
    player_moves++;
    return GOOD;
}
```

The computer's move (handled by computerMove in Listing 14.12) is a bit more complex because the computer must generate the move itself. For this program, the computer generates two random numbers between 1 and 3 and then subtracts 1 from each to bring the values into the correct range for the array's indexes. If the array element indicated by the random values is unoccupied (in other words, it contains a blank), then the computer inserts its marker and increments the number of moves it has made.

Listing 14.12    tttGame::computerMove

```
void tttGame::computerMove()
{
    int row, column;

    row = (rand() / RAND_FACTOR) - 1;
    column = (rand() / RAND_FACTOR) - 1;
    while (grid[row][column] != ' ')
    {
        row ++;
        if (row == ROWS) row = 0;
        if (grid[row][column] != ' ')
        {
            column++;
            if (column == COLS) column = 0;
        }
    }
    grid[row][column] = computer;
    computer_moves++;
}
```

If the randomly selected element is occupied, the computer looks in the next row. If the next row is occupied, it looks in the next column. The process repeats until the computer finds an open element. Notice that the function detects when the "next" index is 3 and resets it to 0 so that the index values don't exceed those available in the array. This is an example of array bounds checking.

**Note**

There are certainly better strategies for picking moves in a tic-tac-toe game. (This one might be described as somewhat brain dead.) However, strategies that analyze the current position of markers on the board require much more code than the random strategy. Since the purpose of this program is to demonstrate how to use two-dimensional arrays rather than to make the computer a good game player, the random strategy has been used.

### Finding Winners and Ties

The status of the game at the end of each move is detected with the `check-Grid` function (Listing 14.13). The function's first job is to look for a winner, a process for which there is no simple algorithm. The function therefore first checks each row to see if the elements aren't blank and if they contain the same marker. If there is no winner across the rows, the function checks down the columns. If there is no winner down the columns, then the function looks diagonally. When the computer finds a winner, it returns a flag indicating that either the computer or the player has won.

**Listing 14.13   tttGame::checkGrid**

```
int tttGame::checkGrid()
{
    int x, y;

    for (x = 0; x < ROWS; x++)    // look for winner across rows
        if (grid[x][0] != ' ' && grid[x][0] == grid[x][1]
            && grid[x][1] == grid[x][2])
            return WIN;

    for (y = 0; y < COLS; y++) // look for winner down columns
        if (grid[0][y] !=+ ' ' && grid[0][y] == grid[1][y]
            && grid[1][y] == grid[2][y])
                return WIN;

    // check for diagonal win
    if ((grid[0][0] == grid[1][1] && grid[1][1] == grid[2][2]
        && grid[0][0] != ' ')
        || (grid[0][2] == grid [1][1] && grid[1][1] == grid[2][0]
        && grid[0][2] != ' '))
            return WIN;

    // 9 moves mean grid is full
    if (player_moves + computer_moves == 9)
        return TIE;
    return PLAY_ON;
}
```

Assuming there is no winner, the function then checks for a tie. If the sum of the number of moves made by the computer and the player is 9, then the grid is full and the game is a draw. Otherwise, play continues.

The checkGrid function doesn't detect whether the computer or the player has won. That is performed by the whoWon function (Listing 14.14), which looks to see which of the two has made more moves. Whoever has made more moves is the winner.

Listing 14.14    tttGame::whoWon

```
int tttGame::whoWon()
{
    if (player_moves > computer_moves)
        return PLAYER;
    else
        return COMPUTER;
}
```

## The Application Class

The declaration of the application class for the tic-tac-toe game can be found in Listing 14.15. Notice that this class has the typical application class constructor and Run function, but that it also has three variables.

Listing 14.15    AppClass.h

```
class AppClass
{
    private:
        int keepPlaying, goes_first;
        char another;
    public:
        AppClass();
        void Run ();
};
```

How do you decide which variables should be part of an application class and which should be handled as local variables in a Run function? There are two criteria:

- Do the values in the variables need to be retained between function calls? If so, then the variables should be part of a class so that their values will remain with an object as long as the object exists, regardless of which member functions are executed.
- Do the variables need to be initialized before any member functions are called and don't need to be reinitialized at any time during the

program run? If so, it is convenient to place those initializations in the class's constructor. In this way, all initializations are in one place, making the class easier to modify.

The variables that are part of the tic-tac-toe game's application class fall into the second category: the values need to be initialized when the object is created, before the Run function is called, and don't need to be reinitialized at any point in the program.

The application class's Run function appears in Listing 14.16. The function begins by creating one object from the tttGame class (inPlay) and then enters a while loop that plays games until the user indicates that he or she wants to quit. At the start of each new game, the function lets the user choose a marker, decides whether the computer or the player goes first, initializes the grid with a call to InitGrid, and then transfers the user's chosen marker to the tttGame object.

The program then begins a second loop that repeats as long as a single game is in play. Based on whether the user or computer goes first, the program accepts a move from the user or generates a move for the computer by calling either playerMove or computerMove, as appropriate. After two moves have been made, the Run function displays the grid using the displayGrid function and calls checkGrid to determine if the game has ended. If the game has ended, the function issues a break statement to exit the inner loop.

To finish the game, the Run function either determines and displays who won (using whoWon) or displays a message indicating that the game has ended in a draw. Finally, the user is given the choice whether to play another game. The user's response determines whether the outer loop continues.

When studying this program, an important point to remember is that because the grid array is a private variable belonging to the inPlay object, the only way the Run function can gain access to the contents of the array, without using pointers, is to pass a member function the row and column indexes of one element at a time. For example, this is the way in which the playerMove function is written.

## Summary

An array is a complex variable that groups more than one value of a single data type. Arrays can be used as class variables or local variables. They can hold data of simple variable types (integers, floating point values, and so on), or they can hold objects declared from the same class.

## Listing 14.16   The Run function for the Tic-Tac-Toe game

```
void AppClass::Run()
{
    tttGame inPlay;  // declare object of game class
    char X_or_O;
    int move_OK;
    int prow, pcol;


    cout << "      C++ Tic Tac Toe Game" << endl;
    cout << "     Let the games begin!!!" << endl << endl;
    while (toupper(another) == 'Y')
    {
        cout << "Choose your weapon (enter X or O): ";
        cin >> X_or_O;
        if (goes_first == COMPUTER)
            goes_first = PLAYER;      // alternate who goes first
        else
            goes_first = COMPUTER;
        inPlay.InitGame();  // initialize the grid for each new game
        inPlay.chooseMarker (toupper(X_or_O));
        while (keepPlaying == PLAY_ON)
        {
            if (goes_first == PLAYER)
            {
                move_OK = BAD;
                while (move_OK == BAD)
                {
                    cout << "\nEnter the row and column where you want";
                        << " to place a marker: ";
                    cin >> prow >> pcol;
                    move_OK = inPlay.playerMove (prow, pcol);
                    if (move_OK == BAD)
                        cout << "\nThat square is already occupied";
                }
            }
            else
            {
                cout << "\nThe computer makes its move." << endl;
                inPlay.computerMove();
            }
            inPlay.displayGrid();
            keepPlaying = inPlay.checkGrid();   // check to see if game is over
            if (keepPlaying != PLAY_ON)
                break;        // break out of loop if game is over
```

Continued next page

**Listing 14.16**(Continued)    The Run function for the Tic-Tac-Toe game

```
if (goes_first == PLAYER)
        {
            cout << "\nThe computer makes its move." << endl;
            inPlay.computerMove();
        }
        else
        {
            move_OK = BAD;
            while (move_OK == BAD)
            {
                cout << "\nEnter the row and column where you want to";
                    << "place a marker: ";
                cin >> prow >> pcol;
                move_OK = inPlay.playerMove (prow, pcol);
                if (move_OK == BAD)
                    cout << "\nThat square is already occupied";
            }
        }
        inPlay.displayGrid();
        keepPlaying = inPlay.checkGrid();
    }
    if (keepPlaying == WIN)  // find out who won the game
    {
        if (inPlay.whoWon() == PLAYER)
            cout << "\nCongratulations!  You've won the game!";
        else
            cout << "\nThe computer won this one. So it goes...";
    }
    else
        if (keepPlaying == TIE)
            cout << "\nThis won ended in a draw.";
    cout << "\nDo you want to play another game? (Y or N): ";
    cin >> another;
    if (toupper(another) == 'Y')
        keepPlaying = PLAY_ON;
    }
}
```

To declare a one-dimensional (one column, many rows) C++ array, place the number of elements in the array within brackets following the name of the array. A two-dimensional array (many columns, many rows) requires two sets of brackets, one for the array index of each dimension.

The elements in a C++ array are numbered beginning with 0. Although the array declaration requires the total number of elements in the array, the index of the highest element in the array is one less than the total number of elements.

To assign a value to an array, a program uses the name of the array followed by brackets containing the index of the element to which the value is to be assigned.

The name of an array is the address of the beginning of the array in main memory.

## Exercises

1.  Write a class that contains an array of the closing Dow Jones Averages for the past two weeks. The program that manipulates an object of this class should allow the user to enter the averages and then initialize the object with those numbers. The program should finish by calling a member function that computes the average of the values in the array and returns that average to the calling function, which should then display the average for the user.

2.  Write a class that contains a two-dimensional array for the credit card purchases made by one employee during a seven-day period. Allow the employee to make up to 10 purchases each day. The program that manipulates an object of this class should prompt the user to enter data for the array and then initialize the object's array. Write member functions to calculate the total purchases made on one day and the total purchases made for the entire seven-day period. Then, prepare a nicely formatted report that shows the purchases made on each day, the total for each day, and—at the end of the report—the grand total of the purchases made.

3.  You have been asked to keep track of the number of people attending a computer trade show that runs for seven days. Create a class that contains an array of the attendance each day. The program that manipulates an object of this class should allow the user to do the following:

    *   Let the user enter values into the array.
    *   Display the values in the order in which they were entered.

- Compute and display the average attendance.
- Sort the values and display them in sorted order.

4.  Modify the program you wrote for Exercise 3 so that it makes a copy of the array of attendance figures and sorts the copy, rather than the original. (*Hint:* To copy data from one array to another, use a for loop. You must copy the elements one at a time!)

5.  Create a class that stores and evaluates a poker hand. The class should contain a two-dimensional array to store the five-card hand. In one column, store the suit (1 = Diamonds, 2 = Hearts, 3 = Clubs, 4 = Spades); in the other column, store the card value (11 = Jack, 12 = Queen, 13 = King). Include a member function that evaluates a hand and reports back to the program calling the function whether the hand contains a flush (all the same suit), a straight (all five cards in numeric order), a straight flush (all five cards in the same suit in numeric order), four of a kind, a full house (three of a kind plus two of a kind), three of a kind, two pair, one pair, or nothing. Write a program that demonstrates that the hand evaluation function works.

6.  Consider the algorithm for the bubble sort that you learned about in this chapter. One of the drawbacks of the process is that a program must make an extra pass through an array when the array is completely sorted to determine that the array is in order and that sorting should stop. What other method could a program use to determine when an array is completely sorted? Your method should avoid making the extra pass through the array without requiring the program to do too much extra work.

# 15

# Arrays of Objects

## OBJECTIVES

In this chapter you will read about:

- How arrays can be used to store multiple objects of the same class.
- Using arrays as function parameters.
- Reading arrays of objects from and writing arrays of objects to a text file.
- Sorting an array of objects.

Business information systems usually deal with data that describe many objects of a single class rather than just a single object. For example, a program to manage a pharmacy's prescriptions must handle many customers, many types of drugs, and many prescriptions.

In this chapter you will begin by reading about general strategies for handling multiple objects of the same class. We will then turn to the details of one of those strategies: placing the objects in an array.

## Strategies for Handling Multiple Objects

A program can manage multiple objects of the same class in many ways, each of which has its benefits and drawbacks. In this book you will be introduced not only to arrays of objects, but also to data structures known as linked lists. To give you a framework for organizing objects, this section introduces some of the possible strategies and discusses their advantages and disadvantages.

### Multiple Individual Objects

You could create a separately named variable for each object created from a class. Unless the number of objects is very small, however, this solution isn't very practical. As you can see in Figure 15.1, the objects aren't necessarily stored next to one another in main memory. To access an object, you must use the object's individual name. If you want to call the same member function for each object, you must write one statement for each object.

### Arrays of Objects

A commonly used alternative to multiple individual objects is an array of objects created for static binding, such as that in Figure 15.2. Such an array is declared as part of the class whose functions will be manipulating the array's contents. Arrays of objects are easy to use but have two drawbacks. First, they can waste storage space because space for an entire array is allocated when the array is declared, regardless of whether the array is completely filled with data. Second, the number of objects is limited to the number of elements declared in the array. Of course, these drawbacks aren't unique to arrays of objects; they are the same issues we raised when discussing arrays in Chapter 14.

Figure 15.1   Storing individual objects from the same class

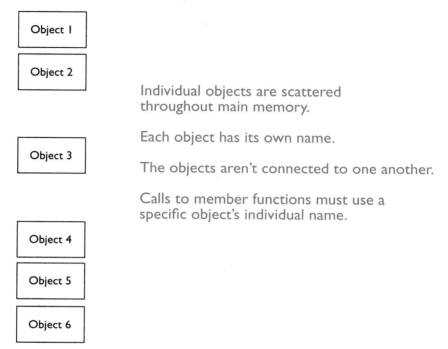

Individual objects are scattered throughout main memory.

Each object has its own name.

The objects aren't connected to one another.

Calls to member functions must use a specific object's individual name.

You might also create an array of pointers to objects (see Figure 15.3). Used with dynamic binding, this technique provides good memory management for objects, but it is still limited to the number of elements in the pointer array.

Arrays of objects or pointers to objects have one additional limitation: The number of elements you can allocate to any array is ultimately limited by the amount of main memory available to the program. Any data structure that is kept totally in main memory will be subject to this limitation. (Disk-based storage structures are beyond the scope of this book, however.)

Arrays of objects or pointers to objects are usually managed by a class designed specifically for that purpose, hiding the details of array manipulation from the class using the array. For example, if the pharmacy program mentioned earlier used an array to store all its customer objects, then the array would be declared in an array manager class. An array manager object would take care of inserting objects into the array, finding objects in the array, and

Figure 15.2    An array of objects

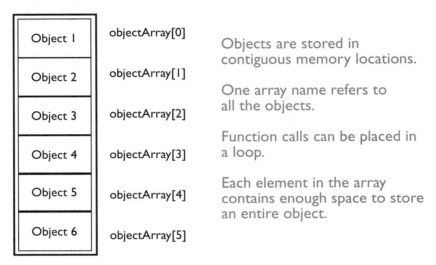

objectArray

removing objects from the array. The program's application object would create one array manager object and would then request array services from the array manager. You will learn how to create and use an array manager in this chapter.

## Linked Lists

You might also decide to manage multiple objects from the same class with a linked list. A *linked list* is a data structure in which objects are chained together by pointing to one another. The list is managed by a special list manager class, which has member functions to insert items into the list, find items in the list, and delete items from the list.

A linked list can be constructed in two ways. In the simplest organization, each object that can become part of a list contains a variable (usually named `next`) that contains a pointer to the logically next element in the list, as in Figure 15.4. The drawback to this arrangement is that the objects in the list must know something about the list. In other words, the pointers that support list membership are actually part of the objects in the list.

Figure 15.3    An array of pointers to objects

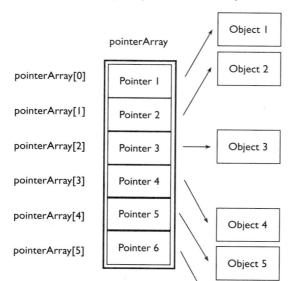

Objects are scattered in main memory.

The pointer array contains the addresses of the objects in main memory.

The pointer array takes up just enough space to hold the pointers.

Figure 15.4    A linked list with pointers in list objects

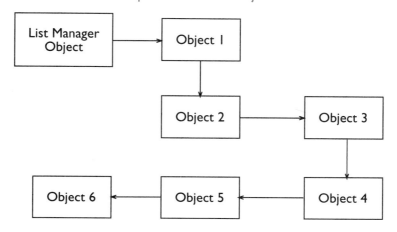

An alternative, though somewhat more complex, structure can be seen in Figure 15.5. The list manager points to special objects called *nodes*, each of which points to an object in the list. In this case, the "next" pointers are part of the node object rather than the objects being linked. The benefit of this arrangement is that the objects that are in the list don't need to know anything about the list.

**Figure 15.5   A linked list using node objects**

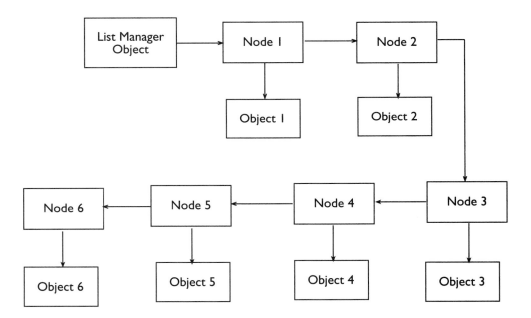

Regardless of which structure you choose, linked lists require dynamic binding (because they use pointers) and provide good memory management. Because objects are chained together, the number of objects that can be added to the list is limited only by available memory space. However, linked lists are more difficult to manipulate than arrays of objects or pointers to objects. You will learn how to program linked lists in Chapter 19.

## The Survey Analysis Program

As an example of a program that handles an array of objects, we will be looking at the survey analysis program that has been mentioned earlier in this book. The purpose of the program is to store and analyze the result of surveys about shoe ownership and purchasing patterns.

A transcript of a sample run of the program can be found in Figure 15.6. Notice that this program uses two menus: one to choose the program function (overall averages, averages by gender, and frequency distributions) and a second to choose the data value that is to be analyzed. The program uses a separate class for each menu (mainMenu and fldMenu in Listing 15.1). Like other menu classes that you have seen to this point, mainMenu and fldMenu have display functions that show menu options and choose functions that return a user's menu selection (see Listing 15.2).

Each survey that was completed is represented as an object of the One-Survey class (Listing 15.3). The class is made up of variables for the survey number, the gender and age of the respondent, and eight values for the number of pairs of shoes that the respondent owns and has purchased in the last year.

With one exception, the member functions for the OneSurvey class perform actions you have seen before (Listing 15.4). The constructor, for example, initializes the integer variables to 0 and sets the single character variable to null. The InitSurvey function accepts data from a function manipulating an object and inserts those data into the OneSurvey object's variables. Other than the copy function, the remaining member functions simply return the contents of one of the object's variables to a calling function.

As you will see later in this chapter, the purpose of the copy function is to copy data from one OneSurvey object to another. It is used when sorting an array of objects. (There is an easier way to copy objects, but because it requires the use of pointers, we'll leave a discussion of that method until Chapter 17.)

The survey analysis program illustrates most of the concepts that will be covered in the rest of this chapter. Nonetheless, it is far from complete. It should do many more things, including computing standard deviations, medians, modes, and statistics based on groupings of respondents by age. In addition, the program needs better error checking and more I/O capabilities. (You will get a change to add some of the missing pieces for the exercises at the end of this chapter.)

Figure 15.6   Sample output from the survey analysis program

```
Choose an option:

1. Compute averages
2. Compute averages by gender
3. Frequencies
9. Quit

Which one? 1

This function computes the average for the entire sample.

Choose the field to analyze:

1. Number of pairs of athletic shoes owned
2. Number of pairs of athleitic shoes purchased
3. Number of pairs of dress shoes owned
4. Number of pairs of dress shoes purchased
5. Number of pairs of boots owned
6. Number of pairs of boots purchased
7. Number of pairs of sandals owned
8. Number of pairs of sandals purchased
9. Exit without making a choice

Which one? 4

The average is 5.333333

Choose an option:

1. Compute averages
2. Compute averages by gender
3. Frequencies
9. Quit

Which one? 4

Choose the field to analyze:

1. Number of pairs of athletic shoes owned
2. Number of pairs of athleitic shoes purchased
3. Number of pairs of dress shoes owned
4. Number of pairs of dress shoes purchased
5. Number of pairs of boots owned
6. Number of pairs of boots purchased
7. Number of pairs of sandals owned
8. Number of pairs of sandals purchased
9. Exit without making a choice

Which one? 4

The average for men is 6.400000
The average for women is 4.363636

Choose an option:

1. Compute averages
2. Compute averages by gender
3. Frequencies
9. Quit

Which one? 3

Choose the field to analyze:

1. Number of pairs of athletic shoes owned
2. Number of pairs of athleitic shoes purchased
3. Number of pairs of dress shoes owned
4. Number of pairs of dress shoes purchased
5. Number of pairs of boots owned
6. Number of pairs of boots purchased
7. Number of pairs of sandals owned
8. Number of pairs of sandals purchased
9. Exit without making a choice

Which one? 4

VALUE COUNT
  0     2
  1     1
  2     1
  3     3
  5     1
  6     5
  7     3
  8     4
```

### Listing 15.1 The mainMenu and fldMenu classes

```
class mainMenu
{
    private:
        int option;
    public:
        mainMenu();
        void display();
        int choose();
};


class fldMenu
{
    private:
        int option;
    public:
        fldMenu();
        void display();
        int choose();
};
```

## Declaring and Referencing Arrays of Objects

In principle, an array of objects isn't much different from any other array. To declare an array of objects for use with static binding, you add the number of objects in the array to the declaration:

```
type_of_object array_name [#_of_objects];
```

The array that holds objects for the survey analysis program is declared in the array manager class (Listing 15.5):

```
OneSurvey theSurveys[NUMB_SURVEYS];
```

This allocates space for 50 objects of the class `OneSurvey`. Each individual object can then be referenced by the name of the array and the index of the object's position in the array. The third object, for example, is specified with:

```
theSurveys [2];
```

## Listing 15.2   Menu class member functions

```
mainMenu::mainMenu()
{
    option = 0;
}

void mainMenu::display()
{
    cout << "\nChoose an option:" << endl << endl;
    cout << "1. Compute averages" << endl;
    cout << "2. Compute averages by gender" << endl;
    cout << "3. Frequencies" << endl;
    cout << "9. Quit" << endl << endl;
}

int mainMenu::choose()
{
    cout << "Which one? ";
    cin >> option;
    return option;
}

fldMenu::fldMenu()
{
    option = 0;
}

void fldMenu::display()
{
    cout << "\nChoose the field to analyze:" << endl << endl;
    cout << "1. Number of pairs of athletic shoes owned" << endl;
    cout << "2. Number of pairs of athletic shoes purchased" << endl;
    cout << "3. Number of pairs of dress shoes owned" << endl;
    cout << "4. Number of pairs of dress shoes purchased" << endl;
    cout << "5. Number of pairs of boots owned" << endl;
    cout << "6. Number of pairs of boots purchased" << endl;
    cout << "7. Number of pairs of sandals owned" << endl;
    cout << "8. Number of pairs of sandals purchased" << endl;
    cout << "9. Exit without making a choice" << endl << endl;
}

int fldMenu::choose()
{
    cout << "Which one? ";
    cin >> option;
    return option;
}
```

## Listing 15.3 Survey.h

```
class OneSurvey
{

    private:
        int Survey_numb;
        char Gender;
        int Age, AthleticOwned,
            AthleticBought,DressOwned,DressBought,BootsOwned,BootsBought,
            SandalsOwned, SandalsBought;


    public:
        OneSurvey(); // constructor
        void InitSurvey (int, char, int, int, int, int, int, int, int,
            int, int);
        char getGender();
        int getAge();
        int getAthleticOwned();
        int getAthleticBought();
        int getDressOwned();
        int getDressBought();
        int getBootsOwned();
        int getBootsBought();
        int getSandalsOwned();
        int getSandalsBought();
        // copy data from another object of the same type
        void copy (OneSurvey);

};
```

In other words, the name of an object that is part of an array of objects includes the object's array index. This means that when a member function of the array manager references an object in the array, it must use the object's entire name, including the array index. For example, to retrieve the value in the Gender variable, the array manage class uses

```
LGender = theSurveys[index].getGender();
```

where LGender is a local character variable and index contains the index of the desired array element.

## Listing 15.4    Survey.cpp

```cpp
#include "survey.h"

OneSurvey::OneSurvey()    // constructor
{
    Survey_numb = 0;
    Gender = '\0';
    Age = 0;
    AthleticOwned = 0;
    AthleticBought = 0;
    DressOwned = 0;
    DressBought = 0;
    BootsOwned = 0;
    BootsBought = 0;
    SandalsOwned = 0;
    SandalsBought = 0;
}

void OneSurvey::InitSurvey (int iSurvey_numb, char iGender, int iAge, int
    iAOwned, int iABought, int iDOwned, int iDBought, int iBOwned, int
    iBBought, int iSOwned, int iSBought)
{
    Survey_numb = iSurvey_numb;
    Gender = iGender;
    Age = iAge;
    AthleticOwned = iAOwned;
    AthleticBought = iABought;
    DressOwned = iDOwned;
    DressBought = iDBought;
    BootsOwned = iBOwned;
    BootsBought = iBBought;
    SandalsOwned = iSOwned;
    SandalsBought = iSBought;
}

char OneSurvey::getGender()
    { return Gender; }

int OneSurvey::getAge()
    { return Age; }

int OneSurvey::getAthleticOwned()
    { return AthleticOwned; }

int OneSurvey::getAthleticBought()
    { return AthleticBought;}
```

Continued next page

Listing 15.4(Continued)    Survey.cpp

```
int OneSurvey::getDressOwned()
    { return DressOwned; }

int OneSurvey::getDressBought()
    { return DressBought; }

int OneSurvey::getBootsOwned()
    { return BootsOwned; }

int OneSurvey::getBootsBought()
    { return BootsBought; }

int OneSurvey::getSandalsOwned()
    { return SandalsOwned; }

int OneSurvey::getSandalsBought()
    { return SandalsBought; }

void OneSurvey::copy (OneSurvey inputObject)   // copy one object into another
{
    Survey_numb = inputObject.Survey_numb;
    Gender = inputObject.Gender;
    Age = inputObject.Age;
    AthleticOwned = inputObject.AthleticOwned;
    AthleticBought = inputObject.AthleticBought;
    DressOwned = inputObject.DressOwned;
    DressBought = inputObject.DressBought;
    BootsOwned = inputObject.BootsOwned;
    BootsBought = inputObject.BootsBought;
    SandalsOwned = inputObject.SandalsOwned;
    SandalsBought = inputObject.SandalsBought;
}
```

## Array Manipulation by an Array Manager

Because the array of objects is declared as a private variable of the array manager class, only an object of the ArrayMgr class has direct access to the contents of the array. Nonetheless, the array manager *doesn't* have access to the contents of the OneSurvey objects. It must call OneSurvey class member functions, just like any other class.

For example, consider the array manager class's insert function (Listing 15.6). The purpose of this function is to initialize one of the objects in the array. The values themselves are passed in as parameters. .The insert

## Listing 15.5    ArrayMgr.h

```
const NUMB_SURVEYS = 50;
const SWAP_MADE = 1;
const NO_SWAP = 0;

class ArrayMgr
{
    private:
        int lastIndex;
        OneSurvey theSurveys[NUMB_SURVEYS];
    public:
        ArrayMgr();
        void insert(int, char, int, int, int, int, int, int, int, int, int);
        void sort(int);  // pass in field number to sort by
        // pass in array index wanted, field number wanted
        int getValue (int, int);
        char getGender (int);
        int getCount ();
};
```

## Listing 15.6    ArrayMgr::insert

```
void ArrayMgr::insert (int iSurvey_numb, char iGender, int iAge, int iAOwned,
    int iABought, int iDOwned, int iDBought, int iBOwned, int iBBought, int
    iSOwned, int iSBought)
{
    ++lastIndex;
    theSurveys[lastIndex].InitSurvey (iSurvey_numb, iGender, iAge, iAOwned,
        iABought, iDOwned, iDBought, iBOwned, iBBought, iSOwned, iSBought);
}
```

function therefore increments the count of items in the array and calls the OneSurvey class member function InitSurvey, passing all the input values along as parameters

The survey analysis program's application object needs access to individual values stored in the OneSurvey objects. To obtain a value, the application object makes a request to the array manager, sending it an identifier for the survey variable wanted and the array index of the survey object wanted. As you can see in Listing 15.7, the array manager's getValue function first determines the variable whose value is being requested, and then calls the appropriate OneSurvey class "get" function, using the array index received as an input parameter.

Listing 15.7   ArrayMgr::getValue

```
int ArrayMgr::getValue (int index, int whichField)
{
    int Value;

    switch(whichField)
    {
        case 1: Value = theSurveys[index].getAthleticOwned(); break;
        case 2: Value = theSurveys[index].getAthleticBought(); break;
        case 3: Value = theSurveys[index].getDressOwned(); break;
        case 4: Value = theSurveys[index].getDressBought(); break;
        case 5: Value = theSurveys[index].getBootsOwned(); break;
        case 6: Value = theSurveys[index].getBootsBought(); break;
        case 7: Value = theSurveys[index].getSandalsOwned(); break;
        case 8: Value = theSurveys[index].getSandalsBought(); break;
    }
    return Value;
}
```

**Note**

The field numbers in the getValue function are keyed to the menu choices in the fldMenu class.

## Interacting with the Array Manager

The array manager class hides the details of the array from the survey analysis program's application object. Therefore, the application object must request data from the array manager each time it needs a value. For example, consider the application class function that computes the average for a single OneSurvey class variable (Averages in Listing 15.8).

To compute the average, the function must sum the values and then divides that sum by the total number of values. The Averages function therefore begins by letting the user make a choice from the field menu. It then enters a for loop that processes objects in the array of objects. To obtain a value, the function calls the getValue function you saw earlier, passing in the array index and the field number chosen from the field menu.

The application object uses a similar strategy to compute separate averages based on gender. The GAverages function (Listing 15.9) lets the user makes a choice from the field menu, just like Averages. However, GAverage's for loop is more involved. First, the for loop retrieves a respondent's gender by calling the array manager function getGender, passing in an array

### Listing 15.8    AppClass::Averages

```
void AppClass::Averages()
{
    fldMenu theMenu; // create field menu object
    int sum = 0, i;

    cout << setiosflags (ios::showpoint) << setprecision(6);
    cout << "\nThis function computes the average for the entire sample."
        << endl;

    theMenu.display();
    choice = theMenu.choose();

    // this gets the user out without doing computations
    if (choice == 9) return;

    for (i = 0; i <= theArray.getCount(); i++)
        sum += theArray.getValue (i, choice);

    cout << "\nThe average is " << (float) sum / (theArray.getCount() + 1)
        << endl;
}
```

index to identify the specific object from which a value should be retrieved. Then, based on the gender, the `for` loop increments the correct counter (`countM` or `countF`) and adds to the correct sum (`sumM` or `SumF`). When the entire array has been processed, the function computes and displays the two averages.

## Sorting Arrays of Objects

One of the most commonly performed types of statistical analysis is the generation of frequency distributions. Typically, frequency distributions list all the unique values in a given variable, ordered from low to high, along with the number of times the value occurs.

Probably the easiest way to produce a frequency distribution is to sort the values and then scan them from low to high, counting how many times each value occurs. The `Frequencies` function of the survey analysis program (Listing 15.10) must therefore ask the array manager to sort the array by any of the eight variables dealing with pairs of shoes. To implement the sort, we'll use the bubble sort method that you first read about in Chapter 14. However, in this case, we'll be moving entire objects based on the value of one of the object's variables.

## Listing 15.9    ArrayMgr::GAverages

```
void AppClass::GAverages()
{
    fldMenu theMenu;  //create field menu object
    int i, sumM = 0, sumF = 0, countM = 0, countF = 0;
    char Lgender;

    cout << setiosflags (ios::showpoint) << setprecision(6);

    theMenu.display();
    choice = theMenu.choose();

    if (choice == 9) return;  // get the user out without doing computations

    for (i = 0; i <= theArray.getCount(); i++)
    {
        Lgender = theArray.getGender(i);
        if (Lgender == 'M')
        {
            countM++;;
            sumM += theArray.getValue (i, choice);
        }
        else
        {
            countF++;
            sumF += theArray.getValue (i, choice);
        }
    }
    cout << "\nThe average for men is " << (float) sumM / countM << endl;
    cout << "The average for women is " << (float) sumF / countF << endl;
}
```

Sorting for the survey analysis program is performed by the array manager's `sort` function (Listing 15.11). Although the logic of the sort is exactly the same as what we used in Chapter 14, there are some differences in how we handle the swaps of array elements becauase we are dealing with objects rather than individual values.,

To perform the swap, the `sort` function declares a local object from the `OneSurvey` class named `tempSurvey`. (This is not an array; it is a single object.) Then, the program calls the `OneSurvey` class's `copy` function to transfer data from the array to the temporary object with the syntax:

```
tempSurvey.copy(theSurveys[i]);
```

## Listing 15.10   AppClass::Frequencies

```
void AppClass::Frequencies()
{
    fldMenu theMenu; // create field menu object
    resetiosflags(0);
    int i;

    theMenu.display();
    choice = theMenu.choose();

    theArray.sort(choice); // sort the array on the chosen field

    // scan sorted array to generate frequency distribution
    int Value, howMany = 1, ValueBelow;
    Value = theArray.getValue (0, choice); // get first value
    cout << "\nVALUE COUNT" << endl;
    for (i = 1; i <= theArray.getCount(); i++)
    {
        ValueBelow = theArray.getValue (i, choice);
        if (ValueBelow == Value)
            howMany++;
        else
        {
            cout << "  " << setw(2) << Value << "     " << setw(2) << howMany <<
    endl;
            Value = ValueBelow;
            howMany = 1;
        }
    }
}
```

This takes one object from the array of objects and uses it as an input parameter to the copy function, which acts on the tempSurvey object. The copy function (look back at Listing 15.4) transfers the data one variable at a time.

The next step is to copy up the value below:

```
theSurveys[i].copy(theSurveys[i+1]);
```

In this case, the object below the one that was just placed in temporary storage is copied into the preceding element in the array. Finally, the object in temporary storage is copied into its new location in the array:

```
theSurveys[i+1].copy(tempSurvey);
```

## Listing 15.11   arrayMgr::sort

```
void ArrayMgr::sort (int whichField)
{
    OneSurvey tempSurvey; // temporary object for use when swapping objects
    int result, Value, ValueBelow, i;

    result = SWAP_MADE;
    while (result == SWAP_MADE)
    {
        result = NO_SWAP;
        for (i = 0; i <= lastIndex; i++)
        {
            Value = getValue (i, whichField);
            ValueBelow = getValue (i+1, whichField);
            if (Value > ValueBelow)
            {
                // put current data into temporary object
                tempSurvey.copy(theSurveys[i]);
                // copy in object below
                theSurveys[i].copy(theSurveys[i+1]);
                // copy original from temporary object
                theSurveys[i+1].copy(tempSurvey);
                result = SWAP_MADE;
            }
        }
    }
}
```

# Loading Objects from a Text File

The survey analysis program's Run function (Listing 15.12) reads its data from a text file (Sample). Unfortunately, the program has no way of knowing how many objects are represented in the text file. It therefore can't use a for loop to read one set of data after another. One solution to this problem is to read data until the computer detects that it has reached the end of the file, until an *end-of-file* condition arises. An end-of-file condition indicates that a program has attempted to read beyond the last valid data in a file.

The ifstream class contains a flag (eof) that indicates the end-of-file condition. You can test to determine that the flag has been set (an end-of-file has occurred) with the syntax

```
if (stream_name.eof)
```

## Listing 15.12    AppClass::Run

```
void AppClass::Run()
{
    mainMenu theMenu; // create main menu object
    int
    LSurvey_numb,LAge,LAthleticOwned,LAthleticBought,LDressOwned,LDressBought,
        LBootsOwned,LBootsBought,LSandalsOwned,LSandalsBought;
    char LGender;

    // attempt to open the text file containing the data
    ifstream readFile ("Survey");
    if (!readFile.is_open()) // if data file can't be found, exit the program
    {
        cout << "\nThe survey data file wasn't found.";
        return;
    }

    while (readFile)   // keep going until an error occurs
    {
        readFile >> LSurvey_numb >> LGender >> LAge >> LAthleticOwned
            >> LAthleticBought >> LDressOwned >> LDressBought >> LBootsOwned
            >> LBootsBought >> LSandalsOwned >> LSandalsBought;

    theArray.insert(LSurvey_numb,LGender,LAge,LAthleticOwned,LAthleticBought,
        LDressOwned,LDressBought,LBootsOwned,LBootsBought,LSandalsOwned,
        LSandalsBought);
    }

    if (!readFile.eof)
    {
        // something other than end-of-file enountered. Quit program
        cout << "\nError occurred while reading input file. ";
        cout << "Unable to continue.";
        return;
    }
    while (choice != QUIT)
    {
        theMenu.display();
        choice = theMenu.choose();
        switch(choice)
        {
            case AVGS:
                Averages();
                break;
```

Continued next page

**Listing 15.12**(Continued)   AppClass::Run

```
    case GENDERAVGS:
        GAverages();
        break;
    case FREQS:
        Frequencies();
        break;
    case QUIT:
        break;
    default:
        cout << "\nYou've entered an unavailable option.";
    }
  }
}
```

By the same token, you might decide to read repeated groups of data from a file with a `while` loop such as

```
while (!stream_name.eof)
{
    // read from the file
}
```

However, there is a major risk in doing so: If an error other than an end-of-file arises when reading from the file, the program will be stuck in an infinite loop. Therefore, programs typically loop until *any* error arises and then determine exactly what error occurred. The survey analysis program, for example, contains the loop

```
while (readfile)
{
    read one object's data
    copy data to object by calling ArrayMgr::insert
}
```

Each iteration of the loop reads one survey's worth of data from the file. It then calls the array manager's `insert` function to insert the data into an object in the array of objects. Counting the number of objects as they are read is handled by the array manager object.

The preceding loop stops whenever any file error occurs. At that point, it is up to the program to check the exact type of error. In this case, the program looks for an error that isn't an end-of-file:

```
if (!readfile.eof)
{
    display error message
    return; // exit program
}
```

If an unexpected error condition has arisen, the program displays an error message to the user and then quits. There isn't any requirement that a program stop execution if an unexpected file error occurs, but the way the survey analysis program is written, it will have no data to analyze if a problem with the file occurs.

## Arrays as Function Parameters

Because the name of an array contains the address of the starting location of the array in main memory, using arrays as function parameters is somewhat different than using the simple variable types you have encountered to this point. In this section you will read declaring arrays as function parameters, passing the arrays, and "returning" arrays.

## Passing One-Dimensional Arrays

As an example of a one-dimensional array as a function parameter, we'll look at a very simple program that generates a set of random numbers. The numbers are generated by the `randoms` class (Listing 15.13). The constructor initializes the random number generator; the `loadArray` function generates random numbers and places them into an array for the application object (see Listing 15.14). The array is the `loadArray` function's first parameter; the number of random numbers to be generated is passed in the second parameter.

## Listing 15.13    randoms.h

```
class randoms
{
    public:
        randoms();
        void loadArray (int [], int);
};
```

## Listing 15.14    randoms.cpp

```
#include "randoms.h"
#include <stdlib.h>
#include <time.h>

randoms::randoms()
{
    // initialize random number generator
    srand (time (NULL) % 37);
}

void randoms::loadArray (int numbers[], int howMany)
{
    for (int i = 1; i <= howMany; i++)
        numbers[i] = rand();
}
```

The syntax for handling arrays as formal parameters is different from that used with simple variables. First, the prototype of the function that will be accepting the array must indicate that the parameter is an array. For a one-dimensional array, the prototype doesn't need to specify the number of elements in the array; it just needs to include the brackets that normally surround the index. The prototype for the loadArray function is therefore:

```
void loadArray (int [], int);
```

The function implementation also doesn't need to indicate the number of elements in the array. The function header of the loadArray function is therefore written as

```
void randoms::loadArray (int numbers[], int howMany)
```

When the array arrives in the function, it will be called numbers. Notice that the parameter list contains the data type—in this case integers—along with the name to be given the parameter in the function. The brackets next to the parameter's name indicate that it's an array.

The function that receives the array doesn't need to know how many elements are in the array. It only needs to know the data type of the array's value. This is because C++ accesses elements in a one-dimensional array by multiplying the array index by the number of bytes in each element and then adding that offset to the starting main memory address of the array.

**Warning**

The major implication of the way in which C++ accesses an array is that it really doesn't keep track of the size of an array. Once space is allocated when an array is declared, all C++ does is perform its multiplication and addition to generate an address for data access. This means you can read data beyond the end of an array or write data beyond the end of an array. Reading the data gives you a wrong value, whereas writing the data may well destroy the contents of a memory location actually allocated to another variable. As you read in Chapter 14, it is therefore up to the programmer to ensure that a program doesn't overflow the bounds of an array; C++ won't do it for you!

When you call a function that has an entire array as a formal parameter, use the array's name, without any brackets. For example, the random number program's application object's Run function (Listing 15.15) calls the loadArray function with:

```
theNumbers.loadArray (numbers, count);
```

## Listing 15.15    AppClass::Run

```
void AppClass::Run()
{
    int count, numbers [MAX_NUMBS];
    randoms theNumbers;

    cout << "How many random numbers do you want? ";
    cin >> count;

    theNumbers.loadArray (numbers, count);

    cout << "\nThe numbers are:" << endl << endl;
    cout << setiosflags (ios::right);
    for (int i = 0; i < count-1; i++)
        cout << setw(10) << numbers [i] << endl;
}
```

Passing an array as a formal parameter may appear to be similar to passing a simple variable, but what gets passed is very different. When you pass a simple variable, such as the loadArray function's count parameter, the program sends the function a *copy* of the parameter's value, leaving the contents of the original variable untouched. However, *the name of an array is the main memory address of the beginning of the array.* When you pass an entire array, you are actually sending the array's starting address into the function; no copy of the array is made and transferred into the function. In other words, *arrays are always passed by reference*. (It's impossible to pass an array by value.)

To help illustrate the difference, take a look at Figure 15.7. At the top of the figure, we are passing by value. The program makes a copy of the value (in this case, 25) and sends the copy to the function being called, leaving the original unchanged in main memory. If the function makes any changes to the value it has received as a parameter, only the copy is modified. The original value in main memory is untouched.

However, at the bottom of the figure we are passing an array by reference. Instead of making a copy of the contents of the array, the program sends the function the main memory address where the first element of the array is located, which in this example is 2050. The function being called therefore has access to the original array; no copy has been made.

This means that when a function modifies the contents of an array, the modifications are made to the original array in main memory. You therefore never need to return an array to a calling function using the `return` statement. Because all modifications are made to a single copy of the array in main memory, the function passing in the array has access to the array and its changed contents after the function into which it was passed finished executing. Notice in the random numbers program that the Run function declares its own `numbers` array, which is passed into `loadArray`. The `loadArray` function places values into the array and stops execution; the function contains no `return` statement. Nonetheless, because `loadArray` modified the single copy of the array, the Run function can access its contents to display the list of random numbers.

## Passing Two-Dimensional Arrays

A two-dimensional array presents a bit of a challenge to a function: It must be able to figure out where one row ends and another begins. If you don't give a function some idea as to how many columns there are in each row, then the function won't know how to interpret any array indexes. Thus, when you pass a two-dimensional array into a function, you can leave the number of rows empty, but you must indicate the number of columns. A prototype therefore includes the number of columns, as in:

```
void someFunction (int [][NUM_COLUMNS]);
```

Figure 15.7    Pass by value versus pass by reference

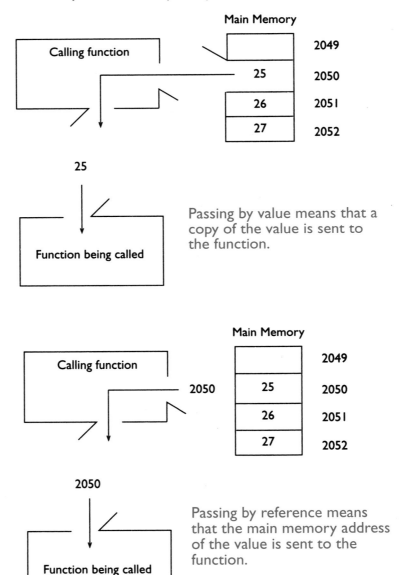

Passing by value means that a copy of the value is sent to the function.

Passing by reference means that the main memory address of the value is sent to the function.

By the same token, the function header must also include the number of columns:

```
void someFunction (int myArray[][NUM_COLUMNS]);
```

When you call the function, it is called using just the name of the array as an input parameter:

```
anObject.someFunction (myArray);
```

The function can then use the starting address of the array, the size of the elements in the array, and the number of columns to calculate the starting address of any element in the array.

## Summary

One strategy for handling multiple objects of the same class is to create an array to hold the objects. In an object-oriented program, an array of objects is handled by an array manager object. The array manager takes care of initializing objects in its array and returning data from objects in the array.

The name of an array is the address of the beginning of the array in main memory. When an array is passed into a function, the array's address is passed, rather than a copy of the array's contents. Because arrays are always passed by reference in this way, modifying the contents of an array in a function changes the array in main memory.

Arrays of objects can be loaded from a text file. In most cases, data are read from the file until an error condition occurs. The program then checks to see if an end-of-file condition has arisen. Any other type of error indicates an unexpected problem with file input.

## Exercises

1. Write a class that contains summary information for a bank. The class should include the customer's number. It should also include a two-dimensional array that holds an account number and a deposit account balance (checking account, CD, NOW account, passbook savings account). Write a program to test the class that includes an array of customer objects. The program should do the following:

   - Permit interactive entry of data.
   - Compute the total worth of each customer. Display each customer's number and the sum of all of his or her account balances. At the end of the report, compute the total amount on deposit at the bank.

2. Create a class that stores information about the salespeople for a cosmetics company. The class should include the salesperson's ID number and the dollar value of sales made during each of the past five weeks (one month). Write a program to test the class that computes the amount paid each salesperson for the month, based on the following rules:

- Base pay is $250 a week plus 10% of sales.
- If a salesperson sells over $10,000 in the month, he or she receives a bonus of $500.

The program should include an array of objects that store data entered interactively. Once the data are in the array, compute and display the number of salespeople receiving pay in the following ranges:

- Less than $1000
- $1000–$2499.99
- $2500–$4999.99
- $5000 or more

Store the counts in an array in your program and display the result once all computations are completed.

3. Create a class that stores the results of a political survey. Each object that you create from the class should store at least the number of voters surveyed who will be voting for a particular candidate. Create an array manager class to hold objects of the preceding class.

Write a program to manage the political survey results. The program should provide menu options that do the following:

- Enter a value into each object.
- Compute the total people surveyed and then compute the percentage voting for each candidate. (You decide: should the percentage be a part of the object storing the number of voters or should it be computed and displayed when needed?)
- Sort the array of objects by number of voters and display the results of the survey in descending order (most votes first). Show the number of voters and the percentage of voters voting for each candidate.

(*Hint:* You're going to need to make a very simple change to a logical condition in the bubble sort to sort in descending rather than ascending order.)

4.  Write a program that tracks which rooms in a hotel are currently occupied. Base the program on a class that describes a room (room number, maximum number of occupants, and an integer flag indicating whether the room is occupied). Include member functions to indicate when a room becomes occupied and when a room becomes unoccupied. Demonstrate that the class and its member functions work by writing a program to manipulate an array of room objects. The program should do the following:

    - Allow interactive entry of data to initialize room objects. (File storage is also useful.)
    - Display the total number of unoccupied rooms.
    - Display the number of unoccupied rooms of each size (size = maximum number of occupants).
    - Find an unoccupied room of a given size and set that room as occupied.
    - Set a room as unoccupied.

5.  As you know, the survey data analysis program that was used as an example isn't complete. Along with additional functionality, it also needs more error trapping and I/O. Add the following to the program:

    - Error trapping when reading the data file: Add code that stops reading the data file when the array is full. Display an appropriate error message. Then give the user the choice of proceeding with data currently in the array or exiting the program.
    - Interactive I/O: Add code that accepts data for new objects from the keyboard and inserts them into the array of objects. Be sure to check to make sure that the array isn't full.
    - File save: Once interactive I/O has been added to the program, the contents of the array of objects must be written back to the text file when the program ends. Add code to write to the file.

- Standard deviation: The standard deviation is a measure of the degree of spread of data values around the average. It has the formula:

$$s = \sqrt{\frac{\Sigma(X_i - \bar{X})^2}{N}}$$

In this formula, $X$ is a data value, $\bar{X}$ is the average (mean) of all data values, and $N$ is the total number of data values. The symbol $\Sigma$ means to sum all the values. The formula therefore tells you first to compute the mean. Then subtract the mean from each data value and square that difference. Add up all the differences and divide them by the total number of values. Finally, take the square root. (*Hint*: Use the `sqrt` function that is prototyped in `math.h`.)

Add computations for the standard deviation to the `Averages` and `GAverages` functions.

- Median and mode: The median is a data value chosen so that half the values are above it and half below it. The mode is that data value (or values) that have the highest frequency. Add code that produces median and mode to the frequency distribution functions.
- Statistics grouped by age range: Add a function that creates groups of objects based on the age of the respondent. For example, age ranges might be defined as all people under 16, 17–21, 22–30, 31–40, and so on. Then, compute means, medians, and modes for each age group.

# 16

# Strings

## OBJECTIVES

In this chapter you will read about:
- Defining and initializing strings.
- Performing string I/O.
- Reading strings from and writing strings to files.
- Using functions that manipulate strings.
- Using strings to create a generic menu class.

By its very nature, business data contain a lot of text: names, phone numbers, addresses, product descriptions, and so on. It is therefore extremely important that business application programmers who are working in C++ be proficient in handling strings.

In this chapter you will learn how C++ represents strings. You will also be introduced to performing string I/O, manipulating arrays of strings, and passing arrays to and from functions. In addition, you will see a generic menu class that you can use in your programs to simplify support for a text-based menu-driven interface.

## The Sample Programs

The major examples in this chapter are drawn from a single program. (You will also see some shorter sample programs.) To help you become accustomed to longer programs, we'll be looking at a program to manage the office supplies inventory. (You were introduced to this program in Chapter 4.) The program lets the user enter new items into the inventory, update the quantities on hand each month, and print a reorder list. The program also saves the inventory to disk each time the program ends and reads it back into memory whenever the program is run.

When a program run begins, the program asks the user for the name of the inventory items data file. Once the user supplies a valid file name, a program run might look something like Figure 16.1.

The supply inventory program uses four classes:

- An application class (`AppClass` in Listing 16.1)
- A class of supply items (`Item`, whose declaration you will see shortly)
- An array manager (`ArrayMgr` in Listing 16.2)
- A generic menu class (`menu`, about which you will read in depth later in this chapter)

## Declaring Strings

As you read earlier in this book, C++ has no "string" data type. Instead, strings are stored as arrays of type `char`. The end of the string is marked with a null, the character '\0'. Although this character might look like two characters, it is

Figure 16.1    Output from the supply inventory program

```
Please choose a menu option:

1. Enter a new item
2. Update inventory
3. View the reorder list
9. Quit

Which one? 1
Description: Pencils, #2
Item number: 9
Amount currently in inventory: 20
Reorder point: 3

Description:

Please choose a menu option:

1. Enter a new item
2. Update inventory
3. View the reorder list
9. Quit

Which one? 2
Enter current inventory amount for each item (-1 = no change)
Pens, red (15): -1
Pens, blue (10): 15
Pens, black (15): -1
Tablets, yellow lined (25): 50
Envelopes, #10 (500): 10
Tape, masking (5): 1
Staples (3): 1
Tape, cellophane (1): -1
Pencils, #2 (20): -1

Please choose a menu option:

1. Enter a new item
2. Update inventory
3. View the reorder list
9. Quit

Which one? 3

ITEMS TO REORDER
-----------------

Envelopes, #10: On hand (10)  Reorder point (25)
Tape, masking: On hand (1)  Reorder point (2)
Staples: On hand (1)  Reorder point (5)
Tape, cellophane: On hand (1)  Reorder point (5)
```

### Listing 16.1    Application class for the supply inventory program

```
class AppClass
{
    private:
        ArrayMgr itemArray;
        void newItem ();
        void monthlyUpdate ();
        void reorderList ();
        int load (); // read from a text file
        void unload (); // write to a text file
    public:
        AppClass ();
        void Run ();
};
```

### Listing 16.2    Array manager class for the supply inventory program

```
const MAX_ITEMS = 50;

class ArrayMgr
{
    private:
        int item_count;
        Item theSupplies [MAX_ITEMS];
    public:
        ArrayMgr();
        int loadArray (char []);
        void unloadArray (char []);
        int initItem (int, int, int, char []);
        int getMaxItemNumb ();
        int getCount ();
        void displayCurrent (int);
        void displayReorder (int);
        void modOnHand (int, int); // pass in array index and new value
};
```

actually stored as one—the ASCII code for null. The \ preceding the 0 is the escape character, telling the compiler that what follows isn't a zero, but should instead be interpreted as a special character.

When defining an array to hold a string, you must allocate one extra element beyond the maximum number of characters in the string to hold the terminating null. For example, if you want to define a 12-character string, you will use the following declaration:

```
char oneLine [13];
```

Although the storage space is 13 characters long, a string needn't use all of it. As you can see in Figure 16.2, a string occupies only as much of the allocated storage space as needed to hold its characters. The null in the last position simply marks the ending position, wherever it may fall.

**Figure 16.2   String storage in main memory**

0                                                                    12

| S | H | O | R | T |   | S | T | R | I | N | G | \0 |

| S | H | O | R | T | E | R | \0 |   |   |   |   |   |

**Note**

The special way in which strings are stored means that you can't use the normal operators for operations such as assignment and logical comparisons. Because a string is an array and its name is a main memory address, if you attempt to assign a value using the assignment operator you'll be assigning an address to the variable, rather than changing its contents. If you use the comparison operators with a string name, you'll be comparing the address of the string, not its contents. You'll therefore be using functions from the C libraries to perform string operations.

If a program contains many strings that need the same amount of storage space, you can simplify string declaration by defining a new data type with `typedef`. (As you will see later in this chapter, this is particularly useful for working with arrays of strings.) To define a "string" data type, use something like

```
typedef char string[81];
```

The result is a data type named `string` that can be used to define other variables, just like any of the simple variable types.

The class for the supply inventory program (Listing 16.3) uses an 80-character string to store the supply item's description. As you can see from the header file, the remainder of the variables are integers.

## Listing 16.3    supplies.h

```
class Item
{
    private:
        int Item_numb, On_hand, Reorder_pt;
        char Desc[81];

    public:
        Item(); // constructor
        void InitItem (int, int, int, char[]);
        int getItem_numb ();
        int getOn_hand ();
        int getReorder_pt ();
        char * getDesc ();
        void ModOn_hand(int);
};
```

Because a string is really an array of characters, C++ compilers don't detect operations that attempt to assign or retrieve values beyond the end of a string. The name of an array (or the first element in an array) is a pointer to the array's starting location in main memory. Access to other elements in the array is computed by multiplying the number of bytes occupied by an element by the element number and then adding that to the array's starting address. This is exactly the way a C++ program accesses data in any other type of array.

If a program does store data beyond the end of a string, it will overwrite the storage for another variable, just as happens when you overflow any other array. With strings, however, the result can be rather devastating if the overflow erases the null that marks the end of a string. Remember: A C++ program looks for the "next" null to detect the end of a string, regardless of how many bytes the next null might be from the beginning of a string.

To make this a bit clearer, take a look at Figure 16.3. At the left you will see some consecutive memory locations that have been used to store two strings, Sample1 and Sample2. Both have been declared to hold a maximum of seven characters (eight memory locations including the terminating null). The program manipulating these strings performs a strcpy operation, placing "This is a test" into Sample1. Although the string constant is longer than the amount of space declared for `Sample1`, the computer executes the function. As a result, the string overlays the original values for `Sample2`. The effect is to place "This is a test" in `Sample1` and "a test" in `Sample2`.

**Figure 16.3  The effect of string overflow**

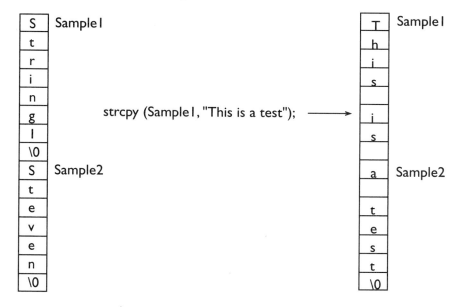

The most common indication that a program has overflowed a string storage location is when the values of variables change without direct modification by a program. To identify where the problem is occurring, use a debugger and view the contents of variables whose contents are mysteriously changing. Step through the program line by line, checking to see which action causes the value of the variables to change. In many cases, it will be a statement that assigns a value to a string. Once you know which string is at fault, you can check the length of the string's array against the length of values being assigned to that array.

## Accessing Strings

As arrays of characters, string variables behave much like other arrays. The name of the string variable represents the starting address of the string in main memory. Each individual character in the string can also be accessed like a single element in any other type of array. For example, `arrayName[0]` is a single-character variable that also happens to be the first element in a string. You can assign a value to it just as you would any other simple variable or array element:

```
arrayName[0] = 'J';
```

In contrast, `arrayName` represents the starting address of the array. You can also obtain the starting address of the array by using the notation `&arrayName[0]`. The ampersand operator tells the computer that you want the address of a variable rather than its contents. That being the case, the notation `&arrayName[5]` gives you the starting address of a substring of the original that begins at the sixth position in the string and continues until the terminating null. (You will learn more about using this operator in Chapter 17.)

## Initializing and Assigning Values to Strings

Strings can be initialized when they are declared, just like any other variable. However, you can't assign a value to a string using an assignment operator; you must use a library function for that purpose.

## Initializing Strings

To initialize a string at the time it is declared, surround the string with double quotes and assign it to the string variable, as in

```
char menuTitle[] = "MAIN MENU";
```

Notice that when you initialize a string in this way, you don't need to tell C++ how much space to allocate for the string array. The compiler will allocate exactly enough space to hold the string.

There is a very important difference in surrounding a single character with single quotes and with double quotes. If you initialize a variable with

```
char yes_no = 'y';
```

you are requesting a single-byte storage location. The single quotes generate a simple character variable, without the trailing null. However, if you initialize a variable with

```
char yes_no[] = "y";
```

you are requesting two bytes of storage, one for the character and the other for the terminating null.

## Assigning Values to Strings

To assign a value to a string, you must use the strcpy function. Like most other string functions, its prototype is in the header file *string.h*. The function has the general syntax

```
strcpy (destination_string, source_string);
```

The destination string is a string variable. The source string can be another string variable or a string constant (characters surrounded by double quotes).

The supply inventory program uses the strcpy function in its constructor and in the member function that initializes an object. (You can find those functions, along with the rest of the program's member functions, in Listing 16.4.) Notice that in the constructor, the strcpy function places a null (the characters \0 surrounded by single quotes) in the Desc variable. In the InitItem function, however, the strcpy function assigns the value in the input parameter (iDesc) to the object's variable.

If you don't want to copy an entire string, but just part of a string, use strncpy, a variant of strcpy that lets you specify exactly how many characters you want to copy:

```
strncpy(destination_string,source_string,#characters);
```

For example, if string1 contains "This is a test," then the following expression copies "This is ":

```
strncpy (string2, string1, 7)
```

To change the starting position in the source string, use the ampersand notation to specify a specific character with which to begin:

```
strncpy (string2, &string1[7], 7)
```

## Listing 16.4  supplies.cpp

```cpp
#include "supplies.h"
#include <string.h>


Item::Item()
{
    Item_numb = 0;
    On_hand = 0;
    Reorder_pt = 0;
    strcpy (Desc, '\0');
}


void Item::InitItem (int iItem_numb, int iOn_hand, int iReorder_pt,
    char iDesc[])
{
    Item_numb = iItem_numb;
    On_hand = iOn_hand;
    Reorder_pt = iReorder_pt;
    strcpy (Desc, iDesc);
}


int Item::getItem_numb ()
    { return Item_numb; }


int Item::getOn_hand ()
    { return On_hand; }

int Item::getReorder_pt ()
    { return Reorder_pt; }


char * Item::getDesc ()
    { return Desc; }


void Item::ModOn_hand (int newAmount)
    { On_hand = newAmount; }
```

After the preceding function call is completed, string2 contains " a test" (including the blank preceding *a*). The strncpy function copies as many characters as specified in the function call or until the computer encounters a terminating null in the source string.

## Concatenating Strings

A common operation performed with strings is to create a long string by combining two strings, one after the other. Known as *concatenation*, this operation copies the source string onto the end of the destination string. The destination string's storage allocation must therefore be long enough to hold the combined string.

The strcat function has the general syntax

```
strcat (destination_string, source_string);
```

As an example, consider the following:

```
char One[30] = "First string";
char Two[30] = "Second string";
strcat (One, Two);
```

The contents of Two will be unaltered; the contents of Two will be "First stringSecond string." To get a space between the words, it needs to be inserted explicitly. If a program executes

```
strcat (One, " ");
strcat (One, Two);
```

the result will be "First string Second string."

To explore how string concatenation can be used, let's look at a program that takes data about a customer stored in individual variables and formats output strings that have correct spacing for a mailing label. This is a common task that many business programs perform. In general, data are stored in the smallest units possible and are combined for output. For example, rather than storing city, state, and zipcode in one variable, they are stored in three. This makes it easier to sort and search the data on any one of the variables.

As you can see in Figure 16.4, this program asks the user for the individual elements of the customer information and then displays a properly formatting mailing label. The program is based on the Customer class (Listing 16.5), which has individual variables for the pieces of the customer's information and three member functions (a constructor, a function to initialize an object, and a function to format and display the label)

The member functions for this program can be found in Listing 16.6. The constructor copies a null (two double quotes directly next to one another) into each variable; the init function copies data from input strings into each

Figure 16.4   Output of the address label program

```
First name: John
Last name: Doe
Street: 125 85th Place
City: Anytown
State: MA
Zip: 12346


John Doe
125 85th Place
Anytown, MA 12346
```

Listing 16.5   labels.h

```cpp
typedef char string80[81];
typedef char string50[51];
typedef char string25[26];

class Customer
{
    private:
        string25 first, last, city;
        string50 street;
        char state[3], zip[6];
    public:
        Customer ();
        void init (string25, string25, string50, string25, char [], char[]);
        void displayFormatted ();
};
```

variable. Formatting and display of the mailing label occurs in displayFor-
matted. (The cout statements appear inside the function because we haven't
yet discussed returning strings from functions.)

As you study displayString, notice that when the function formats
a line for the address label, it begins by *copying* the first piece of data into the
output string. This is essential because you want to erase any previous contents
in the output string. Then, the remainder of the data are *concatenated* onto the
string. Formatting, such as blanks and commas, are added as literal strings;
other values are taken from class variables.

The application class Run function that drives the address label program
can be found in Listing 16.7. It collects the data used to initialize the object
onePerson and then calls the init function to send the input data to the
object. (We'll talk about the string input statements used in this function a bit

## Listing 16.6   labels.cpp

```cpp
#include <iostream.h>
#include <string.h>
#include "label.h"

Customer::Customer()
{
    strcpy (first,"");
    strcpy (last,"");
    strcpy (street,"");
    strcpy (city,"");
    strcpy (state,"");
    strcpy (zip,"");
}

void Customer::init (string25 ifirst, string25 ilast, string50 istreet,
    string25 icity, char istate[], char izip[])
{
    strcpy (first,ifirst);
    strcpy (last,ilast);
    strcpy (street,istreet);
    strcpy (city,icity);
    strcpy (state,istate);
    strcpy (zip,izip);
}

void Customer::displayFormatted ()
{
    string50 wholeName;
    string80 CSZ;

    cout << endl << endl;
    strcpy (wholeName, first);
    strcat (wholeName, " ");
    strcat (wholeName, last);
    cout << wholeName << endl;
    cout << street << endl;

    strcpy (CSZ, city);
    strcat (CSZ, ", ");
    strcat (CSZ, state);
    strcat (CSZ, " ");
    strcat (CSZ, zip);
    cout << CSZ;
}
```

later in this chapter.) In this case, the strings are passed by name, just as any other array. The function finishes by calling the `displayFormatted` function to perform this program's actual work.

**Listing 16.7    Application class Run function for the address label program**

```
void AppClass::Run ()
{
    Customer onePerson;  // delcare an object

    string25 ifirst, ilast, icity;
    string50 istreet;
    char istate[3], izip[6];

    cout << "First name: ";
    cin.getline (ifirst,26);
    cout << "Last name: ";
    cin.getline (ilast,26);
    cout << "Street: ";
    cin.getline (istreet, 51);
    cout << "City: ";
    cin.getline (icity, 26);
    cout << "State: ";
    cin.getline (istate, 3);
    cout << "Zip: ";
    cin.getline (izip, 6);

    onePerson.init (ifirst, ilast, istreet, icity, istate, izip);
    onePerson.displayFormatted();
}
```

## Finding the Length of a String

Because the end of a string is marked with a null, a string doesn't have to fill every position in its array. After you have been playing with strings using the `strcpy` and `strcat` functions, you may not know exactly how many characters are in a string. Nonetheless, you may need to access each character in the string individually. The easiest way to do this is to set up a `for` loop that begins at array element 0 and continues until it reaches the length of the string.

The key to finding the length of a string is the `strlen` function. Its only input parameter is the name of a string variable:

```
strlen (string_variable_name)
```

It returns an integer that represents the number of characters in the string, excluding the trailing null. In other words, if a string variable contains `abcdefghij\0`, the string length is 10, not 11.

To use the function, you can assign its result to an integer variable or place it in any expression that expects an integer. For example, the following code displays each character of a string on a separate line:

```
char aString[50] = "This is a test";
for (int i = 0; i <= strlen(aString); i++)
    cout << "Character #: " << aString[i] << endl;
```

## Comparing Strings

Because strings are arrays, they can't be compared like simple data types. If you attempt something like `if (Array1 > Array 2)`, C++ will assume that you are asking for an analysis of the starting addresses of the arrays, not their contents.

The solution is a function called `strcmp`, which has the following general syntax:

```
result = strcmp(first_string, second_string);
```

If the two strings are identical, `result` is 0. However, if `first_string` follows `second_string` in alphabetical order, the result is greater than 0 (usually 1); if `first_string` precedes `second_string`, the result is less than 0 (usually -1).

**Warning**

Although most `strcmp` functions return 1 for a greater than result and -1 for a less than result, don't count on it; you never know when you'll encounter one that returns some other value. It is therefore much better programming to test for greater than 0 and less than 0 rather than equal to 1 or -1.

As an example of comparing strings, we'll be looking at a program that compares dates stored as strings in the format YY/MM/DD. (Because string comparisons are made in alphabetical rather than numeric order, this is the only string date format that will also be evaluated in correct chronological order.)

**Note**

The date comparison program is simply a demonstration of string comparison; it isn't a good way to manage dates because YY/MM/DD isn't a commonly used date format. You will see a much more effective way to handle dates in Chapter 20.

The program (Figure 16.5) collects a date from the user that it stores in an object created from a class named Date (Listing 16.8). It then stores that date in a class object. The program collects a second date from the user, compares it to the date stored in the object, and then reports back to the user which date comes first.

Figure 16.5   Output of the date comparison program

```
Enter a date in the format YY/MM/DD: 96/10/05
Enter a date to compare: 95/09/12
The date in the class is later.
```

Listing 16.8   date.h

```
const BAD_MON = 1;
const BAD_DAY = 2;
const OK = 0;

class Date
{
    private:
        char stringDate[9];
    public:
        Date ();
        int init (char []);
        int compareDates (char []);
};
```

The function that initializes an object created from the Date class (init) performs some basic validation on the input date. It returns an integer that indicates whether the month or day is out of range. (The logic is incomplete, however, because it doesn't match the number of days in a month to the specific month.) As you can see in Listing 16.9, the program displays an error message and terminates if the date intended for storage in the class isn't valid.

**Listing 16.9   Application class Run function for the date comparison program**

```
void AppClass::Run ()
{
    char iDate[9];
    int result;
    Date oneDay; // declare an object

    cout << "Enter a date in the format YY/MM/DD: ";
    cin.getline (iDate,9);
    result = oneDay.init (iDate);
    if (result == BAD_MON)
    {
        cout << iDate << " contains an invalid month";
        return;
    }
    else if (result == BAD_DAY)
    {
        cout << iDate << "contains an invalid day.";
        return;
    }

    cout << "Enter a date to compare: ";
    cin.getline (iDate,9);
    result = oneDay.compareDates (iDate);

    if (result == 0)
        cout << "The dates are the same.";
    else if (result < 0)
        cout << "The date in the class is earlier.";
    else if (result > 0)
        cout << "The date in the class is later.";
    else
        cout << "An error has occurred when comparing strings.";
}
```

After initializing the object, the Run function collects a date for comparison from the user and then calls the compareDates member function to perform the comparison. It finishes by evaluating the result returned by compareDates and displays an appropriate message to the user.

The member functions that perform the actual work for this program can be found in Listing 16.10. First take a look at the init function. It uses strncpy to isolate the characters for the month into a separate variable. It then compares those two characters to string constants that represent valid months. Assuming the check for the month is passed, the function then isolates the characters that represent the day and compares them to string constants that represent valid months. If the check for the day is passed, the function finishes by copying the input date into the object and returns a value that signals the calling function that the date is valid.

Listing 16.10    date.cpp

```
#include <string.h>
#include "dates.h"

Date::Date()
    { strcpy (stringDate,""); }

int Date::init (char iDate[])
{
    char MM[3], DD[3];

    strncpy (MM,&iDate[3],2);
    if (strcmp(MM,"01") == -1 || strcmp (MM,"12") == 1)
        return BAD_MON;
    strncpy (DD,&iDate[6],2); // isolate the day
    if (strcmp(DD,"01") == -1 || strcmp (DD,"31") == 1)
        return BAD_DAY;
    strcpy (stringDate,iDate);
    return OK;
}

int Date::compareDates (char iDate[])
    { return strcmp (stringDate,iDate); }
```

The compareDates function is quite simple. It performs a strcmp and returns the result. Why then use this function rather than just performing the comparison in the main function? Because the stringDate variable is a private variable and therefore not directly accessible to a function outside the class. It would need to be sent to the calling function by a member function. It is therefore simpler to perform the comparison in a member function.

## String I/O

Strings present special challenges for stream I/O because streams use spaces or commas to separate values. Therefore, although you can use cin with the stream extraction operator to read in one word, you can't use it to read in an entire sentence. The same problem arises when you are attempting to read data from a text file. In this section you will be introduced to the special techniques used to manage stream I/O when strings are involved.

## Interactive Output

To display the contents of a string variable on the screen, simply insert the variable's name into the `cout` stream. For example, assuming that `iDesc` has been declared as an 80-character string,

```
cout << iDesc;
```

writes the contents of the variable on the screen. The `cout` stream displays characters until it reaches the terminating null. It does not pad the output field to the width of the array.

## Interactive Input

Although there are several ways to perform interactive string input, probably the easiest to use is the stream input `getline` function, which you can use with the `cin` stream object. For example, the supply inventory program accepts a value into the `iDesc` variable with the following:

```
cout << "Description: ";
cin.getline (iDesc, 81);
```

When performing keyboard input, the `getline` function takes two parameters: the name of a string variable into which the computer should place the string and the maximum number of characters to be read. The computer will then accept characters until either the user presses Enter or the maximum number of characters has been entered. Because the press of the Enter key is counted as a character, the number of characters entered as a parameter should be one more than the maximum number of characters you actually want to allow in your string. Note that the Enter is not translated into a null. However, the computer does automatically insert the null when it stores the string in the variable you provided.

You can combine `getline` with the function that checks the length of a string (`strlen`) to let a user indicate the end of input with a press of the Enter key. The `strlen` function returns an integer value, the number of characters in a string, not including the terminating null. Therefore, if a program checks the length of a string and finds that the length is zero, the user has pressed Enter without entering any characters. The supply inventory program's application class's `Run` function (Listing 16.11) uses this technique for interactive input of new supply items.

Listing 16.11    AppClass::newItem for the supply inventory program

```
void AppClass::newItem()
{
    int iItem_numb, iOn_hand, iReorder_pt;
    char iDesc[81];

    cout << "\nDescription: ";
    cin.getline (iDesc,81);

    // keep going until "Enter" signals end of input
    while (strlen(iDesc) != 0)
    {
        // generate unique item number
        iItem_numb = itemArray.getMaxItemNumb() + 1;
        cout << "Item number: " << iItem_numb << endl;
        cout << "Amount currently in inventory: ";
        cin >> iOn_hand;
        cout << "Reorder point: ";
        cin >> iReorder_pt;

        int result = itemArray.initItem (iItem_numb, iOn_hand,
            iReorder_pt, iDesc);
        if (!result)
        {
            cout << "\nThe array is full; can't add any more items.";
            return;
        }

        cout << "\nDescription: ";
        cin.getline (iDesc,81);
    }

}
```

Notice that this function collects a value for iDesc before entering the while loop. This gives the user a chance to prevent any input. If the user presses Enter in response to the first cin.getline, the while loop never executes.

## Text File Output

When you insert a string into an output stream, the terminating null isn't included. That means that when you write a string to a text file, you must explicitly write the null. In addition, you need to explicitly write a blank after each value that comes from a simple variable. For example, the supply inventory program's array manager uses the code in Listing 16.12 to write the contents of one Item object to a text file.

Listing 16.12    ArrayMgr::unloadArray

```
void ArrayMgr::unloadArray (char fileName [])
{
    ofstream writeFile (fileName);
    if (writeFile.is_open())
        cout << "Unexpected file error occurred when opening output file.";
    else
    {
        // write the number of items in the array
        writeFile << item_count << ' ';
        for (int i = 0; i <= item_count; i++)
        {
            writeFile << theSupplies[i].getDesc() << '\0';
            writeFile << theSupplies[i].getItem_numb() << ' ';
            writeFile << theSupplies[i].getOn_hand() << ' ';
            writeFile << theSupplies[i].getReorder_pt() << ' ';

        }
    }
}
```

Notice that the unloadArray function begins its writing with the number of objects in the array. This integer is placed at the beginning of the file, and is followed by all the object data. Storing this value will greatly simplify reading in objects.

## File Input

Input from text files that contain strings is subject to the same problems as keyboard input: stream extraction assumes that a space marks the end of a value. The solution is to use a version of the getline function to read a block of data. When reading from a file, the getline function has the following general syntax:

```
stream_name.getline (buffer, size, terminator);
```

The "buffer" is the string variable that will hold the result of the input. The size parameter is the number of characters to be read. Unlike keyboard input, this value doesn't need to include extra space for an Enter or a null; it should be exactly equal to the number of characters.

The third parameter is optional. If included, it contains the character that marks the end of the string. In that case, the size parameter indicates the maximum number of characters to be read; getline reads characters either until it encounters the terminator or until the maximum number of characters has been read.

The supply inventory program's array manager uses the code in Listing 16.13 to read one Item object from a file. Notice that the first thing the function does after opening the file is to read the number of objects from the file. The function can then use that count in the for loop that reads objects from the file into the array of objects.

Inside the for loop, the first statement is a call to the getline function that reads either 80 characters or until a null is encountered. The second statement uses the stream extraction operator to retrieve the three integer values. At this point, the space marking the end of the reorder point value is still in the file. If the program issues another getline call immediately, the string read in will have a leading blank that really isn't part of the string. (No, you can't leave out the final blank; it is needed to mark the end of the third integer value.)

The trick is therefore to read the blank, placing it in a variable whose value is probably never used. The easiest way to read the character is to use the ifstream member function get, which reads just one character.

**Note**

To be completely accurate, in some circumstances you can get away without a blank between the end of a number and the beginning of a string. The program stops reading the number when it encounters a character that isn't part of a legal number (for example, a letter). However, this isn't a good programming practice because there is always the chance that a string will begin with a number or a period. It also introduces ambiguity into the file. If you look at it with a text editor, for example, it will be difficult to determine where one data value ends and another begins. Therefore, always put a blank after a number and before a string. Use the get function to gobble up the extra blank during input as demonstrated in this chapter.

## Listing 16.13   ArrayMgr::loadArray

```
int ArrayMgr::loadArray (char fileName [])
{

    int iItem_numb, iOn_hand, iReorder_pt;
    char iDesc[81], white_space, yes_no;

    ifstream readFile (fileName);

    // handle situation where data file can't be found
    if (!readFile.is_open())
    {
        cout << "No data file could be found. Do you want to continue? ";
        cin >> yes_no;
        if (toupper(yes_no) == 'N')
            return FALSE;
    }
    else
    {
        // The following strategy simplifies working with text files that
        // contain strings

        readFile >> item_count; // get number of objects from beginning of file

        for (int i = 0; i <= item_count ; i++) // load data in from the file
        {
            readFile.getline (iDesc, 80, '\0');
            readFile >> iItem_numb >> iOn_hand >> iReorder_pt;
            readFile.get (white_space);
            theSupplies[i].InitItem (iItem_numb, iOn_hand, iReorder_pt, iDesc);
        }

        if (!readFile)   // file error occurred
        {
            cout << "Unexpected file input error occurred.";
            cout << "Do you want to continue? ";
            cin >> yes_no;
            if (toupper(yes_no) == 'N')
            return FALSE;
        }
    }
    return TRUE;

}
```

## Strings and Functions

Passing a string into a function as a formal parameter is straightforward. However, returning a string from a function with the `return` statement can't be performed without using a pointer. You will see how to perform both of these actions in this section.

## Passing Strings into Functions

Because strings are arrays, they are passed into functions just like other arrays. Therefore, using the name of an array as a formal parameter passes the starting address of the array in main memory. Given that this is a pass by reference, any modification you make to the string in the receiving function is made in main memory to the string's original storage location. The change is therefore available to the calling function.

The supply inventory program's application class uses this technique to send the name of its input and output files to the array manager. For example, consider the application class's `load` function in Listing 16.14. The function asks the user for the name of the file, accepts the file name from the keyboard into a string variable using `getline`, and then sends that file name into the `loadArray` function by placing its name in the function call's parameter list.

Listing 16.14    AppClass::load

```
int AppClass::load()
{
    char fileName[81];
    int result;

    cout << "\nEnter the data file name: ";
    cin.getline (fileName,81);
    return itemArray.loadArray (fileName);
}
```

## Returning Strings Via the return Statement

When you return an array from a function using the `return` statement, you actually return the array's address, not the data themselves. This value is a pointer to the array's location. You must therefore use pointer notation when declaring a function that returns an array. As a first example, consider the `getDesc` member function used by the `Item` class. Its prototype is as follows:

```
char * getDesc ();
```

The * in the return data type means that you will be returning a pointer. In this case, it's a pointer to character data.

**Note**

There is a bit of a "which came first? the chicken or the egg?" problem when it comes to teaching C++ arrays and pointers. It's tough to explain pointers without first knowing about arrays, but it's also virtually impossible to deal with arrays without dealing with pointers. This book has chosen to look at arrays first. You will therefore find much more about pointers in Chapter 17.

The function declaration also uses the pointer notation for its return data type.

```
char * Item::getDesc ()
{
    return Desc;
}
```

To return the Desc variable, which holds the description of an office supply item, the name of the variable is placed after the return statement. As you would expect, this returns the address of the starting point of the array.

## Arrays of Strings: A Generic Menu Class

The menu classes that we have used to this point have a major drawback: They're not reusable. In other words, each menu class has been specifically designed for one specific program. Unless two programs need exactly the same menu options, they can't share the same menu class.

This situation practically defeats the purpose of having a menu class. What we really need is a menu class that can be used by any program with a text-based interface. All we should have to do is supply the class with the name of the menu and its options. Now that you know something about strings, we can do exactly that.

In Listing 16.15 you will find the header file for a menu class that can be reused. The name of the menu is stored in the variable menutitle, a 25-character string. The number of items in the menu is stored in count.

The text of the menu options is stored in an array of strings menuitems. An array of strings is a two-dimensional array in which each row is one string. Although you can access such an array using two index values, it

Listing 16.15   menu.h

```
const MENU_ITEM_LEN = 41;
const MAX_MENU_ITEMS = 20;

typedef char menuoption [MENU_ITEM_LEN];

class menu      // class for a menu of up to MAX_ITEMS
{
    private:
        char menutitle[26];
        menuoption menuitems [MAX_MENU_ITEMS];   // array to hold the items
        int count; // # of options in the menu

    public:
        menu (char [], menuoption [], int); // constructor
        void displaymenu (void);
        int chooseoption (void);
};
```

is generally easier to eliminate the column subscript by using a `typedef` statement to create a string data type. As an example, consider the following statements:

```
typedef char string [81];
string children [10];
```

The `children` array holds 10 strings, each of which can be up to 80 characters long plus a terminating null. To reference the third string in the array, you would then use `children[2]`. This produces the starting address of the array's third element, which in turn is an array 81 elements long.

The `menu` class defines a data type called `menuoption`, a 40-character string. The `menuitems` array therefore consists of up to 20 rows of 40-character strings.

A `menu` object knows how to do three things: initialize itself, display its title and options, and accept a choice of menu option from a user. As you can see in Listing 16.16, the constructor requires a string for the menu's title, the array containing the menu options (an array of strings), and a count of the number of menu items.

From where do these values come? Typically, specifications of elements of the user interface are placed in a *resource file*. (A *resource* is a program element, such as a menu or window, used by a program.) Although resource definitions could be placed in the main function file or in the application class

Listing 16.16 menu.cpp

```cpp
#include <iostream.h>
#include <string.h>
#include "menu.h"

menu::menu (char title [], menuoption menutext[], int numbitems)
{
    strcpy (menutitle, title);
    count = numbitems;
    for (int i = 0; i <= count; i++)
        strcpy (menuitems[i], menutext[i]);
}

void menu::displaymenu ()
{
    cout << endl;
    cout << "---------- " << menutitle << " ----------" << endl << endl;
    for (int i = 0; i <= count; i++)
        cout << menuitems[i] << endl;
    cout << endl;
}

int menu::chooseoption ()
{
    int choice;

    cout << "Enter an option: ";
    cin >> choice;
    return choice;
}
```

implementation file, the main function and application class files will be
cleaner and shorter if resources are defined in their own file. In addition, keeping resources separate from the code that uses them hides the details of the
interface from the rest of the program, making it easier to change resources
without modifying other parts of the program. Resource files also make it
much easier to port a program from one graphic user interface to another and
provide a way to incorporate resources developed by other programmers into a
program.

The resource file for the supply inventory program appears in
Listing 16.17. In general, a resource file contains one string for each menu title
and one array of menu options for each menu. Notice that to initialize the
arrays of strings, the values are placed inside braces and that the individual
strings are separated by commas. The resource file also takes care of initializing

variables for the number of options in each menu. In addition, it sets up constants that can be used in switch statements to make identifying menu options easier.

## Listing 16.17   menu.rsc

```
#include "menu.h"

menuoption maintitle = "MAIN MENU";
menuoption mainmenu [] = {"1. Enter a new item",
                          "2. Update inventory",
                          "3. View the reorder list",
                          "9. Quit"};

int mainmenucount = 4;

const NEW_ITEM = 1;
const UPDATE = 2;
const VIEW_LIST = 3;
const MAIN_QUIT = 9;
```

How a resource file is used is highly dependent on the environment in which you are working. In this particular case, the resource file is actually nothing more than a special-purpose header. It is therefore included in the application class's implementation file with a #include directive. The variables defined in the resource file are then available to the application object, which can use them when it declares menu objects.

To see how the supply inventory program handles the menu object, take a look at the application class's Run function in Listing 16.18. The function first declares an object of the menu class (mainMenu). The variables declared in the resource file (maintitle, mainmenu, and maincount) are passed in as parameters.

When the menu object is created, its constructor copies the input data into the class's variables. In Listing 16.16 notice how the menu items are copied from the input array into the class's array. Each string is copied individually using strcpy. Although this is technically a two-dimensional array, the program can handle it as if it were a one-dimensional array, treating each row as a string.

## Listing 16.18    AppClass::Run for the supply inventory program

```
#include "menu.rsc"

void AppClass::Run()
{
    menu mainMenu (maintitle, mainmenu, mainmenucount); // create a menu object

    int result = load(); // read data from file
    if (!result) return; // no file; user chose to quit

    int choice = 0;
    while (choice != 9)
    {
        mainMenu.displaymenu();
        choice = mainMenu.chooseoption();
        switch (choice)
        {
            case NEW_ITEM:
                newItem();  // enter new items
                break;
            case UPDATE:
                monthlyUpdate();
                break;
            case VIEW_LIST:
                reorderList();
                break;
            case MAIN_QUIT:
                break;
            default:
                cout << "\nYou've entered an unavailable option.";
        }
    }
}
```

To display a menu, the application object uses the menu object's dis-playmenu function. If you look at Listing 16.16, you'll see that the menu object uses a for loop to access each string in the array of strings in order. Placing the name of a string array element in a cout stream causes the program to display the string.

To let the user make a choice from a menu, the application object calls the menu object's chooseoption function. As you can see in Listing 16.16, this function simply prompts the user to make a choice, collects the value from the keyboard, and returns it to the calling function.

Why should you bother to implement menus in this way? First, once you have the menu class and its member functions declared, you can use them in any text-based program, without having to rewrite menu code each time you create a new program. All you have to do is create a resource file that is tailored to a given program's specific needs. In fact, we will be using this menu class in nearly every sample program in this book from now on. Because you know how the class works, we won't bother to discuss it directly.

Using the menu class also further separates platform-dependent I/O code from other parts of the program. Should you choose to port your program to another environment, you can use other menu objects and resource files, reducing (but not eliminating) the amount of modification you need to make to other parts of the program.

## Summary

C++ implements strings as arrays of characters. Each string is terminated by a null, which is represented as the character '\0'. An array declared to contain a string should therefore be one character longer than needed to provide room for the terminating null.

The fact that strings are arrays has numerous implications for how they are stored and manipulated. In particular, most string operations are performed using C library functions rather than the standard operators. The most commonly used functions include

- `strcpy` (copy a string from one storage location to another)
- `strcat` (concatenate one string on the end of another)
- `strlen` (determine the number of characters in a string)
- `strcmp` (compare to strings to determine their relative position in an alphabetical ordering sequence)

String I/O is complicated by the presence of blanks, which the default I/O streams view as the end of a value. To input an entire string from the keyboard, use the `cin.getline` function, which takes everything up to the press of the Enter key as part of one string. To output a string to the screen, simply include the string variable's name in the `cout` stream.

When working with text files, strings must be explicitly followed by nulls; the values of simple variables written to the same file must be explicitly followed by blanks. When reading such files, the blank preceding a string must be read and discarded. The strings themselves are read with the `ifstream` member function `getline`.

Like other arrays, the name of a string variable is the address of the beginning of the array in main memory. All strings are passed to functions by reference. When a string is a return value from a function, its address is passed to the calling function.

Arrays of strings are two-dimensional arrays. Working with them can be simplified by using `typedef` to define a data type for a string, which can then be used when declaring the array. This makes it possible to reference entire strings within the array using only a single index.

## Exercises

1.  Create a class that holds a string of up to 80 characters. Include a member function that reverses the order of the characters in the string. Write a program that demonstrates that the reversal function works.

2.  Write a program that manipulates a class that stores a person's name. The name is entered in the format "Last, First." The class should include a member program that reformats the name so that it is displayed in the format "First Last." Create the program so that it demonstrates that the name reversal function works.

3.  Assume that you are an industrial spy trying to break the data encryption scheme used by one of your employer's competitors. One of your basic techniques is to examine the frequency of characters in a block of text. Create a class that holds a string of up to 256 characters. Include a member function that scans the string and counts the frequency with which each letter in the string appears. (Ignore spaces and punctuation marks; treat uppercase and lowercase letters the same.) When the scan is finished, display the frequency counts. Write a program that demonstrates that the frequency count member function works.

4. Create a class that manages a game of Hangman (the word guessing game). The class should store the solution word (the word the player is trying to guess), the correct guesses so far, the number of guesses made, and the maximum guesses allowed. (Maximum guesses are equal to the length of the solution word plus seven.) Write a program that plays the game. Create a text file for the program that contains a list of words to be used as solutions. When the program begins, read those words into an array of strings. At the beginning of each game, randomly select a word from the solutions array and store it in the game object. Member functions of the class should include evaluating a guess against the solution, storing a correct guess in its proper position in the word (use this string for output after each guess), and storing the number of guesses made. After each guess, the game object should determine the game status (won, in progress, or maximum number of guesses exceeded). After each guess that doesn't result in a win or a loss, print out the letters guessed correctly in their correct position in the word, using underscores (_) as placeholders for letters not yet guessed. Be sure to allow the player to play many games without exiting the program.

5. Write a program that performs simple arithmetic (add, subtract, multiply, divide) using Roman numerals. The class on which this program is based should include a string for a Roman numeral and an integer for its integer equivalent. The class will need functions to convert from a Roman numeral to an integer and from an integer to a Roman numeral.

   The program that manipulates objects created from the class should let users enter expressions in typical arithmetic format, such as

   XXX- XV

   The program should then scan the string to find the Roman numerals and the operator. You should consider writing functions that scan a string for a specific character and, once the character has been found, extracting parts of a string based on the position of that character in the string. (*Note*: There are C library functions that do these things, but you will learn much more about manipulating strings if you write them yourself.)

   Once the program has performed the arithmetic, it should convert the result back to a Roman numeral for display.

6. Write a program that grades true/false exams of up to 30 questions. The key to the exam should be stored in a single string, such as "TFT-FFFFFFF." Student data should be stored in objects created from a class that contains the student ID, a string for the student's responses on the exam, and the number of correct responses. The class should include a member function that scores the exam. The program that manipulates objects should include an array for student objects. After scoring all the exams, the program should prepare and display a frequency distribution of correct responses along with a display of the ID number and score for each student, sorted in descending order by score.

7. The HHH Hardware House employs a number of salespeople, each of whom works within one of the company's five sales territories. At the end of each year, the company prepares an annual sales summary. Write a program that produces this summary. The program should be based on a class that stores a salesperson's name, territory, and total sales for the year. Use an array to store objects created from the class.

   The summary report should be organized by sales territory. Within each territory, display the salespeople and their total sales, sorted in descending order by sales. Compute the total sales for each territory (displayed immediately after all the salespeople from that territory). At the end of the program, display the total sales for the entire company.

# 17

# Pointers

## OBJECTIVES

In this chapter you will learn about:
- Declaring and initializing pointer variables.
- Accessing data in pointer variables.
- Using the "this" pointer.
- Using dynamic binding to create objects and access member functions.
- Returning multiple values from functions.
- Using the addressing of I/O streams as function parameters.

As you know, a pointer is the starting address of a value in main memory. A pointer can point to a simple variable type (for example, an integer or a character), to an array, or to an object. Pointers make it possible to return more than one value from a function. They can also be used to ease and speed access to objects and arrays.

In this chapter you will be introduced to using pointers and pointer variables, manipulating pointers to access memory, using dynamic binding to create objects, and using pointers to pass values to and from functions. Chapter 19 looks at using pointers to implement a linked list, the data structure to which you were introduced in Chapter 15.

To show you how pointers work, we will be looking at a modified version of the supply inventory program to which you were introduced in Chapter 16, along with some small programs that demonstrate the use of pointers. These samples include two versions of a program that counts the number of vowels in a string. The vowel statistics program produces output like that in Figure 17.1. (The difference between the two versions of the program lies in how values are passed into and returned from a function; the output is the same.)

**Figure 17.1    Output from the vowel statistics program**

```
Enter a string of up to 80 characters:
Then, several people ran up to him and sang a joyous song

The vowels in the string are:
  A: 5
  E: 5
  I: 1
  O: 5
  U: 2

There are 18 vowels.
```

A *pointer variable* is a variable that is declared to hold a pointer to some type of data storage. The contents of a pointer variable are therefore interpreted as a main memory address rather than a data value. To make this a bit clearer, consider Figure 17.2, which contains a portion of a computer's memory. This memory segment contains a group of 16-bit integers. Therefore, the addresses on the left increase by two. (Remember that main memory addresses are assigned to individual bytes. A 16-bit integer therefore occupies two bytes, and a block of integers in main memory will have starting addresses two bytes from each other.)

Figure 17.2   Sample contents of memory locations

| Main Memory Addresses | Main Memory Contents | |
|---|---|---|
| 500 | 109 | |
| 502 | 009 | |
| 504 | 516 | |
| 506 | 010 | integer1 |
| 508 | 113 | integer2 |
| 510 | 195 | |
| 512 | 820 | |

Two of the memory locations are referenced by the variables `integer1` and `integer2`. When a program uses `integer1`, the computer accesses memory location 506 and uses the 010 that it finds in that location. By the same token, when a program uses `integer2`, the computer accesses memory location 508 and uses the 113 it finds in that location. In the next section, you will see exactly how pointer variables can provide access to the same locations but in a different way.

## Declaring Pointer Variables

Pointer variables can be local variables or they can be part of a class. To declare a pointer variable for either purpose, use the following general syntax:

```
data_type * variable_name;
```

The asterisk tells the compiler that the following variable will hold a pointer to the specified type of storage. For example, you could declare pointer variables that would ultimately hold the addresses of `integer1` and `integer2` with

```
int * integer1Ptr, * integer2Ptr;
```

Although there is no formal naming convention for pointer variables, we often append the characters *Ptr* to the name of the variable to which the pointer variable will point.

One version of the vowel statistics includes the following declarations in its application class:

```
int A, * APtr, E, * EPtr, I, * IPtr, O, * OPtr,
    U, * UPtr, theTotal, * TotalPtr;
```

This statement sets aside six integer variables (A, E, I, O, U, theTotal) that will hold the counts of the vowels in a string. It also sets aside a pointer variable for each integer variable (APtr, EPtr, IPtr, OPtr, Uptr, TotalPtr). Notice that an asterisk precedes each pointer variable.

## Pointers to Objects

One of the most common uses of pointer variables in an object-oriented program is to hold pointers to objects. For example, the array manager of the pointer-based version of the supply inventory program uses an array of pointers to hold references to Item objects:

```
Item * theSupplies[MAX_ITEMS];
```

The preceding declaration sets up an array named theSupplies. Each element in the array contains a pointer to an object of class Item. Each of those pointers indicates the starting location in memory for an object created from the Item class. (The objects are created with dynamic binding, and their addresses are assigned to elements in this array. You will see how to do this later in this chapter.)

## Initializing Pointer Variables

To initialize a pointer variable, a program uses the assignment operator to copy the address of a storage location into the pointer variable. Placing an ampersand (&) in front of a variable name indicates that you want the address of a variable rather than its contents. For example, you could initialize the integer pointer variables that we've been considering with

```
integer1Ptr = &integer1;
integer2Ptr = &integer2;
```

After the initialization, `integer1Ptr` contains 506; `integer2Ptr` contains 508.

The following statements from one version of the vowel statistics program place the address of an integer variable into a variable that holds an integer pointer:

```
APtr = &A;
EPtr = &E;
IPtr = &I;
OPtr = &O;
UPtr = &U;
TotalPtr = &theTotal;
```

A pointer variable can also be initialized by assigning it the result of a function that returns a pointer. As you will see shortly, this is exactly what happens when you create an object using dynamic binding.

Because the name of an array is a pointer to the start of the array in main memory, you can use the name of an array, without any array indexes, as if it were a pointer variable. However, as you will see shortly, some uses of pointers include modifying the value of the pointer itself. If the pointer variable happens to be the name of an array, changing it in any way will cause the program to lose track of where the array's contents are actually stored. To avoid that problem, declare a separate pointer variable to hold the array's address and initialize it to the address of the array:

```
char stringArray[81];
char * stringArrayPtr;
stringArrayPtr = stringArray;
```

Once `stringArrayPtr` has been initialized, it points to the same location as `stringArray`. However, because `stringArrayPtr` is a separate variable from `stringArray`, you can modify the contents of `stringArrayPtr` without losing track of the original beginning of the array.

## Accessing Values Using the Contents of Pointer Variables

To access a value in a location that a pointer variable points to, you must tell the C++ compiler that you want the contents of the storage location rather than the address of the location. This is known as *dereferencing* the pointer.

Dereferencing is performed by placing an asterisk in front of the pointer variable's name. For example, you can gain access to the contents of `integer1Ptr` and `integer2Ptr` with:

```
*integer1Ptr
*integer2Ptr
```

Using the first expression in a program provides 010 (the contents of location 506); using the second expression provides 113 (the contents of location 508).

Dereferencing can occur on the right or left side of an assignment operator. For example, the member function that computes vowel statistics initializes the variables that count the number of vowels with the following statements:

```
*A = 0;
*E = 0;
*I = 0;
*O = 0;
*U = 0;
*total = 0;
```

As you have just seen, the * operator has two distinct meanings, depending on how it is used. In a declaration, it means "pointer to"; in an executable statement, when it is being used to dereference a pointer variable, it means "the contents of." Telling the difference can sometimes be a bit tricky. Assume that you see the following statements in a C++ program:

```
int count;
int * countPtr = &count;
```

The first statement is a simple declaration. However, the second contains both a declaration (`int * countPtr`) and an executable statement (`countPtr = &count`). A compiler, however, views this entire statement as a declaration. In other words, the variable is being declared and initialized in the declaration. Therefore the * is interpreted as declaring a pointer variable to which the address of `count` is assigned.

Why bother to use a pointer variable? Wouldn't it be easier to simply use the original variable? If a variable is going to be used locally within only one function, then it is certainly easier to use the variable without working with a pointer. However, if the variable needs to be passed into a function where it will be modified and returned, you may want to use pointer notation to return multiple values from the function. (You will be introduced to this technique later in this chapter.)

## Pointer Arithmetic

One of the most common uses of dereferencing pointers is to simplify stepping through blocks of storage in main memory. You do this by performing *pointer arithmetic* (any arithmetic operation performed on a main memory address). As an example, let's look at a program that performs two operations on a string. The first is to determine where one string begins within another; the second generates a substring. The program collects a string that is stored in an object. It then asks the user for a shorter string for which it is to search and reports where the shorter string begins in the object's string. Finally, the program asks for the starting position and length of a substring and finishes by displaying a substring. A sample run of this program can be found in Figure 17.3.

Figure 17.3    Output of the String Stuff program

```
Enter a string to store: This is the string being tested
Enter a string to match: the string being
The first string begins at position 8 in the second.

Enter starting position for substring: 8
Enter length of substring: 5

The substring is "the s"
```

The data handling class on which the String Stuff program is based appears in Listing 17.1. It has just one class variable—a string. The four member functions are the constructor, an initialization function that assigns data to the string, the function that searches for one string within the other (search-String), and the function that produces the substring (subString).

The application class Run function that controls the String Stuff program is relatively simple. (Most of the work in the program takes place in the stringStuff class member functions.) As you can see in Listing 17.2, it gathers the string that is to be stored in a stringStuff object and initializes the object. Then, it collects the string for the matching function, calls the function, and displays the result. The Run function then immediately accepts the data for the substring function. It calls the function and shows the substring (it if was possible to extract a substring.)

## Listing 17.1 match.h

```
class stringStuff
{
    private:
        char theString[81];
    public:
        stringStuff();
        void init (char []);
        int searchString (char []);
        char * subString (int, int);
};
```

## Listing 17.2 AppClass::Run for the String Stuff program

```
void AppClass::Run ()
{
    char ustring[81]; // utility string
    char * stringPtr;
    int matchPos, istart, ilength;

    cout << "Enter a string to store: ";
    cin.getline (ustring,81);
    oneString.init (ustring); // initialize the object

    cout << "Enter a string to match: ";
    cin.getline (ustring,81);

    // Call the function that searches for one string within another
    matchPos = oneString.searchString(ustring);

    cout << "The first string begins at position " << matchPos
        << " in the second.";

    cout << "\n\nEnter starting position for substring: " ;
    cin >> istart;
    cout << "Enter length of substring: ";
    cin >> ilength;

    // Call the subsctring function
    stringPtr = oneString.subString (istart, ilength);

    if (stringPtr == 0)
        cout << "\nCouldn't take the substring.";
    else
        cout << "\nThe substring is \"" << stringPtr << "\"";
}
```

## Taking a Substring

As just mentioned, the real work of the String Stuff program occurs in the member functions. To begin examining how pointer arithmetic is used to access the contents of arrays, let's look first at the subString function, which extracts a portion of a string, given a starting position in the original string and the number of characters to extract (Listing 17.3).

Listing 17.3   stringStuff::subString

```
char * stringStuff::subString (int start, int length)
{
    static char SubString[81]; // storage for substring; must be static
    char * SubStringPtr; // need to be able to step through string
    char * theStringPtr; // don't want to modify value stored in class

    theStringPtr = theString;
    SubStringPtr = SubString;
    if (start < strlen(theString))
    {
        theStringPtr = theStringPtr + start;
        while ((length--) && (*theStringPtr != '\0'))
            *SubStringPtr++ = *theStringPtr++;
        *SubStringPtr = '\0'; // add terminating null
        return SubString;
    }
    return 0; // couldn't take substring
}
```

The function begins by declaring a variable in which the substring will be stored (SubString). Notice that this variable's storage class has been changed from the default auto to static. This has been done to make sure that the variable isn't destroyed when the function terminates. The function returns a pointer to the substring. The string itself therefore must be left in main memory so that there are meaningful data in the pointer's location when the calling function attempts to access it.

The subString function also uses two pointer variables. The first, SubStringPtr, is initialized to the address of the SubString variable. Although the name of an array can be used as a pointer variable, the function is going to be doing arithmetic with the pointer. Using this pointer variable means that the address of SubString remains unchanged and can therefore be used as the function's return value.

The second pointer variable (theStringPtr) is initialized to the address of the class variable theString. The function uses this variable, rather than the class variable, because pointer arithmetic would change the location of an object's data, making the entire string inaccessible.

To begin, the subString function performs a simple error check: If the starting position of the substring is greater than or equal to the length of theString, then it isn't possible to create a substring. In that case, the program returns 0.

However, if the substring can be taken, then the program enters a while loop that copies characters from theString into SubString. It does so by using the pointer variables. A single character in theString is referenced by writing *theStringPtr; a single character in SubString is referenced by *SubStringPtr. The increment operator (++) following each pointer variable name increases the values in the pointer variables by one byte after copying a character.

The important thing to keep in mind about pointer arithmetic is that the amount that is added to or subtracted from a pointer depends on the type of data to which the pointer points. For example, if you have set up a pointer to an array of long integers and your computer uses 32-bit long integers, then incrementing the pointer adds four bytes to the pointer; adding 2 to the pointer adds eight bytes. If your pointer variable points to an array of floating point values, then each increment of 1 adds the number of bytes in your computer's floating point format. In the String Stuff program, each array element is a character. The increment therefore adds one byte to the address stored in each pointer variable.

**Note**

The preceding explains why you need to declare pointer variables to point to a specific type of data. Each pointer variable takes up 32 bits (the size of a main memory address), but when you are doing pointer arithmetic, the compiler needs to know how much to add to the pointer to reach the next value.

Once all the characters have been copied, the subString function appends a null to the end of the substring. It can then return the address of the SubString variable. If you look back at Listing 17.2, you'll notice that the Run function has declared a pointer to a string variable into which the return value is placed.

## Looking for One String Within Another

The `searchString` function, which looks for one string within another, can be found in Listing 17.4. To determine whether the input string (stored in `iString`) is completely contained within `theString`, the function compares every character in `iString` to every character in `theString`. However, it's not enough to begin the comparison with the first character of `theString`. Because `iString` could begin anywhere within `theString`, the function must perform repeated comparisons, beginning with each character in `theString`.

The `searchString` function uses three pointer variables:

- `theStringPtr`: a pointer to `theString` that can be used in pointer arithmetic so that the address of `theString` doesn't need to be changed.
- `moveablePtr`: another pointer to `theString` that can be used in pointer arithmetic.
- `iStringPtr`: a pointer to `iString` that can be used in pointer arithmetic, leaving the address of `iString` intact.

The function also uses two variables (`theStringCount` and `iString-Count`) that hold the length of the two strings.

Before checking to see if the input string is contained within the class's string, the `searchString` function needs to figure out at what point it should stop checking. When fewer characters are left in `theString` than in the input string, there's no reason to continue; it would be impossible for the input string to be contained within `theString`. The computation of the stopping point is stored in the variable `charCount`, which is decremented as the outer `while` loop iterates. If `charCount` drops to zero without finding a match, then the function returns a -1 to indicate that no match was found.

Inside the outer while, `searchString` uses an empty `while` loop (a loop with nothing in its body) to step through the characters being compared. The loop's control condition dereferences each of the string pointers to compare the contents of individual storage locations. The control condition also keeps track of how many characters in the input string have been checked. After evaluating the control condition, the computer increments each pointer variable and decrements the counter. If the counter drops to zero and the

## Listing 17.4    stringStuff::searchString

```
// locate where input string begins inside theString
// return index of where first matching character occurs (-1 if not found)
int stringStuff::searchString (char iString[])
{
    // create pointer variables for the strings so we don't modify the
    // original strings in main memory
    char * theStringPtr, * moveablePtr, * iStringPtr;
    int theStringCount, iStringCount; // variables to hold lengths of strings
    int theStringPos = 0, charCount, iStringPos;

    theStringCount = strlen(theString);
    iStringCount = strlen(iString);

    charCount = theStringCount - iStringCount + 1;
    moveablePtr = theString;

    while (charCount--)
    {
        theStringPtr = moveablePtr++; // moves beginning of theString
        iStringPtr = iString; // start over each time @ beginning of iString
        iStringPos = iStringCount;

    // compare against current state of theString (pointed to by theStringPtr)
    // this loops through every character in iString
        while ((*(iStringPtr++) == *(theStringPtr++)) && (iStringPos--))
            ; // this is an empty while loop

        if (iStringPos == 0) // match was found
            return theStringPos;
        else
            theStringPos++;
    }
    return -1;
}
```

characters in the two strings have been identical, a match has been found. The function can then return an integer that represents the position in theString where the match begins.

## The this Pointer

A C++ program maintains a special pointer that contains the address of the object with which the program is currently working: this. The this pointer can be used in several ways. For example, it can greatly simplify copying one object to another. Remember the laborious variable-by-variable `copy` function used in the bubble sort of an array of objects in Chapter 15? That entire function can be replaced with the following:

```
void OneSurvey::copy (OneSurvey inputObject)
{
    *this = inputObject;
}
```

The assignment statement that now forms the body of the function takes each variable in the object that is being passed in as a formal parameter and assigns those values to the current object. Notice that the `this` pointer is dereferenced, indicating that the assignment is not to assign the address of `inputObject` to the current object, but instead to modify the contents of the current object.

The assignment you have just seen is actually provided by the compiler. In other words, the compiler includes code in the object file that copies the contents of each variable from the source object to the destination object, just as the `copy` function from Chapter 15 acted. If this happens to be what you want, then use this type of assignment. However, if you aren't doing a direct copy, but instead are manipulating the data in some other way as you perform the copy, then you'll need to handle the copying of each variable individually.

## Dynamic Binding

Dynamic binding is a technique for creating objects while a program is running. It has two major advantages over static binding. First, a programmer doesn't need to be able to predict how many objects will be needed; they can be created on the fly. Second, dynamic binding provides better memory management. No storage is set aside for objects that might not be used; memory can be released when objects are no longer needed. In this section you will learn how to create objects using dynamic binding and how to access member functions for objects that are created in this way.

As one example of dynamic binding, we will be examining a version of Chapter 16's supply inventory program that has been modified to use dynamic binding. The first major change occurs in the array manager class. If you look at Listing 17.5, you'll notice that the array of `Item` objects has been replaced with an array of *pointers* to `Item` objects. When this program is run, the computer allocates enough space for 50 pointers, rather than space for 50 objects. The program can then create only as many objects as it actually needs.

### Listing 17.5    ArrayMgr.h modified to support dynamic binding

```
class ArrayMgr
{
    private:
        int item_count;
        Item * theSupplies [MAX_ITEMS];
    public:
        ArrayMgr();
        int loadArray (char *);
        void unloadArray (char *);
        int createItem (int, int, int, char *);
        int getMaxItemNumb ();
        int getCount ();
        void displayCurrent (int);
        void displayReorder (int);
        void modOnHand (int, int); // pass in array index and new value
};
```

## Creating Objects for Use with Dynamic Binding

To create an object using dynamic binding, use the keyword new, followed by the name of the class from which the object is to be created and a parameter list that matches one of the class's constructors. The new operator returns a pointer to the object just created.

In the modified supply inventory program, for example, the initItem function from the original has been replaced by the createItem function (Listing 17.6). Like the original, createItem receives data from the application object that calls it. However, no object exists into which the data can simply be placed. Instead, createItem uses the new operator to create and initializes the object. The pointer returned by new is assigned to the array manager's array of pointers.

### Listing 17.6    ArrayMgr::createItem

```
int ArrayMgr::createItem (int iItem_numb, int iOn_hand, int iReorder_pt,
    char iDesc[])
{
    item_count++; // increment counter
    if (item_count > MAX_ITEMS)
        return FALSE;
    theSupplies[item_count] = new Item (iItem_numb, iOn_hand, iReorder_pt,
        iDesc);
    return TRUE;
}
```

The `new` operator therefore does three things:

- It allocates memory for a new object.
- It takes the input parameters and passes them into the new object's constructor.
- It returns a pointer to the memory location of the new object.

Note that the `new` operator doesn't call the new object's constructor. The constructor is executed when the object is created, regardless of whether the object is created for static or dynamic binding.

The vowel statistics program also uses dynamic binding. The program is based on one class: `string` (Listing 17.7), which is the same for both versions of the program. The application class `Run` function for either version can therefore create an object from the class with the following:

```
cout << "Enter a string of up to 80 characters:" << endl;
    cin.getline (itext, 81);
    theString = new string (itext);
```

Note that the `theString` variable must be declared as a pointer to an object of the `string` class with `string * theString;`.

## Listing 17.7   stats.h

```
class string
{
    private:
        char text[81];
        int length;

    public:
        string (char *);
        void stats (int *, int *, int *, int *, int *, int *);
};
```

## Removing Objects Created for Use with Dynamic Binding

When a program no longer needs an object created with dynamic binding, it can be removed from memory, freeing up the space to be used by other objects. To remove an object from memory, use the following general syntax:

```
delete object_name;
```

The vowel statistics program, for example, removes an object from memory with

```
delete theString;
```

## Accessing Objects and Member Functions Created for Use with Dynamic Binding

In addition to changing the way objects are created, using dynamic binding changes the way in which a program calls a member function. Instead of using a period between the object name and the name of the member function, dynamic binding uses an arrow made up of a hyphen and a greater than symbol (->, the *arrow operator*). For example, one version of the vowel statistics program uses the following statement to call the member function that counts vowels:

```
theString->stats (APtr, EPtr, IPtr, OPtr, UPtr, TotalPtr);
```

The arrow operator tells the computer to dereference the pointer to the object. In other words, the following two expressions are equivalent:

```
pointer2object->functioName();
(*pointer2object).functionName();
```

This means that you can use the arrow operator with objects that are declared as variables. All you need to do is create a pointer variable for the object. For example, the following statements let you use the arrow operator with an object that was allocated space in main memory when the program was run:

```
className someObject;
className * someObjectPtr;
someObjectPtr = &someObject;
someObjectPtr->functionName();
```

## Pointers and Function Parameters

One of the most important things you can do with pointers is return more than one value from a function. To be completely accurate, a function can only return one value. However, a function *can* make modifications directly to a variable's original storage location in main memory.

There are actually two ways to pass parameters so that modifications to variables are made to the original storage locations. The first method, a pass by reference, involves sending the *address of a regular variable* into a function. This is the way in which we have been passing arrays to functions (pass by reference). The second involves sending the *contents of a pointer variable* into a function. In most cases, you'll use the address of a regular variable when there is no reason to create a pointer variable. You'll use a pointer variable when you've created the pointer variable for other purposes.

The difference between these two methods is somewhat subtle. To make it a bit clearer, take a look at Figure 17.4. In the top portion of the illustration, you can see a portion of memory occupied by regular integer variables (named A. E, I, O, U, and `theTotal`) initialized to 0 and pointer variables (named `APtr`, `EPtr`, `IPtr`, `OPtr`, `UPtr`, and `TotalPtr`) that are initialized to hold the main memory addresses of the regular variables. Notice that the main memory addresses aren't contiguous; they represent the beginning of the storage for each variable. Each integer variable takes up two bytes, and each pointer variable takes up four bytes. In this case, when we want to pass the addresses of the integer variables to a function, we send the function the contents of the pointer variables.

However, in the pass by reference example at the bottom of Figure 17.4, we send the addresses of the regular variables directly to a function, without first storing the addresses in separate pointer variables. This illustrates the advantage of pass by reference: You don't need to take up main memory space or waste programming time dealing with pointer variables. However, as you will see throughout the rest of this chapter, pointer variables can make it easier to manipulate many types of data, including objects created for dynamic binding. If you happen to have pointer variables for data manipulation purposes, then you might as well use them as function parameters.

To illustrate the difference between programming with these methods, we will be looking at the two versions of the vowel statistics program. Both programs use the same member functions for the `string` class. As you can see in Listing 17.8, the `stats` function, which counts the vowels in a string, expects six addresses as input parameters. Each of these parameters identifies the location of a variable declared in the main program. Whether the main program variable is a regular variable or a pointer variable depends on the way in which you decide to send the address to the member function.

Figure 17.4  Two ways to pass addresses to functions

| Address | | Variable Name | To Called Function |
|---|---|---|---|
| 2050 | 0 | A | |
| 2052 | 2050 | APtr | ────────→ 2050 |
| 2056 | 0 | E | |
| 2058 | 2056 | EPtr | ────────→ 2056 |
| 2062 | 0 | I | |
| 2064 | 2062 | IPtr | ────────→ 2062 |
| 2068 | 0 | O | |
| 2070 | 2068 | OPtr | ────────→ 2068 |
| 2074 | 0 | U | |
| 2076 | 2074 | UPtr | ────────→ 2074 |
| 2080 | 0 | theTotal | |
| 2082 | 2080 | TotalPtr | ────────→ 2080 |

Passing the contents of pointer variables

| | | | To Called Function |
|---|---|---|---|
| 2050 | 0 | A | ────────→ 2050 |
| 2052 | 0 | E | ────────→ 2052 |
| 2054 | 0 | I | ────────→ 2054 |
| 2056 | 0 | O | ────────→ 2056 |
| 2058 | 0 | U | ────────→ 2058 |
| 2060 | 0 | theTotal | ────────→ 2060 |

Pass by reference

## Listing 17.8   stats.cpp

```cpp
#include <string.h>
#include <iostream.h>
#include "stats.h"

string::string (char * itext)
{
    strcpy (text, itext);
    length = strlen (text);
}

void string::stats (int * A, int * E, int * I, int * O, int * U, int * total)
{
    *A = 0;
    *E = 0;
    *I = 0;
    *O = 0;
    *U = 0;
    *total = 0;
    for (int i = 0; i < length; i++)
    {
        *total += 1;
        switch (text[i])
        {
            case 'A':
            case 'a':
                *A += 1;
                break;
            case 'E':
            case 'e':
                *E += 1;
                break;
            case 'I':
            case 'i':
                *I += 1;
                break;
            case 'O':
            case 'o':
                *O +=+ 1;
                break;
            case 'U':
            case 'u':
                *U += 1;
                break;
            default:
                *total -= 1;  // not a vowel
        }
    }
}
```

Notice that because the member function expects addresses as parameters, all modifications to those parameters in the member function are made using pointer notation. In other words, whenever the member function modifies a value, it uses an asterisk to dereference the pointer.

## Passing by Reference

Passing by reference is the simplest way to return multiple values from a function. As you can see in Listing 17.9, the application class function for the pass by reference version of the vowel statistics program declares an integer variable for each of the six counts the stats member function will produce. Then, to pass the address of those variables into the string class member function, the application class's Run function (Listing 17.10) prefaces each variable with an ampersand.

**Listing 17.9   AppClass.h for the pass-by-reference version of the vowel statistics program**

```
class AppClass
{
    private:
        string * theString; // pointer variable for new string object
        int A, E, I, O, U, theTotal;
    public:
        AppClass ();
        void Run ();
};
```

When you pass by reference, the program doesn't send a copy of the contents of a variable into the called function. Instead, it sends just the main memory address of the variable. Modifications of those variables are made directly to the variable in main memory, thus making the changes available to the calling function or object in which the variables were declared.

## Passing Pointer Variables

The second way to pass the address of a variable into a function is to use a pointer variable as a parameter. To see how this differs from passing by reference, take a look at Listing 17.11. This version of the application class for the vowel statistics program includes both a regular variable and a pointer variable for each vowel count.

**Listing 17.10   AppClass::Run for the pass-by-reference version of the vowel
statistics program**

```
void AppClass::Run ()
{
    char itext[81];

    cout << "Enter a string of up to 80 characters:" << endl;
    cin.getline (itext,81);

    // Create an object using dynamic binding
    theString = new string (itext);

    // Call the stats function, passing the addresses of the application class variables
    theString->stats(&A,&E,&I,&O,&U,&theTotal);

    // Display the result using local variables that were modified in the member function call
    cout << "\nThe vowels in the string are:" << endl;
    cout << "   A: " << A << endl;
    cout << "   E: " << E << endl;
    cout << "   I: " << I << endl;
    cout << "   O: " << O << endl;
    cout << "   U: " << U << endl;
    cout << "\nThere are " << theTotal << " vowels." << endl;
    delete theString;
}
```

**Listing 17.11   AppClass.h for the pointer variable version of the vowel
statistics program**

```
class AppClass
{
    private:
        string * theString;
        int A, * APtr, E, * EPtr, I, * IPtr, O, * OPtr, U, * UPtr, theTotal,
            * TotalPtr;
    public:
        AppClass ();
        void Run ();
};
```

The application class's constructor initializes the pointer variables (see
Listing 17.12). Then, all the Run function needs to do is pass those variables to
the string class member function, as in Listing 17.13. Notice that because
the pointer variables contain addresses, there is no need to use an ampersand in
front of them. In fact, if you did use the ampersand, you would be sending the
address of the pointer variables, not the address of the regular variables.

Listing 17.12   AppClass::AppClass for the pointer variable version of the
             vowel statistics program

```
AppClass::AppClass ()
{
    APtr = &A;
    EPtr = &E;
    IPtr = &I;
    OPtr = &O;
    UPtr = &U;
    TotalPtr = &theTotal;
    theString = 0;
}
```

Listing 17.13   AppClass::Run for the pointer variable version of the vowel
             statistics program

```
void AppClass::Run ()
{
    char itext[81];
    cout << "Enter a string of up to 80 characters:" << endl;
    cin.getline (itext, 81);

    // Create the new object using dynamic binding
    theString = new string (itext);

    // Call the stats function, passing the contents of application class pointer variables
    theString->stats(APtr,EPtr,IPtr,OPtr,UPtr,TotalPtr);

    cout << "\nThe vowels in the string are:" << endl;
    cout << "  A: " << A << endl;
    cout << "  E: " << E << endl;
    cout << "  I: " << I << endl;
    cout << "  O: " << O << endl;
    cout << "  U: " << U << endl;
    cout << "\nThere are " << theTotal << " vowels." << endl;
    delete theString;
}
```

## Using I/O Streams as Function Parameters

The addresses of data or data handling objects are not the only types of addresses that a C++ program can handle. An I/O stream object, such as a file stream, also has an address that can be passed into a function as a parameter, allowing the function to interact with an I/O stream that was created elsewhere. There are two useful things you can do with this capability. The first is to allow objects to save themselves to a file and to read themselves back from that file, using an I/O stream created by a main program. The second is to allow objects to format output in main memory and then return the formatted output to the calling function, where it can be displayed as needed. Both operations are discussed in the following section.

## I/O Streams and Persistent Objects

One of the biggest problems with most of the short programs you have seen thus far in this book is that the objects created by those programs disappear when the program stops running. However, most business applications operate on stored data, data that must exist from one program run to another. The obvious way to handle the problem is to store objects in a file before a program ends and read them in again the next time a program is run. You have already seen one way to do this in Chapter 7.

The drawback to the methods presented in Chapter 7 is that the application object needs to know about the structure of the file containing the objects. A more "object-oriented" way to deal with saving and restoring objects is to write *persistent objects*. A persistent object is an object that reads itself in from a file when it is created and writes itself to a file when it is destroyed.

To support persistent objects, a program opens an I/O stream and then passes the address of that stream into a class's constructor when an object is created. The constructor can then use that stream to read in and initialize the newly created object.

To see how this works, consider a constructor for the modified version of the supply inventory program's Item class. The constructor has the following prototype:

```
Item (ifstream &);
```

This prototype defines its single input parameter as an object of class ifstream (an input file stream). The ampersand indicates that the function expects a reference to that stream to be passed in.

The function that corresponds to the preceding prototype can be found in Listing 17.14. Notice that the declaration's formal parameter list includes the class (ifstream), the ampersand indicating that a reference to the stream is coming, and a name for the stream to be used within the function (fin). Notice also that the local name of the stream is used within the function without pointer notation. This is therefore different from the way the addresses of data or data handling objects are handled.

## Listing 17.14  Item::Item for file input

```
Item::Item(ifstream & fin)    // file input constructor
{
    char white_space;

    fin.getline (Desc, 80, '\0');
    fin >> Item_numb >> On_hand >> Reorder_pt;
    fin.get (white_space);
}
```

To initiate the constructor in Listing 17.14, the supply inventory program's array manager creates a new Item object with the following statement:

```
theSupplies[i] = new Item (readfile);
```

In this example, theSupplies[i] is a pointer to an object of class Item; readFile is a file input stream defined for the file storing drug data. Notice that the stream is passed simply by including its name in the parameter list. Like an array, the name of a stream is an address rather than the contents of the stream.

The preceding new statement is a part of the modified array manager's loadArray function (Listing 17.15). Notice that the new statement has been placed in a for loop that reads the data from the file, one object at a time, creating space for the objects in main memory as needed.

The modified array manager's unloadArray function (Listing 17.16) also passes a reference to an I/O stream to an Item class member function, in this case, write. As you can see in Listing 17.17, the write function accepts the fstream object created in unloadArray and uses it to transfer the current object's data to the file.

## Formatting I/O Streams in Main Memory

A C++ output stream can be formatted in main memory, without immediately displaying the contents of the stream. The formatted stream can then be sent from one function to another to be displayed or printed whenever needed. This is particularly useful when you want to output data contained in an object's private variables and want to avoid having to retrieve and format those values directly.

We can, for example, rework the mailing label program you first saw in Chapter 9 so that the Customer object formats the label in main memory by modifying an output stream. Because the stream is passed by reference, just like

## Listing 17.15    ArrayMgr::loadArray modified for dynamic binding

```
int ArrayMgr::loadArray (char * fileName)
{
    int iItem_numb, iOn_hand, iReorder_pt;
    char iDesc[81], yes_no;

    // Create the input stream, using a file name stored in a string variable that was received by the
    // function as an input parameter.
    ifstream readFile (fileName);

    // handle situation where data file can't be found
    if (!readFile.is_open())
    {
        cout << "No data file could be found. Do you want to continue? ";
        cin >> yes_no;
        if (toupper(yes_no) == 'N')
            return FALSE;
    }
    else
    {
    // The following strategy simplifies working with text files that contain
    // strings

        readFile >> item_count; // get number of objects from beginning of file
        for (int i = 0; i <= item_count ; i++) // load data in from the file
            theSupplies[i] = new Item (readFile);
    }
    return TRUE;
}
```

## Listing 17.16    ArrayMgr::unloadArray modified for dynamic binding

```
void ArrayMgr::unloadArray (char * fileName)
{
    ofstream writeFile (fileName);

    if (writeFile.is_open())
        cout << "Unexpected file error occurred when opening output file.";
    else
    {
        // write the number of items in the array
        writeFile << item_count << ' ';
        for (int i = 0; i <= item_count; i++)
            theSupplies[i]->write (writeFile);
    }
}
```

## Listing 17.17 Item::write

```
void Item::write (ofstream & fout)
{
    fout << Desc << '\0';
    fout << Item_numb << ' ';
    fout << On_hand << ' ';
    fout << Reorder_pt << ' ';
}
```

the file stream you saw in the preceding section, the function that is manipulating the Customer object has access to the formatted stream and can display or print it as needed.

Output streams for in-memory use are created as objects of the ostrstream class. (There is also a related istrstream class.) The declaration of the class is stored in *strstream.h*. However, because *strstream* is longer than the eight characters allowed for MS-DOS/Windows 3.1 file names, many compilers have shortened the name of the header file to *strstrea.h*.

To prepare for formatting the label, mailing label program's application object's Run function contains a statement to create an object from the ostrstream class:

```
ostrstream label;
```

This in-memory stream object can then be passed into a function as a formal parameter.

The function, which is a member function of the Customer class, has the following prototype:

```
void formatLabel (ostrstream &);
```

The middle sole parameter is a reference to the ostrstream object. Notice that this reference uses the ampersand notation, just as the function you saw previously did for its ifstream and ofstream object references.

To call the function, the Run function places the names of the stream object to be passed into the function's parameter list:

```
onePerson.formatLabel (label);
```

In this example, onePerson is an object of class Customer.; label is the ostrstream object created earlier.

The function that accepts the `label` stream as an input parameter formats the stream using the stream insertion operator, just as a program would format a `cout` or `ofstream` object. As you can see in Listing 17.18, the statements look very much like `cout` statements. The major difference is that nothing appears on the screen; the stream is assembled in main memory.

### Listing 17.18   Customer::formatLabel

```
void Customer::formatLabel (ostrstream & label)
{
    string50 wholeName;
    string80 CSZ;

    label << endl << endl;
    label << first << " " << last << endl;
    label << street << endl;
    label << city << ", " << state << " " << zip << endl;
}
```

To display the contents of an in-memory stream, a program uses the stream's `str` member function, inserting it into a `cout` stream, as in:

```
cout << label.str();
```

**Warning**

The `str` function initializes a pointer to the head of the in-memory stream and also freezes the stream so it can't be modified. This latter characteristic of in-memory streams can be a bit of a "gotcha" if you want to repeatedly modify and display an in-memory stream. Unless the stream is destroyed or unfrozen, you won't be able to modify it. Like other local variables, a stream is destroyed when the function in which it was created exits.

This isn't a problem for the mailing label program we've been using as an example because it only creates one label at a time. However, if a program happens to be repeatedly calling a member function that formats a stream, the frozen stream will prevent modifications to the stream after it is initially formatted.

There are two possible solutions. The first is to put the code that deals with the in-memory stream in a small function all its own. This way, when the function ends, the stream object will be destroyed. Recreating it again will provide an unfrozen stream. Alternatively, a program can unfreeze a stream with the `freeze` member function. If you pass the function a parameter of 0, it will unfreeze the stream:

```
label.freeze(0);
```

## Binary Files

To this point, all the files used by the programs you have seen are text files. Text files are relatively easy to program, but they have one major drawback: They can be opened and read by a word processor or text editor. If you are storing data that should be protected from unauthorized viewing, then you should consider a type of file storage that is unintelligible to the casual viewer. Although not as secure as using data encryption, using binary files is an effective way to protect your data against many attempts at unauthorized access.

A *binary file* stores data as a stream of bits that don't translate into readable ASCII characters. The file is therefore unintelligible to a word processor or text editor. By the same token, a program can't use the standard stream insertion and extraction operators to write and read data.

### Creating and Opening Binary Files

Creating and opening a binary file is similar to creating and opening a text file. Because a text file is the default, a program must specifically indicate that it wants a binary file. To do so, add the flag ios::binary to the statement that opens the file, as in

```
ifstream fin (fileName, ios::binary);
ofstream fout (fileName, ios::binary);
```

### Writing to Binary Files

In x you will find a function that writes an Item object from the supply inventory program to a binary file. It uses the member function write to output a stream of unformatted bytes of characters (arrays of characters). The write function has the following general syntax:

```
stream.write (address_of_data, #_characters);
```

### Listing 17.19   Writing to a binary file

```
void Item::write (ofstream & fout)
{
    fout.write (Desc, sizeof (Desc));
    fout.write ((unsigned char *) &Item_numb, sizeof (Item_numb));
    fout.write ((unsigned char *) &On_hand, sizeof (On_hand));
    fout.write ((unsigned char *) &Reorder_pt, sizeof (Reorder_pt));
}
```

The `write` function requires the starting address of the characters to be written to the file. If a program is writing from an array of characters (a string), then the name of the variable is sufficient. However, if the data are stored in a simple variable (for example, an integer or floating point variable), then the variable's name must be preceded by the ampersand to indicate the address of the variable.

The `write` function doesn't recognize the null that terminates a string. A program must therefore tell `write` how many characters are to be output. For example, to write an item description to the file, the program uses

```
fout.write (Desc, sizeof(Desc));
```

The `sizeof` function returns the number of bytes in a C++ data structure (even an object). Although you could certainly use the length of the `Desc` string as a constant, the use of the `sizeof` function means that the `write` will not need to be modified if the length of the `Desc` variable ever changes.

Because `write` only outputs characters, the address of numeric data must be typecast into a character pointer as the data are written. For example, the following syntax typecasts the address of an integer variable:

```
(unsigned char *) &Item_numb
```

## Reading from Binary Files

Reading from a binary file is precisely the opposite of writing to the file. It uses the function `read`, which has the following general syntax:

```
stream.read (address_of_storage, #_characters);
```

The function expects two parameters: the address of the storage location where the data should be stored as they are input and the number of characters to input. Notice in Listing 17.20, a function to read an office supply item from a binary file, that the addresses of variables that aren't character arrays must once more be typecast into character pointers. Because the first element of a character array is a pointer, the name of a character array can be used without typecasting.

## Listing 17.20   Reading from a binary file

```
Item::Item (ifstream & fin)
{
    fout.write (Desc, sizeof (Desc));
    fout.write ((unsigned char *) &Item_numb, sizeof (Item_numb));
    fout.write ((unsigned char *) &On_hand, sizeof (On_hand));
    fout.write ((unsigned char *) &Reorder_pt, sizeof (Reorder_pt));
}
```

## Summary

In this chapter you have learned about using pointers to access data and objects. C++ provides two mechanisms for handling addresses. The first uses ampersand notation: placing an ampersand in front of a variable name or the name of an object created with static binding generates the address at which that variable or object's storage begins in main memory. The exception to this is arrays, whose names are addresses without being preceded by an ampersand.

The second mechanism stores an address in a variable declared to hold a pointer. Pointer variables are used to return multiple values from a function and to hold pointers to objects created with dynamic binding.

To access the data pointed to by a pointer variable, a program must dereference the pointer by placing an asterisk in front of the variable's name. For example, `*Data` refers to the contents of the main memory location stored in the `Data` variable.

C++ maintains a special pointer called `this`, which holds a pointer to the current object. The `this` pointer can be used, for example, to simplify copying one object into another.

Dynamic binding lets a program create and destroy objects as needed, rather than having to declare all objects when the program is written. The `new` keyword creates a new object using dynamic binding and returns a pointer to that object. To access member functions of objects created with dynamic binding, use arrow notation (`->`).

To return multiple values from a function, the function must expect pointer to variables as input parameters. It must then use pointer notation to modify values. The calling function can either pass in the address of a variable (using ampersand notation) or the contents of a pointer variable.

The addresses of I/O streams can be passed into functions as parameters. The streams can be modified by the functions. Because the name of a stream is the main memory address of its starting location, a stream is passed simply by using its name. The function to which the stream is a parameter uses ampersand notation in its parameter list because the function is expecting a reference to the stream. The stream name is then used dereferencing in the function.

Binary files store bytes of unformatted character data. To write to a binary file, a program uses the `write` function, which uses the address of the data to be written along with the number of bytes to write. The `read` function works in exactly the opposite manner to input data from a binary file. In either case, addresses of noncharacter array variables must be typecast into character pointers before writing data to or reading data from a binary file.

## Exercises

1. Create a class that manages payroll information about employees who are paid hourly. The class should store the employee's ID number, his or her hourly pay rate, and the hours worked during a given week. Include a member function that computes an employee's weekly pay. Each employee is paid according to the following schedule:

   - For the first 40 hours worked, pay is equal to the hourly rate times the number of hours worked.
   - For hours over 40, pay is equal to 1.5 times the hourly rate times the number of overtime hours worked.

   The pay computation function should return the pay for the first 40 hours of work, the overtime pay amount, and the total gross pay. Write a program that demonstrates that the class and its payroll computation function work.

2. Create a class that includes an array variable that stores up to 25 floating point values. Include a member function that uses pointer arithmetic to sum the values in the array and returns the sum to the calling function. Write a program that demonstrates that the sum function works correctly.

3. Add a member function to the String Stuff program you read about in this chapter that converts a number stored as a string to an integer. The function should accept a string array as an input parameter and return the equivalent integer value. Be sure to check the input string to determine if it contains only characters that constitute a valid integer. Use pointer

arithmetic to examine the characters in the string one by one, checking and converting them as you go. Add code to the program's `main` function that demonstrates that your conversion function works.

4. To help the local tax assessor, create a class that describes properties in a town. The class should include the ID number of the property and the market value of the property. Include a function that computes and returns the assessed value of the property and the tax owed. The computations use the following rules:

   - A property's assessed value is 33% of its market value.
   - The tax rate is 130 mils for each dollar of assessed value. (One mil = 0.1 cent.)

   Write a program that demonstrates that your class and the tax computation function work.

5. Create a class that can be used to help surgical patients manage their medication schedule after they are released from the hospital. The class should store the name of the medication, the dosage of the medication, and the times at which the medication must be taken (e.g., 2:00 PM, 6:00 PM). Write a program that uses an array of objects to store data about all of a patient's medication. Include a function in the program that prints a daily medication schedule for the patient, showing which medication(s) should be taken each hour during the day and the dosage for each of the medications. The program's output should be organized by hour rather than by type of medication. (*Hint:* This is a bit trickier than it looks, because most medications are taken more than once a day. Consider carefully how you're going to store the times within the class.)

# 18

# Inheritance

## OBJECTIVES

In this chapter you will read about:
- Using inheritance to allow similar classes to share data and functions.
- Where inheritance is appropriate and where it isn't.
- How polymorphism, implemented through virtual functions, allows objects from related classes to react differently to the same message.

This chapter introduces one of the most important features of the object-oriented paradigm: inheritance. Inheritance makes it possible for similar objects to share variable and function definitions. Inheritance also supports *polymorphism*, through which different objects can respond to the same message in different ways.

The example used throughout this chapter is the program that computes loan repayment tables for three types of loans that you first read about in Chapter 4. For example, in Figure 18.1, you can see the payment table for a fixed-payment loan. The program also handles variable-payment and mortgage loans, each of which has different algorithms for calculating payment amounts and interest.

**Figure 18.1    Sample output from the loan program**

|    | PAYMENT | INTEREST | REMAINING PRINCIPAL |
|----|---------|----------|---------------------|
| 1  | 60.00   | 7.29     | 947.29              |
| 2  | 60.00   | 6.91     | 894.20              |
| 3  | 60.00   | 6.52     | 840.72              |
| 4  | 60.00   | 6.13     | 786.85              |
| 5  | 60.00   | 5.74     | 732.59              |
| 6  | 60.00   | 5.34     | 677.93              |
| 7  | 60.00   | 4.94     | 622.87              |
| 8  | 60.00   | 4.54     | 567.41              |
| 9  | 60.00   | 4.14     | 511.55              |
| 10 | 60.00   | 3.73     | 455.28              |
| 11 | 60.00   | 3.32     | 398.60              |
| 12 | 60.00   | 2.91     | 341.51              |
| 13 | 60.00   | 2.49     | 284.00              |
| 14 | 60.00   | 2.07     | 226.07              |
| 15 | 60.00   | 1.65     | 167.72              |
| 16 | 60.00   | 1.22     | 108.94              |
| 17 | 60.00   | 0.79     | 49.73               |
| 18 | 50.10   | 0.36     | 0.00                |

## Where Inheritance Makes Sense

As you read in Chapter 4, using inheritance creates a hierarchy of classes through which the variables and functions for classes higher in the hierarchy are passed down to classes below. This means that when similar classes share variables and functions, you only need to declare them once, rather than repeating them for each class in which they appear.

The idea of inheritance can be a bit confusing, especially if you've studied data management. Although inheritance initially looks a lot like the relationships between entities in a database system, it is a different concept. To help you understand where inheritance is appropriate and where inheritance hurts rather than helps, let's take a look at the design of some classes that could be used to manage the operations of a video store.

The first thing to understand about a video store is that it needs to store data about the type of merchandise it carries. However, the store doesn't rent a type of merchandise; it rents *copies* of those types. Therefore, a video store program must handle two major groups of classes: classes about the types of merchandise and classes about merchandise copies.

In Figure 18.2, each box represents a class. (A video store program also needs a class to describe its customers, but because that class isn't part of the inheritance hierarchy, it doesn't appear in the diagram.) The hierarchy at the top of the diagram, connected by solid lines, describes types of merchandise carried by the store. The hierarchy at the bottom of the diagram, also connected by solid lines, describes the copies of the types of merchandise that are actually rented to customers. The dashed lines in the middle of the diagram indicate where inheritance isn't appropriate. You'll read more about this shortly.

The base class of the type of merchandise hierarchy is a generic Merchandise Item. As you can see in Figure 18.2, it contains data that are applicable to movies, other videos, *and* video games (the three types of merchandise rented by the store). Two classes are derived from the Merchandise Item class, one for videos and another for video games. The Video Game class inherits all the variables from the Merchandise Item class and adds two variables that are specifically applicable to games. The Video class also inherits the Merchandise Item's class variables and adds variables of its own. In contrast, the Video class has two classes derived from it (Movie and Other Video). Video is therefore both a base class and a derived class.

Objects are created from only three of the classes in the merchandise item hierarchy: Movie, Other Video, and Game. Notice that these classes are at the bottom of the hierarchy, classes from which no other classes are derived. Although this is not always the case, it is not uncommon for objects to be created only from classes at the bottom of a hierarchy.

The copy hierarchy begins with the base class Item Copy. It contains variables that apply to all copies of merchandise items, regardless of the type of item. The Video Copy derived class adds variables that apply only to videos.

Figure 18.2   Class hierarchy for a video store program

The Game Copy class doesn't need any additional data. As with the merchandise item hierarchy, objects are created only from the two classes at the bottom of the hierarchy and never from the Item Copy class.

One question arises at this point. If the Other video and Game Copy classes don't add any variables to those they inherit from their respective base classes, why include these classes in the design at all? Because the classes behave differently even when they receive the same message. For example, the Other Video class behaves differently from the Movie class when it receives the message "write yourself to a file."

If you have taken a database course, then you are probably also wondering why the Item Copy class and its derived classes aren't part of the merchandise item hierarchy. It is true that the store stocks many copies of each merchandise item. In fact, a database system would represent this as a one-to-many relationship. Keep in mind, however, that inheritance *copies* all the variables from a base class into a derived class.

If Video Copy, for example, was derived from Movie, each copy of a given movie would repeat all the data about the movie, including its title, distributor, producer, director, stars, and rating. The result would be a great deal of unnecessary duplicated data. The fact that the extra data waste disk space is the least of the problems. As you may know from your database course, the presence of unnecessary duplicated data sooner or later leads to data inconsistency, a situation in which data that should be the same are not. A search for a movie by title would never find any copy that had even one incorrect letter in its title, perhaps causing someone at the store to believe that no copies of a given title were in stock.

In this situation, inheritance isn't appropriate. Use inheritance where the derived classes need every variable from their base classes. (A copy of a merchandise item doesn't need all the data describing the item; it only needs an identifier, such as an inventory number, that can be used to locate the object that contains the descriptive data.) Use inheritance where the inherited variables don't represent unnecessary duplicated data.

Another way to help determine when inheritance is appropriate is to recognize that in most cases, inheritance represents the special relationship "is a," in which a derived class is a more specific example of its base class. In other words, a Video "is a" Merchandise Item; a Movie "is a" Video. If you can express the relationship between two classes using the "is a" relationship, then inheritance is probably appropriate.

## Declaring Derived Classes

As you may remember from Chapter 4, where you were first introduced to inheritance, the loans program has four classes: the base class `Loan` and three classes derived from it (`Fixed_payment`, `Variable_payment`, and `Mortgage`). The base class (Listing 18.1) is declared like any class you have seen to this point, although the `CreatePaymentTable` function's prototype contains features that we will discuss later in this chapter.

## Listing 18.1    The Loans class

```
class Loan
{
    protected:
        float principal;
        float interest_rate;

    public:
        Loan (float, float) ;
        virtual int CreatePaymentTable (float [MAX_TERM][NUM_COLUMNS]) = 0;
};
```

The declaration of derived classes is very similar. The major difference is that the declaration must include the name of the class from which the new class is derived and the type of inheritance that is in effect. As an example, consider the three derived loan classes in Listing 18.2. Notice that the first line of each declaration has the following format:

```
class class_name : inheritance_type base_class_name
```

Because the derived classes inherit all the variables declared in their base class, the `principal` and `interest_rate` variables aren't repeated in the derived classes. However, keep in mind that the inherited variables are as much a part of an object created from a derived class as those variables declared inside the derived class.

## Types of Inheritance

To this point, you have worked with public and private variables and functions. Public items are accessible to all functions; private items are accessible only to members of the class in which they are defined. Inheritance can also be public and private, although private is used very rarely. In addition, inheritance can take advantage of a third type of variables and functions (*protected*).

Regardless of the type of inheritance, a derived class cannot access private variables and functions of its base class. To get around this problem and still hide the internals of the base class from classes and functions outside the class hierarchy, a base class usually uses protected items rather than private items. Assuming public inheritance, protected items are accessible to member functions in all derived classes. Notice in Listing 18.1, for example, that the

### Listing 18.2    Classes derived from the Loan class

```
class Fixed_Payment : public Loan
{
    private:
        float payment;        // amount customer will be paying each month

    public:
        Fixed_Payment (float, float, float);
        int CreatePaymentTable (float [MAX_TERM][NUM_COLUMNS]);
};

class Variable_Payment : public Loan
{
    private:
        // percentage of principal to be paid each month
        float payment_percent;
        // minimum payment to be used when principal gets low
        float minimum_payment;
        float minimum_interest;    // minimum interest assessed

    public:
        Variable_Payment (float, float,float, float, float);
        int CreatePaymentTable (float [MAX_TERM][NUM_COLUMNS]);
};

class Mortgage : public Loan
{
    private:
        int num_periods;
        int periods_per_year;
        float payment;

    public:
        Mortgage (int, int, float, float, float);
        int CreatePaymentTable (float [MAX_TERM][NUM_COLUMNS]);
};
```

Loan class has protected rather than private variables. The derived classes, which are at the bottom of the hierarchy, however, have private variables to hide them from the outside world.

In general, public inheritance means that a derived class has access to the public and protected items of its base class. Public items are inherited as public items; protected items remain protected. Private inheritance, however, means that a derived class has no access to any of its base class's items. Types of inheritance and derived class accessibility are summarized in Table 18.1.

Table 18.1    Variable and function access based on type of inheritance

| Type of Inheritance | Type of Item | Accessible to Derived Class? |
|---|---|---|
| public | public | yes |
| | protected | yes |
| | private | no |
| private | public | no |
| | protected | no |
| | private | no |

**Warning**

By default, inheritance is private. If you accidentally leave out the keyword `public`, base class items will be inaccessible. The type of inheritance is therefore one of the first things you should check if a compiler returns an error message that says variables or functions are inaccessible.

We rarely use private inheritance. Even if you currently don't see a need for a derived class to access variables or member functions from its base class, you can't be certain that you won't need to modify the program in the future in such a way that you *do* need to access base class contents.

## Limitations to Inheritance

A derived class inherits all of its base class's public and protected variables, but it doesn't inherit all of its functions. The following functions aren't inherited:

- constructors
- destructors
- overloaded operators (discussed in Chapter 20)
- friends (discussed in Chapter 20)

# Inheritance and Constructors

Although constructors aren't inherited, the situation isn't as limiting as it might appear. When an object is created from a derived class, the program automatically calls the base class's constructor. When the hierarchy is more than two levels deep, the program calls constructors all the way up the hierarchy.

When constructors take input parameters, the compiler has no way of knowing which parameters should be passed to a base class constructor and which are intended only for local use. In such a case, a program needs to indicate explicitly how parameters should be transferred.

You can find the interactive constructors for the three derived loan classes in Listing 18.3. Notice that the input parameter list for each constructor is followed by a colon and a call to the base class constructor. This is the *only* circumstance under which a derived function can explicitly call its base class's constructor. Once the constructors have been run, the base class constructor becomes inaccessible.

## Listing 18.3   Derived class constructors for the Loans program

```
Fixed_Payment::Fixed_Payment (float i_principal, float i_interest_rate,
    float i_payment)
        : Loan (i_principal, i_interest_rate)
{
    payment = i_payment;
}


Variable_Payment::Variable_Payment (float i_principal, float i_interest_rate,
    float i_payment_percent, float i_minimum_payment, float i_minimum_interest)
        : Loan (i_principal, i_interest_rate)
{
    payment_percent = i_payment_percent;
    minimum_payment = i_minimum_payment;
    minimum_interest = i_minimum_interest;
}

Mortgage::Mortgage (int i_num_periods, int i_periods_per_year,
    float i_principal,float i_interest_rate, float i_payment)
        : Loan (i_principal, i_interest_rate)
{
    num_periods = i_num_periods;
    periods_per_year = i_periods_per_year;
    payment = i_payment;
}
```

## Using Base Class Pointers

One of the most useful aspects of inheritance is the ability to reference an object created from a derived class with a base class pointer. This means that the loan program's application object can use a pointer variable declared to point to an object of the Loan class to contain a pointer to any of the three derived classes. As you can see in Listing 18.4, the application class maintains a single pointer variable that points to the loan with which the program is currently working. Because the variable is declared as a pointer to the base class, the current loan can be created from any of the three derived classes and then manipulated by the base class pointer variable. This means that once a loan object is created and a pointer to it stored in the theLoan variable, the application class doesn't need to pay attention to the type of loan.

### Listing 18.4    AppClass.h for the Loans program

```
class AppClass
{
    private:
        Loan * theLoan; // base class pointer for use throughout program
        float payment_table [MAX_TERM][NUM_COLUMNS];
        void createLoan ();
        void createFixed ();
        void createVariable ();
        void createMortgage ();
        void displayTable ();
    public:
        AppClass();
        void Run ();
};
```

To create a base class pointer, you simply assign a pointer to a derived class object to a base class pointer variable. As an example, look at the loan program's application class's createFixed function (Listing 18.5). The function collects the data needed to initialize the object from the user and then creates an object of the Fixed_payment class for use with dynamic binding. Finally, the function assigns the Fixed_payment class pointer to the base class pointer variable (theLoan). C++ typecasts the derived class pointer to a base class pointer when it performs the assignment.

Why this is useful may not be immediately obvious, but consider what happens when the time comes to create and display a repayment table for a loan. Each derived class has a function named CreatePaymentTable. If the

## Listing 18.5   AppClass::createFixed

```
void AppClass::createFixed()
{
    float i_principal, i_interest_rate, i_payment;
    Fixed_Payment * objptr;

    cout << "\nPrincipal: ";
    cin >> i_principal;
    cout << "\nInterest rate: ";
    cin >> i_interest_rate;
    cout << "\nMonthly payment: ";
    cin >> i_payment;

    // Create object for use with dynamic binding
    objptr = new Fixed_Payment (i_principal, i_interest_rate, i_payment);
    theLoan = objptr; // typecast to base class pointer
}
```

loans program uses a base class pointer to call this function, the computer correctly identifies the type of object and executes the correct function that has been bound to that object; the programmer doesn't need to figure out which type of loan is involved. As you can see in Listing 18.6, the call to Create-PaymentTable is made using the contents of theLoan, the base class pointer variable.

## Listing 18.6   AppClass::displayTable

```
void AppClass::displayTable ()
{
    int num_payments = theLoan->CreatePaymentTable (payment_table);
    cout << "                         REMAINING" << endl;
    cout << "       PAYMENT " << " INTEREST " << "PRINCIPAL" << endl;
    cout << "       ------- " << " --------" << " ---------" << endl;

    for (int i = 0; i <= num_payments; i++)
    {
        cout << setiosflags(ios::showpoint | ios::fixed | ios::right);
        cout << setw(3) << i+1
             << setw(10) << setprecision(2) << payment_table[i][PAYMENT]
             << setw(10) << setprecision(2) <<payment_table[i][INTEREST]
             << setw(10) << setprecision (2) <<payment_table[i][PRINCIPAL] <<
    endl;
    }
    cout << endl;
}
```

**Note**

Base class pointers can also make it possible to place objects derived from the same base class into the same data structure. For example, if the loans program were rewritten to handle more than one loan at a time, an array or linked list that managed multiple loan objects could contain all three types of loans, as long as the data structure was declared to hold base class pointers. You will see an example of doing this in Chapter 19.

## Polymorphism

One of the most powerful capabilities of inheritance is its support for *polymorphism*, the ability to have classes in the same inheritance hierarchy respond differently to the same message. A program is using polymorphism when member functions in different classes have the same signature but differ in the content of the function body. As an example, consider the three `CreatePaymentTable` functions (Listing 18.7, Listing 18.8, and Listing 18.9). Each is defined in a different class and has exactly the same signature. However, the body of each function is different. In other words, the functions receive the same message and yet behave in a different way.

**Note**

It's important to keep in mind the difference between function overloading and polymorphism. Function overloading occurs when more than one function in the same class has the same name but a different signature. Polymorphism occurs when functions in different classes in the same inheritance hierarchy have the same signature but different bodies.

## Virtual Functions

A program uses *virtual functions* to implement polymorphism. A virtual function is a function that needs to be called with a pointer (dynamic binding) so that the program will know exactly which function to use. The pointer to an object that precedes the -> and the name of the function identifies the class from which the correct function should be taken.

To declare a function virtual, precede its prototype with the keyword `virtual`, just as was done with the `CreatePaymentTable` function in Listing 18.1. Once declared, a function is virtual all the way down the inheritance hierarchy. A derived class can redefine a virtual function, giving that

### Listing 18.7    Fixed_Payment::CreatePaymentTable

```
int Fixed_Payment::CreatePaymentTable (float
    payment_table[MAX_TERM][NUM_COLUMNS])
{
    int i = 0;
    float monthly_interest;

    while (principal >= payment)
    {
        payment_table[i][PAYMENT] = payment;
        monthly_interest = principal * (interest_rate/12.0);
        payment_table[i][INTEREST] = monthly_interest;
        principal = principal - (payment - monthly_interest);
        payment_table[i++][PRINCIPAL] = principal;
    }

    if (principal > 0.0)
    {
        payment_table[i][INTEREST] = principal * (interest_rate/12.0);
        payment_table[i][PAYMENT] = principal + payment_table[i][INTEREST];
        payment_table[i][PRINCIPAL] = 0.0;
    }
    return i;
}
```

function behavior appropriate to the derived class, or it can simply inherit the function from its base class. In the loans program, the `CreatePaymentTable` function is redefined by the `Fixed_payment`, `Variable_payment`, and `Mortgage` classes.

Once a function has been declared virtual in a base class, it isn't necessary to include the keyword `virtual` in any derived classes. However, many programmers choose to do so because it makes class definitions easier to understand.

## Pure Functions and Abstract Classes

In some circumstances, you may want to use a base class only as a source for derived classes; you never intend to create objects from that class. (`Loan` is such a class.) To prevent any program from ever creating objects from a class, make it an *abstract class*. (A program can only create objects from *concrete classes*, classes that aren't abstract.) Note, however, that making a class abstract does not prevent you from declaring a base class pointer variable that points to an object of

### Listing 18.8 Variable_Payment::CreatePaymentTable

```
int Variable_Payment::CreatePaymentTable (float
    payment_table[MAX_TERM][NUM_COLUMNS])
{
    int i = 0;
    float interest, payment;

    while (principal >= minimum_payment)
    {
        interest = principal * (interest_rate/12.0);
        if (interest < minimum_interest) interest = minimum_interest;
        payment_table[i][INTEREST] = interest;
        principal = principal + interest;
        payment = principal * payment_percent;
        if (payment < minimum_payment) payment = minimum_payment;
        principal = principal - payment;
        payment_table[i][PRINCIPAL] = principal;
        payment_table[i++][PAYMENT] = payment;
    }

    if (i == 0)
        payment_table[i][INTEREST] = 0;
    else
    {
        payment_table[i][INTEREST] = principal * (interest_rate/12.0);
        if (payment_table[i][INTEREST] < minimum_interest)
            payment_table[i][INTEREST] = minimum_interest;
    }

    payment_table[i][PAYMENT] = principal + payment_table[i][INTEREST];
    payment_table[i][PRINCIPAL] = 0.0;
    return i;
}
```

that class. Although a program will never have an object from that class, the base class pointer can nonetheless be created by typecasting a pointer to an object of a derived class.

An abstract class is a class that contains at least one *pure function*, a virtual function that is declared in a class but not defined. In other words, the function has only a prototype. Pure functions are identified by following their prototypes with = 0. The Loan class declaration, for example, includes the following declaration for the CreatePaymentTable function:

```
virtual int CreatePaymentTable (float [MAX_TERM][NUM_COLUMNS]) = 0;
```

## Listing 18.9   Mortgage::CreatePaymentTable

```
int Mortgage::CreatePaymentTable (float payment_table[MAX_TERM][NUM_COLUMNS])
{
    int i = 0;
    float period_interest_rate, PVIFA;

    period_interest_rate = interest_rate/periods_per_year;
    PVIFA = (1/period_interest_rate) -
        (1/(period_interest_rate * pow((double) 1 +
        period_interest_rate,(double) num_periods)));
    if (payment == 0)
        payment = principal/PVIFA;
    else
        if (principal == 0)
            principal = payment * PVIFA;
        else
        {
            cout << "\nYou must enter either principal or payment.";
            return (0);
        }
    while (principal > payment)
    {
        payment_table[i][INTEREST] = principal * period_interest_rate;
        payment_table[i][PAYMENT] = payment;
        principal = principal - (payment - payment_table[i][INTEREST]);
        payment_table[i++][PRINCIPAL] = principal;
    }
    payment_table[i][INTEREST] = principal * period_interest_rate;
    payment_table[i][PAYMENT] = principal + payment_table[i][INTEREST];
    payment_table[i][PRINCIPAL] = 0.0;
    return i;
}
```

Pure functions are ultimately redefined in concrete classes. For example, the CreatePaymentTable function is redefined by Fixed_payment, Variable_payment, and Mortgage, the three concrete classes in the loan class hierarchy.

Why bother to use polymorphism, virtual functions, and abstract base classes? Because they simplify a program, providing a consistent interface to the programmer. They also generalize object behavior. With a polymorphic CreatePaymentTable function such as that used by the loans program, the programmer knows that to generate a repayment table, he or she can simply use a function named CreatePaymentTable, regardless of the details needed to perform the output. This not only makes a program easier to write, debug, and understand, but also makes it easier to reuse classes in multiple programs.

## Summary

Inheritance provides a mechanism that allows similar classes to share variables and functions in a hierarchical manner. Inheritance is appropriate when the classes are related by the "is a" relationship. A derived class "is a" more specific instance of a base class.

By default, inheritance is private. Private inheritance means that no variables or functions of a base class are accessible to its derived classes. However, in most cases inheritance is public. With public inheritance, public items in the base class are inherited as public items and protected items are inherited as protected. However, even with public inheritance private items are inaccessible to a derived class.

Not everything can be inherited. Constructors, destructors, overloaded operators, and friends can't be inherited. However, when an object is created from a derived class, the base class constructor is called automatically, along with the derived class constructor.

Pointers to base classes can be used to provide a generic way to access objects created from classes derived from the same base class.

Polymorphism allows objects created from different classes to respond to the same message in different ways. Polymorphism is implemented using virtual functions, functions that must be referenced with a pointer (using dynamic binding). Polymorphic functions must have the same signature. This is in direct contrast to function overloading, in which functions that are part of the same class have different signatures.

Base classes from which no objects can be created are known as abstract base classes; classes from which objects can be created are called concrete classes. An abstract base class contains at least one pure virtual function (a function whose prototype ends with the initialization = 0). Pure functions are declared but not defined; they have a prototype but no body. Pure functions are redefined by concrete classes in the hierarchy.

## Exercises

1. Create a class hierarchy to manage the live animal inventory for a pet shop that handles cats, dogs, aquarium fish, reptiles, and small mammals (for example, rabbits, gerbils, and hamsters). Include data such as the type of animal, its living conditions, its feeding and care requirements, and the number of individuals currently in stock. Write member functions that display data about a given type of animal, enter new individuals into

inventory, and remove individuals from inventory when sold. Create a single array of pointers to objects to manage the entire inventory. Write a program that demonstrates that the classes and their member functions work.

2.  Create at least one class hierarchy to manage a corporation's office furniture and equipment, which includes items such as desks, chairs, file cabinets, computers, copiers, and fax machines. (Consider carefully whether there should be one or two class hierarchies.) Classes should include variables for the name of an item, its manufacturer, a description of the item (using as many variables as necessary), an internal corporate identification number, the date of purchase, purchase price, and current value. Develop necessary data structures to manage objects. Include member functions to enter new items and to display data describing items of a given type (e.g., desks). In addition, include member functions to compute the total current value of all assets of a given type, of all assets, and of all assets organized by type (a control break report).

3.  Create classes to manage the "cars wanted" list of an exotic car dealership. The classes should handle data about the customers along with descriptions of the vehicles for which customers are searching. Decide which classes can be part of a class hierarchy and which need to be related to others using data structures. Include member functions to enter customers and customer requests, display the requests of a specific customer, and find out whether a specific car matches any request currently stored. Write a program that demonstrates that the classes and their member functions work.

4.  Create a class hierarchy to manage an investment portfolio, including stocks, bonds, CDs, and mutual funds. Include data about the name of the investment, the amount held, and the current unit value. Include member functions to enter new investments, modify the current value of all investments held, and the total value of the portfolio. Use an array of pointers to manage the objects. Write a program that demonstrates that the classes and their member functions work.

5.  Modify the program you wrote for Exercise 4 so that it handles multiple investment profiles. Also add a class to manage the investors. Allow a single investor to own multiple portfolios; allow a single portfolio to be owned by multiple investors. Consider carefully how this "many-to-many" relationship can be implemented, either through a class hierarchy or through data structures.

# 19

# Linked Lists

## OBJECTIVES

In this chapter you will read about:
- Creating list manager objects to handle linked lists.
- Using node objects to point to objects in a list.
- Inserting objects into and removing objects from a list.
- Using an iterator to traverse a list.

As you first read in Chapter 15, a linked list is a dynamic data structure that chains together objects by having one object point to the "next" object in the list. Because you can lengthen the list by simply adding another object to the chain, the number of objects in a linked list theoretically is limited only by the amount of main memory available for the program's data storage.

In this chapter you will learn how an object-oriented program creates and manages a linked list. The sample program handles a linked list of the illustrations used in a book someone is writing. As you can see in the sample run in Figure 19.1, the user enters a four-digit figure number, the source of the illustration, whether the publisher needs to obtain permission to reprint the illustration, and whether the illustration is currently available. The new illustration is then added to the list in alphabetical order by figure number. (Because the figure numbers are stored as strings, you must always enter four digits for the figure number, using leading 0s where necessary.) The program can also remove illustrations from the list and display the entire list.

## Linked List Classes

In Chapter 15 you read that there were two ways to put together an object-oriented linked list. The first included "next" pointers in each of the objects that were part of the list. The second used a special "node" object, which pointed both to the object that was part of the list and to the next node in the list (see Figure 19.2). The benefit of the second strategy is that although it requires an extra object (the node), it keeps pointers to data structures out of the objects that belong to the data structure. This can become very important when the same object belongs to many data structures, because it keeps the objects being managed much simpler. For this reason, we will be examining a linked list that uses node objects.

## The List Manager

A linked list requires a list manager class that controls all access to the list. The list manager points to the first object in the list. For example, in Listing 19.1 the list manager's only variable is a pointer variable that points to an object of class node. In addition, a list manager class will have functions to:

- Insert items into the list.
- Remove items from the list.
- Find items in the list.
- Return the address of the first item in the list.

Figure 19.1 Sample run of the book illustration program

```
---------- MAIN MENU ----------

1. Enter a new illustration
2. Remove an illustration
3. View illustration list
9. Quit


Enter an option: 1
Figure number: 05.08
Source: Author
Permission needed? N
Do we have the art? N

---------- MAIN MENU ----------

1. Enter a new illustration
2. Remove an illustration
3. View illustration list
9. Quit


Enter an option: 1
Figure number: 04.10
Source: Times/Mirror
Permission needed? Y
Do we have the art? N

---------- MAIN MENU ----------

1. Enter a new illustration
2. Remove an illustration
3. View illustration list
9. Quit


Enter an option: 3

Figure 04.10:
Source: Times/Mirror
Permission needed? Y    On hand? N

Figure 05.08:
Source: Author
Permission needed? N    On hand? N
```

Notice in Listing 19.1 that the ListMgr class declaration includes references to objects of two other classes (node, the objects that form the list, and Art, the objects that are being linked by the list). When you start including pointers to objects of a different class within a class declaration, you can run into a problem. The compiler won't accept a pointer to a class until the class has been declared. The objects that manipulate data structures have to be declared before they can be used in other classes, but the other classes need to include

Figure 19.2   A linked list using node objects

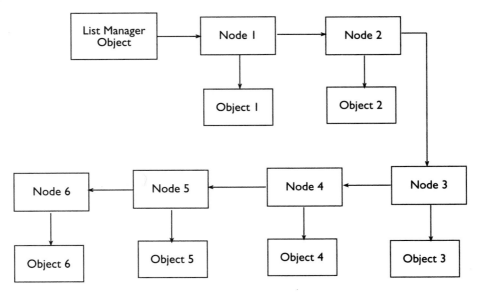

## Listing 19.1   ListMgr.h

```
// Forward declarations of classes used by the ListMgr whose declarations appear elsewhere
class node;
class Art;

class ListMgr
{
    private:
        node * first; // List manager only knows about the first node in the list
    public:
        ListMgr ();
        void insert (Art *);
        Art * find (char *); // traverse list to locate by figure number
        int remove (char *); // use figure number to locate for removal
        node * getFirst();
};
```

pointers to the objects that manipulate the data structures. (Yes, that is very cir-
cular …) There is a simple way around this problem: include a *forward reference*
to a class in a header file, before the class is actually declared.

A forward reference includes the keyword `class` and the name of the class. It tells the compiler that a class by that name will be declared later. For example, the header file for the list manager class includes the following statements:

```
class node;
class Art;
```

By placing these statements before the definition of the `ListMgr` class, the compiler won't flag an error when it encounters references to the `node` and `Art` classes prior to their declaration.

## The Node Class

The linked list we are creating is made up of a set of nodes chained together by pointers. Each node (Listing 19.2) therefore contains two pointer variables, one to point to the next node and another to point to the object being managed by the list (an object of class `Art`).

Listing 19.2   Node.h

```
class Art;

class node
{
    private:
        Art * theArt; // pointer to object being linked
        node * next; // pointer to next node in list
    public:
        node (Art *);
        node * getNextPtr ();
        Art * getArt ();
        void setNext (node *);
};
```

A node class typically contains functions to:

- Return a pointer to the object being managed by the list.
- Return a pointer to the next node in the list.
- Set the value of the pointer to the next node in the list.

## The Art Class

As mentioned earlier, one of the benefits of creating a linked list that uses separate node objects is that the objects being managed by the list are unaware of the list. Consider, for example, the Art class in Listing 19.3. The class has variables to store data about an illustration, and member functions to return the figure number and to display an object's data. There is absolutely nothing special or different about this class; it is blissfully unaware that multiple objects from the class will be logically linked together into a list.

Listing 19.3    Art.h

```
class Art
{
    private:
        char fig_numb[6];   // format: CC.NN
        char source[26];
        char permission_needed, on_hand;
    public:
        Art (char [], char [], char, char);
        char * getFigNumb ();
        void display();
};
```

## Searching a Linked List

A linked list is a *sequential* data structure. That is, its nodes can only be accessed in order, beginning with the first node, moving to the next, and the next, and so on. To search a linked list—regardless of whether the search is simply to retrieve an object from the list, find a place to insert a new object, or find an object to be removed—the strategy is the same: A program begins by obtaining the first node in the list from the list manager and then retrieving a pointer to the next node from each node in turn.

To help you see how this works, take a look at the list manager's find function in Listing 19.4. The function's single parameter is the figure number of the Art object to be found. Using that value, the search is performed in the following way:

1. Initialize the current node as the first node in the list.
2. If the current node is 0, return 0 to the calling function. (The list is empty or the program has reached the end of the list without finding a match.)

## Listing 19.4   ListMgr::find

```
Art * ListMgr::find (char * searchNumb)
{
    Art * currentArt;
    node * current, * next;
    current = first;  // start at head of list

    while (current != 0)
    {
        currentArt = current->getArt();
        if (strcmp (searchNumb, currentArt->getFigNumb()) == 0)
            return currentArt;
        current = current->getNextPtr();
    }
    return 0;  // not found
}
```

3. Retrieve a pointer to the illustration pointed by the current node.
4. Compare the figure number of the illustration pointed to by the current node to the figure number for which we are searching.
5. If the figure numbers match, return a pointer to the illustration pointed to by the current node.
6. If the figure numbers don't match, obtain the contents of the current node's next variable and make that the new current node.
7. Continue with Step 2.

It is then up to the calling function to determine whether find returned a valid address or a 0, indicating that the search was unsuccessful.

**Note**

As written, the book illustration program's application class doesn't use the find function because the program doesn't provide an option to find an illustration by figure number. However, the function has been included in the list manager class to make the class complete. This means that the book illustration program could be modified at any time to support the added capability, without needing to make any changes to the list manager.

## Inserting Objects into a Linked List

Objects are inserted into a linked list under two circumstances: either data are being read in from a file or an object is being created interactively. Why does a program need to recreate a list if the objects in the list are stored in a file before the program ends? Because the pointer that created a linked list won't be the same each time the program is run. There is no way to guarantee that a program always loads in memory at the same place. (A program's location in memory depends on what other programs are running when the program is launched.) Each time an object is created, it will almost certainly be located at a main memory address different from where it was the last time the program was run. In fact, using pointers from a previous program run will corrupt any other program running concurrently that happens to be occupying the memory locations pointed to by the stored pointers. A program must therefore recreate the pointers that define linked lists as data are read in from a file. By the same token, a program shouldn't bother to store the pointers that define a linked list in a data file.

Several strategies can be used to insert a new object into a linked list. New objects can always be placed at the beginning of the list. Alternatively, they can be placed at the end of the list. (If you are inserting new objects at the end of a list, it helps a great deal if the list manager maintains a pointer to the last object as well as to the first.) Often, however, linked lists are kept in a particular order, such as alphabetical or chronological. The list used by the book illustration program, for example, is kept in alphabetical order by figure number.

Regardless of where a new object is inserted into a linked list, at least two pointers have to be modified to make the insertion:

- The "next" pointer in the preceding object must be modified to point to the new object. If the object is being inserted at the beginning of the list, the "first" pointer in the list manager object must be modified.
- The "next" pointer in the new object must be modified to point to the next object in the list.

As an example, take a look at Figure 19.3. In this case, the new node (Node 7) is being placed between existing nodes 4 and 5. To perform the insertion, a program must break the existing link between nodes 4 and 5. This break occurs when the value in Node 4's next pointer variable is changed. A program must therefore make Node 4 point to Node 7. Then, Node 7 must point to Node 5.

The procedure about which you have just read makes one major assumption: we know the location in the list where the new node is to be inserted. Before beginning an insert, a program must find that location. The function to insert an illustration into the linked list of illustrations

Figure 19.3   Inserting a node into a linked list

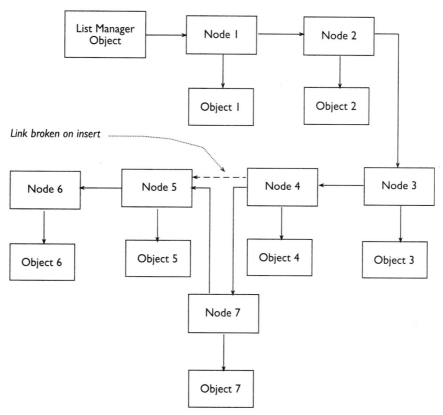

(Listing 19.5) therefore includes code that looks similar to the find function. The search begins at the first object in the list and continues until either the end of the list is reached or the figure number of the new illustration is alphabetically greater than the figure number of the illustration just checked. When the latter condition arises, the new illustration is inserted between the illustration just checked and the object that follows it.

Because this list is using node objects, the insertion function must also create new nodes. The process to perform the insertion is therefore as follows:

1.  Create a new node object, initializing it with a pointer to the illustration object.

## Listing 19.5   ListMgr::insert

```
void ListMgr::insert (Art * theArt)
{
    node * newNode, * current, * previous;
    char * newFigNumb;
    Art * currentArt;

    newNode = new node (theArt); // create a node object
    newFigNumb = theArt->getFigNumb();

    if (first == 0) // list is empty
        first = newNode;
    else
    {
        int firstNode = TRUE;
        current = first; // start at head of list
        while (current != 0)
        {
            currentArt = current->getArt();
            if (strcmp (newFigNumb, currentArt->getFigNumb()) <= 0)
                break; // spot found
            // save preceding node
            previous = current;
            current = current->getNextPtr();
            firstNode = FALSE; // not the first node
        }

        // set previous node to point to new node except when first in list
        if (!firstNode)
            previous->setNext (newNode);
        else
            first = newNode; // have new first in list

        // set new node to point to following node
        newNode->setNext (current);
    }
}
```

2. Retrieve the figure number from the new illustration object.
3. If the list is empty (the `first` pointer in the list manager object is 0), insert the new node as first in the list by setting `first` to the address of the new node. Return to the calling function.
4. Set a flag to indicate that the new node will be first in the list.
5. Initialize the current node as the first node in the list.
6. If the current node is 0 (end of list has been reached), go to Step 11.
7. Retrieve a pointer to the illustration pointed to by the current node.

8. Compare the figure number of the illustration pointed to by the current node to the figure number for which we are searching. If the figure number of the new illustration is greater than the figure number of the current illustration, go to step 11.

9. Save the current node as the previous node.

10. Retrieve the contents of the current node's `next` variable and make it the current node.

11. Set the flag to indicate that the new node won't be first in the list.

12. Go to step 5.

13. If the new node won't be first in the list, set the previous node to point to the new node.

14. If the new node is first in the list, set the list manager to point to the new node.

15. Set the new node to point to the current node.

This process handles two special cases. The first arises when the program is inserting the first node into the list. If that is the case, there is no need to perform a search. The function can simply set the list manager's `first` pointer to point to the first node.

The second special case arises when a new illustration must be inserted at the head of the list. (In other words, its figure number alphabetically precedes all other figure numbers in the list.) In that situation, the function modifies the list manager object to point to the new illustration's node and the new node to point to the node that was previously first in the list.

The creation of a new `Art` object and its insertion into the linked list are coordinated by the application object. As you can see in Listing 19.6, the application object collects the data needed for an `Art` object, creates the object, and then asks the list manager to insert the new object into the list.

## Removing Objects from a Linked List

Removing an object from a linked list is just the opposite of inserting it. Assuming that the program has found the node that is to be removed, it isolates that node by modifying the pointer in the previous node to point to the following node. For example, in Figure 19.4 the "next" pointer in Node 4 has been changed to point to Node 6. The effect is the removal of Node 5. Note that as long as Node 5 remains in main memory, it will continue to point to Node 6. However, because the link between 4 and 5 no longer exists, the pointer from Node 5 has no impact on the list.

## Listing 19.6    AppClass::addArt

```
void AppClass::addArt()
{
    Art * newArt;
    char iFigNumb[6], iSource[26];
    char iperm, ionHand;

    cout << "Figure number: ";
    cin.getline (iFigNumb, 6);
    cout << "Source: ";
    cin.getline (iSource,26);
    cout << "Permission needed? ";
    cin.get (iperm);
    cout << "Do we have the art? ";
    cin.get (ionHand);
    newArt = new Art (iFigNumb, iSource, iperm, ionHand);
    theList->insert (newArt);
}
```

## Figure 19.4    Removing a node from a linked list

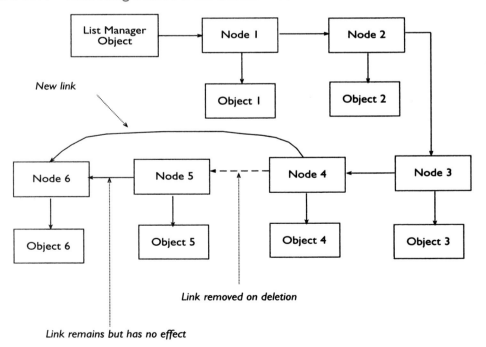

To program the node removal (Listing 19.7), the list manager searches through the list until it finds the node that is to be removed. Once it has found the node, it sets the previous node to point to the node following the node being removed. However, if the node being removed happens to be the first node in the list, the function must modify the list manager so that the node following the node being removed becomes the new first node.

An insertion into a linked list isn't likely to fail. Either a new node goes at the beginning, in the middle, or at the end of the list, regardless of how many nodes are currently in the list. However, a removal can fail. First, the list may be empty. Second, the node that the program has been asked to remove may not be in the list. Therefore, the remove function returns a value that indicates whether the removal was successful. It is up to the calling function to interpret that return value and take appropriate action. For example, the book illustration's application class displays a message to the user when removal has failed (see Listing 19.8).

## Traversing a Linked List

Although the list insertion and removal functions traverse the linked list to examine nodes in order, they aren't capable of returning the nodes one at a time to a calling function for processing. To present a listing of all the nodes in the list, a program needs a class that keeps track of the last node accessed. Such a class would then feed the "next" node to a calling function when asked.

A class that traverses a data structure and returns nodes one at a time to a calling function is known as an *iterator*. For the linked list in our example, the iterator class (Listing 19.9) needs to keep track of only two things: the list whose nodes it is accessing (theList) and the most recent node accessed (current). The only thing the iterator needs to know how to do is find a pointer to the Art object being referenced by its current node.

To see how this works, let's first look at how the list iterator is used. The application object begins by creating a list iterator object (Listing 19.10), passing it a pointer to the list manager object.

The iterator object's constructor then takes over. As you can see in Listing 19.11, it sets the current node to 0 and stores the pointer to the list manager object.

The application object begins the traversal by obtaining a pointer to the first Art object. If the list is empty, the call to the list iterator's getNext function will return 0 and the following while loop will never execute. However, if

## Listing 19.7   ListMgr::remove

```
int ListMgr::remove (char * searchNumb)
{
    Art * currentArt;
    node * current, * previous, * next;

    if (first == 0)
        return FALSE; // list is empty

    int firstNode = TRUE;
    current = first;

    while (current != 0)
    {
        currentArt = current->getArt();
        if (strcmp (searchNumb, currentArt->getFigNumb()) == 0)
            break; // jump out of loop
        // save preceding because there aren't backward pointers
        previous = current;
        current = current->getNextPtr();
        firstNode = FALSE; // not the first node
    }

    if (current == 0)
        return FALSE; // node not found

    if (!firstNode)
    {
        next = current->getNextPtr(); // gets node after node being removed
        previous->setNext (next);
    }
    else
        // sets first to node after node being removed
        first = current->getNextPtr();

    delete current->getArt(); // remove art object from memory

    delete current; // remove node object from memory

    return TRUE; // remove was successful
}
```

there is at least one node in the list, the function enters the loop and displays data about the current illustration. Then, the function gets a pointer to the next illustration.

## Listing 19.8   AppClass::removeArt

```
void AppClass::removeArt()
{
    char iFigNumb[6];

    cout << "Figure number to remove: ";
    cin.getline (iFigNumb, 6);
    int result = theList->remove (iFigNumb);
    if (result)
        cout << "Remove successful";
    else
        cout << "Remove unsuccessful";
}
```

## Listing 19.9   ListItr.h

```
class ListMgr;
class node;
class Art;

class ListItr
{
    private:
        node * current;
        ListMgr * theList;
    public:
        ListItr (ListMgr *);
        Art * getNext ();
};
```

## Listing 19.10   AppClass::viewArt

```
void AppClass::viewArt()
{
    Art * current;
    ListItr * theIterator;

    theIterator = new ListItr (theList);
    current = theIterator->getNext();
    cout << endl;  // just a blank line for spacing
    while (current != 0)
    {
        current->display();
        current = theIterator->getNext();
    }
}
```

### Listing 19.11  ListItr::ListItr

```
ListItr::ListItr (ListMgr * whichList)
{
    current = 0;
    theList = whichList;
}
```

Notice that the first call to getNext actually returns the first element in the linked list. The getNext function (Listing 19.12) detects the beginning of a traversal by looking for the 0 that was placed in current by the constructor.

### Listing 19.12   ListItr::getNext

```
Art * ListItr::getNext ()
{
    if (current == 0)
        current = theList->getFirst();
    else
        current = current->getNextPtr();

    if (current != 0)
        return current->getArt();
    else
        return 0;
}
```

Because the list iterator stores the last accessed node in current, it is able to keep track of where it is in the list. The iterator object is destroyed when the viewArt function terminates. This means that if the function is executed again, even during the same program run, the function creates a brand new list iterator object that is reinitialized to start again at the beginning of the list.

## Summary

A linked list is a sequential data structure that links objects together by having each object point to the next object in the list. A linked list has no preset limit on the number of objects that can be added to the list. (The limit is usually the amount of memory available to the program.) However, because it is a sequential data structure, it can only be searched sequentially (from first, to next, to next, and so on.)

An object-oriented linked list is handled by a list manager object. The list manager takes care of inserting items into the list, removing items from the list, and locating items in the list. An object called an iterator is responsible for traversing the list, returning the objects in the list, in order.

There are two general strategies for creating an object-oriented linked list. The first embeds the pointer to the next object in the list directly in the objects being linked. The second uses a node object that points to the object being linked. The node contains a pointer to the next node; there are no pointers in the objects being linked.

## Exercises

1. Create two classes, one to store data about a college student and another to store the courses taken by a student. The course class should include the name and number of the course, the semester/quarter in which the course was taken, the number of course credits, and the grade earned. Create a class that manipulates a linked list that connects course objects to a student object. Also create a class that manipulates an array of student objects. Write a program that tests the classes. The program should do the following:

   • Permit interactive entry of student and course data. The constructor for the student class should insert the student into the array of student objects; the constructor for the course class should insert the course into the correct student's linked list of courses. Optionally, write member functions that store the classes in a data file when the program ends and read the objects into main memory when the program begins.
   • Compute a student's grade point average (GPA) and store the value in the student object. The program should recalculate the GPA each time a new course is added.
   • Display a student's transcript.
   • Determine if or when a specific student has taken a specific course. The user enters the student number and the course number; the program does the rest.

2.  Write a program that provides lists of the passengers scheduled to fly on an airline's flights. This program needs three classes: a flight (flight number, date, time, and maximum number of passengers), a passenger (name, address, and phone number), and a list manager to handle a linked list of passengers for each flight. Allow users to create new flights, add passengers to a flight, remove passengers from a flight, and display a list of a flight's passengers. Be sure to avoid overbooking!

3.  The Suddenly Summer Bathing Suit Company needs a program to manage telephone messages that come into the home office for its salespeople. The telephone is answered by a secretary, who types the message into a computer. Write a program that can be used to store and retrieve messages. The program is based on three classes: a salesperson class (name and password), a message class (the text of the message—up to 256 characters, the date and time of the message, whether the message has been read), and a class to manipulate a linked list of the messages waiting for a given salesperson. The program should allow a secretary to enter messages. A salesperson should be able to retrieve his or her unread messages, all messages (read and unread), and delete messages. Note that a secretary can enter messages for any salesperson. However, a salesperson must supply a recognized name and password to retrieve or delete messages. To make this practical, of course, salesperson data and messages must be maintained in data files that are read when the program is run and written when the program stops.

# 20

# Overloading

## OBJECTIVES

In this chapter you will read about:

- How overloading can give functions and operators more than one meaning.
- Simplifying date manipulations with overloaded operators.
- Simplifying string manipulations with overloaded operators.

*Overloading* is a technique that gives operators and functions multiple definitions so that using the same operator or calling the same function results in different actions, depending on how the operator or function is used. The major benefit of overloading is that it simplifies the use of classes by helping to present a consistent interface to the programmer.

Although you may not be aware of it, you have already used overloaded operators. For example, the stream insertion and extraction operators are redefinitions of the C++ operators that shift the bits in a storage location to the right (>>) or left (<<). The classes you have seen that have more than one constructor are examples of function overloading.

In this chapter we will summarize and extend your knowledge of function overloading. However, the primary thrust of this chapter is to introduce you to operator overloading so that you can simplify the way in which your programs manipulate objects.

## Overloading Functions

When a C++ compiler compiles member functions, it identifies a function by more than just its name. A function's *signature* is made up of its name along with the number, type, and order of its parameters. It is therefore acceptable to define more than one function by the same name in the same class, as long as the functions have the same signature. For example, a C++ compiler recognizes the following functions as different:

```
Object * find (char *, int);
Object * find (int, char *);
```

Although the two functions return the same type of value and have the same name, number of parameters, and parameter types, the order of their parameters is distinct. When you define two or more member functions in the same class with the same name, distinguishing them by their parameters, you are using function overloading.

**Note**

Using the same function name in different classes isn't precisely the same as overloading within a single class. A C++ compiler identifies member functions in terms of the classes in which they are defined. You can therefore define two functions with exactly the same name and parameter list for two distinct, unrelated classes without a problem. The program knows which class's member function to used based on the type of object issuing the function call.

# Overloading Constructors

One of the most common uses of overloading is to provide multiple constructors for the same class. The supply inventory program, for example, has two constructors for its Item class—one for data entered from the keyboard and the other for data read from a file. As you can see, the function signatures are significantly different:

```
Item (ifstream &); // file input constructor
Item (int, int, int, char *); // interactive constructor
```

The first constructor has only one parameter—an input stream reference. The second constructor's parameters are three integers and a character pointer.

As you can see in Listing 20.1, the implementations of the two functions are also considerably different. Keep in mind, however, that the C++ compiler knows which function to bind to an object based on the entire function signature, not just the function name.

## Listing 20.1    Overloaded constructors for the Item class

```
// file input constructor
Item::Item(ifstream & fin)
{
    char white_space;

    fin.getline (Desc, 80, '\0');
    fin >> Item_numb >> On_hand >> Reorder_pt;

    // Need to skip over blank at the end of the reorder point value to prepare for reading next object,
    // which begins with a string.
    fin.get (white_space);
}

// interactive constructor
Item::Item (int iItem_numb, int iOn_hand, int iReorder_pt, char * iDesc)
{
    Item_numb = iItem_numb;
    On_hand = iOn_hand;
    Reorder_pt = iReorder_pt;
    strcpy (Desc, iDesc);
}
```

**Note**

Because C++ compilers identify functions by the entire function signature and not just the name of the function, compilers can identify many errors that involve the wrong types and/or numbers of parameters passed to functions by comparing the parameter list in a function call to the parameter list in a prototype. In most cases, the compiler's error message will tell you that the compiler can't find a function that matches the signature in a function call. It's then up to you to figure out where the function call's parameter list differs from that of the function's prototype.

## Copy Constructors

Many classes contain a third type of constructor known as a *copy constructor*. It is an overloaded member function, just like the constructors you have seen for interactive and file input. The purpose of a copy constructor is to initialize a new object with data copied from another object of the same class. For example, the Item class might declare a copy constructor as

```
Item (Item);
```

The function can then be implemented simply with

```
Item::Item (Item copyItem)
    { *this = copyItem; }
```

Using the default assignment in the preceding example will work only if the class contains no pointers. If the class contains pointers, then you will end up having two objects pointing to the same place in main memory because the contents of pointer variables will be copied along with the contents of regular variables. Therefore, if a class contains pointers, a copy constructor must initialize each variable individually.

For example, assume that a class named sampleClass contains the following variables:

```
someClass * anObject;
int ID_numb;
char name[31], address[81;
```

If you attempt to use the default *this assignment for these variables, you will end up with two objects pointing to the same object created from someClass because the assignment will copy the address of the someClass object rather than creating a new one. This means that you can't use *this to copy from one object to another but must write a copy constructor that creates an object from someClass. A sample copy constructor might appear like the one in Listing 20.2. Notice that the regular variables are copied using an assignment statement but that the anObject pointer is filled by using the new statement to create the object.

### Listing 20.2   A copy constructor

```
sampleClass::sampleClass (sampleClass & original)
{
    ID_numb = original.ID_numb;
    strcpy (name, original.name);
    strcpy (address, original.address);
    anObject = new someClass();
}
```

You can invoke a copy constructor when you declare an object as a variable. For example, assume that a program contains the following:

```
sampleClass firstObject (0, "", "");
sampleClass secondObject = firstObject;
```

The first declaration creates an object from sampleClass and passes the data for the class into a constructor designed for interactive input. (The ID_numb variable receives the 0; the two string variables receive nulls.) Although the second declaration looks like an assignment statement, it actually creates secondObject and invokes the copy constructor, passing firstObject into the constructor.

## Overloading Operators

Overloading functions is easy: all you need to do is make sure that the overloaded functions have different signatures. There are no other restrictions on the overloaded functions. Overloading operators is very different. Although overloaded operators are implemented as functions, there are significant restrictions on where they are defined and the number and type of parameters they can accept.

If operator overloading is surrounded by more restrictions than function overloading, why bother to do it at all? Because overloaded operators can greatly simplify the interface between a programmer and the classes he or she is using. For example, we often use overloaded operators to make it easier to work with dates and strings. Wouldn't it be nice if you could do the following?

```
String firstString, secondString;
:
:
if (firstString == secondString) ...
```

You wouldn't ever need to work explicitly with string functions again. And wouldn't it be nice if you could enter a date in MM/DD/YY format and have date comparisons work correctly?

In the rest of this chapter you will learn about two utility classes—`date` and `String`—that make it possible for you to manipulate these two types of data as if they were simple data types. You can use these classes in many programs you write. (The sample application class `Run` functions that you see in this chapter are included only to demonstrate the operation of the utility classes.)

In Figure 20.1 you will find the sample output of a program that tests the `date` class. The class accepts either a current system date or a string in the format MM/DD/YY to initialize an object. It can add an integer to a date, such as the 30 days that have been added to the current date. It can also use the normal relationship operators to make comparisons between dates.

## Figure 20.1   Using the date class

```
Today is 5/14/1996.
30 days from today will be 6/13/1996.

Enter a date (MM/DD/YY): 10/13/2020
Enter another date (MM/DD/YY): 01/07/2100

The first date is earlier than the second date.
```

The `String` class, whose test program generates a output like that in Figure 20.2, has constructors that accept either a literal string or another string object as input (a copy constructor). Overloaded operators allow a program using the class to assign literal strings to a string object, use normal relationship operators to compare strings, and perform concatenation with the += operator. In addition, the String class overloads the unary * (pointer to) operator so that a String object can be used anywhere a char * is required.

**Figure 20.2   Using the String class**

```
Enter a string: This is a test string
The string you just entered is: This is a test string

Enter another string: Another test string
The string you just entered is: Another test string

The second string is alphabetically first.

A third string has been initialized to: Another test string

Enter the first half of a string: This is a

Enter the second half of a string: silly way to test strings

The concatenated string is: This is a silly way to test strings
```

## Operators Available for Overloading

Most of C++'s operators are available for overloading, including those in Table 20.1. Notice that the operators are divided into two types, unary and binary. Unary operators are those that work in a single value. For example, the + operator can be used to preserve the sign of a single value, as in +sales. However, when the same operator is used between two other values, as in sales + tax, it is a binary operator that adds the two values together.

The distinction between unary and binary operators may seem trivial. However, as you will see shortly, the rules for where you define overloaded operator functions and the number of parameters they can take depend in some part on whether the operator is unary or binary.

**Note**

The idea behind overloaded operators is to define new behavior for operators that are consistent with the operators' default behaviors. It is confusing to the programmer if operator overloading drastically changes an operator's behavior. For example, overloading a multiplication operator to perform addition is confusing. However, overloading a multiplication operator so that it multiplies the values contained in two objects makes sense.

Table 20.1   Some of the C++ operators available for overloading

| Operator | Type | Operator | Type | Operator | Type |
|----------|------|----------|------|----------|------|
| + | Unary | ++ | Unary | ! | Unary |
| - | Unary | -- | Unary | ( ) | Unary |
| * | Unary | [ ] | Unary | | |
| + | Binary | * | Binary | | |
| - | Binary | / | Binary | % | Binary |
| == | Binary | = | Binary | & | Binary |
| != | Binary | += | Binary | && | Binary |
| < | Binary | -= | Binary | \| | Binary |
| <= | Binary | *= | Binary | \|\| | Binary |
| >= | Binary | /= | Binary | << | Binary |
| > | Binary | %= | Binary | >> | Binary |

## The Rules for Operator Overloading

As mentioned earlier, the implementation of operator overloading is rather restrictive. The rules that you will be encountering as we go through examples of operator overloading include the following:

- Operator overloading can be used only to redefine the behavior of existing operators. It cannot be used to define new ones.
- Overloading for a unary operator can be declared as a member function with no parameters. The operator then always acts on the current object.
- Overloading with a unary operator can be declared as a *friend* function (a function that's not part of the class but has access to the entire class) with one parameter, which must be an object of the class or a pointer to an object of the class.
- Overloading for a binary operator can be declared as a member function with one parameter. In this case, the current object must always be used on the left of the operator. The object or value on the right of the operator is taken from the parameter passed into the function.

- Overloading for a binary operator can be declared as a friend function with two parameters, one of which must be an object of the class or a pointer to an object of the class. The first parameter is the value or object that is used on the left of the operator; the second parameter is the value or object that is used on the right.

How do you choose whether to implement an overloaded operator as a member function or a friend function? The answer is tied to the nature of friend functions and the flexibility you need for the overloaded operator. A friend function has access to all the private variables and functions in the class for which it is declared as a friend. Using friend functions therefore violates the object-oriented principle of information hiding. Many programmers therefore prefer not to use friend functions if they can be avoided.

However, when you overload a binary operator as a member function, it can only take one parameter. For example, if you want to compare a string object to a literal string, an overloaded operator can be declared as

```
int operator== (char *);
```

The problem with this declaration is that when the overloaded operator is used, the object must always be on the left side of the operator as in

```
Object_name == "Comparison string"
```

In other words, the operation isn't commutative. If you want it to be commutative, so that the object and the constant can be on either side of the operator, then you must implement the overloading using two friend functions, each of which can take two parameters:

```
friend int operator==(String, char *);
friend int operator==(char *, String);
```

Because the overloaded operator sends the object or value on the left side of the operator into the first parameter and the object or value on the right side of the operator into the second parameter, the compiler chooses whichever of the two functions above matches the use of the operator in a program. When you want an overloaded operator to be commutative, you have no alternative but to use friend functions in the above fashion.

## Declaring Overloaded Operators

The date and string classes use both member functions and friend functions to overload operators. As you can see in Listing 20.3, the date class has two friend functions, both of which allow a program to add an integer to a date. The rest of the operators—the relationship and assignment operators—are overloaded as member functions.

### Listing 20.3  Date.h

```
class date
{
    friend date operator+ (int, date);
    friend date operator+ (date, int);

    typedef char date_string[11];
    private:
        int month, day, year;
        void itoa (int, char *); // convert integer back to ASCII
    public:
        date (char *);
        date (tm *); // constructor that works off tm structure
        int getMonth ();
        int getDay ();
        int getYear ();
        char * showDate (date_string);
        // overloaded operators
        int operator== (date);
        int operator!= (date);
        int operator> (date);
        int operator>= (date);
        int operator< (date);
        int operator<= (date);
        // assignment--lets you copy one date to another
        void operator= (date *);
};
```

The string class (Listing 20.4) uses friend functions to overload the relationship operators when a string object is compared to a literal string. However, it uses member functions when a string object is compared to another string object. The remaining operators (assignment, type conversion, and individual character access) are overloaded as member functions.

Notice that this class declaration combines both function and operator overloading. There are as many as three functions for each overloaded operator. Each function for a given operator, however, has a different signature, making them different functions as far as the compiler is concerned.

## Listing 20.4    stringClass.h

```
class String
{
    // operators overloaded as friend functions

    // equal to
    friend int operator== (String, char *);
    friend int operator== (char *, String);

    // not equal to
    friend int operator!= (String, char *);
    friend int operator!= (char *, String);

    // greater than
    friend int operator> (String, char *);
    friend int operator> (char *, String);

    // greater than or equal to
    friend int operator>= (String, char *);
    friend int operator>= (char *, String);

    // less than
    friend int operator< (String, char *);
    friend int operator< (char *, String);

    // less than or equal to
    friend int operator<= (String, char *);
    friend int operator<= (char *, String);

private:
    char cString[256]; // 255 character C string
public:
    String (); // default constructorl
    String (String &); // copy constructor
    String (char *); // initialize to literal
    char * getcString (); // return pointer to the string itself
    int len (); // get length of string

    // overloaded operators

    // assignment
    void operator= (String *); // assignment between two C string objects
    void operator= (char *); // assignment from a literal
```

Continued next page

**Listing 20.4**(Continued)    **stringClass.h**

```
// relationship
int operator== (String);
int operator> (String);
int operator>= (String);
int operator< (String);
int operator<= (String);
int operator!= (String);

// concatenation
void operator+= (String);
void operator+= (char *);

// character access
// program sends in array index; use on right side of =
char operator[] (int);

// type conversion (lets you use String in place of char *)
operator char*();
};
```

To declare an overloaded operator as a member function, create a public function prototype in which the name of the function is the keyword `operator` followed by the operator being overloaded. The function's return data type will depend on the type of operator. For example, relationship operators should return an `int` or `bool` (if the latter is supported by your compiler) because a relationship operator produces a result of either true or false (1 or 0). By the same token, assignment operators don't need to return any value, while the functions to add a constant to a date should return the modified date.

To declare an overloaded operator as a friend function, place the function prototype within the class but before the public or private elements of the class. Precede the prototype with the keyword `friend`.

## Overloading Operators for Date Manipulation

The overloaded operators that handle dates require objects of class `date`. This means that before a program can use overloaded operators to simplify date manipulation, dates must be transformed into date objects. We will therefore begin by looking at how date objects are initialized and then examine the overloaded operators that manipulate them.

## Creating Date Objects

A date object can be initialized either by passing a constructor a string in the format MM/DD/YY (or YYYY) or by passing a constructor a data structure containing the current system date.

### Constructing Dates from a String

In Listing 20.5 you will find the date class constructor that breaks a string into month, day, and year parts and converts those parts to integers for storage. This process—scanning a string to break it into its constituent parts—is known as *parsing*.

### Listing 20.5   Constructing dates from a string

```
date::date (char * stringDate)
{
    char Tstring[5];
    int i = 0, j = 0;

    while (stringDate[i] != '/' && stringDate[i] != '-')
        Tstring[i++] = stringDate[i]; // copy month
    Tstring[i] = '\0';
    month = atoi (Tstring); // convert to integer
    i++; // skip over delimeter
    while (stringDate[i] != '/' && stringDate[i] != '-')
        Tstring[j++] = stringDate[i++];   // get day; need to start over at 0 with Tstring
    Tstring[j] = '\0';
    day = atoi (Tstring); // convert to integer
    i++; // skip over delimeter
    strcpy (Tstring, &stringDate[i]); // get rest of string for year
    year = atoi (Tstring); // convert to integer
}
```

The parsing logic used in this constructor is based on the knowledge that a user will type either a / or - to separate the parts of the date. The constructor therefore looks at each character in the string, beginning with the first character, checking to see if it is one of the two *delimiters* (characters that separate identifiable parts of a string).

Once the constructor finds a delimiter, it knows that the preceding character or characters (those encountered after the last delimiter) represent a part of the date that should be saved. The constructor therefore copies those characters into a separate string variable and converts them to an integer using the `atoi` function. (The `atoi`—ASCII to integer—function is part of the C libraries, and its header file can be found in *stdlib.h*.)

Notice that this type of parsing—looking for the delimiters—has one major advantage: The user can enter one- or two-digit days and months, or two- or four-digit years, and the parsing will work correctly.

## Constructing Dates from the Current System Date

ANSI C++ provides a somewhat convoluted way for a program to read and manipulate the current system date and time. The ultimate target of the sequence of library function calls is a structure called `tm`. A *structure* is a variable that groups together other variables of different data types. In some ways, it is like a class that has variables but no member functions. Although structures are used frequently in C programs (which have no object capabilities), C++ programs typically use them only when interacting with functions from the C libraries.

The `tm` structure (found in the header file *time.h*) is declared as follows:

```
struct tm
{
    int tm_sec;
    int tm_min;
    int tm_hour;
    int tm_mday;
    int tm_mon;
    int tm_year;
    int tm_wday;
    int tm_yday;
    int tm_isdat;
}
```

To use the structure, a program can declare a variable from the structure, much as you would declare an object for static binding:

```
struct tm dateTime;
```

Alternatively, a program can declare a pointer to the structure for use by a library function that returns a `tm` pointer:

```
struct tm * todayPtr;
```

The C library function that returns the current date and time is `time`, which we used in Chapter 13 as part of the seed for the random number generator. Unfortunately, `time` doesn't place its result into a `tm` structure, but returns data in a custom data type called `time_t` that contains the number of seconds that have elapsed since 00:00:00 GMT, January 1, 1970. This means that the `time_t` value must be converted into a `tm` structure. The process therefore requires the following steps:

```
struct tm * today;
time_t seconds;

time (&seconds);
today = localtime (&seconds);
```

First, we declare a pointer to a `tm` structure and a variable of type `time_t`. Then we call the `time` function, passing it the address of the `time_t` variable into which the result should be placed. Then, the result is converted to a `tm` structure by calling `localtime`. This function expects the address of a `time_t` variable as input and returns a pointer to the `tm` structure it produces.

The pointer to the `tm` structure can then be passed into a `date` class constructor (Listing 20.6) with the following syntax:

```
theDate = new date (today);
```

Notice that because we are working with a pointer to the structure, the constructor uses arrow notation to access the variables in the structure. If the program were working with the structure itself, then it would use dot notation.

## Listing 20.6   Constructing a date from a tm structure

```
date::date (tm * today)  // works off tm structure returned by localtime
{
    month = today->tm_mon + 1;  // months numbered beginning with 0
    day = today->tm_mday;
    year = today->tm_year + 1900;  // year in structure is - 1900
}
```

The `tm` structure stores dates in a slightly different way than the `date` class. For example, the `tm` structure numbers months beginning with 0 and subtracts 1900 from all years. The constructor in Listing 20.6 therefore adjusts for these differences.

If you're a new programmer, how do you figure out which library functions to use to do things like capturing the current system date? Your program development software will be accompanied by an ANSI library reference manual (either in paper or electronic form). The entries in that reference document every library function, including the function's prototype, the header file in which the prototype is declared, and an explanation of how the function is used. It pays to spend some time browsing through the library reference manual so that you get an overall view of what functions are available to you.

## Overloading the Assignment Operator

To overload the assignment operator, create a function that copies the contents of one object into another. As you can see in Listing 20.7, assignment has been implemented as a member function that expects a pointer to a date object as its sole input parameter. The function itself uses arrow notation to call the "get" functions belonging to the input object (the object on the right of the assignment operator). The retrieved values are assigned to the variables of the current object (the object on the left of the assignment operator).

**Listing 20.7    Assigning one date to another**

```
void date::operator= (date * inDate) // copy
{
    month = inDate->getMonth();
    day = inDate->getDay();
    year = inDate->getYear();
}
```

To use the overloaded assignment operator, a program declares two pointer variables, one for each date, as in Listing 20.8. Then, a program can replace the contents of the first date with the contents of the second by writing a simple assignment.

## Overloading the Relationship Operators

When dates are involved, the relationship operators should make their decisions based on chronological order. As you can see in Listing 20.9, the functions must examine each part of the date individually, beginning with the year. Each returns either true or false (1 or 0).

## Listing 20.8    Declaring and copying dates

```
cout << "\nEnter a date (MM/DD/YY): ";
cin.getline (string_date, 11);
theDate = new date (string_date);

cout << "Enter another date (MM/DD/YY): ";
cin.getline (string_date,11);
date * secondDate = new date (string_date);

// Replace the contents of the second date with the contents of the first date
secondDate = firstDate;
```

The relationship operators expect a date object as a parameter, rather than a pointer to an object. This means that when a program is working with pointers to date objects, it must dereference the pointers when invoking overloaded relationship operators. Notice in Listing 20.10, for example, that the-Date and secondDate, both of which have been declared as pointers to objects of class date, are preceded by the * operator when used in a logical expression.

# Overloading the Addition Operator

Date addition is used frequently in business programming to determine, for example, when a payment is due or how long a payment is overdue. Any date class should therefore make it possible to add an integer (a given number of days) to a date.

The date class we have been using as an example overloads the addition operator as friend functions. This way, the functions that provide the overloading can take two parameters, making it possible to have the date object on either side of the operator. Friend functions are not member functions—they don't belong to the class—and therefore do not include a class name and scope resolution operator in their name.

The functions that implement the overloading can be found in Listing 20.11. Because our calendar has months of varying lengths, the addition has to be performed one part of the date at a time. (Yes, you're right; these addition functions don't adjust for leap years ...)

To use the addition, a program must dereference a pointer to a date object, as in

```
*theDate = *theDate + 30;
```

## Listing 20.9    Overloaded relationship operators

```
// Overloading the equality operator
int date::operator== (date inDate)
{
    if (month == inDate.getMonth() && day == inDate.getDay() && year ==
    inDate.getYear())
        return TRUE;
    return FALSE;
}



// Overloading the not equal operator
int date::operator!= (date inDate)
{
    if (month == inDate.getMonth() && day == inDate.getDay() && year ==
    inDate.getYear())
        return FALSE;
    return TRUE;
}



// Overloading the greater than operator
int date::operator> (date inDate)
{
    if (year > inDate.getYear())
        return TRUE;
    if (year == inDate.getYear())
    {
        if (month > inDate.getMonth())
            return TRUE;
        if (month == inDate.getMonth() && day > inDate.getDay())
            return TRUE;
    }
    return FALSE;
}



// Overloading the greater than or equals to operator
int date::operator>= (date inDate)
{
    if (*this > inDate)
        return TRUE;
    if (*this == inDate)
        return TRUE;
    return FALSE;
}
```

Continued next page

Listing 20.9(Continued)   Overloaded relationship operators

```
// Overloading the less than operator
int date::operator< (date inDate)
{
    if (year < inDate.getYear())
        return TRUE;
    if (year == inDate.getYear())
    {
        if (month < inDate.getMonth())
            return TRUE;
        if (month == inDate.getMonth() && day < inDate.getDay())
            return TRUE;
    }
    return FALSE;
}


// Overloading the less than or equal to operator
int date::operator<= (date inDate)
{
    if (*this < inDate)
        return TRUE;
    if (*this == inDate)
        return TRUE;
    return FALSE;
}
```

Listing 20.10   Using overloaded relationship operators

```
cout << endl;
if (*theDate < *secondDate)
    cout << "The first date is earlier than the second date" << ".";
else
    cout << "The second date is earlier than the first date" << ".";
```

Should you choose to use static binding rather than dynamic binding when creating date objects, then the dereference isn't required.

## Overloading Operators for String Manipulation

As with dates, using overloaded operators with string means that a program must work with a string object declared from the class in which the overloading is implemented. For the following discussion, our example will be the String class whose declaration you saw in Listing 20.4.

## Listing 20.11    Overloading the addition operator

```
// Overloading the addition operator
date operator+ (int days2add, date inDate)
{
    inDate.day += days2add;
    if (inDate.month == 2 && inDate.day > 28)
    {
        inDate.day -= 28;
        inDate.month++;
    }
    else if ((inDate.month == 4 || inDate.month == 6 || inDate.month == 9 ||
        inDate.month == 11) && inDate.day > 30)
    {
        inDate.day -= 30;
        inDate.month++;
    }
    else if (inDate.day > 31)
    {
        inDate.day -= 31;
        inDate.month++;
    }
    if (inDate.month > 12)
    {
        inDate.month--;
        inDate.year++;
    }
    return inDate;
}


// Overloading the addition operator
// Same as preceding but parameters are reversed
date operator+ (date inDate, int days2add)
{
    inDate.day += days2add;
    if (inDate.month == 2 && inDate.day > 28)
    {
        inDate.day -= 28;
        inDate.month++;
    }
    else if ((inDate.month == 4 || inDate.month == 6 || inDate.month == 9 ||
        inDate.month == 11) && inDate.day > 30)
    {
        inDate.day -= 30;
        inDate.month++;
    }
```

**Continued next page**

**Listing 20.11**(Continued)   Overloading the addition operator

```
else if (inDate.day > 31)
{
    inDate.day -= 31;
    inDate.month++;
}
if (inDate.month > 12)
{
    inDate.month = 1;
    inDate.year++;
}
return inDate;
}
```

# Creating String Objects

The String class has three constructors (Listing 20.12). The default constructor, which takes no input parameters, produces a string object with null as the contents of its string. The second constructor is a copy constructor, which makes it possible to initialize one string object with the contents of another. The third constructor initializes a new string object with a literal string or string variable.

**Listing 20.12**   String class constructors

```
String::String ()  // default constructor
    { strcpy (cString,""); }  // set string to null

String::String (String & inObject) // copy constructor
    { *this = inObject; }

String::String (char * inString)
    { strcpy (cString, inString); }
```

A program uses the constructors as follows:

```
String firstString; // an empty string
String secondString = "Test string";
String thirdString = secondString;
```

The first declaration produces a string object with no characters (except the terminating null). The second string is initialized with "Test string." The final string is also initialized with "Test string," which is copied from the second-String object.

## Overloading the Assignment Operator

To assign one string to another, you would normally use the strcpy function. Therefore, functions to overload the assignment operator for the String class only need to use strcpy to copy the input string into the string object's cString variable. Notice in Listing 20.13 that there are two overloaded assignment operator member functions, one for copying from another string object and another for copying from a literal string or string variable.

Listing 20.13 Overloading string assignment operators

```
void String::operator= (String * inObject)
    { strcpy (cString, inObject->cString); }

void String::operator= (char * inString)
    { strcpy (cString, inString); }
```

## Overloading the Relationship Operators

In Listing 20.14, you will find three functions overloading each relationship operator. Those functions that compare two string objects can be overloaded as member functions. However, the functions that compare a string object to a string (either a literal string or a string variable) have been overloaded as friend functions so that the string object can appear on either side of the relationship operator.

## Overloading Concatenation

Concatenation has often been called "string addition." It therefore makes sense to overload the + or += operator to perform concatenation. In Listing 20.15 you will find two member functions that overload += to concatenate the contents of another string object or a string onto a string object.

Keep in mind that + and += are two distinct operators. To perform concatenation, a program must use a statement like

```
firstString += secondString;
```

If you want to support the + operator for concatenation, a string class must contain functions specifically written for that operator.

## Listing 20.14   Overloading string relationship operators

```
int String::operator== (String inObject)
    { return (strcmp (cString, inObject.cString) == 0); }

int String::operator> (String inObject)
    { return (strcmp (cString, inObject.cString) > 0); }

int String::operator>= (String inObject)
    { return (strcmp (cString, inObject.cString) >= 0); }

int String::operator< (String inObject)
    { return (strcmp (cString, inObject.cString) < 0); }

int String::operator<= (String inObject)
    { return (strcmp (cString, inObject.cString) >= 0); }

int String::operator!= (String inObject)
    { return (strcmp (cString, inObject.cString) != 0); }

// operators overloaded as friend functions

int operator== (String inObject, char * inString)
    { return (strcmp (inObject.cString, inString) == 0); }

int operator== (char * inString, String inObject)
    { return (strcmp (inObject.cString, inString) == 0); }

int operator != (String inObject, char * inString)
    { return (strcmp (inObject.cString, inString) != 0); }

int operator!= (char * inString, String inObject)
    { return (strcmp (inObject.cString, inString) != 0); }

int operator> (String inObject, char * inString)
    { return (strcmp (inObject.cString, inString) > 0); }

int operator> (char * inString, String inObject)
    { return (strcmp (inObject.cString, inString) > 0); }

int operator>= (String inObject, char * inString)
    { return (strcmp (inObject.cString, inString) >= 0); }

int operator>= (char * inString, String inObject)
    { return (strcmp (inObject.cString, inString) >= 0); }

int operator< (String inObject, char * inString)
    { return (strcmp (inObject.cString, inString) < 0); }
```

Continued next page

### Listing 20.14(Continued)  Overloading string relationship operators

```
int operator< (char * inString, String inObject)
    { return (strcmp (inObject.cString, inString) < 0); }

int operator<= (String inObject, char * inString)
    { return (strcmp (inObject.cString, inString) <= 0); }

int operator<= (char * inString, String inObject)
    { return (strcmp (inObject.cString, inString) <= 0); }
```

### Listing 20.15  Overloading concatenation

```
void String::operator+= (String inObject)
    { strcat (cString, inObject.cString); }

void String::operator+= (char * inString)
    { strcat (cString, inString); }
```

## Overloading the Unary * Operator

Overloading the unary * operator as a *type conversion operator* makes it possible to use an object of the String class anywhere a char * is required. For example, in Listing 20.16, you can see a string object used as a parameter for the getline function and in a cout stream.

### Listing 20.16   Using the overloaded unary * operator

```
// using the type conversion
cout << "Enter a string: ";
cin.getline (firstString, 81);
cout << "The string you just entered is: " << firstString;
```

The implementation of the overloaded operator can be found in Listing 20.17. Notice that the function's header includes the data type to which the * operator points (char) but that it has no return data type. The body of the function then returns the address of the string that is part of the string address (cString).

### Listing 20.17   Overloading the unary * operator

```
String::operator char*()
    { return cString; }
```

## Overloading the [ ] Operator

Overloading the [ ] operator can give a program access to individual characters within a string. For example, if a program needs the third character in a string, it could contain

```
String theString;
char theCharacter;
theCharacter = theString[2];
```

The implementation of the function to return individual characters in a string appears in Listing 20.18.

### Listing 20.18 Overloading the [ ] operator

```
char String::operator[] (int Index)
    { return cString[Index]; }
```

As declared in the String class, the [ ] operator can only be used on the right side of an assignment operator. To understand why this is so, consider the following statement:

```
theString [4] = 'c';
```

To perform the assignment, the program must have a main memory address on the left of the assignment operator. In other words, it must know where to put the character being assigned. However, the overloaded operator returns a char, not a pointer, and you can't assign something to a character.

## Summary

In this chapter you have learned how overloading of functions and operators is used to provide a simpler, more consistent interface to a programmer. Function overloading occurs when two member functions of the same class have the same name but different parameter lists. The C++ compiler identifies a function based on its signature, which is made up of the function's name along with the number, type, and order of its parameters. As long as the parameters differ in number, type, or order, a compiler will see two functions with the same name as distinct. When a function is called, the compiler uses the function whose signature matches the syntax of the function call.

Function overloading is commonly used to give classes more than one constructor. Typically, one constructor is used for interactive data input, another for input from a file, and a third to copy data into a new object from another object of the same class.

Operator overloading gives alternative meanings to C++ operators. Most C++ operators can be overloaded to make it easier for a programmer to work with objects. Overloaded operators are implemented as functions whose names are made up of the keyword `operator` followed by the operator being over-loaded.

When functions that define binary overloaded operators are declared as member functions, they can take only one input parameter. That parameter must be placed on the right side of the operator when the operator is used; an object of the class in which the overloading is defined must appear on the left side of the operator. The operations of overloaded operators defined as member functions are therefore not commutative.

Functions that define overloaded operators can also be declared as friend functions. A friend function or class has access to the private variables and function of the class to which it is declared as a friend. The drawback to using friends is that they violate the object-oriented principle of information hiding. However, overloaded binary operators defined as friends can take two parameters. By defining two overloaded binary operator functions with parameters in opposite order, an overloaded operator can be made commutative.

## Exercises

1. Create an array manager class that handles an array of integers. Overload the assignment operator so that the contents of one array object can be copied into another with the syntax Array1 = Array2.

2. Modify the program you wrote for Exercise 5 from Chapter 16 (Roman numeral arithmetic) to use operator overloading for arithmetic operators, allowing you to include code in the form Object1 + Object2, Object1 - Object2, and so on.

3. Create an array iterator class. An object of this class should return the contents of the array to a calling function, one element at a time. Overload the () operator so that it performs a "get current element" operation. Overload the ++ operator so that it increments the variable holding the index of the

current element. Overload the ! operator so that it returns true when all elements in the array have been returned, false when some elements still remain to be processed. Include an init function that sets the current element to 0. Then, test your iterator in a program by using it in a for loop:

```
arrayItr theIterator;
int arrayValue;
for (theIterator.init();!theIterator; theIterator++)
{
    arrayValue = theIterator();
    // display arrayValue
}
```

# 21

# Templates

## OBJECTIVES

In this chapter you will read about:

- How templates make it possible to use the same class with different data types.
- Writing template classes.
- Using template classes.

There is one major problem with the linked list classes you studied in Chapter 19: they are designed specifically to handle objects of class `Art`. Does this mean that each time you want to write a program that uses a linked list you need to write a new set of classes (node, list manager, and list iterator) customized for the type of object that will belong to the list? Fortunately, the answer is no.

C++ provides a way of creating generic classes that have placeholders for data types; you specify the data types when you create objects. Such classes are called *template classes*. The major benefit of templates classes is that you can reuse the class definitions in a variety of situations, without needing to redefine the classes from scratch.

## Defining Template Classes

In Listing 21.1 you will find a revised header file for the linked list manager class. There are a number of differences between this implementation and what you originally saw in Chapter 19:

- The class declaration and the implementation of its member functions are all in one file. When you compile a program that uses templates, the compiler uses the templates to generate function definitions with the data types supplied by the program. The template member functions are therefore not really executable code, but a pattern from which executable code will be created. This means that not only must the class declaration be included in a source code file using the class, but the function implementations must be included as well.

- In class and member function declarations, the name of a class is preceded by the keyword `template` and a list of placeholders for data types that will be passed in when an object is created from the class. The list of placeholders is surrounded by < and >. Each placeholder is preceded by the keyword `class`. When there is more than one placeholder, each is preceded by `class` and separated from the following parameter by a comma. Our particular example has only one input parameter: the type of object to be manipulated by the linked list. It is represented by the letter A. Although typically template parameters are single uppercase letters, you can use any legal C++ identifier.

- Whenever the name of the class is used, it is followed by its input parameter list, as in `ListMgr<A>`. Notice in Listing 21.1, for

## Listing 21.1    ListMgr.h

```
template <class A> class node;

template <class A>
class ListMgr
{
    private:
        node<A> * first;
    public:
        ListMgr ();
        void insert (A *);
        A * find (char *); // traverse list to locate by key
        int remove (char *); // use key to locate for removal
        node<A> * getFirst();
};

template <class A>
ListMgr<A>::ListMgr()
{
    first = 0;
}

template <class A>
void ListMgr<A>::insert (A * theObject)
{
    node<A> * newNode, * current, * previous;
    char * Key, * newKey;
    A * currentObject;

    newNode = new node<A> (theObject); // create a node object
    newKey = theObject->getKey();

    if (first == 0) // list is empty
        first = newNode;
    else
    {
        int firstNode = TRUE;
        current = first; // start at head of list
        while (current != 0)
        {
            currentObject = current->getObject();
            if (strcmp (newKey, currentObject->getKey()) <= 0)
                break; // spot found
            // save preceding because there aren't backward pointers
            previous = current;
            current = current->getNextPtr();
            firstNode = FALSE; // not the first node
        }
```

Continued next page

## Listing 21.1 (Continued)   ListMgr.h

```
// set previous node to point to new node except when first in list
        if (!firstNode)
            previous->setNext (newNode);
        else
            first = newNode; // have new first in list

        // set new node to point to following node
        newNode->setNext (current);
    }
}

template <class A>
A * ListMgr<A>::find (char * searchKey)
{
    A * currentObject;
    node<A> * current, * next;
    current = first; // start at head of list
    while (current != 0)
    {
        currentObject = current->getObject();
        if (strcmp (searchKey, currentObject->getKey()) == 0)
            return currentArt;
        current = current->getNextPtr();
    }
    return 0; // not found
}
template <class A>
int ListMgr<A>::remove (char * searchKey)
{
    A * currentObject;
    node<A> * current, * previous, * next;

    if (first == 0)
        return FALSE; // list is empty
    int firstNode = TRUE;
    current = first;

    while (current != 0)
    {
        currentObject = current->getObject();
        if (strcmp (searchKey, currentObject->getKey()) == 0)
            break; // jump out of loop
        // save preceding because there aren't backward pointers
        previous = current;
        current = current->getNextPtr();
        firstNode = FALSE; // not the first node
    }
```

Continued next page

**Listing 21.1**(Continued)   **ListMgr.h**

```
if (current == 0)
        return FALSE; // node not found

    if (!firstNode)
    {
        next = current->getNextPtr(); // gets node after node being removed
        previous->setNext (next);
    }
    else
        // sets first to node after node being removed
        first = current->getNextPtr();

    delete current->getObject(); // remove art object from memory
    delete current; // remove node object from memory

    return TRUE; // remove was successful
}

template <class A>
node<A> * ListMgr<A>::getFirst()
    { return first; }
```

example, that when declaring node objects, member functions use node<A>.

- When the placeholder is used to create objects or as an input parameters, the functions simply use the placeholder, as in A * theObject.
- Variable names have been changed to make them more generic. For example, the variable whose value determines the order of nodes in the list is now the "key." The current object is referred to simply as theObject.

The list manager template class in Listing 21.1 will support a list of any type of object, providing the key used to order the list is a C++ string. This restriction arises because strings require special handling to perform comparisons (the strcmp used in the insert function).

**Note**   You can create a list manager that handles an integer, floating point, or character key by using a second input parameter to the template that stands for the data type of the key.

The node (Listing 21.2) and list iterator (Listing 21.3) classes have been modified much like the list manager class. Everywhere a reference to a template class appears, the class name is followed by the class's input parameter. The placeholder for the input parameter now appears in every place where the original version of the classes referred to the Art class.

## Listing 21.2    Node.h

```
template <class A>
class node
{
    private:
        A * theObject; // pointer to object being linked
        node * next; // pointer to next node in list
    public:
        node (A *);
        node * getNextPtr ();
        A * getObject ();
        void setNext (node *);
};

template <class A>
node<A>::node (A * inputObject)
{
    theObject = inputObject;
    next = 0;
}
template <class A>
node * node<A>::getNextPtr()
    { return next; }

template <class A>
A * node<A>::getObject ()
    { return theObject; }

template <class A>
void node<A>::setNext (node * nextNode)
    { next = nextNode; }
```

Notice also that the forward class declarations have changed slightly. For example, when the list iterator class needs to let the compiler know that node and ListMgr are classes, it uses:

```
template <class A> class ListMgr;
template <class A> class node;
```

## Listing 21.3   ListItr.h

```
template <class A> class ListMgr;
template <class A> class node;

template <class A>
class ListItr
{
    private:
        node<A> * current;
        ListMgr<A> * theList;
    public:
        ListItr (ListMgr<A> *);
        A * getNext ();
};

template <class A>
ListItr<A>::ListItr (ListMgr<A> * whichList)
{
    current = 0;
    theList = whichList;
}

template <class A>
A * ListItr<A>::getNext ()
{
    if (current == 0)
        current = theList->getFirst();
    else
        current = current->getNextPtr();

    if (current != 0)
        return current->getObject();
    else
        return 0;
}
```

## Using Template Classes

To create an object from a template class, you must specify the data type that is to be substituted for each of the template class's input parameters. For example, the application class declaration (Listing 21.4) adds <Art> to the name of the list manager class when declaring a pointer variable for an object of that class. Then, to create the object and save a pointer to that object, the application class's constructor uses the following:

```
theList = new ListMgr<Art>()
```

## Listing 21.4    AppClass.h

```
template <class A> class ListMgr;
class Art;

class AppClass
{
    private:
        ListMgr<Art> * theList;
        void addArt ();
        void removeArt ();
        void viewArt ();
    public:
        AppClass();
        void Run();
};
```

By the same token, the application class declares a pointer to a list iterator and creates the object with

```
ListItr<Art> * theIterator;
    :
    :
theIterator = new ListItr<Art> (theList);
```

The remainder of the application class is unmodified from the original version of the program.

The list manager and list iterator classes must also use the same notation when creating objects of other template classes. As you can see in Listing 21.1 and Listing 21.3, both use pointers to node objects; the list iterator also uses a pointer to a list manager object.

---

**Note**

The Art class is essentially unmodified, although the getFigNumb function has been renamed getKey so that it is consistent with the function expected by the list manager template class.

---

## Summary

Template classes provide a method for creating classes that are independent of specific data types. A template class declaration includes a placeholder for each data type that will be specified whenever an object is created from the class. The major benefit of template classes is that they can be reused in a variety of situations without rewriting the class declarations for different data types.

When a program creates an object from a template class, the compiler makes a copy of the template class's member functions using the date type(s) supplied by the program. A template class therefore doesn't represent executable code, but instead is a pattern from which executable code is generated when the program is compiled.

## Exercises

1. On paper, make a list of programming tasks that could be made simpler through the use of templates. After you have finished, look at your list as a whole. What do the items on your list have in common? What does this tell you about the place of templates in C++ programming?

2. Create a template function that sorts an array of some simple data type (for example, integers, floating point, or characters). Write a simple program that tests your function.

3. Create a set of template classes that manage an array of 100 elements. The array should be able to handle integers, floating point numbers, or characters. Create member functions to:

   - Insert a new element at the bottom of the array.
   - Remove an element from the array.
   - Sort the array based on the value stored in the array. (*Hint:* Can you use the template from Exercise 1?)
   - Display the contents of the array.

4. Create a set of template classes that manages an array of 100 pointers to objects. The objects are ordered by a string key. Create member functions to:

   - Insert a new element at the bottom of the array.
   - Remove an element from the array.
   - Sort the array based on the key.
   - Display the contents of the array.

# Summing Up

## OBJECTIVES

In this chapter you will read about:

- Using all the elements of the object-oriented paradigm and the C++ language that have been discussed throughout this book to prepare a meaningful, useful program.
- Reusing previously developed classes with few or no modifications.

Throughout this book we have used relatively short example programs to demonstrate the characteristics of the object-oriented paradigm and the syntax of the C++ programming language. Before you finish your introduction to this material, you should have a chance to study a longer, meaningful program that uses all of the concepts we have discussed to see how all the elements work together. This chapter therefore sums up everything you have learned with a program that maintains a datebook.

The datebook program is not complete. There are some functions it doesn't perform; some of its code isn't as generic as it could be. You will get a chance to modify the program and remedy some of its deficiencies in the exercises at the end of this chapter.

**Note**

Because the datebook is a rather lengthy program, the listings for classes that are new to this program have been placed at the end of this chapter (after the exercises) rather than being interspersed in the text.

## What the User Sees

The datebook program lets a user enter, remove, and view events that are scheduled on specific dates. When the user runs the program, he or she is first asked to enter the name of the file containing events that have already been scheduled. If there is no file, the user simply presses Enter, at which point the program gives the user the choice of continuing and starting a new file, or exiting the program (see Figure 22.1).

### Figure 22.1  Starting a new data file

```
Input file name:

File not found. Continue?
```

If, however, the user enters a valid file name, the program loads data from the file into main memory. The user, of course, is unaware that the program is building data structures to organize the data as the data are read from the file.

Once data are loaded, the user is presented with the program's main menu (Figure 22.2). As you might expect, this menu is produced by the menu class we have used throughout the latter half of this book.

Figure 22.2    The datebook program's main menu

```
Input file name: File2

---------- MAIN MENU ----------

1. Enter a new event
2. Remove an event
3. View events
9. Quit


Enter an option:
```

The datebook program handles two types of events: special events (occurrences such as birthdays that apply just to a date) and appointments (occurrences that require a time). To enter a special event, the user types the date and a description for the event, as in Figure 22.3. If the user chooses an appointment, he or she then also needs to enter a time (Figure 22.4). The time must be expressed using a 24-hour clock.

Figure 22.3    Entering a special event

```
Enter an option: 1

Date of event: 8/7/96

Event description: Macworld Expo begins
Event type (1: Special event, 2: appointment): 1
```

Figure 22.4    Entering an appointment

```
Enter an option: 1

Date of event: 5/29/96

Event description: Search committee meeting
Event type (1: Special event, 2: appointment): 2
Appointment time: 8:00
```

To remove an event, the user enters the date of the event and the event description. If the event description doesn't match exactly, then the program reports that the event has been found and can't be removed, as in Figure 22.5. However, if a matching event is found, it will be removed.

Figure 22.5    Trying to remove an event

```
Enter an option: 2


Date of event: 6/12/96
Event description: My birthday

The event you entered wasn't scheduled.
```

The datebook program provides four ways of selecting events for viewing (see Figure 22.6). As you can see in Figure 22.7—the result of listing all events—the days on which events are scheduled are maintained in chronological order. A listing of the events on a given date consists of the date with the text of the events listed beneath. (Unfortunately, because we are working with a text-based interface, we can't give the user a calendar-like display.)

Figure 22.6    The view menu

```
---------- VIEW MENU ----------

1. Events on one date
2. Events in a range of dates
3. Events of one type
4. All events
9. Return to main menu


Enter an option:
```

To obtain the events on one date (Figure 22.8), all a user has to do is enter the wanted date. To view dates within a range, the user enters both a starting and ending date (see Figure 22.9). The third listing—events of one type—requires the user to enter just the number for the event type (Figure 22.10).

## Data Handling Classes

The datebook program manages two basic types of objects: days and events. The Day class (Listing 22.1 on page 474) includes an object of class date and a list manager object. Both of these objects are declared from classes you have seen before. The list manager class, and the node class that forms the contents of the list, are unmodified from Chapter 21. The date class is the same as the

Figure 22.7   Viewing all events

```
Enter an option: 4

5/29/96:
Search committee meeting
  at 08:00

6/12/96:
Father's Day
Vacation begins


7/27/96:
Dad's birthday
Department meeting
  at 10:00

8/7/96:
Macworld Expo begins


10/13/96:
My birthday
```

Figure 22.8   Viewing the events on one date

```
Enter an option: 1


Enter date: 6/12/96
Father's Day
Vacation begins
```

Figure 22.9   Viewing the events within a range of dates

```
Enter an option: 2

Enter starting date: 6/1/96
Enter ending date: 8/1/96

6/12/96:
Father's Day
Vacation begins


7/27/96:
Dad's birthday
Department meeting
  at 10:00
```

Figure 22.10    Viewing events of one type

```
Enter an option: 3

Type of event (1: Special event  2: Appointment): 1

6/12/96:
Father's Day
Vacation begins

7/27/96:
Dad's birthday

8/7/96:
Macworld Expo begins
```

date class introduced in Chapter 20 with one exception: the constructor that initializes a date from a tm structure has been replaced with a copy constructor (a constructor that copies data from another date object).

The implementation of the Day class (Listing 22.2 on page 474) includes member functions that do the following:

- Create an object of the class: Runs the appropriate constructor (character, date object, or file input).
- Create a new event (newEvent): Gathers the data for the new event and inserts it into the linked list of events.
- Remove an event (removeEvent): Searches for the event in the linked list of events and, if the event is found, removes it from the list.
- Display all linked events (showAll): Traverses the linked list using the list iterator class you saw in Chapter 19.
- Display events of one type (showOneType): Traverses the linked list using a list iterator, looking for events of a specified type.
- Return the date stored in an object (getDate).
- Write an object to a file (write).

If you look again at Listing 22.1 on page 474, you'll notice that the list manager object is created from the list manager template class with a pointer to an object of class Event. This is actually a base class pointer that lets the program handle multiple types of events in the same linked list.

Event (listing Listing 22.3 on page 478) is an abstract base class from which specific types of events can be derived. This implementation includes two derived classes: Appointment and Special. As you can see in Listing 22.3, Appointment adds an object of class Time to the event type and event description variables inherited from the base class.

Special, however, is actually the same as Event; it adds no variables or member functions to its base class. Why, then, should we have the class at all? Why not make Event a concrete class and allow objects to be created from it? Although there is technically no reason why Event couldn't be a concrete class, it makes the program more flexible if we declare the Special class. If we decide later that we do need to add variables to the Special class, we can easily do so without affecting any other class. However, if objects for special events were created directly from Event, adding those variables for a special event would mean modifying the base class, and adding the new variables—which apply only to special events—to all classes derived from that base class (for example, Appointment). We therefore obtain a better object-oriented design by declaring and using the Special class.

The event classes, implemented in Listing 22.4 on page 479, have member functions that do the following:

- Create an object of the class: Runs the appropriate constructor (interactive or file input).
- Display data (display): Formats and displays all of an object's stored data.
- Return the type of event (getType).
- Return the key by which objects are ordered when objects are part of a linked list (getKey).
- Write the object to a file (write).

Event, Special, and Appointment have objects as data. In particular, Event uses an object of the String class to store the event description. Appointment uses an object of class Time to store the time of an appointment.

The Time class (declared in Listing 22.5 on page 481) maintains time using a 24-hour clock. Hours and minutes are stored as integers in separate variables. Its member functions (Listing 22.6 on page 481) provide the following capabilities:

- Create an object from the class: Runs the appropriate constructor to initialize the object from two integers, another time object, a character string, or file input.
- Display the time (showTime): Uses the private function itoa (integer-to-ASCII) to convert the parts of the time from integers to characters and formats the time with a colon separating the hours and minutes.

**Note**

This is the same itoa function used by the date class. Although some C++ implementations do provide an itoa function, that function isn't part of the ANSI standard.

- Return the hours (getHours).
- Return the minutes (getMins).
- Write the time to a file (write).

## The Array Manager

The Day objects are managed by an array manager template class (Listing 22.7 on page 483). As written, the array can handle 500 days. All you need to do to increase that number, however, is to change the ARRAY_SIZE constant in the first line of the file.

Like the template classes for the linked list, the class declaration and member function implementations for the array manager class have been placed in a single header file that can be included in the file that will be created objects from the template.

This array manager is designed to handle objects that use dates as their key. As you can see in Listing 22.7, the insert function places a new day object at the bottom of the array and then sorts the array to place it in chronological order.

In addition to inserting new elements into the array, the array manager template class does the following:

- Creates an object of the class.
- Returns the contents of one array element (returnOne).
- Searches for an object that contains a specified date (find).
- Manages removing an event from a day (removeOne).

**Note**

Keep in mind that the `removeOne` function handles removing a single event from one day. It does not remove a day object from the array.

- Returns the last index used in the array (`getLastIndex`).

## The Application Class

The application class (declared in Listing 22.8 on page 485 and implemented in Listing 22.9 on page 486) takes care of the following:

- Managing the main menu using the resource file in Listing 22.10 on page 491, capturing user menu choices, and calling functions to process menu choices (the `Run`) function.
- Managing loading data from the data file (`load`). This includes building the array of day objects and the linked lists of event objects as data are loaded.
- Managing saving data to the data file (`unload`).
- Entering new events (`newEvent`). This includes determining whether the date of the new event is already stored in a day object and, if the date has not been stored, creating a day object and inserting it into the array of days before creating the event.
- Viewing events, including managing the view menu (`viewEvents`).
- Deleting events (`deleteEvent`).

## A Final Note

How long did it take an experienced programmer to write and debug the date-book program? Less than six hours. If you think that's a short time, you're right. Why was the development time so short? It wasn't simply because the person writing the program was a good programmer. It was because so much of the code had already been developed and tested.

Consider all the classes used in the datebook program that you have seen before:

- `String`
- `date`
- `menu`

- `ListMgr`
- `Node`
- `ListItr`

Although the `Time` and `ArrayMgr` classes are new to this program, they, too, fit into the category of generic, reusable classes. This is what object-oriented programming is all about: the ability to create a collection of classes that can be reused in a variety of ways, therefore shortening software development time considerably.

In addition to taking advantage of reusable classes, the datebook program provides an easily expandable hierarchy of objects to contain data (the `Event` hierarchy). Inheritance makes it easy to add different types of events and to modify those that are already part of the program.

## Exercises

1. The datebook program currently has no way to remove data for dates that have passed. To add this capability, you will need to:

   - Add an option to the main menu.
   - Add trapping and a function for the new option to the application class. The application class function should ask the user for the date to be removed. It could also allow the user to enter a range of dates.
   - Add a function to the array manager template class that deletes items from the array. (Be sure to move items up to fill in the hole left by the deleted item.) Before deleting the item from the array, remove all events linked to that item. As items are removed from data structures, delete them from main memory.

2. As currently written, the array manager template class isn't as generic as it could be because it expects the key by which the array is ordered to be a date object. Rework this class so that it is more generic. Consider the following as you do so:

   - What change(s) will need to be made to the date class so that it will work with the modified array manager template class?
   - How will you handle the need to dereference pointers to date objects when using the overloaded relationship operators?

3. Currently, the time class works only with 24-hour times; it doesn't recognize A.M. or P.M. Modify the class so that users can work with either a 24- or 12-hour clock. Add a constructor that initializes an object from the current system time, using the tm structure. Make any changes necessary to the datebook program to accommodate your modifications. If you want to make the time class complete, consider overloading relationship operators to allow comparison of times. Also consider overloading the addition operator to allow a program to add a unit of time (hours and minutes) to a time object.

4. To remove an event, the user must enter the description of the event exactly as it was entered; even the case of the characters must match. If the user has forgotten the description of an event, finding the event to remove it can be a problem. Consider how you could rework the application class's remove function to make it easier for the user to identify which event should be removed. Then, implement your ideas.

5. Many datebook programs let the user indicate that an event should be repeated (once a week, once a month, once a year). Add this capability to the datebook program. Let the user specify how often and how many times the event should repeat. Then add days to the starting date (using the overloaded date addition operator) based on the user's input. Create one new event for each repeat, adding day objects as needed to the array of days.

## Source Code for the Datebook Program

### Listing 22.1    Day.h

```
template <class A> class ListMgr;
class date;
class Event;
class ifstream;
class ofstream;

typedef char date_string[9];

class Day
{
    private:
        date * theDay;
        ListMgr<Event> * theList; // list of events for this date; uses base class pointer
        int eventCount;
    public:
        Day (char *); // input a string date
        Day (date *); // input a date object
        Day (ifstream &);
        void newEvent ();
        void removeEvent (char *);
        void showAll (); // display all linked events
        void showOneType (int); // display one type
        date * getDate ();
        void write (ofstream &);
};
```

### Listing 22.2    Day.cpp

```
#include <string.h>
#include "day.h"
#include "listmgr.h"
#include "listitr.h"
#include "node.h"
#include "date.h"
#include "event.h"
#include "timeclass.h"
#include <fstream.h>
#include <iostream.h>
```

Continued next page

## Listing 22.2(Continued)   Day.cpp

```cpp
Day::Day (char * inString)
{
    theDay = new date (inString);
    theList = new ListMgr<Event> ();
    eventCount = 0;
}

Day::Day (date * inDate)
{
    theDay = new date (inDate);
    theList = new ListMgr<Event> ();
    eventCount = 0;
}

Day::Day (ifstream & fin)
{
    char dummy;
    Special * theSpecialEvent;
    Appointment * theAppointment;
    int Type;

    date_string inString;
    fin.getline (inString,80,'\0');
    theDay = new date (inString);
    theList = new ListMgr<Event> ();
    fin >> eventCount;
    for (int i = 1;i <= eventCount; i++)
    {
        fin >> Type;
        fin.get (dummy);
        switch (Type)
        {
            case SPECIAL:
                theSpecialEvent = new Special (fin, Type);
                theList->insert (theSpecialEvent);
                break;
            case APPOINTMENT:
                theAppointment = new Appointment (fin, Type);
                theList->insert (theAppointment);
                break;
        }
    }
}
```

Continued next page

## Listing 22.2 (Continued)   Day.cpp

```cpp
void Day::newEvent ()
{
    String inDesc, inString;
    int Type;
    Time * inTime;

    cout << endl;
    cout << "Event description: ";
    cin.getline (inDesc,255);
    cout << "Event type (1: Special event, 2: appointment): ";
    cin >> Type;
    switch (Type)
    {
        case SPECIAL:
            Special * theSpecialEvent = new Special (inDesc,Type);
            theList->insert (theSpecialEvent);
            eventCount++;
            break;
        case APPOINTMENT:
            cout << "Appointment time: ";
            cin.getline (inString,255);
            inTime = new Time (inString);
            Appointment * theAppointment = new Appointment
                (inDesc, Type, inTime);
            theList->insert (theAppointment);
            eventCount++;
            break;
        default:
            cout << "\nInvalid event type" << endl;
    }
}

void Day::removeEvent (char * iDesc)
{
    int result;
    result = theList->remove (iDesc);
    if (!result)
        cout << "\nThe event you entered wasn't scheduled." << endl << endl;
    else
        cout << "\nEvent removed." << endl << endl;
}
```

Continued next page

## Listing 22.2(Continued)    Day.cpp

```cpp
void Day::showAll ()
{
    ListItr<Event> * theIterator = new ListItr<Event> (theList);
    Event * current;
    current = theIterator->getNext();
    while (current)
    {
        current->display();
        current = theIterator->getNext();
    }
}

void Day::showOneType (int theType)
{
    ListItr<Event> * theIterator = new ListItr<Event> (theList);
    Event * current;
    int header = false;
    date_string requestedDate;
    current = theIterator->getNext();
    while (current)
    {
        if (current->getType() == theType)
        {
            if (!header)
                cout << theDay->showDate (requestedDate) << ":" << endl;
            current->display();
            header = true;
        }
        current = theIterator->getNext();
    }
}

date * Day::getDate () { return theDay; }

void Day::write (ofstream & fout)
{
    Event * current;
    date_string outDate;
    fout << theDay->showDate (outDate) << '\0';
    fout << eventCount << ' ';
    ListItr<Event> * theIterator = new ListItr<Event> (theList);
    current = theIterator->getNext();
    while (current)
    {
        current->write (fout);
        current = theIterator->getNext();
    }
}
```

## Listing 22.3   Event.h

```
class ifstream;
class ofstream;

#include "stringclass.h"

const SPECIAL = 1;
const APPOINTMENT = 2;

class Event
{
    protected:
        String eventName;
        int eventType;
    public:
        Event (String, int);
        Event (ifstream &, int);
        virtual void display ();
        int getType ();
        virtual void write (ofstream &);
        char * getKey();
};

// Don't need write and display functions;
// Use functions inherited from base class
// This subclass is the same as the base class,
//   but we include it anyway to make it easier
//   to modify the class at a later time.

class Special : public Event
{
    public:
        Special (String, int);
        Special (ifstream &, int);
};

class Time;

class Appointment : public Event
{
    private:
        Time * apptTime;
    public:
        Appointment (String, int, Time *);
        Appointment (ifstream &, int);
        void display ();
        void write (ofstream &);
};
```

## Listing 22.4    Event.cpp

```cpp
#include "event.h"
#include "timeclass.h"
#include <fstream.h>
#include <iostream.h>

// *******************************************************
//    • Event class
// *******************************************************

Event::Event (String inString, int Type)
{
    eventName = inString;
    eventType = Type;
}

Event::Event (ifstream & fin, int Type)
{
    eventType = Type;
    char tString[256], dummy;

// event type is read by the Day object

    fin.getline (tString,255,'\0');
    eventName = tString;
}

void Event::display ()
{
    cout << eventName << endl;
}

int Event::getType ()
    { return eventType; }

void Event::write (ofstream & fout)
{
    fout << eventType << ' ';
    fout << eventName << '\0';
}

char * Event::getKey ()
    { return eventName; }
```

Continued next page

## Listing 22.4(Continued)    Event.cpp

```
// *****************************************************
//    • Special class
// *****************************************************

Special::Special (String inString, int Type)
    : Event (inString, Type)
{
    // just calls base class constructor
}

Special::Special (ifstream & fin, int Type)
    : Event (fin, Type)
{
    // just calls base class constructor
}


// *****************************************************
//    • Appointment class
// *****************************************************

Appointment::Appointment (String inString, int Type, Time * inTime)
    : Event (inString, Type)
{
    apptTime = new Time (inTime);
}

Appointment::Appointment (ifstream & fin, int Type)
    : Event (fin, Type)
{
    apptTime = new Time (fin);
}

void Appointment::display ()
{
    char timeString[6];
    Event::display(); // call base class function
    cout << "  at " << apptTime->showTime (timeString);
}

void Appointment::write (ofstream & fout)
{
    Event::write (fout);
    apptTime->write (fout);
}
```

## Listing 22.5    Timeclass.h

```
class ofstream;
class ifstream;
class Time
{
    private:
        int hours, mins;
        void itoa (int, char *);
    public:
        Time (int, int);
        Time (Time *); // copy constructor
        Time (char *);
        Time (ifstream &);
        char * showTime (char *);
        int getHours ();
        int getMins ();
        void write (ofstream &);
};
```

## Listing 22.6    Timeclass.cpp

```
#include "timeclass.h"
#include <string.h>
#include <stdlib.h>
#include <fstream.h>
#include <fp.h>

Time::Time (int ihours, int imins)
{
    hours = ihours;
    mins = imins;
}

Time::Time (Time * inTime)
{
    hours = inTime->getHours();
    mins = inTime->getMins();
}

Time::Time (char * timeString)
{
    char temp[3];
    strncpy (temp,timeString,2);
    hours = atoi (temp);
    strcpy (temp,&timeString[3]);
    mins = atoi (temp);
}
```

Continued next page

## Listing 22.6(Continued)   Timeclass.cpp

```
Time::Time (ifstream & fin)
{
    char dummy;
    fin >> hours >> mins;
    fin.get (dummy);
}

char * Time::showTime (char * timeString)
{
    char digits[3];
    itoa (hours, digits);
    strcpy (timeString, digits);
    if (hours == 0) strcat (timeString,"0"); // make sure 00 shows
    strcat (timeString, ":");
    itoa (mins, digits);
    strcat (timeString, digits);
    if (mins == 0) strcat (timeString,"0"); // make sure 00 shows
    return timeString;
}

void Time::itoa (int integer, char * string)
{
    // characters, not a string
    char numbers[] = {'0','1','2','3','4','5','6','7','8','9'};
    int digit, power = 0, divisor, temp, i;

    temp = integer;
    while (temp > 0) // find highest power of 10
    {
        power++;
        temp /= 10;
    }

    if (power > 1) power--;
    divisor = pow (10,power);

    for (i = 0; i <= power; i++)
    {
        digit = integer / divisor;
        string[i] = numbers[digit];
        integer = integer % divisor;
        divisor = divisor / 10;
    }
    string[i] = '\0';
}
```

Continued next page

Listing 22.6(Continued)    Timeclass.cpp

```
int Time::getHours ()
    { return hours; }

int Time::getMins ()
    { return mins; }

void Time::write (ofstream & fout)
{
    fout << hours << ' ' << mins << ' ';
}
```

## Listing 22.7    ArrayMgr.h

```
const ARRAY_SIZE = 500;
const SWAP_MADE = 1;
const NO_SWAP = 0;

class date;
class String;

template <class T>
class ArrayMgr
{
    private:
        T * theArray[ARRAY_SIZE];
        int lastIndex;
    public:
        ArrayMgr ();
        void insert (T *);
        T * returnOne (int); // return a pointer from the array
        T * find (date *); // find out if a date is in the array
        void removeOne (date *, String);
        int getLastIndex ();
};

template <class T>
ArrayMgr<T>::ArrayMgr()
{
    lastIndex = -1;
    for (int i = 0; i < ARRAY_SIZE; i++)
        theArray[i] = 0;
}
```

Continued next page

## Listing 22.7(Continued)   ArrayMgr.h

```
template <class T>
void ArrayMgr<T>::insert (T * inObject)
{
    date * thisDate, * nextDate;
    theArray [++lastIndex] = inObject;
    if (lastIndex == 0) return; // no need to sort when there is just one
    // now sort in chronological order
    int result = SWAP_MADE;
    int i;
    while (result == SWAP_MADE)
    {
        result = NO_SWAP;
        for (i = 0; i < lastIndex; i++)
        {
            thisDate = theArray[i]->getDate();
            nextDate = theArray[i+1]->getDate();
            if (*thisDate > *nextDate)
            {
                inObject = theArray[i];
                theArray[i] = theArray[i+1];
                theArray[i+1] = inObject;
                result = SWAP_MADE;
            }
        }
    }
}


template <class T>
T * ArrayMgr<T>::returnOne (int index)
    { return theArray [index]; }

template <class T>
T * ArrayMgr<T>::find (date * inDate)
{
    for (int i = 0; i <= lastIndex; i++)
    {
        date * searchDate = theArray[i]->getDate ();
        if (*searchDate == *inDate)
            return theArray[i];
    }
    return 0;
}
```

Continued next page

## Listing 22.7(Continued)   ArrayMgr.h

```
template <class T>
void ArrayMgr<T>::removeOne (date * theDate, String theEvent)
{
    T * theDay = find (theDate);
    if (T == 0)
    {
        cout << "\nThere are no events on that date." << endl;
        return;
    }
    theDay->remove (theEvent);
}


template <class T>
int ArrayMgr<T>::getLastIndex ()
    { return lastIndex; }
```

## Listing 22.8   AppClass.h

```
template <class T> class ArrayMgr;
class Day;

typedef char date_string[9];

class AppClass
{
    private:
        ArrayMgr<Day> * ArrayOfDays;
    public:
        AppClass ();
        void Run();
        void load ();
        void unload ();
        void newEvent ();
        void viewEvents ();
        void deleteEvent ();
};
```

## Listing 22.9   AppClass.cpp

```cpp
#include <iostream.h>
#include <fstream.h>
#include "appclass.h"
#include "arraymgr.h"
#include "menu.rsc"
#include "day.h"
#include "date.h"
#include "event.h"
#include <ctype.h>
#include <string.h>

AppClass::AppClass ()
{
    ArrayOfDays = new ArrayMgr<Day> ();
}

void AppClass::Run ()
{
    menu theMenu (maintitle, mainmenu, mainmenucount); // create menu object
    int choice = 0;

    load (); // load stuff from file

    while (choice != QUIT)
    {
        theMenu.displaymenu();
        choice = theMenu.chooseoption();
        switch (choice)
        {
            case INSERT:
                newEvent();
                break;
            case REMOVE:
                deleteEvent ();
                break;
            case VIEW:
                viewEvents ();
                break;
            case QUIT:
                break;
            default:
                cout << "\nInvalid menu option";

        }
    }
    unload (); // save stuff back in the file
}
```

Continued next page

Listing 22.9(Continued)    AppClass.cpp

```
void AppClass::load ()
{
    String fileName;
    char yes_no;

    cout << "\nInput file name: ";
    cin.getline (fileName,31);
    ifstream fin (fileName);

    if (!fin.is_open())
    {
        cout << "\nFile not found. Continue? ";
        cin >> yes_no;
        if (toupper(yes_no) == 'N')
            return;
    }
    else
    {
        Day * theDay;
        int lastIndex;
        char dummy;

        fin >> lastIndex; // read number of day objects
        fin.get (dummy); // skip over blank

        for (int i = 0; i <= lastIndex; i++)
        {
            theDay = new Day (fin); // reading day also reads linked events
            ArrayOfDays->insert (theDay);
        }
    }
}

void AppClass::newEvent ()
{
    date_string requestedDate;
    date * theDate;
    Day * foundDay;

    cout << "Date of event: ";
    cin.getline (requestedDate,15);
    if (strlen(requestedDate) == 0) return; // error exit
```

Continued next page

## Listing 22.9(Continued)   AppClass.cpp

```
    theDate = new date (requestedDate);
    foundDay = ArrayOfDays->find (theDate);  // see if date is already in array
    if (foundDay == 0)
    {
        foundDay = new Day (theDate);
        ArrayOfDays->insert (foundDay);  // insert new day if not there
    }
    foundDay->newEvent();  // create the new event
    delete theDate;  // done with this one
}

void AppClass::deleteEvent ()
{
    date_string requestedDate;
    date * theDate;
    String iDesc;

    cout << "\nDate of event: ";
    cin.getline (requestedDate, 15);
    theDate = new date (requestedDate);
    Day * theDay = ArrayOfDays->find (theDate);
    if (theDay == 0)
    {
        cout << "\nDate not found";
        delete theDate;
        return;
    }
    cout << "Event description: ";
    cin.getline (iDesc, 255);
    theDay->removeEvent (iDesc);
    delete theDate;
}

void AppClass::viewEvents ()
{
    menu theMenu (viewtitle, viewmenu, viewmenucount);
    int choice = 0;
    date_string requestedDate;
    date * theDate, * endDate, * startDate;
    Day * theDay;

    while (choice != RETURN)
    {
        theMenu.displaymenu();
        choice = theMenu.chooseoption();
```

Continued next page

Listing 22.9(Continued)    AppClass.cpp

```cpp
switch (choice)
{
    case ONE_DATE:
        cout << "\nEnter date: ";
        cin.getline (requestedDate, 15);
        if (strlen(requestedDate) == 0) break; // error exit

        theDate = new date (requestedDate);
        theDay = ArrayOfDays->find (theDate);
        if (theDay == 0)
            cout << "Date not found";
        else
            theDay->showAll ();
        break;
    case DATE_RANGE:
        cout << "Enter starting date: ";
        cin.getline (requestedDate, 15);
        if (strlen(requestedDate) == 0) break; // error exit
        startDate = new date (requestedDate);

        cout << "Enter ending date: ";
        cin.getline (requestedDate, 15);
        if (strlen(requestedDate) == 0) break; // error exit
        endDate = new date (requestedDate);

        for (int i = 0; i < ArrayOfDays->getLastIndex(); i++)
        {
            theDay = ArrayOfDays->returnOne(i);
            theDate = theDay->getDate();
            if (*theDate >= *startDate && *theDate <= *endDate)
            {
                cout << endl;
                cout << theDate->showDate (requestedDate)
                    << ": " << endl;
                theDay->showAll();
                cout << endl; endl;
            }
        }
        break;
    case ONE_TYPE:
        int Type;
        cout << "Type of event (1: Special event  2: Appointment): ";
        cin >> Type;
```

Continued next page

## Listing 22.9(Continued)    AppClass.cpp

```
                for (int i = 0; i < ArrayOfDays->getLastIndex(); i++)
                {
                    cout << endl;
                    theDay = ArrayOfDays->returnOne(i);
                    theDate = theDay->getDate();
                    theDay->showOneType (Type);
                }
                break;
            case ALL:
                for (int i = 0; i <= ArrayOfDays->getLastIndex(); i++)
                {
                    theDay = ArrayOfDays->returnOne(i);
                    theDate = theDay->getDate();
                    cout << endl;
                    cout << theDate->showDate (requestedDate) << ": " << endl;
                    theDay->showAll();
                    cout << endl; endl;
                }
                break;
            case RETURN:
                break;
            default:
                cout << "\nUnrecognized menu option.";
        }
    }
}

void AppClass::unload ()
{
    String fileName;
    Day * theDay;
    cout << "\nOutput file name: ";
    cin.getline (fileName,31);
    ofstream fout (fileName);

    if (!fout.is_open())
    {
        cout << "\nOutput file error.";
        return;
    }
    int lastIndex = ArrayOfDays->getLastIndex();
    fout << lastIndex << ' ';
    for (int i = 0; i <= lastIndex; i++)
    {
        theDay = ArrayOfDays->returnOne(i);
        theDay->write (fout);
    }
}
```

## Listing 22.10    Menu.rsc

```
#include "menu.h"

menuoption maintitle = "MAIN MENU";
menuoption mainmenu [] = {"1. Enter a new event",
                "2. Remove an event",
                "3. View events",
                        "9. Quit"};

int mainmenucount = 4;

const INSERT = 1;
const REMOVE = 2;
const VIEW = 3;
const QUIT = 9;

menuoption viewtitle = "VIEW MENU";
menuoption viewmenu [] = {"1. Events on one date",
                "2. Events in a range of dates",
                "3. Events of one type",
                "4. All events",
                "9. Return to main menu"};

int viewmenucount = 5;

const ONE_DATE = 1;
const DATE_RANGE = 2;
const ONE_TYPE = 3;
const ALL = 4;
const RETURN = 9;
```

# Glossary

**Abstract class:** A class from which objects are never created; a class that contains at least one pure virtual function.

**Access mode:** A designation that determines the accessibility of the variables in a class by other functions.

**Address (of a byte):** A unique number assigned to a byte of main memory.

**Algorithm:** A process used for solving a specific problem or arriving at a specific type of output.

**Application object:** An object that represents a computer program.

**Application software:** Software that does useful work for a user.

**Arithmetic expressions:** Expressions that perform some calculation that produces a numeric value.

**Arithmetic operator:** Operators that specify what action the computer should take with numeric values.

**Array:** A complex variable that can store multiple values of the same data type.

**Arrow operator:** The operator used to reference a variable or member function of an object using dynamic binding.

**ASCII:** The character coding scheme used in most computers.

**Assembler:** A program that translates an assembly language program into machine language.

**Assembly language:** A programming language in which a programmer uses a mnemonic code in place of a binary instruction code.

**Assignment:** Placing a value into a variable across an equals sign.

**Assignment operator:** The operator used to assign a value to a variable; an equals sign.

**Attribute:** A piece of data that describes an object.

**Base (of a number system):** In a place value system, the number that is raised to a power to generate the value of any given digit position in a number.

**Base class:** A class from which other classes are derived; a parent class in a class hierarchy.

**Binary:** Anything that has two states (e.g., off/on, 0/1, yes/no).

**Binary file:** A file that stores data as an unorganized stream of bits.

**Binary operators**: Operators that perform actions on two values.

**Binding**: Linking an object to the member functions of its class.

**Bit**: One binary digit (a 0 or a 1).

**Bit-wise AND operator**: An operator (&) that performs a logical AND operation on pairs of bits in two storage locations.

**Bit-wise OR operator**: A C++ operator ( | ) that logically ORs the individual bits of two storage locations.

**Bottom-up design**: Designing a program beginning with detailed functional modules and assembling them into a complete program.

**Breakpoint**: A marker used by a debugger to indicate a line of source code at which execution will be stopped.

**Bubble sort**: A sorting algorithm that examines successive pairs of values and swaps them if they are in the wrong order. The sort makes repeated passes through the values until no swapping occurs, indicating that the values are in the correct order.

**Bug**: A glitch in a program that prevents the program from operating properly.

**Byte**: Eight bits.

**Class**: The template from which objects of the same type are created.

**Class library**: A collection of previously compiled classes that can be used in an object-oriented program.

**Comment statement**: A line of explanation that is added to a program when it is written.

**Compiler**: A program that translates a high-level language program into machine code all at once, before the program is run.

**Compiler directive**: An instruction to the compiler that is processed when a file is being compiled.

**Concatenation**: Creating a longer string by combining two shorter strings, one on the end of the other.

**Concrete class**: A class from which objects can be created; a class that isn't an abstract class.

**Constant**: A variable whose contents can't be changed.

**Constructor**: A function that has the same name as its class. It is executed automatically whenever an object is created from the class.

**Control condition**: The logical expression that determines whether a loop will continue to execute.

**Copy constructor**: A constructor that initializes a new object with data copied from another object of the same class.

**Data structures**: Program structures that organize multiple, related values.

**Data type**: A specification of the type of data to be stored in a variable.

**Delimiters**: Characters that separate identifiable parts of a string.

**Dereference (a pointer)**: To access the location pointed to by the contents of a pointer variable.

**Derived class**: A class that is defined as a more specific instance of another class; a child class in a class hierarchy.

**Dot operator**: A period that indicates which object variables and/or member functions belong to.

**Dynamic binding**: Allocating space for objects while a program is running.

**Emulation**: Using software to translate from the instruction set of one type of CPU to another.

**End-of-file**: A condition that arises when a program attempts to read beyond the last data stored in a data file.

**Escape character**: A character used to send formatting information to an output device.

**Expression**: Any part of a C++ statement that can be evaluated to produce a single value.

**Formal parameter**: A value that is passed into a function when the function is called by another function.

**Forward reference**: Naming a class in a header file, indicating that a definition will follow later.

**Function**: A self-contained block of C++ source code.

**Function prototype**: A declaration of a function's name and the data the function needs from the outside world to perform its work.

**Function signature:** The name of a function along with the number, type, and order of its parameters, used to uniquely identify a function.

**Gigabyte:** $2^{30}$, or 1,073,741,824 bytes.

**Global variable:** A variable defined so that it is accessible to an entire program.

**Header file:** A file with a *.h* extension used by C++ to store constants and data structures.

**Hexadecimal:** Base 16; a shorthand for binary in which each place represents four binary places.

**High-level language:** A programming language with an English-like syntax.

**Infinite loop:** A loop that never stops repeating.

**Information hiding:** Hiding the details of a class from other classes and/or programs.

**Inline function:** A member function whose body is defined with the class definition.

**Instance (of a class):** An object created from a class.

**Instantiate (an object):** Create an object from a class.

**Instruction:** An action that a computer knows how to perform.

**Instruction set:** The collection of instructions known to a computer.

**Interpreter:** A program that translates a high-level language program into machine language while a program is running.

**Iteration:** Repeating sets of actions in a program.

**Iterator:** A class designed to process all the nodes in a data structure (an array, list, or tree).

**Kilobyte:** $2^{10}$ or 1024 bytes.

**Libraries:** Collections of pre-compiled programs that can be used by a program that you write.

**Linking:** The process of combining all the object code modules of a program into a single executable program.

**Literal values:** Values that are coded directly into a program, without placing them in main memory under a variable name.

**Local variable:** A variable defined within a function or compound statement (delimited by braces) that can be used only within the function or compound statement.

**Logic (of a program):** The step-by-step process used by a program to handle everything that happens while the program is running.

**Logical expressions:** Expressions that evaluate values and return either "true" (some value other than 0, but usually 1) or "false" (0).

**Loop:** A set of program actions that are repeated.

**Looping:** Repeating sets of actions within a program.

**Machine language:** A programming language made up of binary codes that a computer can understand without translation.

**Manipulators:** Functions in the `ios` class hierarchy that format I/O stream output.

**Megabyte:** $2^{20}$, or 1,048,576 bytes.

**Member function:** The actions an object knows how to perform.

**Message:** Instructions sent to an object telling it to perform one of the actions it knows how to do.

**Method:** An action an object knows how to perform.

**Mnemonic code:** A two- to five-character code that represents an instruction in a computer's instruction set.

**Multiple inheritance:** Deriving a class from more than one base class.

**Node:** An object in a data structure.

**Object:** An entity in a data processing environment that has data that describe it and actions that it can perform.

**Object code:** The machine language translation of a source program.

**Object-oriented programming:** A paradigm for designing and developing application programs that encapsulate data and the actions data can perform into objects.

**OOP:** The abbreviation for object-oriented programming.

**Overloading:** A technique for giving operators and functions more than one meaning so that they react differently to different messages.

**Paradigm:** A theoretical model that can be used as a pattern for some activity.

**Parameter:** Data passed into and/or out of a function.

**Parameter list:** A definition of the values passed into a function.

**Parameter passing:** Sending data into a function through the function's parameter list.

**Parsing:** Scanning a string to break it into its constituent parts.

**Pass by reference:** Including the address of a variable in a function's parameter list so that if the value is changed in the function, the modified value will be returned to the calling function.

**Pass by value:** Sending values to a function such that modifying those values in the function does not modify them anywhere else in the program.

**Persistent object:** An object that reads itself in from a file when it is created and saves itself to a file when it is destroyed.

**Pointer:** A main memory address, usually the location of data used by a program.

**Pointer arithmetic:** Any arithmetic operation performed on a main memory address.

**Pointer variables:** Variables that contain the addresses of where data are stored.

**Polymorphism:** The ability to have classes in the same inheritance hierarchy respond differently to the same message.

**Program:** A specific, detailed set of directions to a computer.

**Programming:** The task of designing, writing, and debugging a program.

**Project:** A collection of all the source code files (and possibly the libraries) that should be linked into a single program.

**Pure function:** A function that is declared but not defined in a class; a virtual function that is initialized with = 0.

**Resource:** A program element, such as a window or menu, used by a program.

**Resource file:** A file containing resource specifications.

**Scope (of a variable):** The portion of a program in which a variable is recognized.

**Selection:** Elements of a program that make choices between alternative sets of actions.

**Services:** The actions an object knows how to perform.

**Signature:** A function's name and parameter list.

**Software development life cycle:** An organizational process used to develop software that meets the needs of its users.

**Source code:** A text file containing programming language statements.

**Static binding**: Allocating space for objects when a program is compiled.

**Stream extraction operator**: The operator (>>) that takes a value from an I/O stream and places it into a variable.

**Stream I/O**: Operations that view I/O as a stream of characters coming to or from some destination, such as the screen, keyboard, or a file.

**Stream insertion operator**: Two less than signs (<<) that insert a value into an I/O stream.

**Structure**: A variable that groups together other variables of different data types.

**Structure member operator**: A period that indicates which object variables and/or member functions belong to.

**Structured programming**: A programming paradigm in which programs are built from only three structures (simple sequence, iteration, and selection).

**System development life cycle**: The process used by systems analysts to design and implement information systems.

**Systems software**: Software that manages a computer's operations.

**Template class**: A class written with placeholders for data types that are specified when an object is created from the class.

**Top-down design**: A process for designing a program in which the high-level design of the program is created first; the design is then fleshed out in detail.

**Unary operators**: Operators that work with a single value.

**User interface**: The portion of a program that interacts with a user.

**Variable**: A piece of data that describes an object; a label on a main memory storage location.

**Virtual function**: A function that will probably need to be called using a pointer so the program can determine exactly which function to use.

**Weak data typing**: Minimal checking of the type of data assigned to variables.

# Index